Contents

ISBN 0-75256-639-3

© 2001, Chronosports Editeur
Jordils Park, Chemin des Jordils 40, CH-1025 St-Sulpice, Suisse. Tél.: (++41 21) 694 24 44. Fax: (++41 21) 694 24 46.

This is a Parragon Book

This edition published in 2001

Parragon
Queen Street House
4 Queen Street
Bath BA1 1HE, UK

FORMULA 1 YEARBOOK
2001-02

Pictures: LAT Photographic
Steven Tee, Clive Rose, Lorenzo Bellanca, Charles Coates, Michael Cooper,
Martyn Elford, Jeff Bloxham, Chris Dixon, M. Griffiths, Peter Spinney

Additional photographers
Thierry Gromik
Steve Domenjoz

Conception and Grands Prix reports
Luc Domenjoz

Translated by
Eric Silbermann

Statistics, results and page layout
Sidonie Perrin
Aline Zwahlen

Drawings 2001 and circuit maps
Pierre Ménard

Gaps charts
Michele Merlino

Technical summary
Paolo Filisetti

Page layout
Cyril Davillerd, (i)(om.idesign
Solange Amara

PHOTOGRAPHIC CREDIT

Foreword

"*Writing the preface to the "Formula 1 Yearbook" for the second consecutive year gives me great pleasure, because it is a symbol of Scuderia Ferrari's extraordinary 2001 season.*

A season which saw us take our third consecutive Constructors' Championship title also allowed Michael Schumacher to be crowned Drivers' Champion for the second year in a row, bringing his personal tally of titles to four.

For Ferrari, the 2001 season was a record breaking one. We beat the record for the number of points scored in a season in the Constructors' Championship, while Michael beat the equivalent record in the Drivers' category. This season did not come down to the traditional duel, as it turned into a three-way fight, at the end of which Ferrari can pride itself on having won over half the honours, while our two adversaries shared the others equally between them. We scored nine wins, while our rivals took four each.

The mood within the Ferrari team this year was extraordinary once again. I am happy that we made liars of those who thought we might have lacked motivation after the results obtained in 2000. On the contrary, our irrepressible will to win was stronger than ever in 2001.

The past season has also been very important in terms of consolidating the structure of Scuderia Ferrari. Contracts with Michael Schumacher and the senior personnel have all been extended to the long term. The future has been one of our main considerations this year, as we have been working for several months now on our car for 2002.

We are well aware of the difficulties which await us next year. Several major constructors are returning to Formula 1 and that will make our task even more arduous, if that is possible. But our will to win is as strong as ever. Believe me when I say that Ferrari will do all in its power to maintain its position as the reference point of the sport. That way, we can ensure that, next year, our car will once again feature on the cover of "Formula 1 Yearbook."

Enjoy the read,"

Jean Todt

Red Zone

by Didier Braillon
«L'Équipe»

Michael Schumacher was by far the most talked about driver in the media. His every word was swallowed up by a mass of journalists.

▽▷

DIDIER BRAILLON
47 years old. A journalist at L'Equipe for the past ten years, he first tackled F1 in1979. In 1982, he became the editor of the prestigious Grand Prix International magazine. When this folded in 1984, he worked as a press officer, first for the RAM team and then for Larrousse. In 1989, he joined the France-Soir newspaper, before moving to Course Auto in 1991. The magazine had a short life and so he moved to the motor racing pages of L'Equipe in time for the start of the 1992 season.

By the end of the Hungarian Grand Prix, it was pretty much all over bar the shouting. As he crossed the finish line, Michael Schumacher was able to give his famous victory cry over the Ferrari radio of, "*I love you, I love all guys!*" He had good reason, as this fifty first win not only put him level with Alain Prost at the top of the list of all-time winners, it also handed him his fourth world championship title, coming back to back after his 2000 performance for the Scuderia. There was more to celebrate as, thanks to Barrichello's second place, Ferrari picked up the Constructors' title for the third consecutive year.

Right from the start of the season, it was clear that the team run by Jean Todt, was well on the way to adding to past successes, thanks to the qualities of the F2001. McLaren boss Ron Dennis had hoped the Italian crew would lack motivation and rest on its laurels. On the contrary, Ferrari was keen to maintain its dominance. For the moment, and without knowing what 2002 will bring, it does seem as though we are in the middle of a Ferrari era. The only blot on their copybook was in failing to get Rubens Barrichello to the runner-up slot in the Drivers' classification, despite the best efforts of all concerned.

"*If I can help Rubens, I will do it, because that's how things work in a team,*" claimed Schumacher, after he took the title. He was ready to play team tactics, even if it meant sacrificing a win, which would have put him out on his own in terms of grands prix won. But two weeks later, in Spa, where he made his F1 debut ten years earlier at the wheel of a Jordan, he snatched his fifty second win. However, everything possible was done for Rubens

in the last few races. He even had the use of the spare car, as well as extra attention from technical director and strategist, Ross Brawn and help from his team-mate. He was never able to get into a position where he could make the most of it. As for Schumacher, he hit a low at Monza, badly affected by the events in New York and Washington. He fought back in Indianapolis and went on to close the year with a win in Suzuka; his fifty third.

"*A win is the best way to end the season before the winter break,*" he said. "*It is a great motivation for the team and gives confidence for the next race.*"

With eleven pole positions and nine wins, he proved yet again, that given equal equipment, he is unbeatable. Never quickest in qualifying, the best Barrichello could do was pick up second places: three behind his team-mate, in Melbourne, Monaco and Budapest; two behind the BMW-Williams of Ralf Schumacher and two more behind Juan Pablo Montoya in Hockenheim and Monza. He was beaten into third place in the championship by David Coulthard, with fifty six points. That was less than half Michael Schumacher's tally of 123, in itself a new record for points scored in a season.

What is there left for Michael Schumacher to achieve? "*To carry on winning as many races as possible,*" he replies. "*That's my main objective, because every weekend you start from scratch. That's why F1 is so tough and what I think adds to its attraction. I still want more. The fire still burns for me to give the maximum for a good time to come.*"

He will not be able to reach Ayrton Senna's record of sixty five poles in 2002, as he is on forty three, but he could hope to equal Juan Manuel Fangio's all-time record of five world championship titles next season.

"*It's not a real target, because it does not seem*

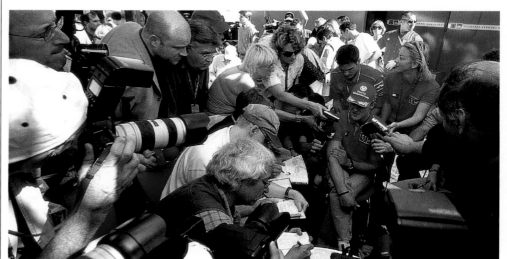

right to make the comparison," claims Schumacher. "*What that man did, at the time he was racing, in the Fifties, with cars that went so quickly and with so little safety, seems exceptional and incredible. I don't think I could have done it. Compared with that, everything the drivers of the modern era can do seems a bit less impressive*". Coming from a driver whom people unfairly reckon is arrogant, this sincere compliment demonstrates some good human qualities. While crushing F1 with his talent, the German is not the sort to blow his own trumpet.

"*You cannot imagine what a great team Ferrari is,*" he insisted after winning in Budapest, evidently ignoring how much of a role he has played in its success since joining the Scuderia in 1996. "*It's an exceptional team, so good and it is a real pleasure to work with them. Everyone puts so much into their work, with so much determination and passion. The human relationships are very good and I really owe them. When I think of everything we have gone through together over the years, I tell myself this team is simply the best!*"

The best, above all, when compared with McLaren-Mercedes, its main rival since 1998. At first the Anglo-German squad was dominant, then the two were about equal, but now McLaren has taken a pasting. Two pole positions and two wins for David Coulthard; no poles and two wins for Mika Hakkinen. That was the story of a season characterised by bad luck and lack of reliability. In Barcelona, Hakkinen had the race in his pocket, leading Michael Schumacher, only to have the clutch fail within sight of the flag.

It was at this very same Spanish Grand Prix that electronic driver aids, such as traction and launch control and automatic transmission, were reintroduced. McLaren-Mercedes suffered all sorts of problems with these gizmos. Despite the competence of its TAG electronics group, these new devices saw its cars stranded on the grid no less than five times, either at the start of the formation lap or the race itself. In these circumstances, the fact David Coulthard managed to fight his way

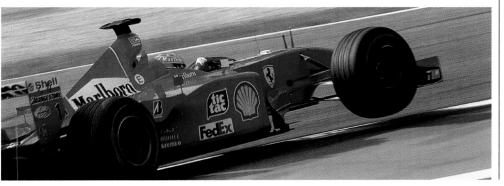

to the runner-up slot in the championship can be seen as a minor triumph.

"*We put all our effort into winning,*" maintains Ron Dennis. "*If we have not managed it very often, there can only be one obvious reason: on several occasions, the job we did just wasn't good enough. Our performance level was good, but reliability was not. The most important thing is to analyse carefully what happened and to take the appropriate measures to ensure it does not happen again. In the end, we have to admit that the best team won.*"

Even if Ron Dennis reckons his cars were quick enough, they were usually out-paced by the BMW-Williams. Fragile and with inconsistent handling, because of the relative inexperience of Michelin, making their F1 comeback, the FW23 nevertheless managed to put up some devastating results: just one pole but three wins for Ralf Schumacher and three pole positions and just one win for Juan Pablo Montoya.

With his first grand prix win, in his fifth F1 season, the Ferrari driver's little brother, the duo finally succeeded in doing what brothers in other families; Stewart, Rodriguez, Fittipaldi, Scheckter, Villeneuve and Fabi had all failed to do. They were the first brothers to win grands prix.

The 1999 CART champion and winner of the rival IRL series' premier event, the Indy 500 in 2000, Juan Pablo Montoya became the first Colombian to win a grand prix. Along with Finland's Kimi Raikkonen in the Sauber camp and Fernando Alonso at Minardi, he was part of a new generation, who showed that right from their first season in the sport, they had the talent to maybe one day challenge Michael Schumacher. Of course, Montoya, as a former F3000 champion and Williams test driver was more experienced than the other rookies.

Ferrari was dominant, McLaren-Mercedes was on the slide and BMW-Williams in the ascendant: these three were the dominant trio: apart from the poles and the wins, between

△
The joy and emotion of a fourth world title, as he steps out of the cockpit (left) and on the podium (right).

◁
The world champion with his two children, Gina Maria and Mick.

them they took all the race fastest laps. Back in 1999, the Mugen powered Jordans had won two races. But now there was a huge gap between the giants and their chasers. Neither the Irish team, despite sharing a works Honda engine with BAR, nor Jaguar, flying the Ford flag, nor Benetton, who partnered a returning Renault, determined to take some brave risks on the engine front, were able to challenge the top three. In fact, against all expectations, it was the Sauber-Petronas crew, with its Ferrari customer engine, which settled into the fourth slot.

Although this year was all about the glory that Michael Schumacher brought to Ferrari, both the driver and the team experienced some scary moments: the barrel roll in practice for the Australian Grand Prix, being hit by Luciano Burti's Prost-Acer at the start in Germany and also two heavy crashes caused by mechanical failure in private testing. The first was at Monza in July, and the second was at Mugello in August, after the titles were won.

Although, Schumacher took a break from work after both these incidents, he emerged uscathed both physically and mentally. "*The main thing is to always understand what caused the accident,*" concluded Schumacher. He always managed to put this type of incident out of his mind and set off on the right foot once again. ∎

David Coulthard finished second in the championship. While he mounted a challenge to Michael Schumacher at the start of the season, it did not last long.

Juan Pablo Montoya was making his F1 debut this year. After a running-in period, he had the measure of his teammate by the end of the season.

Sauber: on the way up

Having been supported by Mercedes in Sports Cars, Peter Sauber entered F1 in 1993 with backing from the German company, but after two seasons, Mercedes switched allegiance to McLaren. The Swiss team made do with Ford power for two years.
Then in 1997, it signed up for Ferrari customer engines.
Re-badged Petronas, the name of Malaysia's national oil company, these power units are the ones that Ferrari used in the previous season.

In theory, they are therefore at a disadvantage and less evolved than the competition. On top of that, they cost between twenty and thirty million dollars, which does not leave much money for development in other areas.
However, this year, Sauber was surprisingly successful, taking fourth place in the championship. It scored 22 points, four more than its previous best in 1995.
It might be a long way off the 179, 102 and 80 of the top trio, but it was enough to get

the better of BAR and Jordan, both benefiting from freely supplied factory engines. As Peter Sauber says with satisfaction, he is the first of the independents.
Having started off relying on Mercedes, the team's independence has indeed proved its strength.
However, in order to move up, a new strategy will be required, involving a tie-up with a manufacturer of its own. With its very Swiss outlook on life, Sauber has just completed its greatest season.

△
Once again, all the grands prix, with the exception of Indianapolis, were run in front of full houses. F1 is a global success at the start of the millennium.

Peter Sauber and his Petronas-badged Ferrari engine. One of the pleasant surprises of the season.
▽

When a team has to put its own name on the cars' side-pods, it is a bad sign. Usually, that is one of the prized slots for a sponsor. But, from Melbourne to Suzuka, "Prost Grand Prix," meant to be just a temporary fill-in, obstinately stayed painted on the side of the cars. After a tempestuous bust up with Peugeot at the end of 2000, several of the sponsors, who had been there since the team was formed in 1997, disappeared as well: Gauloises, Bic, Yahoo!, Agfa and PlayStation had all been there in 2000 on the AP03-Peugeot, but were missing on the AP04. It had to carry the impressive cost of running a Ferrari customer engine, renamed Acer, after the computer company. South American television was there, in the form of PSN, although they did not meet all their contractual obligations and Adecco and Parmalat, brought along by Pedro Diniz. Having hung up his helmet, the Brazilian and his father were actually owners of forty percent of the team. With the team floundering in debt, to the extent that it had to cea-

Prost: money troubles

se testing during the summer, Diniz offered to buy Alain Prost out of the team. Understandably, Prost refused and fought to find any solution possible, struggling from day to day to keep the team afloat. It is possible that Bernie Ecclestone helped out by giving Alain an advance on the TV revenues he was owed. The situation was so serious that Prost himself did not come to the final race in Japan, preferring to stay in Europe chasing funds. He was determined not to let the team slip from his grasp.

Honda: a lack of power

An ill wind blew through the Blues this year. Nothing worked for the Prost team, from the budget to the relations with the drivers (below, Alain Prost with Jean Alesi).
▽

Times have certainly changed. The last time it was in F1, from 1983 to 1992, Honda was the reference point.
With its V6 turbo and then its normally aspirated V10 and V12, the Japanese company racked up sixty nine wins, powering Lotus, Williams and especially McLaren, with whom, in 1988, they won all but one of the races.
It was a dominant performance from Ayrton Senna and Alain Prost. Honda's engines were reliable and powerful.
When they quit, they tackled CART in the States on the racing front and confronted the new stringent anti-pollution laws with their road cars. In the meantime, its satellite company, Mugen, kept things ticking over in a discrete fashion, picking up four wins on the way.

Then Honda returned in 2000 with BAR and then added Jordan to the list this year. Honda wanted to win and, as usual, wanted to use the programme to train its young engineers on a regular rota system. But the sport has moved on at a pace in the last decade. Up against the Fiat group, in the shape of Ferrari, Mercedes, with McLaren and BMW with Williams, Honda has so far only met failure. The only slight relief came from Jacques Villeneuve's two podium finishes, with third place in Barcelona and Hockenheim.
Its engine was out-dated, too heavy and lacking in power. Now they must raise their game. While their technical knowhow is there, finance could be a problem.
Because alongside the giants of the car industry, including new arrivals Toyota, Honda is just a very small constructor.

Bridgestone/Michelin: the war is on...

Bridgestone had enjoyed the challenge of competing against Goodyear, but when the American company pulled out at the end of 1998, the Japanese tyre manufacturer found itself in a monopoly situation.
So this year, it was with a mixture of pleasure and anxiety that it welcomed Michelin back to the party. Absent since the end of 1994, the French firm tackled this new era under the direction of its totemic leader, Pierre Dupasquier, who had been in charge during their previous F1 foray.
Bridgestone already had the two top teams, Ferrari and McLaren, so Michelin adopted Williams as its lead team. The remaining eight outfits were split equally, with Benetton, Jaguar, Minardi and Prost running on Michelin. It did not take long for them to make their mark, thanks mainly to Ralf Schumacher, who gave them a trio of important firsts: a fastest race lap in round 3 in Sao Paulo; next time round in Imola came the first win and round 10 in Magny-Cours, the German delivered them their first pole position.
In the end, Bridgestone won 13 grands prix to Michelin's four, all of them with Williams. The relentless battle between the two tyre companies inevitably led to a worrying reduction in lap times; sometimes as much as two or three seconds compared with the previous year.
The two companies are therefore very secretive about their work. If a tyre fell into the wrong hands, who knows what secrets it would reveal, which is why security in all the pits seemed to be run by the tyre companies.

2001 WORLD CHAMPIONSHIP

Drivers :

1.	M. Schumacher	123
2.	D. Coulthard	65
3.	R. Barrichello	56
4.	R. Schumacher	49
5.	M. Häkkinen	37
6.	J. P. Montoya	31
7.	J. Villeneuve	12
	N. Heidfeld	12
	J. Trulli	12
10.	K. Räikkönen	9
11.	G. Fisichella	8
12.	E. Irvine	6
	H.-H. Frentzen	6
14.	O. Panis	5
	J. Alesi	5
16.	P. de la Rosa	3
17.	J. Button	2
18.	J. Verstappen	1

Constructors :

1.	Ferrari	179
2.	McLaren Mercedes	102
3.	Williams BMW	80
4.	Sauber Petronas	21
5.	Jordan Honda	19
6.	BAR Honda	17
7.	Benetton Renault	10
8.	Jaguar Racing	9
9.	Prost Acer	4
10.	Arrows Asiatech	1

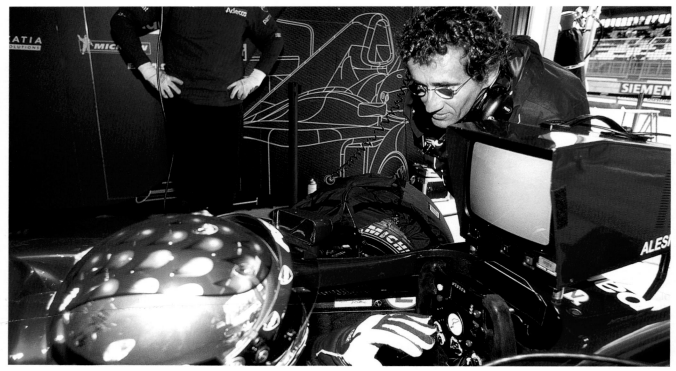

Ferrari F2001: maximum efficiency

by Paolo Filisetti

The 2001 Championship was very interesting from a technical point of view.
The ingredients required to win had increased in number, because of the return of electronic driver aids and the tyre war. However, only one car was truly competitive throughout the entire season and that was the Ferrari F2001. It is hard to describe the development of the F2001, because it did not seem to change very much during the course of the year, whereas it actually evolved almost continuously in every area.
In the opposition, engineers were also very creative.
Here are the most outstanding innovations.

F2001 overview

The car's design was conditioned by changes to the rules regarding aerodynamic limitations to the front and rear wings and more stringent crash test requirements. Although not revolutionary, the Ferrari F2001 pushed every aspect of its design to the limit, with stunning results.

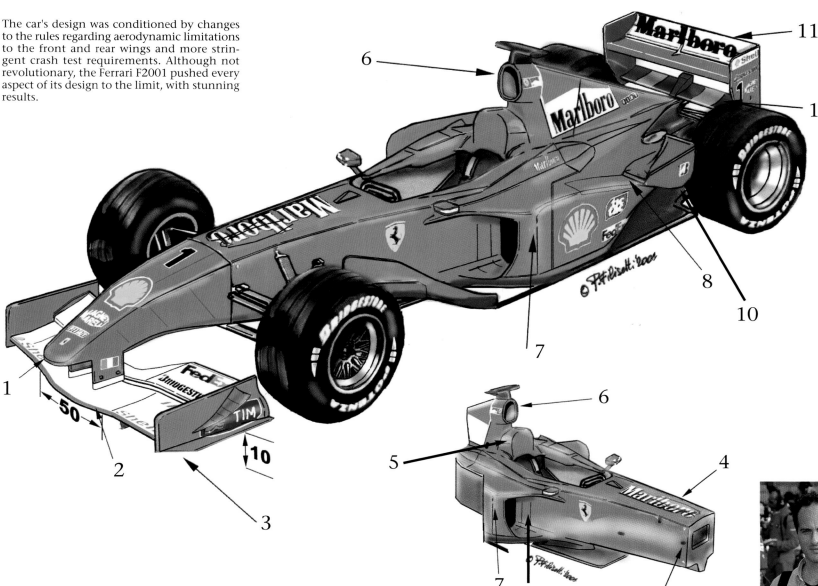

Here is a detailed tour of its main components:

Nose
The nose (1) has a drop down shape, in contrast to three years of running a high nose configuration. As with most of the cars, the front wing sports a central "spoon" profile (2) in the central 50 cm section, as allowed in the rules. The endplates (3) were designed to reduce the pitch sensitivity of the front end and, more importantly, to reduce the loss of wing efficiency caused by the increased distance from the ground (10 cms from the reference plane, instead of the previous 5 cms.)

Chassis
The chassis has a square section, similar to the F1 2000, but with an increase in dimension, especially at the front (4).
The area around the headrest protection was slightly redesigned (5).
The engine air intake (6) underwent a major modification, sporting a round shape to meet the new 2001 crash test requirements and to provide a clean airflow to the engine, in order to obtain constant air pressure values inside the duct.

Aerodynamics
Apart from the "drop down nose", the shape of the car is conventional, with the sidepods (7) about 15 cm longer in comparison to the 2000 version, due to more stringent side impact tests. The sidepods are quite high at the front, dropping down at the rear (8), their air inlets are still thin and vertical (9). At the rear, bodywork is very low and hides a very narrow Coke-bottle shape (10). The rear wing, as demanded by the rules, sports three elements on top (11) and one below (12).

PAOLO FILISETTI,
34 years old, born and lives in Milan, Italy. A Formula 1 fan as a child, he developed an interest in the technical side after studying mechanical engineering. He began working for specialist publications in 1996 and has covered all the grands prix since then. He contributes to several European publications.

Ferrari front uprights cover

This device, introduced at the first race in Australia, is designed to provide a better air flow in the area inside the front wheels. The cover has a cylindrical shape (1) that completely fills the inside of the wheel rim to reduce turbulence. Next to the cover is a very small air intake (2) for disc and caliper cooling, reducing in this way the drag caused by bigger air intakes.

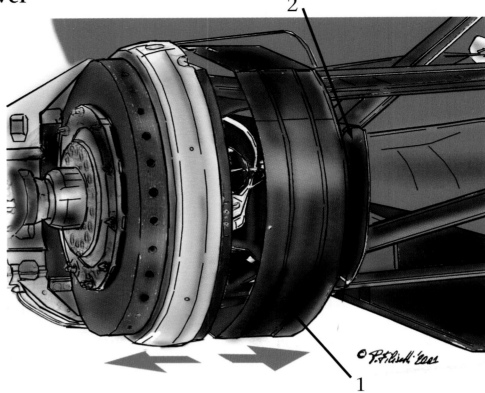

Williams FW23 steering wheel

Throughout the season, additional buttons and switches florished on all F1 steering wheels. Here is the FW23 example and Williams is second to none in this area, thanks to its partnership with BMW.

Here is an explanation of all the functions on the steering wheel

1 - Main button, to cut off the current to the engine
2 - Mixture button and display mode change
3 - Speed limiter and catflap button to close the cover of the fuel tank aperture)

4 - Decremental button in various settings (e.g. fuel mix, traction etc.)
5 - Brake balance between rear (R) and front (F)
6 - Fuel pump button (on/off)
7 - Gear display
8 - Main display (speed, sector times, temperatures: oil, water, etc.)
9 - Drink pump button
10 - Incremental button in various settings (e.g. fuel mix, traction, etc.)
11 - Neutral, clutch calibration (basic on traction, and launch control system)
12 - Radio button
13 - Recovery button in case of malfunction of a programme (returning to manua control)

Evolution of the Ferrari steering wheel after Monza

Following the continous evolution of the electronic devices that were allowed from Spain onwards, in Monza, Ferrari introduced a slight change to its steering wheel.
In fact the upper section of the rim was characterised by a changed cover which included four buttons, two at the sides and two on the top.
At this point only the side buttons were active, used to change the set up of the traction control. They sport a minus (left) and a plus (right) sign in order to increase or decrease the "slip" ratio.

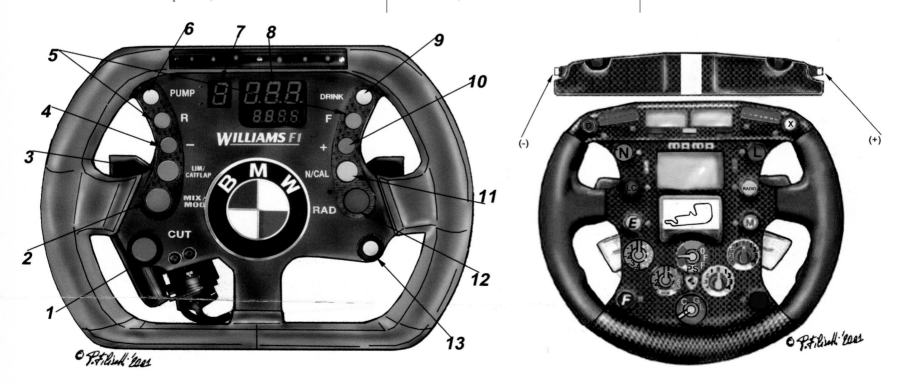

Williams FW23 diffuser in Austria

Further to other competitors' requests for clarification of the FIA technical delegate's report on a diffuser used by Williams, since the second half of the 2000 season, the team had to change it before the Austrian Grand Prix.

All cars have their step in the bottom that tapers to a vee, behind the rear wheel centre line.

Williams engineers found a different interpretation of the rule, placing this vee ahead of the rear wheel centre line. In this way, by the sides of the gear box, the step included two openings (1, in blue) that effectively increased the length of the diffuser, improving the air flow extraction.

The red line (2) is the imaginary line placed 33 cms ahead of the rear wheel centre line, where the step can have a side opening, starting the proper diffuser section.

The dotted red line (3) indicates the old V that tapered far ahead of this imaginary line.

New Williams FW23 chassis and barge boards

Williams introduced a new, lighter chassis construction at the Belgian Grand Prix. It feature an increased strength of the cockpit sides, so as to comply with the new more stringent rules concerning the side intrusion test for 2002.

The shape of the join between the chassis and the sidepod opening was also slightly changed in comparison to the previous model.

One can see from the curved shape of the Castrol sticker (1) the visual effect of increased dimensions of the chassis in this area.

Other interesting elements frequently developed during this season are the front barge boards, composed of three elements instead of the previous two since the last race in Japan.

In fact, a further element shaped as a wing profile (2) was placed at the front of the main shield and inside it, very close to the chassis.

In this way the air flow has been efficiently diverted outside the sidepods, providing a better efficiency of the car's undertray and of course to the revised rear diffuser characterised by new sections following the adoption of the high exhausts configuration.

Monaco: Arrows additional front wing, and Jordan cockpit wing

The Monaco circuit is the slowest track of the championship, so all the teams try to increase as much as they can the downforce provided by their cars.

This time, some of the designers came up with some really weird and wonderful aero devices. Two teams stood out: Arrows and Jordan.

Arrows used a very strange additional front wing which was mounted on Thursday. This new device was a scale copy of the rear wing, connected to the foremost point of the nose by means of two pillars diverting to the top, to reach the maximum width of the wing profiles of 50 cms, as "allowed by the rules".

Jordan was the other team which introduced an interesting solution. On Thursday, a small wing 50 cm wide was placed right in front of the cockpit, connected to the chassis by a single thin pillar right over the front roll over structure.

This solution and the Arrows front wing passed scrutineering from a dimensional point of view, but were banned by the technical delegate Jo Bauer, on safety grounds, as per article 2.3 of the technical regulations.

The players

Twenty years ago, a team would send around fifteen people to each grand prix.

Today a top team will field nearer to a hundred personnel to defend its colours. From chefs to marketing experts, mechanics, engineers and others, there are now thousands working in Formula 1.

Of these, the general public is usually only aware of the 22 drivers. After all, they are the ones who take all the risks, once the red lights go out.

Ferrari

1. Michael SCHUMACHER

DRIVER PROFILE

- Name : *SCHUMACHER*
- First name : *Michael*
- Nationality : *German*
- Date of birth : *January 3, 1969*
- Place of birth : *Hürth-Hermühlheim (D)*
- Lives in : *Vufflens-le-Château (CH)*
- Marital status : *married to Corinna*
- Kids : *one girl and one boy (Gina & Mick)*
- Hobbies : *karting, watches, cinema, karaoke*
- Favourite music : *Tina Turner, rock*
- Favourite meal : *italian food*
- Favourite drinks : *apple juice with mineral water*
- Height : *174 cm*
- Weight : *75 kg*

- Web : *www.michael-schumacher.de*

STATISTICS

- Nber of Grand Prix : 162
- Victories : 53
- Pole-positions : 43
- Best laps : 44
- Accident/off : 22
- Not qualified : 0
- Laps in the lead : 3097
- Km in the lead : 14318
- Points scored : 801

PRIOR TO F1

1984-85 : *Karting: Champion junior (D)*
1986 : *Karting: 3rd (D & EUR)*
1987 : *Karting: Champion (D & EUR)*
1988 : *Champion F. Koenig, F. Ford 1600 (EUR) (2nd) F. Ford 1600 (D) (6th)*
1989 : *F3 (D) (3rd)*
1990 : *Champion F3 (D)*
1990-91 : *Sport-prototypes Mercedes (5th & 9th)*

F1 CAREER

1991 : *Jordan/Ford, Benetton/Ford. 4 points. 12e of champ.*
1992 : *Benetton / Ford. 53 points. 3rd of championship.*
1993 : *Benetton / Ford. 52 points. 4th of championship.*
1994 : *Benetton / Ford. 92 points.* **World Champion.**
1995 : *Benetton/Renault. 102 points.* **World Champion.**
1996 : *Ferrari. 49 points. 3rd of championship.*
1997 : *Ferrari. 78 points. Excluded of championship (2nd).*
1998 : *Ferrari. 86 points. 2nd of championship.*
1999 : *Ferrari. 44 points. 5th of championship.*
2000 : *Ferrari. 108 points.* **World Champion.**
2001 : *Ferrari. 123 points.* **World Champion.**

2. Rubens BARRICHELLO

DRIVER PROFILE

- Name : *BARRICHELLO*
- First names : *Rubens Gonçalves*
- Nationality : *Brazilian*
- Date of birth : *May 23, 1972*
- Place of birth : *São Paulo (BR)*
- Lives in : *Monte Carlo (MC)*
- Marital status : *married to Silvana*
- Kids : *one boy (Eduardo)*
- Hobbies : *jet-ski, golf*
- Favourite music : *pop, rock*
- Favourite meal : *pasta*
- Favourite drinks : *Pepsi light*
- Height : *172 cm*
- Weight : *77 kg*

- Web : *www.barrichello.com.br*

STATISTICS

- Nber of Grand Prix : 147
- Victories : 1
- Pole-positions : 3
- Best laps : 3
- Accident/off : 23
- Not qualified : 0
- Laps in the lead : 210
- Km in the lead : 979
- Points scored : 195

PRIOR TO F1

1981-88 : *Karting (5 times Brazilian Champion)*
1989 : *F. Ford 1600 (3rd)*
1990 : *Champion Opel Lotus Euroseries, F. Vauxhall (11th)*
1991 : *Champion F3 (GB)*
1992 : *F3000 (3rd)*

F1 CAREER

1993 : *Jordan / Hart. 2 points. 17th of championship.*
1994 : *Jordan / Hart. 19 points. 6th of championship.*
1995 : *Jordan / Peugeot. 11 points. 11th of championship.*
1996 : *Jordan / Peugeot. 14 points. 8th of championship.*
1997 : *Stewart / Ford. 6 points. 13th of championship.*
1998 : *Stewart / Ford. 4 points. 12th of championship.*
1999 : *Stewart / Ford. 21 points. 7th of championship.*
2000 : *Ferrari. 62 points. 4th of championship.*
2001 : *Ferrari. 56 points. 3rd of championship.*

He picked up a fourth crown in Budapest, along with his 51st win, to equal Alain Prost in terms of title and race wins. But Michael Schumacher did not rest on his laurels. Next time out, in Spa, he celebrated ten years in F1 with his 52nd win, setting a new record, which he extended to 53 in Suzuka. However, behind the implacable war machine, with every passing year, one realises that here is a sensitive man and not a cold unfeeling monster. Deeply affected by the events of 11th September, at Monza, he drove only out of a sense of obligation and without any brio. In different circumstances, he would have done everything in his power to give the tifosi the chance to cheer him on the top step of the podium.

Yes, he is good. Yes he deserves his place at Ferrari and his masters are happy with him. Yes, he has driven some great races and is capable of winning fair and square. The proof? He says it himself! He is the master of self-persuasion, except that the results, when compared with those of his team-mate, simply do not stack up. Rubens Barrichello ends up being irritating, simply because he is such a nice guy. It is never easy for a driver to admit the superiority of a rival, but now he should follow the example of the previous incumbent of the Number 2 seat at Ferrari, Eddie Irvine, and resolve to do so. Because, once he can get over this hurdle, we will be able to believe in him again.

Ross Brawn

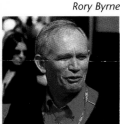

Nigel Stepney

Rory Byrne

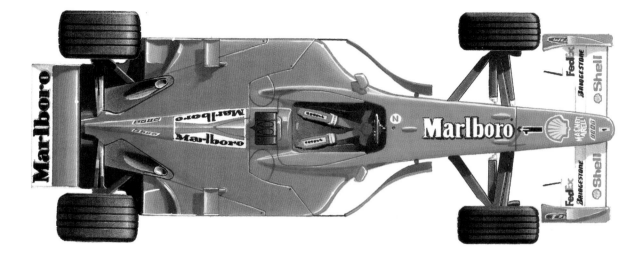

FERRARI F2001
MICHAEL SCHUMACHER
MALAYSIAN GRAND PRIX

P.MÉNARD

Ferrari F2001

SPECIFICATION

- Chassis : *Ferrari F2001*
- Engine : *Ferrari 050- V10 (90°)*
- Displacement : *2997*
- Electronic Ignition system : *Magneti-Marelli*
- Tyres : *Bridgestone*
- Fuel / Oil : *Shell*
- Brakes (discs) : *Brembo*
- Brakes (calipers) : *Brembo*
- Transmission : *Ferrari 7 gears, semi-autom.*
- Radiators : *not revealed*
- Plugs : *SKF*
- Shock absorbers : *not revealed*
- Wheels : *BBS*
- Suspensions : *push rods (ft/bk)*
- Dry Weight : *600 kg, including driver/camera*
- Wheelbase : *not revealed*
- Total length : *4445 mm*
- Total height : *959 mm*
- Front track : *1470 mm*
- Rear track : *1405 mm*

TEAM PROFILE

- Address : *Ferrari SpA*
  Via A. Ascari 55-57
  41053 Maranello (MO)
  Italia
- Telephone : *(39) 0536 94 91 11*
- Fax : *(39) 0536 94 64 88*
- Web : *www.ferrari.it*
- Established in : *1929*
- First Grand Prix : *Monaco 1950*
- General Director : *Luca Di Montezemolo*
- Technical Director : *Ross Brawn*
- Engine Director : *Paolo Martinelli*
- Chief Designer : *Rory Byrne*
- General Manager : *Jean Todt*
- Race Technical Manager : *Nigel Stepney*
- Nber of employees : *600*
- Sponsors : *Marlboro, Fiat, Shell, Fedex*

TEST DRIVER 2001

- Luca BADOER (I)

SUCCESSION OF DRIVERS 2001

- Michael SCHUMACHER : *alls Grand Prix*
- Rubens BARRICHELLO : *alls Grand Prix*

STATISTICS

- Number of Grand Prix : 653
- Number of victories : 144
- Number of pole-positions : 148
- Number of best laps during the race : 147
- Number of drivers' world titles : 11
- Number of constructors' titles : 11
- Total number of points scored : 2659,5
  (2703,5)

POSITIONS IN WORLD CHAMPIONSHIP

1958 : *2nd – 40 (57) points*
1959 : *2nd – 32 (38) points*
1960 : *3rd – 24 (27) points*
1961 : *1st – 40 (52) points*
1962 : *5th – 18 points*
1963 : *4th – 26 points*
1964 : *1st – 45 (49) points*
1965 : *4th – 26 (27) points*
1966 : *2nd – 31 (32) points*
1967 : *4th – 20 points*
1968 : *4th – 32 points*
1969 : *5th – 7 points*
1970 : *2nd – 55 points*
1971 : *4th – 33 points*
1972 : *4th – 33 points*

1973 : *6th – 12 points*
1974 : *2nd – 65 points*
1975 : *1st – 72,5 points*
1976 : *1st – 83 points*
1977 : *1st – 95 points*
1978 : *2nd – 58 points*
1979 : *1st – 113 points*
1980 : *10th – 8 points*
1981 : *5th – 34 points*
1982 : *1st – 74 points*
1983 : *1st – 89 points*
1984 : *2nd – 57,5 points*
1985 : *2nd – 82 points*
1986 : *4th – 37 points*
1987 : *4th – 53 points*

1988 : *2nd – 65 points*
1989 : *3rd – 59 points*
1990 : *2nd – 110 points*
1991 : *3rd – 55,5 points*
1992 : *4th – 21 points*
1993 : *4th – 28 points*
1994 : *3rd – 71 points*
1995 : *3rd – 73 points*
1996 : *2nd – 70 points*
1997 : *2nd – 102 points*
1998 : *2nd – 133 points*
1999 : *1st - 128 points*
2000 : *1st - 170 points*
2001 : *1st - 179 points*

A Masterclass

By the end of the Hungarian Grand Prix, the top slots in both Drivers' and Constructors' Championships were already allocated. By the three quarter point of the season, the outfit known the world over as the Scuderia (literally the Team) as though there is no other, had already secured its third consecutive title. Its imperial leader Michael Schumacher claimed his second in a row. At the end of 2000, Jean Todt's stated aim was to see the start of an era of Ferrari domination and, in the short term, that objective seems to have been met. The F2001 proved to be an excellent car in terms of performance and reliability and all its electronic aids tended to work faultlessly. It was maintained by a team, which operated as a close and cohesive unit, utterly devoted to its charismatic champion. For any signs of weakness, one could perhaps look at race strategy. Despite a reputation for excellence over the past few years, there were times when it looked shaky. In terms of choice of tyre type, the number of pit stops and the narrow "window" available in which to make them, the decisions occasionally looked a bit risky.

McLaren-Mercedes

3. Mika HÄKKINEN

DRIVER PROFILE

- Name : *HÄKKINEN*
- First names : *Mika Pauli*
- Nationality : *Finnish*
- Date of birth : *September 28, 1968*
- Place of birth : *Vantaa (Helsinki) (SF)*
- Lives in : *Monte Carlo (MC)*
- Marital status : *married to Erja Honkanen*
- Kids : *one boy (Hugo)*
- Hobbies : *skiing, swimming, tennis, diving*
- Favourite music : *Frank Sinatra, Phil Collins, pop*
- Favourite meal : *finnish food with meat*
- Boissons favorites : *water, Coca-cola*
- Height : *179 cm*
- Weight : *70 kg*

- Web : *www.mika.hakkinen.com*

STATISTICS	**PRIOR TO F1**
- Nber of Grand Prix : 162	1974-86 : *Karting (5x*
- Victories : 20	*Champion of Finland)*
- Pole-positions : 26	1987 : *Champion*
- Best laps : 25	*F. Ford 1600 (SF & S)*
- Accident/off : 17	1988 : *Champion Opel*
- Not qualified : 2	*Lotus Euroseries*
- Laps in the lead : 1490	1989 : *F3 (GB) (7th)*
- Km in the lead : 7201	1990 : *Champion F3*
- Points scored : 420	*West Surrey Racing*

F1 CAREER

1991 : *Lotus / Judd. 2 points. 15th of championship.*
1992 : *Lotus / Ford. 11 points. 8th of championship.*
1993 : *McLaren / Ford. 4 points. 15th of championship.*
1994 : *McLaren / Peugeot. 26 points. 4th of championship.*
1995 : *McLaren / Mercedes. 17 points. 7th of championship.*
1996 : *McLaren / Mercedes. 31 points. 5th of championship.*
1997 : *McLaren / Mercedes. 27 points. 6th of championship.*
1998 : *McLaren / Mercedes. 100 pts.* **World Champion.**
1999 : *McLaren / Mercedes. 76 pts.* **World Champion.**
2000 : *McLaren / Mercedes. 89 pts. 2nd of championship.*
2001 : *McLaren / Mercedes. 37 pts. 5th of championship.*

4. David COULTHARD

DRIVER PROFILE

- Name : *COULTHARD*
- First name : *David*
- Nationality : *British*
- Date of birth : *March 27, 1971*
- Place of birth : *Twynholm (Scotland)*
- Lives in : *Monte Carlo (MC)*
- Marital status : *single*
- Kids : *-*
- Hobbies : *running, cinema, golf*
- Favourite music : *The Cranberries, Oasis, The Corrs*
- Favourite meal : *pasta*
- Favourite drinks : *tea and mineral water*
- Height : *182 cm*
- Weight : *72,5 kg*

- Web : *www.davidcoulthard.com*

STATISTICS	**PRIOR TO F1**
- Nber of Grand Prix : 124	1983-88 : *Karting*
- Victories : 11	1989 : *Champion F. Ford*
- Pole-positions : 12	*1600 (GB)*
- Best laps : 17	1990 : *F. Vauxhall-Lotus (4th),*
- Accident/off : 14	*GM Lotus Euroseries (5th)*
- Not qualified : 0	1991 : *F3 (GB) (2nd)*
- Laps in the lead : 760	1992 : *F3000 (9th)*
- Km in the lead : 3669	1993 : *F3000 (3rd)*
- Points scored : 359	1994 : *F3000 (9th)*

F1 CAREER

1994 : *Williams / Renault. 14 points. 8th of championship.*
1995 : *Williams / Renault. 49 points. 3rd of championship.*
1996 : *McLaren / Mercedes. 18 points. 7th of championship.*
1997 : *McLaren / Mercedes. 36 points. 3rd of championship.*
1998 : *McLaren / Mercedes. 56 points. 3rd of championship.*
1999 : *McLaren / Mercedes. 45 points. 4th of championship.*
2000 : *McLaren / Mercedes. 73 points. 3rd of championship.*
2001 : *McLaren / Mercedes. 65 points. 2nd of championship.*

He began discussing it with his team as far back as Monaco and it was finally announced fifteen weeks later in Monza. Like Alain Prost in 1992, Mika Hakkinen will take a sabbatical in 2002. If the driver gets the itch again, they say he could be back the following year. If he does not, then a career that got off to a slow start, culminating with two world titles, will have come to a lacklustre end. Faced with an unwilling car, repeatedly hobbled with mechanical problems, he was both inconsistent, sometimes blisteringly quick, usually not, and mainly very unlucky. However, he never really complained. If that's it, we will be left with memories of a man who got on with the job in a totally sporting manner. In F1, that is something of a rarity.

Season after season, he progresses and one cannot fail but notice, because he always tells us he is improving! He has to be seen as a serious title contender and at the start of every year, he tells us that is his sole objective. But David Coulthard never goes the distance. Beaten before the flag, he then accepts the fact with a humble speech in which he admits his faults, before saying he will come back even stronger next year. Sadly, he has been the victim of bad timing, because when his team was at its peak, so was his team-mate Mika Hakkinen. And now that he had the beating of the Finn, Ferrari were too strong. But David keeps his chin up and what could be better for the lifestyle magazines than a smiling F1 driver.

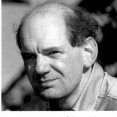

Adrian Newey

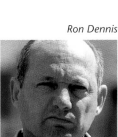

Ron Dennis

McLAREN MP4/16-MERCEDES
DAVID COULTHARD
BRAZILIAN GRAND PRIX

McLaren-Mercedes MP4/16

SPECIFICATION

- Chassis : McLaren MP4-16
- Engine : Mercedes-Benz V10 FO110K (72°)
- Displacement : 2998
- Electronic Ignition system : TAG Star system
- Wheels : Enkei
- Tyres : Bridgestone
- Fuel / Oil : Mobil
- Brakes (discs) : Carbone Industrie
- Brakes (calipers) : AP Racing
- Transmission : McLaren 6 gears, semi-autom.
- Radiators : McLaren / Calsonic / Marston
- Plugs / battery : NGK / GS
- Shock absorbers : Penske/McLaren
- Suspensions : torsion bar/push rods
- Dry Weight : 600 kg, including driver/camera
- Total length : not revealed
- Front track : not revealed
- Rear track : not revealed

TEAM PROFILE

- Address : McLaren International Ltd.
  Woking Business Park
  Albert Drive, Sheerwater
  Woking, Surrey GU21 5JY
  England
- Telephone : (44) 1483 711 311
- Fax : (44) 1483 711 448
- Web : www.mclaren.com
- Established in : 1963
- First Grand Prix : Monaco 1966
- General Director : Ron Dennis
- Technical Director : Adrian Newey
- Team Coordinator : Jo Ramirez
- Chief Designer : Neil Oatley
- Nber of employees : 500
- Sponsors : Reemtsma (West), T-D1, TNT,
  Hugo Boss, SAP-Schüco,
  Tag Heuer, Warsteiner

STATISTICS

- Number of Grand Prix : 526
- Number of victories : 134
- Number of pole-positions : 112
- Number of best laps during the race : 107
- Number of drivers' world titles : 11
- Number of constructors' titles : 8
- Total number of points scored : 2583,5

POSITIONS IN WORLD CHAMPIONSHIP

1966 : 7th – 3 points	1978 : 8th – 15 points	1990 : 1st – 121 points
1967 : 8th – 1 point	1979 : 7th – 15 points	1991 : 1st – 139 points
1968 : 2nd – 51 points	1980 : 7th – 11 points	1992 : 2nd – 99 points
1969 : 4th – 40 points	1981 : 6th – 28 points	1993 : 2nd – 84 points
1970 : 4th – 35 points	1982 : 2nd – 69 points	1994 : 4th – 42 points
1971 : 6th – 10 points	1983 : 5th – 34 points	1995 : 4th – 30 points
1972 : 3rd – 47 points	1984 : 1st – 143.5 points	1996 : 4th – 49 points
1973 : 3rd – 58 points	1985 : 1st – 90 points	1997 : 4th – 63 points
1974 : 1st – 73 points	1986 : 2nd – 96 points	1998 : 1st – 156 points
1975 : 3rd – 53 points	1987 : 2nd – 76 points	1999 : 2nd – 124 points
1976 : 2nd – 74 points	1988 : 1st – 199 points	2000 : 2nd – 152 points
1977 : 3rd – 60 points	1989 : 1st – 141 points	2001 : 2nd – 102 points

Thoroughly beaten

When Ron Dennis' speech patters become ever more convoluted, one knows that excellence is no longer on the agenda. For the third year running, McLaren-Mercedes has failed to claim the Constructors' title and for the second time, the Drivers' crown has eluded its drivers. In the end, the defeated party admitted that Ferrari, its long time rival, had done a better job, but it was hard to swallow. Because internally, a situation already rubbed raw by Adrian Newey's attempted defection to Jaguar, which destabilised the team, was exacerbated by a real rift between McLaren and Mercedes. Afflicted with inconsistent handling, difficult to set up, cruel on tyres, both front and rear, the MP4/16 was far from perfect. Its electrical systems and even the overall mechanical side were surprisingly fragile, to the point that on five occasions, its drivers were left stranded on the grid at the start. Fortunately, there were improvements when it came to race strategy, which allowed them to win sometimes, beating Ferrari, but mainly when the Italians were already struggling.

TEST DRIVER 2001

- Alexander WURZ (A)

SUCCESSION OF DRIVERS 2001

- Mika HÄKKINEN : alls Grand Prix
- David COULTHARD : alls Grand Prix

Williams-BMW

5. Ralf SCHUMACHER

DRIVER PROFILE

- Name : *SCHUMACHER*
- First name : *Ralf*
- Nationality : *German*
- Date of birth : *June 30, 1975*
- Place of birth : *Hürth-Hermühlheim (D)*
- Lives in : *Hallwang (Salzburg) (A)*
- Marital status : *married to Cora*
- Kids : *a boy*
- Hobbies : *karting, tennis, bachgammon*
- Favourite music : *soft rock*
- Plats favoris : *pasta*
- Favourite drinks : *apple juice with mineral water*
- Height : *178 cm*
- Weight : *73 kg*

- Web : *www.ralf-schumacher.net*

STATISTICS

		PRIOR TO F1
Nber of Grand Prix :	83	1978-92 : *Karting*
Victories :	3	1993 : *F3 ADAC Jr. (2nd)*
Pole-positions :	1	1994 : *F3 (D) (3rd)*
Best laps :	6	1995 : *F3 (D) (2nd),*
Accident/off :	21	*winner world final F3*
Not qualified :	0	*Macao*
Laps in the lead :	148	1996 : *Champion F3000 (J)*
Km in the lead :	751	
Points scored :	135	

F1 CAREER

1997 : *Jordan / Peugeot. 13 points. 11th of championship.*
1998 : *Jordan / Mugen-Honda. 14 pts. 10th of champ.*
1999 : *Williams / Supertec. 35 points. 6th of championship.*
2000 : *Williams / BMW. 24 points. 5th of championship.*
2001 : *Williams / BMW. 49 points. 4th of championship.*

6. Juan Pablo MONTOYA

DRIVER PROFILE

- Name : *MONTOYA ROLDAN*
- First name : *Juan Pablo*
- Nationality : *Colombian*
- Date of birth : *September 30, 1975*
- Place of birth : *Bogota (COL)*
- Lives in : *Monte Carlo (MC)*
- Marital status : *engaged to Connie*
- Kids : *-*
- Hobbies : *computers and video games*
- Favourite music : *rock*
- Plats favoris : *pasta*
- Favourite drinks : *orange juice*
- Height : *168 cm*
- Weight : *72 kg*

- Web : *www.jpmontoya.com*

STATISTICS

		PRIOR TO F1
Nber of Grand Prix :	17	1981-91: *Karting (2 times*
Victories :	1	*World Champion Jr.)*
Pole-positions :	3	1992 : *F. Renault (COL)*
Best laps :	3	1993 : *Swift GTI (COL)*
Accident/off :	4	1994 : *Karting-Sudam 125*
Not qualified :	0	*Champ. Barber Saab (3rd)*
Laps in the lead :	122	1995 : *F. Vauxhall (GB)*
Km in the lead :	634	1996 : *F3 (GB)*
Points scored :	0	1997 : *F3000 (2nd)*
		1998 : *Champion F3000*
		1999 : *Champion CART*
		2000 : *CART (9th)*

F1 CAREER

1997 : *Williams / Renault. Test driver.*
2001 : *Williams / BMW. 31 points. 6th of championship.*

At least he does not try and hide his feelings. If he wins, which he feels is perfectly natural, then he doesn't make a fuss, but if he is beaten, he sulks and gets in a very bad mood. Ralf Schumacher moved up a notch by taking his first wins this year, but he still has not rid himself completely of a slight inferiority complex vis a vis his elder brother. Behind the wheel, those feelings disappear, but in public, he seems shy in the presence of big brother. This shyness means he can sometimes snap and his relationship with team-mate Juan Pablo Montoya reflects this trait. Sometimes they appear to stalk one another like cat and dog. For the moment, the team are pleased with this sense of rivalry, but Ralf must learn to handle defeat.

A little bomb! Behind the wheel, he is scared of no one. His thought processes leave no room for self doubt and when he speaks he sounds like a cartoon character, with a high pitched voice, in a hurry to make his point. Juan Pablo Montoya is the first Colombian to win a grand prix and his inaugural season can be divided into two parts. Having over-driven on the track, crashed too often and occasionally upset his peers, the big change came in Montreal. In Canada, he had a major row with Jacques Villeneuve and also smacked the wall. Frank Williams gave him the hard word and the man was transformed. From then on, he drove at "only" a hundred percent and his talent shone through.

Patrick Head

Frank Williams

**WILLIAMS FW23-BMW
RALF SCHUMACHER
SAN MARINO GRAND PRIX**

Williams-BMW FW23

SPECIFICATION

- Chassis : *Williams FW23*
- Engine : *BMW P80 V10 (90°)*
- Displacement : *2998*
- Electronic Ignition system : *BMW*
- Tyres : *Michelin*
- Wheels : *O.Z. Racing*
- Fuel / Oil : *Petrobras / Castrol*
- Brakes (discs) : *Carbone Industrie*
- Brakes (calipers) : *AP Racing*
- Transmission : *WilliamsF1 6 gears, semi-aut.*
- Radiators : *not revealed*
- Plugs : *Champion*
- Shock absorbers : *WilliamsF1*
- Suspensions : *WilliamsF1*
- Dry Weight : *600 kg, including driver/camera*
- Wheelbase : *3160 mm*
- Front track : *1460 mm*
- Rear track : *1400 mm*
- Total length : *4540 mm*

TEAM PROFILE

- Address : *BMW Williams F1*
  Grove, Wantage
  Oxfordshire OX12 0DQ,
  Grande-Bretagne
- Telephone : *(44) 1235 77 77 00*
- Fax : *(44) 1235 77 77 39*
- Web : *www.williamsf1.co.uk*
  www.bmw.williamsf1.com
- Established in : *1969*
- First Grand Prix : *Argentina 1975*
- General Director : *Frank Williams*
- Technical Director : *Patrick Head*
- Team-manager : *Dickie Stanford*
- Chief Mechanic : *Carl Gaden*
- Nber of employees : *380*
- Sponsors : *BMW, Compaq, Allianz, Reuters,*
  Accenture, Nortel Networks…

TEST DRIVER 2001

- Marc GENÉ (E)

SUCCESSION OF DRIVERS 2001

- Ralf SCHUMACHER : *alls Grand Prix*
- Juan Pablo MONTOYA : *alls Grand Prix*

STATISTICS

- Number of Grand Prix : 428
- Number of victories : 103
- Number of pole-positions : 108
- Number of best laps during the race : 110
- Number of drivers' world titles : 7
- Number of constructors' titles : 9
- Total number of points scored : 2105,5

POSITIONS IN WORLD CHAMPIONSHIP

1975 : *9th – 6 points*	1989 : *2nd – 77 points*
1976 : *not classified*	1990 : *4th – 57 points*
1977 : *not classified*	1991 : *2nd – 125 points*
1978 : *9th – 11 points*	1992 : **1st – 164 points**
1979 : *2nd – 75 points*	1993 : **1st – 168 points**
1980 : **1st – 120 points**	1994 : **1st – 118 points**
1981 : **1st – 95 points**	1995 : *2nd – 112 points*
1982 : *4th – 58 points*	1996 : **1st – 175 points**
1983 : *4th – 38 points*	1997 : **1st – 123 points**
1984 : *6th – 25.5 points*	1998 : *3rd – 38 points*
1985 : *3rd – 71 points*	1999 : *5th – 35 points*
1986 : **1st – 141 points**	2000 : *3rd – 36 points*
1987 : **1st – 137 points**	2001 : *3rd – 80 points*
1988 : *7th – 20 points*	

Getting stronger

This was only the second year of the new partnership with BMW, but the team has already proved it is back at the highest level, after going through a barren patch since 1997, when its long collaboration with Renault came to an end.

The engine was blessed with a redoubtable cavalry of horses, reputedly the most powerful in the paddock and it shone, especially on the fast circuits. But the overall package, despite a few weaknesses in the area of aerodynamics, allowed to be in contention for victory at just about every circuit. In its comeback year, Michelin also added to the potential with some startling performances. On weekends when the French tyres had an edge over the Bridgestones on offer to Ferrari and McLaren-Mercedes, the FW23 was definitely the class act of the field. However, reliability was an issue, with the cars often failing to see the flag, sometimes down to the over-exuberance of its drivers. As usual Sir Frank Williams and Patrick Head were happy to see their two young charges battle it out between them.

Benetton-Renault

7. Giancarlo FISICHELLA

DRIVER PROFILE

- Name : *FISICHELLA*
- First name : *Giancarlo*
- Nationality : *Italian*
- Date of birth : *January 14, 1973*
- Place of birth : *Roma (I)*
- Lives in : *Roma and Monte Carlo (MC)*
- Marital status : *married to Luna*
- Kids : *a girl (Carlotta)*
- Hobbies : *fishing, football, skiing, fashion*
- Favourite music : *italiens singers, dance, reggae*
- Plats favoris : *bucatini alla matriciana (pasta)*
- Favourite drinks : *Coca-cola, orange juice*
- Height : *172 cm*
- Weight : *64 kg*

- Web : *www.giancarlofisichella.it*

STATISTICS | PRIOR TO F1

STATISTICS		PRIOR TO F1
• Nber of Grand Prix :	91	*1984-88 : Karting*
• Victories :	0	*1989 : karting: World*
• Pole-positions :	1	*championship (4th)*
• Best laps :	1	*1991 : F. Alfa Boxer; kart*
• Accident/off :	17	*(EUR) (2nd)*
• Not qualified :	0	*1992 : F3 (I) (8th)*
• Laps in the lead :	35	*1993 : F3 (I) (2nd)*
• Km in the lead :	172	*1994 : Champion F3 (I)*
• Points scored :	75	*1995 : DTM/ITC Alfa Romeo*

F1 CAREER

1996 : Minardi / Ford. 0 point.
1997 : Jordan / Peugeot. 20 points. 8th of championship.
1998 : Benetton / Playlife. 16 points. 9th of championship.
1999 : Benetton / Playlife. 13 points. 9th of championship.
2000 : Benetton / Playlife. 18 points. 6th of championship.
2001 : Benetton / Renault. 8 points. 11th of championship.

8. Jenson BUTTON

DRIVER PROFILE

- Name : *BUTTON*
- First name : *Jenson*
- Nationality : *British*
- Date of birth : *January 19, 1980*
- Place of birth : *Frome, Somerset (GB)*
- Lives in : *Bicester (GB)*
- Marital status : *engaged to Louise*
- Kids : *-*
- Hobbies : *surfing the net, to have fun*
- Favourite music : *techno and disco*
- Plats favoris : *pasta*
- Favourite drinks : *orange juice*
- Height : *173 cm*
- Weight : *68 kg*

- Web : *www.jensonbutton.com*

STATISTICS | PRIOR TO F1

STATISTICS		PRIOR TO F1
• Nber of Grand Prix :	34	*1989-1996 : Karting (3rd*
• Victories :	0	*World cup in 1996)*
• Pole-positions :	0	*1997 : Champion Kart*
• Best laps :	0	*Super A (EUR)*
• Accident/off :	11	*1998 : Champion*
• Not qualified :	0	*Formula Ford and Ford*
• Laps in the lead :	0	*Festival (GB)*
• Km in the lead :	0	*1999 : F3 (GB) (3rd)*
• Points scored :	14	

F1 CAREER

2000 : Williams / BMW. 12 points. 8th of championship.
2001 : Benetton / Renault. 2 points. 17th of championship.

There is no denying his talent, but the young Italian seemed to prefer the dolce vita. He would never be the last to leave a test session, never the first to arrive in the paddock for a race weekend. This year, Giancarlo Fisichella lifted his game in every area, knuckling down to work, never complaining about a car which, at first, did not work at all. He got little support on the psychological front from Flavio Briatore, not an expert in driver maintenance. But in qualifying and in the race, he gave it his all, usually out-shining his allegedly "superstar" team-mate. He even learned to speak English properly, having mumbled his way through the language of F1 for the past five years. We now have a new "Fisico" and it might just be a great one.

Last year, he was the standard bearer for a new generation of "baby drivers," discovered by clairvoyant managers who trawled the lower formulae for potential money spinners. He had been the big revelation of the championship. Williams "loaned" the darling of the British media to Benetton and suddenly Jenson Button disappeared from view. Or at least that was the case on the track. Off it, he continued to provide tabloid fodder, photographed with an endless stream of pretty girls, attending chic events or endorsing products. He might be a good F1 driver, but it's a demanding discipline which requires total concentration. Luckily, he finally seems to have realised what is required.

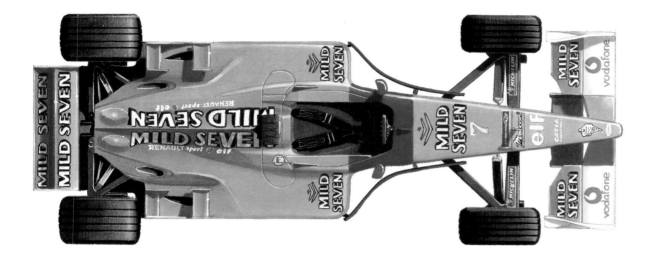

BENETTON B201-RENAULT
GIANCARLO FISICHELLA
SAN MARINO GRAND PRIX

Benetton-Renault B201

SPECIFICATION

- Chassis : *Benetton B201*
- Engine : *Renault RS21 V10 (111°)*
- Displacement : *2998*
- Electronic Ignition system : *Magneti-Marelli*
- Tyres : *Michelin*
- Wheels : *BBS*
- Fuel / Oil : *Elf*
- Brakes (discs) : *Hitco*
- Brakes (calipers) : *AP Racing*
- Transmission : *Benetton 6 gears, semi-autom.*
- Radiators : *Benetton*
- Plugs : *Champion*
- Shock absorbers : *Dynamics*
- Suspensions : *push rods (ft/bk)*
- Dry Weight : *600 kg, including driver/camera*
- Wheelbase : *not revealed*
- Front track : *not revealed*
- Rear track : *not revealed*

TEAM PROFILE

- Address : *Benetton F1 Racing Team*
  Whiteways Technical Centre
  Enstone, Chipping Norton
  Oxon OX7 4EE
  England
- Telephone : *(44) 1608 67 80 00*
- Fax : *(44) 1608 67 86 09*
- Web : *www.benettonf1.com*
- Established in : *1970 (under the name Toleman)*
- First Grand Prix : *Brasil 1986 (Italia 1981)*
- General Director : *Flavio Briatore*
- Technical Director : *Mike Gascoyne*
- Team Manager : *Steve Nielsen*
- Chief Designer : *Mark Smith*
- Nber of employees : *360*
- Sponsors : *Mild Seven, Benetton Group,*
  Playlife, Korean Air, Marconi

TEST DRIVER 2001

- Mark Webber (AUS)

SUCCESSION OF DRIVERS 2001

- Giancarlo FISICHELLA : *alls Grand Prix*
- Jenson BUTTON : *alls Grand Prix*

STATISTICS

- Number of Grand Prix : *317*
- Number of victories : *26*
- Number of pole-positions : *16*
- Number of best laps during the race : *38*
- Number of drivers' world titles : *2*
- Number of constructors' titles : *1*
- Total number of points scored : *877,5*

POSITIONS IN WORLD CHAMPIONSHIP

1981 : *not classified*
1982 : *not classified*
1983 : *9th – 10 points*
1984 : *7th – 16 points*
1985 : *not classified*
1986 : *6th – 19 points*
1987 : *5th – 28 points*
1988 : *3rd – 39 points*
1989 : *4th – 39 points*
1990 : *3rd – 71 points*
1991 : *4th – 38,5 points*

1992 : *3rd – 91 points*
1993 : *3rd – 72 points*
1994 : *2nd – 103 points*
1995 : *1st – 137 points*
1996 : *3rd – 68 points*
1997 : *3rd – 67 points*
1998 : *5th – 33 points*
1999 : *6th – 16 points*
2000 : *4th – 20 points*
2001 : *7th – 10 points*

Flavio Briatore

Betting on the future

For its official return to the sport, having masqueraded behind the names of Mecachrome and Supertec for the past three seasons, Renault opted to go down the route of radical design. The V angle, at 111 degrees, was much wider than the norm, although no technical information was ever divulged. But this adventurous approach cost them dear in the short term. It suffered from a cruel lack of power and was incredibly fragile. The B201 would spend most of a race weekend in the pits or at the side of the track. Because the engines were being continually modified, they never really had enough engines to do any serious work. Despite this major handicap, there were signs of progress in the second half of the season, which brought the team nearer to its goal of hitting the ground running in 2002 in its new clothes. Because, in 2002, Flavio Briatore will no longer be in charge of Benetton, he will be running Renault and the cars will feature even more innovation in the engine department. If the gamble pays off, the opposition will be forced to follow. And at first at least, they will have some catching up to do.

BAR-Honda

9. Olivier PANIS

DRIVER PROFILE

- Name : *PANIS*
- First names : *Olivier Denis*
- Nationality : *French*
- Date of birth : *September 2, 1966*
- Place of birth : *Lyon (F)*
- Lives in : *Varses (Grenoble) (F)*
- Marital status : *married to Anne*
- Kids : *two children (Caroline & Aurélien)*
- Hobbies : *karting, skiing, cycling, tennis, boat*
- Favourite music : *Céline Dion, Florent Pagny, Barry White*
- Favourite meal : *pasta olive oil and parmesan*
- Favourite drinks : *Coca-cola*
- Height : *173 cm*
- Weight : *76 kg*

- Web : *www.olivier-panis.com*

STATISTICS · PRIOR TO F1

Nber of Grand Prix :	108	1981-87 : *Karting*
Victories :	1	1987 : *Champion Volant*
Pole-positions :	0	*Elf Winfield Paul Ricard*
Best laps :	0	1988 : *F. Renault (F) (4th)*
Accident/off :	15	1989 : *Champion F.*
Not qualified :	0	*Renault (F)*
Laps in the lead :	16	1990 : *F3 (F) (4th)*
Km in the lead :	53	1991 : *F3 (F) (2nd)*
Points scored :	61	1992 : *F3000 (10th)*
		1993 : *Champion F3000*

F1 CAREER

1994 : *Ligier / Renault. 9 points. 11th of championship.*
1995 : *Ligier / Mugen-Honda. 16 pts. 8th of championship.*
1996 : *Ligier / Mugen-Honda. 13 pts. 9th of championship.*
1997 : *Prost / Mugen-Honda. 16 pts. 9th of championship.*
1998 : *Prost / Peugeot. 0 point.*
1999 : *Prost / Peugeot. 2 points. 15th of championship.*
2000 : *McLaren / Mercedes. 3rd driver*
2001 : *BAR / Honda. 5 points. 14th of championship.*

10. Jacques VILLENEUVE

DRIVER PROFILE

- Name : *VILLENEUVE*
- First name : *Jacques*
- Nationality : *Canadian*
- Date of birth : *April 9, 1971*
- Place of birth : *St-Jean-sur-Richelieu, Québec, (CDN)*
- Lives in : *Monte Carlo (MC)*
- Marital status : *single*
- Kids : *-*
- Hobbies : *skiing, music, reading, guitar, computer*
- Favourite music : *Coldplay, Fool's garden, David Graw*
- Favourite meal : *pasta*
- Favourite drinks : *milk and "Root beer"*
- Height : *171 cm*
- Weight : *63 kg*

- Web : *www.jv-world.com*

STATISTICS · PRIOR TO F1

Nber of Grand Prix :	99	1986 : *Jim Russel School*
Victories :	11	1987 : *Spenard-David*
Pole-positions :	13	*School*
Best laps :	9	1988: *Champ. Alfa (I)*
Accident/off :	13	1989-91 : *F3 (I) (-, 14th, 6th)*
Not qualified :	0	1992 : *F3 (J) (2nd)*
Laps in the lead :	634	1993 : *F. Atlantic (3rd)*
Km in the lead :	2814	1994 : *IndyCar (6th)*
Points scored :	209	1995 : *Champion IndyCar*

F1 CAREER

1996 : *Williams / Renault. 78 pts. 2nd of championship.*
1997 : *Williams / Renault. 81 pts. **World Champion.***
1998 : *Williams/Mecachrome. 21 pts. 5th of championship.*
1999 : *BAR / Supertec. 0 point.*
2000 : *BAR / Honda. 17 points. 7th of championship.*
2001 : *BAR / Honda. 12 points. 7th of championship.*

Torn apart by an unhappy time with Prost, he risked everything by taking a step backwards to the role of test driver, admittedly with a top team in the shape of McLaren. It paid off and with a rebuilt reputation, Olivier Panis found himself a new motivating force and a seat which, before the season got underway, promised him the chance to shine. But he had to face the disappointment of a bad car, with doubtful reliability. Nevertheless, he remained positive in the face of adversity and proved he was more of a motivator and fine tuner than his team-mate. Respected and listened to, he was therefore the first driver to make his home in the Villeneuve household.

In his Williams days, when the team handed him a world title, he seemed to be capable of rattling Michael Schumacher's cage in fine style. Then, he opted to go for an adventure based on friendship with Craig Pollock which, irrespective of on-track success, was going to be a nice little money earner. Since then, Jacques Villeneuve has slipped unnoticed into the pack. He is wasting his talent, which was perhaps too liberally scattered outside the paddock, with his interest in music or the conquest of famous females. Indeed, how can one be a driver and co-owner of a team, even if he insists on denying the squad was built around him? He seems greedy for all the trappings the sport can bring, without accepting its responsibilities. He is marginalised and incapable of forming a strong unit around him in these difficult times.

Craig Pollock

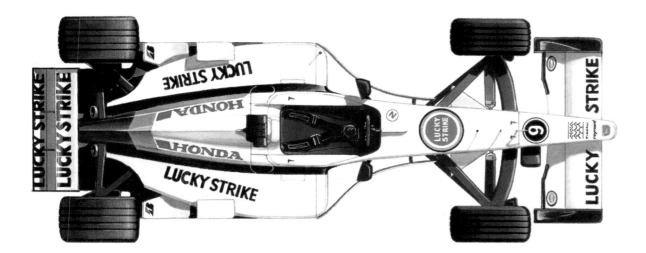

BAR 003-HONDA
OLIVIER PANIS
BRAZILIAN GRAND PRIX

BAR-Honda 003

SPECIFICATION

- Chassis : BAR 003
- Engine : Honda V10 -RA001E (82°)
- Displacement : 3000
- Electronic Ignition system : Honda PGM IG
- Tyres : Bridgestone
- Wheels : OZ
- Fuel / Oil : Nisseki
- Brakes (discs) : Hitco
- Brakes (calipers) : AP Racing
- Transmission : Xtrac 6 gears, semi-autom.
- Radiators : Honda
- Plugs / battery : Champion / Reynard
- Shock absorbers : Koni
- Suspensions : push rods (ft/bk)
- Dry Weight : 600 kg, including driver/camera
- Wheelbase : 3050 mm
- Front track : 1460 mm
- Rear track : 1420 mm
- Total length : 4550 mm
- Total height : 950 mm

TEAM PROFILE

- Address : British American Racing Honda
  Brackley, Northamptonshire
  NN13 7BD
  England
- Telephone : (44) 1280 84 40 00
- Fax : (44) 1280 84 40 01
- Web : www.britishamericanracing.com
- Established in : 1997
- First Grand Prix : Australia 1999
- Managing Director : Craig Pollock
- Technical Director : Malcom Oastler
- Car Designer : Andy Green
- Team Manager : Ron Meadows
- Chief Mechanic : Alistair Gibson
- Nber of employees : 300
- Sponsors : British American Tabacco (BAT),
  Tiscali, Intercond, Sonax,
  Electronic Arts

STATISTICS

• Number of Grand Prix :	50
• Number of victories :	0
• Number of pole-positions :	0
• Number of best laps during the race :	0
• Number of drivers' world titles :	0
• Number of constructors' titles :	0
• Total number of points scored :	37

POSITIONS IN WORLD CHAMPIONSHIP

1999 : not classified   2001 : 6th – 17 points
2000 : 5th – 20 points

TEST DRIVERS 2001

- Patrick LEMARIÉ (F)   • Darren MANNING (GB)
- Takuma SATO (J)   • Anthony DAVIDSON (GB)

SUCCESSION OF DRIVERS 2001

- Olivier PANIS : alls Grand Prix
- Jacques VILLENEUVE : alls Grand Prix

Friendship is not enough

There was not much fun to be had at the BAR. Formed in 1999, thanks to a cash injection from British American Tobacco, which Craig Pollock used to buy out Tyrrell, the team built around Jacques Villeneuve, who still claims to have no financial interest in the equipe, continues to struggle. Having got over a destructive internal power struggle between Pollock and Adrian Reynard, British American Racing has still failed to deliver the goods, despite a more than healthy budget. Not only was the 003 less than brilliant, but the team also made some inadmissible errors of judgement. Having produced an exhaustive study of its weaknesses, it decided to try and resolve them internally, rather than calling in management experts. The drivers found it hard to hide their displeasure from the media and the Honda engine was definitely not up there with the best. In short, this team is keeping its detonators too near its explosives and risks blowing itself apart.

Jordan-Honda

11. Heinz-Harald FRENTZEN

DRIVER PROFILE

- Name : *FRENTZEN*
- First name : *Heinz-Harald*
- Nationality : *German*
- Date of birth : *May 18, 1967*
- Place of birth : *Mönchengladbach (D)*
- Lives in : *Monte Carlo (MC)*
- Marital status : *married to Tanja*
- Kids : *one girl (Léa)*
- Hobbies : *meet and have diner with his friends*
- Favourite music : *U2, The Stones, Simple minds, rap*
- Favourite meal : *paëlla, fish*
- Favourite drinks : *malt beer*
- Height : *178 cm*
- Weight : *63 kg*

- Web : *www.frentzen.de*

STATISTICS

- Nber of Grand Prix : 129
- Victories : 3
- Pole-positions : 2
- Best laps : 6
- Accident/off : 25
- Not qualified : 0
- Laps in the lead : 149
- Km in the lead : 745
- Points scored : 159

PRIOR TO F1

- 1980-85 : *Karting*
- 1986-87 : *F. Ford 2000*
- 1988 : *Champion F. Opel Lotus (D), 6th Euroseries*
- 1989 : *F3 (D) (2nd)*
- 1990 : *F3000 (7th) Sport-prototypes (16th)*
- 1991 : *F3000 (14th)*
- 1992 : *F3000 (J) (14th) Sport-prototypes (13th)*
- 1993 : *F3000 (J) (9th)*

F1 CAREER

- 1994 : *Sauber / Mercedes. 7 points. 13th of championship.*
- 1995 : *Sauber / Ford. 15 points. 9th of championship.*
- 1996 : *Sauber / Ford. 7 points. 12th of championship.*
- 1997 : *Williams / Renault. 42 pts. 2nd of championship.*
- 1998 : *Williams/Mécachrome. 17 pts. 7th of championship.*
- 1999 : *Jordan / Mugen-Honda. 54 pts. 3rd of championship.*
- 2000 : *Jordan / Mugen-Honda. 11 pts. 9th of championship.*
- 2001 : *Jordan / Honda, Prost / Acer. 6 pts. 12th of champ.*

12. Jarno TRULLI

DRIVER PROFILE

- Name : *TRULLI*
- First name : *Jarno*
- Nationality : *Italian*
- Date of birth : *July 13, 1974*
- Place of birth : *Pescara (I)*
- Lives in : *Monte Carlo (MC) and Pescara (I)*
- Marital status : *single*
- Kids : *-*
- Hobbies : *music, tennis, karting, swimming*
- Favourite music : *Vasco Rossi, Elton John*
- Favourite meal : *pizza*
- Favourite drinks : *Coca-Cola*
- Height : *173 cm*
- Weight : *60 kg*

- Web : *www.jarnotrulli.com*

STATISTICS

- Nber of Grand Prix : 80
- Victories : 0
- Pole-positions : 0
- Best laps : 0
- Accident/off : 15
- Not qualified : 0
- Laps in the lead : 38
- Km in the lead : 165
- Points scored : 29

PRIOR TO F1

- 1983-86 : *Karting*
- 1988-90 : *Champion Kart 100 (I)*
- 1991 : *World Champion Kart 100 FK*
- 1992 : *Kart 125 FC (2nd)*
- 1993 : *Kart 100 SA (2nd)*
- 1994 : *World Champion Kart 125 FC and Champion Kart 100 FSA (EUR & North USA)*
- 1995 : *Champion Kart 100 FA (I)*
- 1996 : *Champion F3 (D)*

F1 CAREER

- 1997 : *Minardi/Hart, Prost/Mugen Honda. 3 pts. 15th of champ.*
- 1998 : *Prost / Peugeot. 1 point. 15th of championship.*
- 1999 : *Prost / Peugeot. 7 point. 11th of championship.*
- 2000 : *Jordan / Mugen-Honda. 6 pts. 10th of championship.*
- 2001 : *Jordan / Honda. 12 pts. 7th of championship.*

Right from the early races of the season, the honeymoon period he had enjoyed ever since his race winning days in 1999, had come to an end. It was felt that Heinz-Harald might not have been as fit as he should be and certainly his performance in a race would often tail off in the closing stages. He then got into a state of conflict with Eddie Jordan, who having tried to persuade his charge to up his game, finally decided the German was no longer worth his impressive salary. He was eventually sacked just before the race at Hockenheim. He found refuge in the Prost team, after Jean Alesi stormed out of that particular seat, to end up at Jordan! Frentzen was reborn in his new environment. When he can regard himself as team leader, without coming under threat from his team-mate, his morale is restored and the performance follows. But, if he feels threatened then it's a downward spiral.

Bubbling with energy, he has the ability to find a level of total concentration and pull out a really first class qualifying lap. However, in the race, sometimes his mentality starts to slip out of gear, he becomes less precise and mistakes often follow. Once again this year, Jarno Trulli was unlucky. His equipment was fragile and let him down too often and he was often in the wrong place at the wrong time. But he has been involved in so many incidents, that one begins to doubt his cries of innocence. More sinned against than sinning, one has to ask oneself if he was always the victim. In part, driving a racing car involves an element of predicting what might happen and keeping an eye on others. As he is incapable of allowing himself to lose position, this is something he appears incapable of mastering.

11. Ricardo ZONTA

The Brazilian filled the role of team test driver. He was drafted in to replace Heinz-Harald Frentzen in Montreal and Hockenheim. But, orders to produce a sensible performance meant he never really got the chance to show what he could do.

DRIVER PROFILE

- Name : *ZONTA*
- First name : *Ricardo*
- Nationality : *Brazilian*
- Date of birth : *March 23, 1976*
- Place of birth : *Curitiba (BR)*
- Lives in : *Monte Carlo (MC)*
- Marital status : *single*
- Kids :
- Hobbies : *surf, water skiing*
- Favourite music : *The Corrs, Paralamas do Sucesso*
- Favourite meal : *pasta with chicken*
- Favourite drinks : *orange juice*
- Height : *172 cm*
- Weight : *64 kg*
- Web : *www.ricardozonta.com.br*

PRIOR TO F1

- 1987-92 : *Karting*
- 1993 : *Formula Chevrolet (BR) (6th)*
- 1994-95 : *F3 (BR) (1994: 6th, 1995: Champion)*
- 1996-97 : *F3000 (1996: 4th, 1997: Champion)*

F1 CAREER

- 1997 : *Jordan. -/- 1998 : McLaren. Test driver.*
- 1999 : *BAR / Supertec. 0 point.*
- 2000 : *BAR / Honda. 3 points. 14th of championship.*
- 2001 : *Jordan / Honda. (2 GP) 0 point.*
- Nber of Grand Prix : 29   • Points scored : 3

JORDAN EJ11-HONDA
JARNO TRULLI
BRAZILIAN GRAND PRIX

Jordan-Honda EJ11

SPECIFICATION

- Chassis : Jordan EJ11
- Engine : Honda V10 - RA001E (82°)
- Displacement : 3000
- Electronic Ignition system : Honda
- Tyres : Bridgestone
- Wheels : OZ Racing
- Fuel / Oil : not revealed
- Brakes (discs) : Carbone Industrie / Brembo
- Brakes (calipers) : Brembo
- Transmission : Jordan 7 gears longitudinal...
- Radiators : Secan / Jordan
- Plugs / battery : NGK / Fiamm
- Shock absorbers : Penske
- Suspensions : push rods (ft/bk)
- Dry Weight : 600 kg, including driver/camera
- Wheelbase : 3050 mm
- Front track : 1500 mm
- Rear track : 1418 mm
- Total length : 4650 mm
- Total height : 950 mm

TEAM PROFILE

- Address : Jordan Grand Prix
  Buckingham Road, Silverstone,
  Northants NN12 8TJ
  England
- Telephone : (44) 1327 850 800
- Fax : (44) 1327 857 993
- Web : www.jordangp.com
- Established in : 1981
- First Grand Prix : USA 1991
- Chairman/Team owner : Eddie Jordan
- Technical director : Egbahl Hamidy
- Managing Director : Trevor Foster
- Chief Mechanic : Phil Spencer
- Nber of employees : 231
- Sponsors : Benson&Hedges, Deutsche
  Post, Infineon, Master Card, HP

TEST DRIVER 2001

- Ricardo ZONTA (BR)

STATISTICS

- Number of Grand Prix : 180
- Number of victories : 3
- Number of pole-positions : 2
- Number of best laps during the race : 2
- Number of drivers' world titles : 0
- Number of constructors' titles : 0
- Total number of points scored : 252

POSITIONS IN WORLD CHAMPIONSHIP

1991 : 5th – 13 points	1997 : 5th – 33 points
1992 : 11th – 1 point	1998 : 4th – 34 points
1993 : 10th – 3 points	1999 : 3rd – 61 points
1994 : 5th – 28 points	2000 : 6th – 17 points
1995 : 6th – 21 points	2001 : 5th – 19 points
1996 : 5th – 22 points	

Eddie Jordan

SUCCESSION OF DRIVERS 2001

- Heinz-Harald FRENTZEN : 10 GP (AUS, MAL, BR, SM, E,
  A, MC, EUR, F, GB)
- Ricardo ZONTA : 2 GP (CDN, D)
- Jean ALESI : 5 GP (HON, B, I, USA, J)
- Jarno TRULLI : alls Grand Prix

Fast but fragile

After three years running second division Honda engines under the Mugen banner, Eddie Jordan's team was involved in a civil war with the similarly powered British American Racing squad. Their results were pretty similar. However, their respective qualities and faults were at opposite ends of the spectrum. Fast and even very competitive on some circuits, most notably in qualifying, the EJ11 lacked reliability to a terrible extent in the middle part of the season, the most common cause of failure being the hydraulic systems. 1999 had seen the team climb to third in the classification, but the downward trend was already visible in 2000, with its cars failing to see the flag on too many occasions. In recent times, the team has haemorrhaged technical staff, mainly to Benetton and Williams and it will have to stock up on brain power if it is to move forward and realise its true potential.

Arrows-Asiatech

14. Jos VERSTAPPEN

DRIVER PROFILE
- Name : *VERSTAPPEN*
- First names : *Joshannes Franciscus*
- Nationality : *Dutch*
- Date of birth : *March 4, 1972*
- Place of birth : *Montford (NL)*
- Lives in : *Monte Carlo (MC)*
- Marital status : *married to Sophie*
- Kids : *one girl and one boy (Victoria & Max)*
- Hobbies : *go-kart, moto*
- Favourite music : *UB40, rock*
- Favourite meal : *pasta and dutch dish*
- Favourite drinks : *Coca cola*
- Height : *175 cm*
- Weight : *73 kg*

- Web : *www.verstappen.nl*

STATISTICS | PRIOR TO F1
- Nber of Grand Prix : 91 | 1982-91 : Karting :
- Victories : 0 | **Champion** (NL & Bénélux)
- Pole-positions : 0 | (1984 & 1986),
- Best laps : 0 | Intercontinental A (EUR)
- Accident/off : 20 | (1989), (B) (1991)
- Not qualified : 0 | 1992 : Champion F. Opel
- Laps in the lead : 0 | Lotus (NL)
- Km in the lead : 0 | 1993 : Champion F3 (D)
- Points scored : 17 | F. Atlantic (N-Z) (4th)

F1 CAREER
1994 : Benetton / Ford. 10 points. 10th of championship.
1995 : Simtek / Ford. (5 GP), 0 point.
1996 : Arrows / Hart. 1 point. 16th of championship.
1997 : Tyrrell / Ford. 0 point.
1998 : Stewart / Ford. (9 GP), 0 point.
2000 : Arrows / Supertec. 5 points. 12th of championship.
2001 : Arrows / Asiatech. 1 point. 18th of championship.

15. Enrique BERNOLDI

DRIVER PROFILE
- Name : *LANGUE DE SILVÉRIO E BERNOLDI*
- First names : *Enrique Antônio*
- Nationality : *Brazilian*
- Date of birth : *October 19, 1978*
- Place of birth : *Curitiba (BR)*
- Lives in : *Salzburg (A), Oxford (GB)*
- Marital status : *single*
- Kids : *one child*
- Hobbies : *jet-ski, beach of brazil*
- Favourite music : *Alanis Morisette, All Saint*
- Favourite meal : *italian food*
- Favourite drinks : *Sprite*
- Height : *178 cm*
- Weight : *68 kg*

- Web : *www.enriquebernoldi.com.br*

STATISTICS | PRIOR TO F1
- Nber of Grand Prix : 17 | 1987-93 : karting.
- Victories : 0 | Champion (BR) (1990 & 91)
- Pole-positions : 0 | 1995 : F. Alfa-Boxer (I) (4th)
- Best laps : 0 | 1996 : Champion F.
- Accident/off : 3 | Renault (EUR)
- Not qualified : 0 | 1997 : F3 (GB) (5th)
- Laps in the lead : 0 | 1998 : F3 (GB) (2nd)
- Km en tête : 0 | 1999 : F3000 (18th)
- Points scored : 0 | 2000 : F3000 (15th)

F1 CAREER
2000 : Sauber / Petronas. Test driver.
2001 : Arrows / Asiatech. 0 point.

Without a doubt, he was the undisputed king of the overtaking manoeuvre this year, especially when it came to making up places at the start. He was helped by a car that was often carrying the bare minimum of fuel. Jos Verstappen is a full-on hero in his native land, where his huge fan club have made him their "Boss." Outside his homeland, he is treated with apathy. He is not the stuff of heros and at the start of the year, his physical condition was suspect: he had been spotted scoffing fast food burgers in airports! Despite this, he enjoys an unexpected friendship with none other than Michael Schumacher. It proves he has a brain, which is not always a prerequisite to future success as a Formula 1 driver.

Called into the line-up just before the start of the season, thanks to a heavy bag of Red Bull money, which allowed him to boot Pedro De La Rosa out of a confirmed drive, Enrique Bernoldi at first proved more adept in qualifying than in the races. It was however, during one of the grands prix, the Monaco event, that he managed to get his name splashed all over the papers. He defended his position so well against David Coulthard, who was trying to fight his way up from the back of the grid, that he drew equal amounts of praise and vilification for his driving skill. Over the course of the season, he gradually improved, producing several error-free performances. It was unfortunate therefore, that he did not boost his chances, as he refused to collaborate in any way on the technical front with his team-mate.

Tom Walkinshaw

Mick Ainsley-Cowlishaw

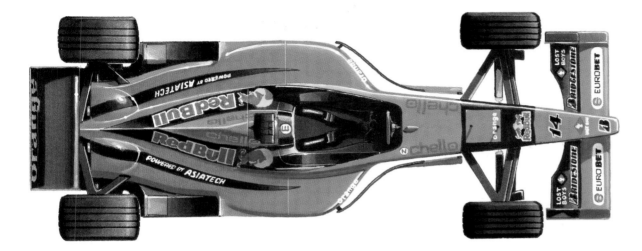

**ARROWS A22-ASIATECH
JOS VERSTAPPEN
MALAYSIAN GRAND PRIX**

Arrows-Asiatech A22

SPECIFICATION

- Chassis : Arrows A22
- Engine : Asiatech 001 V10 (72°)
- Displacement : 2998
- Electronic Ignition system : TAG Electronic
- Tyres : Bridgestone
- Wheels : BBS
- Fuel / Oil : Arrows
- Brakes (discs) : Hitco
- Brakes (calipers) : AP Racing / Arrows
- Transmission : Xtrac/Arrows 6 gears, semi-auto.
- Radiators : not revealed
- Plugs : NGK
- Shock absorbers : Dynamics
- Suspensions : push rods (ft/bk)
- Dry Weight : 600 kg, including driver/camera
- Wheelbase : 2995 mm
- Front track : 1465 mm
- Rear track : 1410 mm
- Total length : 4430 mm
- Total height : 1000 mm

TEAM PROFILE

- Address : Arrows F1 Team
  Leafield Technical Centre
  Witney, Oxon OX8 5PF
  Grande-Bretagne
- Telephone : (44) 1993 87 10 00
- Fax : (44) 1993 87 10 87
- Web : www.arrows.co.uk
- Established in : 1977
- First Grand Prix : Brazil 1978
- Chairman : Tom Walkinshaw
- Technical Director : Mike Coughlan
- Team Manager : Mick Ainsley-Cowlishaw
- Chief Mechanic : Stuart Cowie
- Nber of employees : 200
- Sponsors : Orange, RedBull, Eurobet, Chello, Lost Boys, Repsol, Morgan Grenfell

TEST DRIVERS 2001

- Antonio PIZZONIA (BR)
- Johnny HERBERT (GB)

SUCCESSION OF DRIVERS 2001

- Jos VERSTAPPEN : alls Grand Prix
- Enrique BERNOLDI : alls Grand Prix

STATISTICS

- Number of Grand Prix : 371
- Number of victories : 0
- Number of pole-positions : 1
- Number of best laps during the race : 0
- Number of drivers' world titles : 0
- Number of constructors' titles : 0
- Total number of points scored : 165

POSITIONS IN WORLD CHAMPIONSHIP

1978 : 9th – 11 points		1990 : 9th – 2 points	
1979 : 9th – 5 points		1991 : not classified	
1980 : 7th – 11 points		1992 : 7th – 6 points	
1981 : 8th – 10 points		1993 : 9th – 4 points	
1982 : 10th – 5 points		1994 : 9th – 9 points	
1983 : 10th – 4 points		1995 : 8th – 5 points	
1984 : 9th – 6 points		1996 : 9th – 1 point	
1985 : 8th – 14 points		1997 : 8th – 9 points	
1986 : 10th – 1 point		1998 : 7th – 6 points	
1987 : 6th – 11 points		1999 : 9th – 1 point	
1988 : 4th – 23 points		2000 : 7th – 7 points	
1989 : 7th – 13 points		2001 : 10th – 1 point	

The usual regression

For the second year in succession, this team run by TWR, Tom Walkinshaw's multinational company, which works for a variety of car manufacturers in providing industrial expertise, relied on French motive power, running under a different brand name. In 2000, it was a Renault engine masquerading as a Supertec. This time, his cars were Peugeot-powered, but the engines were badged by the Asian consortium running under the Asiatech banner. Certainly, this instability on the engine supply front did little to help the Arrows team, which has been chasing an elusive first win since 1978 and there was no reason to hope for much. The A22 occasionally made its mark in the early part of the year, mainly through some interesting multi-stop strategies, which saw their cars artificially shoot towards the top of the running order. But after that, the season only served to demonstrate that other sad Arrows tradition, namely sliding inexorably down the order as the championship drew to its close. Yes, the budget is definitely tight, but as Arrows is just one arm of the TWR operation, it is obvious that the heart really isn't in it.

Sauber-Petronas

16. Nick HEIDFELD

DRIVER PROFILE

- Name : *HEIDFELD*
- First name : *Nick*
- Nationality : *German*
- Date of birth : *19 mai 1977*
- Place of birth : *Mönchengladbach (D)*
- Lives in : *Monte Carlo (MC)*
- Marital status : *engaged to Patricia*
- Kids : *-*
- Hobbies : *tennis, golf, cycling, moto, cinema*
- Favourite meal : *hors-d'oeuvre, italian food*
- Favourite music : *Outkast, Moby, Texas, Lauryn Hill*
- Favourite drinks : *orange juice*
- Height : *164 cm*
- Weight : *59 kg*

- Web : *www.nickheidfeld.de*

STATISTICS	PRIOR TO F1
• Nber of Grand Prix : 33	1986-92: *Karting*
• Victories : 0	1993 : *Formule A Laval (F)*
• Pole-positions : 0	1994 : *Champion*
• Best laps : 0	*F. Ford 1600 (D)*
• Accident/off : 7	1995 : *Champion F. Ford*
• Not qualified : 0	*1800 (D), F. Ford (D) (2nd)*
• Laps in the lead : 0	1996 : *F3 (D) (3rd)*
• Km in the lead : 0	1997 : *Champion F3 (D)*
• Points scored : 12	1998 : *F3000 (2nd)*
	1999 : *Champion F3000*

F1 CAREER

1998-99 : *McLaren / Mercedes. Test driver.*
2000 : *Prost / Peugeot. 0 point.*
2001 : *Sauber / Petronas. 12 points. 7th of championship.*

17. Kimi RÄIKKÖNEN

DRIVER PROFILE

- Name : *RÄIKKÖNEN*
- First name : *Kimi*
- Nationality : *Finnish*
- Date of birth : *October 17, 1979*
- Place of birth : *Espoo (SF)*
- Lives in : *Espoo (SF), Chigwell (GB)*
- Marital status : *single*
- Kids : *-*
- Hobbies : *snowboard, jogging, gym*
- Favourite music : *U2*
- Favourite meal : *pasta, finnish dish with reindeer*
- Favourite drinks : *pineapple juice, water and milk*
- Height : *175 cm*
- Weight : *62 kg*

- Web : *www.racecar.co.uk/kimi*

STATISTICS	PRIOR TO F1
• Nber of Grand Prix : 17	1987-99 : *Karting*
• Victories : 0	1998 : *Champion karting*
• Pole-positions : 0	*Formula A (SF & Nordic)*
• Best laps : 0	1999 : *Karting*
• Accident/off : 3	*Formula A (SF) (2nd),*
• Not qualified : 0	*World championship*
• Laps in the lead : 0	*Formula Super A (10th)*
• Km in the lead : 0	2000 : *Champion*
• Points scored : 9	*F. Renault (GB)*

F1 CAREER

2001 : *Sauber / Petronas. 9 points. 9th of championship.*

When he came to Formula 1 with the Prost team, where Mercedes had placed him, it was with a reputation as some sort of mini-genius. F3000 champion with the McLaren Junior team, he was nicknamed "Computer Kid" because of his obsession with analysing the telemetry data with his engineers. Would he be the Michael Schumacher of the next decade? At the end of that first year, he was a nothing and the nickname had been changed to "Charlie Chaplin" because of his mincing walk. Then Sauber took him on and saved him. On the podium in Sao Paulo, Nick Heidfeld consistently demonstrated what he could do. But now he might be bitter. Because despite a Mercedes contract until 2003, it's his teammate who has been chosen to replace Mika Hakkinen at McLaren next season.

Jenson Button's F1 debut with Williams was so successful in 2000 that his management decided to opt for the baby driver syndrome yet again, looking even further down the ladder, going all the way to Formula Renault! When Raikkonen's name appeared on a testing time sheet from Mugello over the winter, one could be forgiven for thinking there had been a typing error. Surely they had meant to write Hakkinen. But he was driving a Sauber and his first name was Kimi, not Mika. He was quickly snapped up and made his F1 debut this year, with only 23 single seater race starts on his cv backed up by an early career in karting of course. Solid, quick and calm, he was a real Finn! Unlike Button, who retrograded at Benetton, Kimi has moved the other way for his second season. He will wear McLaren colours, replacing none other than Hakkinen.

SAUBER C20-PETRONAS
NICK HEIDFELD
BRAZILIAN GRAND PRIX

Sauber-Petronas C20

SPECIFICATION

- Chassis : *Sauber C20*
- Engine : *Petronas 01A V10 (90°)*
- Displacement : *2997*
- Electronic Ignition system : *Magneti-Marelli*
- Tyres : *Bridgestone*
- Wheels : *OZ*
- Carburant : *Petronas*
- Brakes (discs) : *Carbone Industrie / Brembo*
- Brakes (calipers) : *Brembo*
- Transmission : *Semi-auto. 7 gears longitudin.*
- Radiators : *Behr / Secan*
- Plugs : *Champion / SPE*
- Shock absorbers : *Sachs*
- Suspensions : *push rods (ft/bk)*
- Dry Weight : *600 kg, including driver/camera*
- Wheelbase : *3040 mm*
- Front track : *1470 mm*
- Rear track : *1410 mm*
- Total length : *4450 mm*
- Total height : *950 mm*

TEAM PROFILE

- Address : *Red Bull Sauber AG*
  Wildbachstrasse 9
  8340 Hinwil
  Switzerland
- Telephone : *(41) 1 938 83 00*
- Fax : *(41) 1 938 83 01*
- Web : *www.redbull-sauber.ch*
- Established in : *1970*
- First Grand Prix : *South Africa 1993*
- Team Principal : *Peter Sauber*
- Technical Director : *Willy Rampf*
- Team Manager : *Beat Zehnder*
- Chief Mechanic : *Urs Kuratle*
- Nber of employees : *210*
- Sponsors : *Red Bull, Petronas, Credit Suisse*

TEST DRIVER 2001

- None

STATISTICS

- Number of Grand Prix : 146
- Number of victories : 0
- Number of pole-positions : 0
- Number of best laps during the race : 0
- Number of drivers' world titles : 0
- Number of constructors' titles : 0
- Total number of points scored : 111

POSITIONS IN WORLD CHAMPIONSHIP

1993 : 6th – 12 points	1998 : 6th – 10 points
1994 : 8th – 12 points	1999 : 8th – 5 points
1995 : 7th – 18 points	2000 : 8th – 6 points
1996 : 7th – 11 points	2001 : 4th – 21 points
1997 : 7th – 16 points	

Peter Sauber

SUCCESSION OF DRIVERS 2001

- Nick HEIDFELD : *alls Grand Prix*
- Kimi RÄIKKÖNEN : *alls Grand Prix*

A major fourth

It was the big surprise of the year. With two young drivers, which led to concerns the team might falter through lack of experience, Peter Sauber's team, to date quiet and conservative, suddenly took on a new dimension. Despite the handicap of being based in Switzerland, so far away from the sport's home in England, from where just about everything to do with the sport emanates, the C20, with its Petronas badged 2000 model year Ferrari customer engine, instantly proved to be very competitive. Quick, reliable, comfortable on all types of track, it managed to maintain momentum throughout the length season, unlike Arrows for example. This went against the grain, as in the past, Sauber would show strongly in the early races, only to fade away. This time, development work continued apace and was carried out with typically Swiss precision, but without any of the torpor associated with that country. After Ferrari, McLaren-Mercedes and BMW-Williams, all representing major manufacturers, Sauber was the best team; something which, given its status as a "private" team seemed out of its reach.

Jaguar

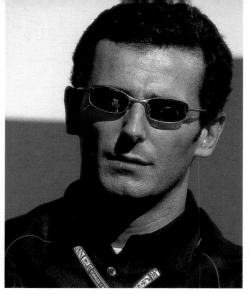

18. Eddie IRVINE

DRIVER PROFILE

- Name : *IRVINE*
- First name : *Edmund*
- Nationality : *British*
- Date of birth : *November 10, 1965*
- Place of birth : *Newtownards (IRL)*
- Lives in : *Dublin (IRL), Milan (I)*
- Marital status : *single*
- Kids : *one girl (Zoé)*
- Hobbies : *fishing, stock exchange, guitar*
- Favourite music : *rock, Van Morrison, U2, Oasis…*
- Favourite meal : *chinese food*
- Favourite drinks : *beer Miller*
- Height : *178 cm*
- Weight : *70 kg*

- Web : *www.eddie365.com*

STATISTICS / PRIOR TO F1

STATISTICS		PRIOR TO F1
• Nber of Grand Prix :	130	1983 : *F. Ford 1600 (IRL)*
• Victories :	4	1984-86 : *F. Ford 1600 (GB)*
• Pole-positions :	0	1987 : *Champion F. Ford*
• Best laps :	1	*1600 (GB)*
• Accident/off :	34	1988 : *F3 (GB) (5th)*
• Not qualified :	0	1989 : *F3000 (9th)*
• Laps in the lead :	156	1990 : *F3000 (3rd)*
• Km in the lead :	838	1991 : *F3000 (J) (7th)*
• Points scored :	183	1992 : *F3000 (J) (8th)*
		1993 : *F3000 (J) (2nd)*

F1 CAREER

1993 : *Jordan / Hart. (2 GP), 1 point. 20th of champ.*
1994 : *Jordan / Hart. 6 points. 14th of championship.*
1995 : *Jordan / Peugeot. 10 points. 12th of championship.*
1996 : *Ferrari. 11 points. 10th of championship.*
1997 : *Ferrari. 24 points. 7th of championship.*
1998 : *Ferrari. 47 points. 4th of championship.*
1999 : *Ferrari. 74 points. 2nd of championship.*
2000 : *Jaguar. 4 points. 13th of championship.*
2001 : *Jaguar. 6 points. 12th of championship.*

19. Pedro de la ROSA

DRIVER PROFILE

- Name : *MARTÍNEZ de la ROSA*
- First name : *Pedro*
- Nationality : *Spanish*
- Date of birth : *February 24, 1971*
- Place of birth : *Barcelona (E)*
- Lives in : *Barcelona (E)*
- Marital status : *engaged to Maria*
- Kids : -
- Hobbies : *karting, mountain-bike, music, reading*
- Favourite music : *Mecano*
- Favourite meal : *paëlla, pasta*
- Favourite drinks : *mineral water*
- Height : *177 cm*
- Weight : *74 kg*

- Web : *www.pedrodelarosa.com*

STATISTICS / PRIOR TO F1

STATISTICS		PRIOR TO F1
• Nber of Grand Prix :	46	1988 : *Karting*
• Victories :	0	1989 : *Champion F. Fiat (E)*
• Pole-positions :	0	1990 : *Champion*
• Best laps :	0	*F. Ford 1600 (E)*
• Accident/off :	12	1991 : *F. Renault (E) (4th)*
• Not qualified :	0	1992 : *Champion*
• Laps in the lead :	0	*F. Renault (GB & EUR)*
• Km in the lead :	0	1993 : *F3 (GB) (6th)*
• Points scored :	6	1994 : *F3 (GB)*
		1995 : *Champion F3 (J)*
		1996 : *F3000 & GT (J) (8th)*
		1997 : *Champion*
		F3000 & GT (J)

F1 CAREER

1998 : *Jordan / Mugen-Honda. Test driver.*
1999 : *Arrows. 1 point. 17th of championship.*
2000 : *Arrows / Supertec. 2 points. 16th of championship.*
2001 : *Jaguar. 3 points. 16th of championship.*

When he left Ferrari at the end of 1999, he forsook the front of stage for the role of spear carrier. For the past two years, Eddie Irvine has kept his pecker up and retained his outspoken manner. He continues to marry the trivial with the consequential with great intelligence. He never misses an opportunity to dismantle the opinions of a Hakkinen or a Barrichello who might feel they are at the same level as Michael Schumacher. During four years alongside the great man, he knows the subject. The problem is that nobody listens anymore. He is anonymous once again: a condemned man, forced to try and get his car and team to progress. But he has not lost heart. Behind the jokey exterior is a hard working driver.

This should have been his third season at Arrows, because he had a contract that said so. But then Enrique Bernoldi turned up with a budget with a month to go to curtain-up and he was out of a drive. Forty eight hours later he was officially a Prost test driver. In the end, De La Rosa opted for an identical role with Jaguar. Except that this post offered the benefit of a guaranteed race seat for 2002, or earlier perhaps, given that Luciano Burti was not expected to shine. It was the right move and from race five, he was lining up on the grid. Since then, the intelligent Catalan, steadily went from strength to strength. In fact, as from Silverstone onwards he became to take the upper hand over his more experienced teammate. His only weakness is that when he makes a mistake, it is never his fault, but always the other driver's.

Bobby Rahal

JAGUAR R2-FORD
EDDIE IRVINE
MONACO GRAND PRIX

Jaguar R2

SPECIFICATION

- Chassis : *Jaguar R2*
- Engine : *Ford-Cosworth V10 CR-3 (72°)*
- Displacement : *2998*
- Electronic Ignition system : *Pi "VCS"*
- Tyres : *Michelin*
- Wheels : *BBS*
- Fuel / Oil : *Texaco / Havoline*
- Brakes (discs) : *Carbone Industrie*
- Brakes (calipers) : *AP Racing*
- Transmission : *Jaguar 6 gears, semi-autom.*
- Radiators : *IMI*
- Plugs / Battery : *Champion / JRL*
- Shock absorbers : *Jaguar / Penske*
- Suspensions : *Upper / Bilstein, carbon fibre*
- Dry Weight : *600 kg, including driver/camera*
- Wheelbase : *not revealed*
- Front track : *1469 mm*
- Rear track : *1408 mm*
- Total length : *4500 mm*

TEAM PROFILE

- Address : *Jaguar Racing Ltd*
  Bradbourne Drive, Tilbrook,
  Milton Keynes, MK7 8BJ
  England
- Telephone : *(44) 1908 27 97 00*
- Fax : *(44) 1908 27 97 11*
- Web : *www.jaguar-racing.com*
- Established in : *2000*
- First Grand Prix : *Australia 2000*
- General Director : *Neil Ressler*
- Technical Director : *Steve Nichols*
- Team Manager : *David Stubbs*
- Chief Mechanic : *Dave Boys*
- Nber of employees : *335*
- Sponsors : *HSBC, Lear, Beck's, HP, AT&T*

TEST DRIVER 2001

- Tomas SCHECKTER (MC)

STATISTICS

- Number of Grand Prix : 34
- Number of victories : 0
- Number of pole-positions : 0
- Number of best laps during the race : 0
- Number of drivers' world titles : 0
- Number of constructors' titles : 0
- Total number of points scored : 13

POSITIONS IN WORLD CHAMPIONSHIP

| 2000 : 9th – 4 points | 2001 : 8th – 9 points |

SUCCESSION OF DRIVERS 2001

- Eddie IRVINE : *alls Grand Prix*
- Luciano BURTI : *4 GP (AUS, MAL, BR, SM)*
- Pedro de la ROSA : *13 GP (E, A, MC, CDN, EUR, F,*
  GB, D, HON, I, EU, J)

Niki Lauda

A political animal

Just as was the case with Jordan, the engineers called upon to evolve the car during the season were not the ones who had designed it in the first place. In this case, not because the staff had defected to pastures new in the paddock, but because Bobby Rahal, put in charge back in September 2000, carried out some executions. In an ironic twist of fate, come the end of August, he too had his head on the block, because of a lack of judgement and his abortive attempt to recruit McLaren's technical director, Adrian Newey. Parachuting in at the end of February, with the backing of Ford's Premier Group, Niki Lauda took over, sending the American back home to look after his interests in CART. Of course, the reason Lauda was looking for work was that he too had been deposed from his own company, Lauda Air, accused of mismanagement. Given the dodgy political climate, it comes as no surprise that Jaguar's second season was no better than its first. Slow in qualifying, sometimes a little bit better in the races, they only shone in Monaco. Just as happened in 2000 actually.

Minardi-European

20. Tarso MARQUES

DRIVER PROFILE

- Name : SANT'ANNA MARQUES
- First names : Tarso Anibal
- Nationality : Brazilian
- Date of birth : January 19, 1976
- Place of birth : Curitiba (Paranà) (BR)
- Lives in : Faenza (I)
- Marital status : single
- Kids : -
- Hobbies : skiing, Harley-Davidson
- Favourite music : Metallica, Pro-Pain, Rolling Stones
- Favourite meal : pasta
- Favourite drinks : orange juice
- Height : 176 cm
- Weight : 76 kg

- Web : www.tarsomarques.com

STATISTICS		PRIOR TO F1
• Nber of Grand Prix :	26	1988-91 : Karting
• Victories :	0	1992 : F. Opel (BR)
• Pole-positions :	0	1993 : F3 (BR &
• Best laps :	0	South America)
• Accident/off :	3	1994 : F3000 (12ʰ)
• Not qualified :	1	1995 : F3000 (2ⁿᵈ)
• Laps in the lead :	0	
• Kil. en tête :	0	1999 : CART
• Points scored :	0	2000 : CART

F1 CAREER

1996 : Minardi / Ford. (2 GP). 0 point.
1997 : Minardi / Hart. (10 GP). 0 point.
2001 : Minardi / European. (14 GP). 0 point.

21. Fernando ALONSO

DRIVER PROFILE

- Name : ALONSO
- First name : Fernando
- Nationality : Spanish
- Date of birth : July 29, 1981
- Place of birth : Oviedo (E)
- Lives in : Oxford (GB)
- Marital status : single
- Kids : -
- Hobbies : football, cycling
- Favourite music : all
- Favourite meal : pasta
- Favourite drinks : mineral water
- Height : 171 cm
- Weight : 68 kg

- Web : www.fernandoalonso.com

STATISTICS		PRIOR TO F1
• Nber of Grand Prix :	17	1984-95 : Karting:
• Victories :	0	Champion (E) (93-94-95)
• Pole-positions :	0	1996 : World Champion
• Best laps :	0	junior Karting
• Accident/off :	2	1997-98: Champion
• Not qualified :	0	Inter-A (E)
• Laps in the lead :	0	1999 : Champion Euro-
• Kil. en tête :	0	Open Nissan
• Points scored :	0	2000 : F3000 (4ʰ)

F1 CAREER

2001 : Minardi / European. 0 point.

There are some drivers who, on arriving in F3000, suddenly appear to have a great future ahead of them. Tarso Marques was quick, but it was said that, on top of this quality, he also had the right mentality. However, as with so many others, this was only a brief illusion. One had to wonder why Minardi chose this year to bring him back to the F1 fold after he had already had a lacklustre attempt back in 1997. On top of that, he was not bringing any backing with him, as he would tell people endlessly. His replacement by Alex Yoong and a healthy Malaysian budget towards the end of the season, at least proved he was right on the money front. But there were so many mistakes and spins that he had definitely been miscast. Although in the end, he maintained he had lost the drive because of people who were against him and ruined his reputation, but the truth is, he lost the drive on the stopwatch.

He came into F1 not yet twenty years old and he has never been seen to smile. In fact, behind the wheel, he never puts on a spectacular show. From a modest background, it was an unhappy childhood which no doubt contributed to his "Buster Keaton" air. However, in the car it was another matter entirely. He knew how to extract every last drop of performance out of his recalcitrant mount. Sometimes, he even managed to get his car off the back row of the grid, where it seemed to want to spend its days, occasionally by quite an impressive margin. It is tempting to compare him with Kimi Raikkonen, who made his debut in a much more favourable technical climate. It is not a valid comparison, but Alonso is yet another good example of this new generation, who are tackling Formula 1 with a natural confidence and a clear mind.

Giancarlo Minardi

20. Alex YOONG

As Marques' successor for the last three races, he neither did better nor worse. However, the first Malaysian driver in F1 is well supported by his country.

DRIVER PROFILE

- Name : LOONG YOONG
- First name : Alexander Charles
- Nationality : Malaysian
- Date of birth : July 20, 1976
- Place of birth : Kuala Lumpur (MAL)
- Lives in : Kuala Lumpur (MAL)
- Marital status : single
- Kids : -
- Hobbies : water-skiing, reading, diving
- Favourite meal : curry laksa
- Favourite drinks : sugar cane
- Height : 178 cm
- Weight : 68 kg
- Web : www.alexyoong.com

- Nber of Grand Prix : 3

PRIOR TO F1

1984-91 : Karting
1992-94 : Production races car
1994 : Formula Asia International Series
1995 : Formula Asia International Series (2ⁿᵈ)
1996-97 : Formula Renault (GB)
1998-99 : F3 (GB)
1999 : F3000, F3000 (I)
2001 : Formula Nippon (J)

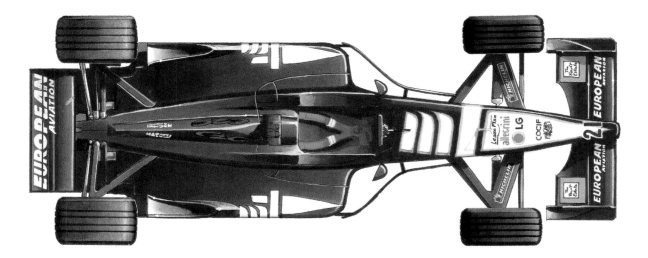

MINARDI PS01-FORD ZETEC R
FERNANDO ALONSO
AUSTRALIAN GRAND PRIX

Minardi-European PS01

SPECIFICATION

- Chassis : *Minardi PS01*
- Engine : *European V10 (72°) (Ford Zetec R)*
- Displacement : *2998*
- Electronic Ignition system : *Magneti-Marelli*
- Tyres : *Michelin*
- Wheels : *OZ*
- Fuel / Oil : *Elf*
- Brakes (discs) : *Brembo*
- Brakes (calipers) : *Brembo*
- Transmission : *Minardi 6 gears, semi-autom.*
- Radiators : *Minardi*
- Plugs / Battery : *Champion*
- Shock absorbers : *Dynamics*
- Suspensions : *push rods coaxials (ft/bk)*
- Dry Weight : *600 kg, including driver/camera*
- Wheelbase : *not revealed*
- Front track : *1480 mm*
- Rear track : *1410 mm*
- Total length : *4509 mm*

TEAM PROFILE

- Address : *Minardi Team SpA*
  Via Spallanzani 21
  48018 Faenza
  Italia
- Telephone : *(39) 0546 696 111*
- Fax : *(39) 0546 620 998*
- Web : *www.minardi.it*
- Established in : *1974*
- First Grand Prix : *Brazil 1985*
- Chairman : *Paul Stoddart*
- Technical Director : *Gustav Brunner*
- Technical Coordinator : *Gabriele Tredozi*
- Chief Mechanic : *Nigel Steer*
- Nber of employees : *155*
- Sponsors : *Lease Plan, Gericom, Sebring, PDP*

SUCCESSION OF DRIVERS 2001

- Tarso MARQUES : *13 GP (AUS, MAL, BR, SM, E, A, MC, CDN, EUR, F, D, HON, B)*
- Alex YOONG : *3 GP (I, USA, J)*
- Fernando ALONSO : *alls Grand Prix*

STATISTICS

- Number of Grand Prix : 271
- Number of victories : 0
- Number of pole-positions : 0
- Number of best laps during the race : 0
- Number of drivers' world titles : 0
- Number of constructors' titles : 0
- Total number of points scored : 28

POSITIONS IN WORLD CHAMPIONSHIP

1985 : *not classified*	1994 : *10th – 5 points*
1986 : *not classified*	1995 : *10th – 1 point*
1987 : *not classified*	1996 : *not classified*
1988 : *10th – 1 point*	1997 : *not classified*
1989 : *10th – 6 points*	1998 : *not classified*
1990 : *not classified*	1999 : *10th – 1 point*
1991 : *7th – 6 points*	2000 : *not classified*
1992 : *11th – 1 point*	2001 : *not classified*
1993 : *8th – 7 points*	

TEST DRIVER 2001

- Andrea PICCINI (I)
- Christijan ALBERS (NL)

Paul Stoddart

New beginnings

Bought out at the end of January by Australian businessman Paul Stoddart, the owner of European Aviation, the little Italian Minardi outfit had been on the verge of bankruptcy for several months. Naturally, the game plan for 2001 was rather hastily thrown together. On the technical side, it was built around the ante-diluvian 1998 Ford engine, rebadged as European, having been called Fondmetal when it powered the Minardis in 2000. In effect, being ready for the season was the first and most important victory of the year for the minnows of the pack. They had to be ready for the opening round in March, in Australia and they only just pulled it off, with the PS01 only managing a brief shakedown before heading for the Antipodes. After that, not helped by the defection in May of technical director, Gustav Brunner, who moved to the Toyota project, and having to rely on obsolete equipment, all the team could do was keep its head above water. Despite an obstinate determination to improve, the cars very rarely managed to hoist themselves off the back of the grid. Doing anything else would have constituted a miracle.

Prost-Acer

22. Jean ALESI

DRIVER PROFILE
- Name : *ALESI*
- First name : *Jean*
- Nationality : *French*
- Date of birth : *June 11, 1964*
- Place of birth : *Avignon (F)*
- Lives in : *Genève (CH)*
- Marital status : *married to Kumiko*
- Kids : *two girls and one boy (Helena, Charlotte and Giuliano)*
- Hobbies : *football, skiing, golf, his vineyard*
- Favourite music : *Madonna, U2, Ricky Martin*
- Favourite meal : *pasta*
- Favourite drinks : *mineral water*
- Height : *170 cm*
- Weight : *74 kg*
- Web : *www.jean-alesi.com*

STATISTICS
		PRIOR TO F1	
• Nber of Grand Prix :	201	1981-82 :	*Karting*
• Victories :	1	1983 :	*Renault 5 Turbo (5th)*
• Pole-positions :	2	1984 :	*F. Renault (F) (10th)*
• Best laps :	4	1985 :	*F. Renault (F) (5th)*
• Accident/off :	34	1986 :	*F3 (F) (2nd)*
• Not qualified :	0	1987 :	*Champion F3 (F)*
• Laps in the lead :	265	1988 :	*F3000 (10th)*
• Km in the lead :	1285	1989 :	*Champion F3000*
• Points scored :	241		

F1 CAREER
1989 : *Tyrrell / Ford. 8 points. 9th of championship.*
1990 : *Tyrrell / Ford. 13 points. 9th of championship.*
1991 : *Ferrari. 21 points. 7th of championship.*
1992 : *Ferrari. 18 points. 7th of championship.*
1993 : *Ferrari. 16 points. 6th of championship.*
1994 : *Ferrari. 24 points. 5th of championship.*
1995 : *Ferrari. 42 points. 5th of championship.*
1996 : *Benetton/Renault. 47 points. 4th of championship.*
1997 : *Benetton/Renault. 36 points. 4th of championship.*
1998 : *Sauber / Petronas. 9 points. 11th of championship.*
1999 : *Sauber / Petronas. 2 points. 16th of championship.*
2000 : *Prost / Peugeot. 0 point.*
2001 : *Prost / Acer, Jordan / Honda. 5 pts. 14th of champ.*

23. Luciano BURTI

DRIVER PROFILE
- Name : *BURTI*
- First name : *Luciano*
- Nationality : *Brazilian*
- Date of birth : *March 5, 1975*
- Place of birth : *São Paulo (BR)*
- Lives in : *Cambridge (GB)*
- Marital status : *engaged*
- Kids : *-*
- Hobbies : *cinema, tennis, shooting*
- Favourite music : *alls, from classical to techno*
- Favourite meal : *pasta*
- Favourite drinks : *orange juice*
- Height : *175 cm*
- Weight : *70 kg*

- Web : *www.lucianoburti.com.br*

STATISTICS
		PRIOR TO F1	
• Nber of Grand Prix :	15	1991-93 :	*Karting*
• Victories :	0	1994 :	*Champion karting Amérique of sud, champ. of monde (8th)*
• Pole-positions :	0		
• Best laps :	0		
• Accident/off :	3	1996 :	*F. Vauxhall Jr. (GB) (3rd)*
• Not qualified :	0	1997 :	*Champion F. Vauxhall (GB)*
• Laps in the lead :	0		
• Km in the lead :	0	1998 :	*F3 (GB) (3rd)*
• Points scored :	0	1999 :	*F3 (GB) (2nd)*

F1 CAREER
2000 : *Jaguar. (1 GP). 0 point.*
2001 : *Jaguar, Prost / Acer. (4 & 10 GP). 0 point.*

Twelve races with Prost, five with Jordan. It was just prior to Hockenheim that Jean Alesi decided that the team he had chosen to drive for had reached such an all-time low and it was time to leave. He slammed the door on them, without really knowing what he would do next. Luckily for him, Heinz-Harald Frentzen had been evicted by Jordan a few days earlier and gave him the opportunity he had been waiting for. He would finally team up with Eddie Jordan again, the man he drove for on the way to the 1989 F3000 title. Despite his speed and enthusiasm which remained undiminished after over a decade in the sport, he learned just before Suzuka that the team would not be taking up the option on his services for 2002. It meant that his long and illustrious career came to a rather sudden end.

Having been given the chance to race in Austria in 2000, when he stood in for an unwell Eddie Irvine, Luciano Burti glided from the role of test driver to full time racer for the Jaguar team. But after four races, he was released to Prost, where he replaced Gaston Mazzacane, making room at Jaguar for Pedro De La Rosa. His performance was nothing to write home about, but he made plenty of mistakes - spins, crashes and had two huge accidents. The first came at the start of the German Grand Prix, when he barrel rolled over Michael Schumacher's Ferrari. The second came at Spa, where he tried a very clumsy and high speed overtaking move on none other than former team-mate Eddie Irvine. It was a huge impact, requiring a few days in hospital and he has not been seen since.

23. Gaston MAZZACANE

His drive was paid for by PSN, the South American television channel, but the Argentinian's contract had a performance clause attached. It only took four races for him to fail to live up to it and he was out on his ear. Ouch!

DRIVER PROFILE
- Name : *MAZZACANE*
- First name : *Gastón*
- Nationality : *Argentinian*
- Date of birth : *May 8, 1975*
- Place of birth : *La Plata (RA)*
- Marital status : *single*
- Kids : *-*
- Height : *173 cm*
- Weight : *69 kg*
- Web : *www.gaston-mazzacane.com*
- Nber of Grand Prix : *21*

F1 CAREER
2000 : *Minardi / Fondmetal. 0 point.*
2001 : *Prost / Acer. (4 GP). 0 point.*

23. Tomas ENGE

The first Czech driver in F1, he was called in to deputise for the injured Burti for the last three races. Chosen for his budget, he emerged from the experience with honour.

DRIVER PROFILE
- Name : *ENGE*
- First name : *Tomás*
- Nationality : *Czech*
- Date of birth : *September 11, 1976*
- Place of birth : *Liberec (CZ)*
- Marital status : *single*
- Kids : *-*
- Height : *171 cm*
- Weight : *68 kg*
- Web : *www.tomas-enge.cz*
- Nber of Grand Prix : *3*

Pedro Paulo Diniz

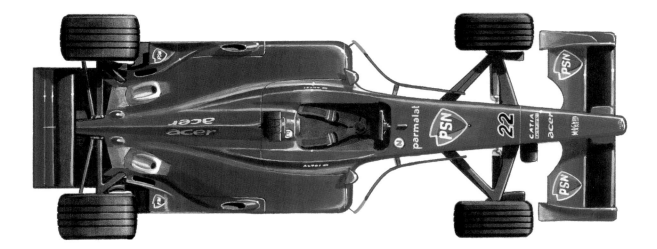

PROST AP04-ACER
JEAN ALESI
MONACO GRAND PRIX

Prost-Acer AP04

SPECIFICATION

- Chassis : *Prost AP04*
- Engine : *Acer 01A (Ferrari 049) V10 (90°)*
- Displacement : *2997*
- Electronic Ignition system : *Magneti-Marelli*
- Tyres : *Michelin*
- Wheels : *BBS*
- Fuel / Oil : *Shell*
- Brakes (discs) : *Carbone Industrie*
- Brakes (calipers) : *AP Racing*
- Transmission : *Prost/Xtrac 7 gears, semi-auto.*
- Plugs / Battery : *NGK / Fiamm*
- Shock absorbers : *Sachs*
- Suspensions : *push rods (ft/bk)*
- Dry Weight : *600 kg, including driver/camera*
- Wheelbase : *not revealed*
- Front track : *not revealed*
- Rear track : *not revealed*
- Total length : *not revealed*

TEAM PROFILE

- Address : *Prost Grand Prix*
  7, Avenue Eugène Freyssinet
  78280 Guyancourt
  France
- Telephone : *(33) 1 39 30 11 00*
- Fax : *(33) 1 39 30 11 01*
- Web : *www.prostgp.com*
- Established in : *1997*
- First Grand Prix : *Australia 1997*
- Chairman : *Alain Prost*
- Technical Director : *Henri Durand*
- Team Manager : *Eric Vuillemin*
- Chief mechanic : *Gabriele Pagliarini*
- Nber of employees : *250*
- Sponsors : *PSN, Acer, Adecco, Parmalat,*
  Dark dog, Brastemp, Catia…

SUCCESSION OF DRIVERS 2001

- Jean ALESI : *12 GP (AUS, MAL, BR, SM, E, A, MC, CDN, EUR, F, GB, D)*
- Heinz-Harald FRENTZEN : *5 GP (HON, B, I, USA, J)*
- Gaston MAZZACANE : *4 GP (AUS, MAL, BR, SM)*
- Luciano BURTI : *10 GP (E, A, MC, CDN, EUR, F, GB, D, HON, B)*
- Tomas ENGE : *3 GP (I, USA, J)*

STATISTICS

- Number of Grand Prix : 83
- Number of victories : 0
- Number of pole-positions : 0
- Number of best laps during the race : 0
- Number of drivers' world titles : 0
- Number of constructors' titles : 0
- Total number of points scored : 35

POSITIONS IN WORLD CHAMPIONSHIP

1997 : 6th - 21 points	2000 : not classified
1998 : 9th - 1 point	2001 : 9th - 4 points
1999 : 7th - 9 points	

TEST DRIVER 2001

- Stéphane SARRAZIN (F)
- Jonathan COCHET (F)

Henri Durand

Survival situation

Using the same Ferrari customer engine as Sauber, in this case re-badged Acer, the Prost team created the big illusion prior to the start of the season. In February in Barcelona and Estoril, it was tasked with choosing the tyres that the Michelin runners would all use in Melbourne. Thanks to the softer compound, in qualifying trim, the AP04 set times which promised more laughs than the team had enjoyed in its Peugeot days. However, once the championship got underway and they were running in similar trim to their rivals, the sad truth was revealed. Indeed, there were those who suspected Prost had deliberately run under-weight in testing, in order to encourage its sponsors. Not that there were any, apart from the odd investor or two. At the end of the year, Alain Prost was still in business, having gone through the summer with a huge deficit which seemed impossible to overcome. The atmosphere within the team was always electric, as characterised by the stormy departure of Jean Alesi back in August. The team got through a total of five drivers and not all of them were of the highest quality. It was yet another handicap which the team could have done without.

Spotlight

As always, "Formula 1 Yearbook" presents analyses by journalists from Italy, England, Germany, Japan and Canada. Different viewpoints to provide various insights into this 2001 season.

On the historic front, our resident historian has marked the death of John Cooper by paying homage to the man and his famous team.

A year of Red emotion

2001 : punto di vista dall'Italia

by Barbara Premoli
«F1 Racing Italia»,

In Italy, Ferrari is Formula 1. Sure, there are fans of other teams and other drivers, but even those who do not have the Prancing Horse in their hearts, must have felt some emotion, faced with such a level of success delivered by the Scuderia and its men. After a long 21 year wait, Michael Schumacher and his boys lifted the 2000 Drivers' and Constructors' championship titles. The task facing them this year seemed, if it was possible, even harder than in the past. It had been a long time since Ferrari had started a season, not in the position of the hound, but instead, in that of the hare, fighting off the challenge of others, most notably McLaren. They did not waste any time. In Melbourne, Schumi, Barrichello et al, set a very fast pace with the F2001 proving competitive right from the word go. From then on, they improved steadily throughout the season, thanks to an ongoing development programme.

What was the secret of success in 2001? The car, the strategy, Ferrari's organisation and the work of the entire team. Worth a special mention was the huge support of test driver Luca Badoer, who virtually lived at the Fiorano test track. But above all, it came down to Michael Schumacher. Like all virtuosi, he elicits mixed reactions, from the real F1 fans to the Ferrari supporters who wish he could be more "latin" and extrovert. But no one can argue about his talent and his ability, not just on the track but off it too.
Michael has built a group around him, a true team which revolves around his captaincy. The German's charisma and his closeness to everyone in the team has given strength to the outfit and united everyone in it. Even the smallest gesture from him, like thanking

every member of the team after every grand prix, makes a big difference in terms of motivation. And motivation in F1, just as in life in general, is a fundamental element of success.

Victory on the track and off it

The 2001 World Championship will be remembered in the annals of F1 for the speed with which it was decided. Schumi and Ferrari had it all sewn up by Budapest, with four races remaining. While Suzuka did not get to hold the key, there was still plenty of emotion and tension in the paddock at the races following the Hungarian Grand Prix. The dramatic events which unfolded in the States naturally affected everyone in Formula 1, leaving an indelible mark on the final part of the season. It went against the generally held view that drivers are from another planet, unaware of events outside their own microcosmic world, only interested in the personal fortunes. The Italian Grand Prix at Monza will mainly be remembered for events off the track. But it will also be remembered as the race where Juan Pablo Montoya took his first ever grand prix win at his fifteenth attempt. It was seen as a sign, as a changing of the old guard, as the dawning of a new era.
The Monza weekend was characterised by tension, heightened further because of Alessandro Zanardi's accident at the Lausitzring. It was a timely reminder that these men love taking risks and are courageous beyond the understanding of lesser mortals. However, they are not automatons who are incapable of thought or opinion or the power of speech. Michael Schumacher and those who side with him, are aware of the dangers they face every time they get into the cockpit, but that does not stop them from wanting to minimise or avoid unnecessary risks. In Monza, this led to the idea of not racing through the first two chicanes on the opening lap. This idea was misunderstood by many, who thought the drivers did not want to race. There is a lot of talk about safety, of ways of improving both passive and active ways of protecting the drivers and all those who work in the F1 environment. In the past few years, huge steps forward have been taken in this area, even if they have met resistence on the way.

A very Italian will to win

Apart from Ferrari, Italy has other knights in armour to follow and in whom to take pride. The country boasts another Scuderia worthy of note, namely Minardi, or more correctly, European-Minardi F1. The Italian team has a fine past since it made its F1 debut in 1985, but it lived through difficult times in the early part of 2001. Right up to the eve of the race in Melbourne, its future on the world stage was in doubt. Then the Australian, Paul Stoddart came along, with his business sense and his funding and he changed the course of the squad's history. Stoddart is a unique investor, with a true passion for the sport. Having taken control of the team, he decided to merge it with his European Formula Racing

BARBARA PREMOLI
Born in Milan (29/9/1963), Barbara has always been interested in cars, especially F1. She graduated in languages and intended becoming a teacher, a small Situations Vacant advertisement in "La Gazzetta dello Sport" changed her life. In the space of a few days, she found herself working for "Motociclismo" magazine, where she enjoyed working for ten years. Then, from January 1999, she accepted the challenge of launching the Italian version of "F1 Racing". Today she is proud to be the editor of this publication.

set up, in Ledbury, while ensuring the Minardi team's unique identity remained intact. Australia was in fact the start of a new era for Giancarlo Minardi's boys, as they kicked off with a clean sheet of paper, but with the same enthusiasm and dedication as usual. Fernando Alonso was a symbol of this desire to start afresh. Very young, determined, very quick and promising, he never managed to leave the back of the grid, but he fought tooth and nail without ever complaining about the limitations of the equipment at his disposal. He finished the season taking the flag in Suzuka in eleventh place.

Even the smallest gesture from Michael Schumacher, ike thanking every member of the team after every grand prix, makes a big difference in terms of motivation.

This result can be regarded as something of a victory. This great team needed Fernando's talent. The word "great" is not to be scoffed at when applied to Minardi, as over the years it has launched many a driver's career, especially that of Michele Alboreto. Because one of the Faenza team's strong points is the way it forms the character of those who work for it, not just in the pits but also out on the track. Minardi is a great school for learning to deal with the hard knocks in life, to fight for results and to keep going despite any disadvantages of being the minnows of the pack.

Two other examples of this will to fight, whatever the cicumstances, are Jarno Trulli and Giancarlo Fisichella, two young, quick drivers who are only 27 and 28 years old respectively. They have already matured and have plenty of experience in F1, even if their great efforts have not yet been rewarded with major results. They both lived through a 2001 season which was far from easy. Jarno fought all 17 rounds at the wheel of a Jordan that was competitive in performance terms but had reliability issues. Fantastic qualifying results would inevitably be followed 24 hours later by a disappointing race with too many mechanical failures. But the man from Pescara is a tough nut and he never gave up. Losing his three points for fourth place in Indianapolis was a major blow. He had richly deserved the result, but the FIA disqualified him as the plank under the Jordan had worn too much. Luckily, Jordan's appeal against the decision was successful and the precious points were returned, providing a great morale booster for Jarno and recognition of all his efforts.

Giancarlo lived through a difficult season, which signalled the changing of the guard from Benetton to Renault. The car was new of course, but the engine was very radical with a 111 degree V angle. His contract was expiring and his team-mate Jenson Button was heavily supported by the media, especially the British, after his great debut season in 2000. Fisico emerged above all these problems, head held high. Thanks to his efforts, the car progressed enormously, if unexpectedly towards the end of the season. He even made it to the step of the podium in Spa. More importantly, he always had the legs of young Jenson, both in qualifying and the race. There was no dealing with Flavio Briatore however, when it came to renewing his contract. But the interesting news is that for 2002, our Italian heros will swop colours, with Jarno moving to the new Renault team, run by Briatore, who is actually his manager, while Giancarlo will drive for the colourful Eddie Jordan; the second time in his career he has been part of the Irish team. Who is favou-

rite to succeed out of these two? At the moment, it would have to be Trulli, who will be handed a car in the middle of a rapid phase of development, a team with a more solid budget and all the tradition and expectations that come from an association with Renault. But above all, he will be working for a boss, Flavio Briatore, who despite his hankering for the glamorous lifestyle, is known for his abilities as an organiser and a motivator. European-Minardi F1, Jarno and Giancarlo have a great deal of support in Italy, true fans who stick by their drivers through thick or thin. Of course, it is easier to attract a following when you are picking up the trophies, but their fans will not lose heart and cannot wait for the day when they will be able to cheer their drivers on the top most step of the podium. Surely that day can no longer be too far away.

A moment to reflect

In a season rich in novelty, enthusiasm and great sporting moments, it seems appropriate to remember some of F1's darker moments, when emotion turned to fear. In the course of the year, there have been some miraculous escapes, with drivers emerging unscathed from big accidents: Jacques Villeneuve in Melbourne, Luciano Burti in Hockenheim and Spa, Michael Schumacher in Australia and in private testing in Monza, Jean Alesi and Kimi Raikkonen in Suzuka and Mika Hakkinen in Monza, to name the most spectacular incidents, which caused the biggest intake of breath from those watching from the sidelines.

Formula 1 is a sport which transcends the narrow confines of the race tracks, as everyone who follows it as a fan or works in the environment on a daily basis knows only too well.

In all cases, no driver was injured. That was due in no small part to the increased safety regulations introduced by FIA. They really proved effective. It would be wrong to ignore the danger of this sport and there is still

much work to do to ensure we do not have repeats of the type of incident, which led to the death of a marshal in Melbourne, in the accident involving Jacques Villeneuve and Ralf Schumacher. Villeneuve was lucky to walk away with nothing worse than pains in his back.

It was a busy year, sadly marked by the deaths of several people who loved Formula 1 and had made their mark in various ways on the sport. Some of these were particularly linked to Italy: Michele Alboreto, Vittorio Brambilla, Gabriele Rumi.

Others no longer with us include Paul Morgan from Ilmor and the journalists Pepi Cereda and Derek Wright. Ken Tyrrell leaves a huge void in the sport for fans all over the world. All these men gave their all to the sport they loved. Formula 1 is a sport which transcends the narrow confines of the race tracks, as everyone who follows it as a fan or works in the environment on a daily basis knows only too well. They and others, like Alex Zanardi, who has vowed to start afresh, are the true champions of 2001.

Scuderia Ferrari's master helmsman managed to steer his team to success for the third consecutive year.
▽

Jaguar: the poisoned chalice

by Nigel Roebuck
«Autosport»

Seventeen races, 34 starts, 10 points. Jaguar's 2001 season did not add up to much, particularly when you considered how much had been spent on it.

Perhaps, though, it was not surprising, for the team lacked many of the engineering facilities - including its own wind-tunnel - which others took for granted.

Nor did it have a true umber one driver. Eddie Irvine, never burdened with modesty, suggested in a midseason interview that Michael Schumacher was the best driver in the world - followed by himself. That being so, there was some surprise when the second best driver in the world was six times out-qualified by journeyman Pedro de la Rosa...

The crowning glories of Jaguar's season were a good third place by Irvine at Monte Carlo, a fourth at Indianapolis, and a fine run to fifth by de la Rosa at Monza. If the team had little to show, in terms of results, however, for Macchiavellian intrigue it was unapproached. It was in December 2000 that Bobby Rahal, one of the legends of Indycar racing as both driver and team owner, took up the job of Chief Executive Officer of Jaguar Racing. He had been appointed by the Ford CEO, Jac Nasser, on the recommendation of Neil Ressler, the Ford senior executive who had run the team in 2000. The initial contract was for three years, and Ressler himself was to continue as chairman of Jaguar Racing, and also of Cosworth Racing and Pi Research.

In 2000 the Jaguar team achieved remarkably little, and the lack of success was amplified by an over-hyped marketing operation, which gave the impression, from the outset, that Ferrari had better watch out. It was an invitation to ridicule.

When Rahal arrived at Milton Keynes, he found an outfit in disarray, a level of morale desperately low, and perhaps only then came fully to appreciate the extent of the task before him.

"*There's a lot to do here,*" he mused in February. "*It's like a supertanker - I read somewhere it takes five miles to stop a supertanker. Well, I've got the brakes on here, and I'm trying to turn it around.*"

NIGEL ROEBUCK, 54 years old, decided to quit his industrial job and enter journalism at the age of 24. In 1971, he starts writing for the American magazine «Car & Driver», before joining the British weekly motor racing magazine «Autosport» in 1976. He is covering Formula One since 1977, while workingfor the «Sunday Tmes», for the «Auto Week» and the Japanese magazine «Racing On».

Not long afterwards, the serious illness of a member of his family caused Ressler to relinquish his commitments, and soon it was announced that Niki Lauda, freshly out of the airline business, would be coming on board.

"*I'll be doing the old Neil Ressler job,*" Lauda said, and the curiosity was that he had been appointed, not by Ford itself, but by the dramatically ambitious Wolfgang Reitzle, president of the company's Premier Automotive Group, which includes Jaguar.

An over-hyped marketing operation, which gave the impression, from the outset, that Ferrari had better watch out. It was an invitation to ridicule.

In February Rahal and Lauda entertained the English press to lunch. "*My job here,*" said Niki, "*is to work with Bobby, and get the other groups - Cosworth, Pi, etc - to make sure they all work in one direction. My job is to coordinate the group's efforts towards Bobby's team.*" The following day I spoke to Keke Rosberg, and told him all seemed very amicable between Lauda and Rahal. He laughed. "*I'll give it six months.*" Why? "*Because Niki isn't going to share power with anybody...*"

At the first race, in Melbourne, Lauda, having stressed he would play no direct role in running 'Bobby's team', announced that Pedro de la Rosa, recently signed as test driver, would definitely race for Jaguar in 2002. This was not the kind of incentive Luciano Burti, beginning his first F1 season, needed. Rahal began to wonder just how much this was 'Bobby's team'.

The high card in his hand, though, was Adrian Newey, with whom he had worked in Indycar racing in the '80s, and a man he considered among his closest friends. When Rahal accepted the Jaguar job, he had good reasons to believe he could persuade Newey to work with him, and through the spring negotiations progressed to a point that, by May, Adrian had signed a letter of agreement to join Jaguar, as technical director, following the expiry of his McLaren contract in the summer of 2002.

Undoubtedly - financial attractions notwithstanding - what appealed strongly to Newey was the idea of working with his old friend. What worried him, conversely, was the thought that he might finish up working for Lauda; thus, in the agreement (which was with Ford, rather than Jaguar) there was a clause permitting him, in the event of Rahal's departure, to leave also.

That being so, had the deal with Newey gone through, Rahal's position at Jaguar would have been immeasurably strengthened. From his point of view, it was therefore unfortunate - to say the least - that the story leaked before the agreement with Newey could be set in contractual stone. When Ron Dennis learned of it, not surprisingly he spared no effort to change Newey's mind, and ultimately he was successful.

"*We had a legally binding agreement with Adrian,*" said Bobby, "*and then he went and signed an extension to his McLaren agreement. That's disappointing professionally, obviously, and there's another thing, too: while it's probably an unimportant issue for most people, a friendship has been put at terminal risk. It's a shame.*" In the end, you have to say it's an unfortunate reflection on reputation and character. When you deal in good faith, and that faith is violated, of course you're disappointed.

I guess McLaren offered Adrian something we couldn't, but that's neither here nor there: when you sign an agreement, you sign an agreement.

"Still, you know, one man doesn't make a team - I don't care who he is. Jaguar Racing is going to succeed, and, as a result of what's happened, we're probably even more determined to do it. The sun's still going to come up tomorrow; we just have a little bit more work to do, that's all."

What worried him, conversely, was the thought that he might finish up working for Lauda.

Perhaps, though, after that Rahal was always walking on quicksand. Apart from the podium at Monaco, Jaguar's performances had not notably improved, compared with those of the year before, but then there was little reason to expect otherwise: in the quest for reliability, the R2 was conservative in concept, and it wasn't as though a Nuvolari had been found to drive it. Everything to do with the 2001 season was fundamentally in place by the time Rahal arrived - as Lauda had acknowledged in February.

"We have to find a quick way to get up to the top," Niki said then, "but I think the minimum time you can ask us to do it is three years; this year, as Bobby says, the team is basically set, so all you can do is see what is there, and, if necessary, start changing it. If we can win a race in our third year, I think we're doing a good job."

That had tallied with Rahal's assessment, but as the summer progressed, it began to look increasingly as though he would not be allowed three years - or anything like it - to turn Jaguar around, and that worried many of his colleagues, who privately confided they thought he had done much to right a

sinking ship, put many good things in place for the future.

The signs were, though, that he was being frozen out, not least by a clear alliance between Lauda and Eddie Irvine, men of similar social interests.

In interviews, 'Bobby' became 'Rahal', and eventually not so much as mentioned. The messages may have been unspoken, but they were there.

As well as that, it was Lauda who had the friends and contacts in F1, Rahal who was the outsider, the American, coming in from CART.

Ultimately, Bobby decided that the situation between the two of them was untenable, that he couldn't run a company while having to look over his shoulder all the time, and so he asked for a meeting with Reitzle, which took place in late August.

The funding for Jaguar Racing comes from Ford, and perhaps, had the company not been through such a catastrophic year, in so many ways, F1 might have raised a blip on some screen in Detroit, prompting those who hired Rahal to come to his defence. As it was, Ressler was no longer a Ford employee, so the outcome of the Reitzle meeting was a foregone conclusion.

The following day, a press release announced that Rahal had decided he had too much on his plate, that he was leaving Jaguar to concentrate on his CART team, and other business interests in the USA. The parting, it was stressed, was 'amicable'.

That morning I spoke to a member of the team. "It's a travesty, isn't it?" he said. "What the hell does Niki Lauda know about running a race team?"

Time will tell.

In January, Bobby Rahal was still all smiles at the team launch. After that, it was the retreat from Moscow, as Niki Lauda was brought in to manage the team. The "love you hate you" relationship between the two of them only lasted a couple of months.

BMW - Mercedes: opposite philosophies

by Anno Hecker
«Frankfurter Allgemeine Zeitung»

«*And where are the Mercedes?*" asked *Mario Theissen after qualifying for the European Grand Prix at the Nurburgring. "Out of sight, out of mind," so the saying goes, because only Michael Schumacher had done better than the two BMW-Williams.* While there was no malice intended in the BMW boss' remark, the fact he insisted on that, almost added to this impression. Especially as, at that time, Mercedes was the butt of all sorts of derogatory remarks and sarcasm in Germany. Instead of referring to them as the "silver arrows," they were being called the "broken arrows," or the "silver whistles," while the noise of the Mercedes engines was described in one paper as a "dead man's wail." The strengths and weaknesses of the two German engine suppliers was at the centre of a debate just as heated as the usual one about the relative merits of the two Schumacher brothers: BMW versus Mercedes, Munich versus Stuttgart, this was the theme that the German press was making a meal of.

The Munich marque had already racked up some impressive performances, including a third place in its first race, the 2000 Australian Grand Prix, third place in the constructors' classification, its first win at its 21st attempt, courtesy of Ralf Schumacher's Imola victory. It was a mighty comeback after a thirteen year absence and it showed no sign of stopping there. BMW would be a serious contender for the 2002 titles.

But there is little point in investing a fortune, running into millions of dollars, if you don't reap the benefit in the marketplace. BMW had been aware of this problem for a while and had made sure it did not apply to them. They would not stand for being a mere appendix to a team, like Renault had been in its heyday with Williams, when its name was often forgotten. That is why BMW took top billing in the team's name, a hyphen separating it from Sir Frank's surname. It certainly made a prominent appearance. In commercial terms, BMW had therefore guaranteed exposure in a campaign every bit as successful as Mercedes' 1998 plans, when the Stuttgart marketeers resurrected the old "silver arrows" theme, taking its name from the Mercedes team that raced in the Thirties. It was certainly evocative and not a bad ruse, given that the McLaren-Mercedes is anything but a German car.

Which is the best?

And which has the best engine? "We do," claims BMW driver Ralf Schumacher, during a press conference at the Nurburgring. In the Mercedes corner, David Coulthard made the same claim for his own engine supplier, although one had to ask if there was a touch of irony in the Scotsman's reply. Data proved who was right, with the BMW pumping out 850 horsepower, the Mercedes only 830. The BMW can also run at 18,000 rpm, far better than the Mercedes. "*Anyone looking at the sub-*

ANNO HECKER,
37 years old, worked first as a physical education instructor befor turning to journalism in 1986. After working as a political correspondent for a Bonn news agency, he joined "Frankfurter Allgemeine Zeitung" in 1991 to cover motor sports. He specialised in stories combinig politics and sport.

ject objectively, can see the BMW is best," said an engine expert, who works for Daimler. "*It's well known that BMW is dominant when it comes to engine design, at least in the case of four and six cylinder units.*"

Low profile

BMW's sporting director Mario Theissen just shrugs his shoulders. What more can he say? There is more to its success than its name, the Bayerische Motoren Werke and indeed its six cylinder three litre engine even won an award in the USA during the season.

MW's success forces one to reassess a long held belief that England is the only source of motor sport expertise

---

But BMW has been wary about promoting its products by referring to its F1 successes. It was a wise move as the car world might have found it hard to swallow and considered the company was being arrogant, if one looked at their appalling performance in Spa-Francorchamps, where Juan Pablo Montoya

stalled on the grid and was sent to the back of the class, when he had just secured his first ever pole position, and where Ralf Schumacher was left stranded on the jacks at the second start, like a man on a rowing machine. The mechanics had been unable to replace a faulty wing in time.

Five engine failures will not help their battle with Mercedes, who suffered four, on their way to finishing second behind Ferrari. But as a TV commercial for their sponsor Allianz declared once the season was over, "*We were quick in our first year and quicker still in the second.*" The next stage seems logical: to be the quickest in 2002.

Home-made

If they did win in their third year back in Formula 1, it would also be a victory for the "built at home" concept which BMW has adopted, as opposed to Mercedes' policy of farming out the work. BMW sticks to its guns. "*We build our engines ourselves.*" The Mercedes engine is the work of Swiss Engineer Mario Ilien and his team in England, but BMW produce their own units in and around Munich. Theissen does not cling blindly to the "made in Germany" tag, but he does feel it has an effect on the road engines. "*BMW engineers build this engine. Less than ten of the 220 employees at Munich have worked for other F1 teams. Their experience will be used at a later date to build road car engines. It was a condition of our management committee, before they would let us take part in F1. There has to be a technology transfer.*" Thus, departments which work on road cars are involved in producing parts for the F1 engine and its electronics systems.

England is no longer the answer

The engineers at DaimlerChrysler are affected by this missed opportunity. "*We could have also done it here in Stuttgart. BMW's performance and its Munich team has taken some of the sheen off Mario Illien as Mercedes' engine builder.*" It's nothing to do with the man himself, who is always modest, but more because the original decision taken in Stuttgart no longer holds water. They had felt the only way to win in F1 was by using small specialist firms, who could react more quickly to change than a large company. "*When Mercedes started in 1994, things were a bit different,*" reckons Theissen. "*That's why I don't want to say which method is best.*" But BMW's success forces one to reassess a long held belief that England is the only source of motor sport expertise. Both Ferrari and Sauber have proved that in recent times. "*On the contrary, I see Munich as the ideal base. With us, the employees do not feel linked only to F1, but also to BMW. It's very different in England,*

Mario Theissen and
Mario Ilien back to back,
just like their
philosophies.

where seven teams all work almost within sight of one another. People switch from one team to another, whereas here people feel more loyal." However, BMW's return, which was announced at the Frankfurt Motor Show in 1997, has not been as easy as the results would lead one to believe. They broke a lot of engines before they started racing. *"During 1999, our last year of preparation, Williams were not sure we would make it,"* admitted Theissen. *"Then we had a lot of broken engines in January 2000. I wasn't sure if we would be ready for the first race. And if we were, how we would get on."* Williams helped the Germans meet the deadline and they were both at the same level, come the start of the 2001 season. *"We both motivated one another,"* reckons Theissen.

Mercedes counter-attacks

Jurgen Hubbert was also piling on the pressure. Mercedes' F1 boss announced that, after a restructuring in the motor sport department, he expected McLaren and Mercedes to get back on top soon. *"We are Mercedes and we ask a lot of ourselves, as do our customers. Therefore we also want to be among the best in Formula 1,"* he declared in Indianapolis. He also said that the engine failures during the 2001 season, especially on David Coulthard's car, where it happened three times, were not part of their company philosophy. But he does not feel this weakness is down to their system. *"There were several factors. There was an inevitable loss*

of concentration after the death of Ilmor's Paul Morgan."
Ilmor boss, Mario Illien had to respect the decision taken by the teams to stop using beryllium, a very light yet strong metal. *"That caused us some problems,"* claimed Hubbert.

The Stuttgart men are so sure of themselves that they refuse to consider this first year with the new engine, even without Mika Hakkinen in the driver line-up, as a transitional year

---

BMW had already stopped using it in 2000 and made the most of that in 2001, as well as benefiting from a new engine design. The basics of this engine left a lot of room for further development. Quite the opposite in the Ilmor camp, as their power unit was based on the FO110, which had already won two constructors' titles in 1998 and 1999 and then went on for another ten events, so there was not much room for improvement. The company has now come up with something completely new for 2002. It has a bigger V angle; 90 degrees instead of 72, making the engine flatter. That will allow the engineers to lower the car's centre of gravity, which should improve its handling. Mercedes motorsport chief would neither confirm nor deny this rumour. *"All I know is that it will be very powerful."*
The Stuttgart men are so sure of themselves

that they refuse to consider this first year with the new engine, even without Mika Hakkinen in the driver line-up, as a transitional year. Mercedes reckon that Kimi Raikkonen is strong enough to put David Coulthard under pressure right from the word go, which should be productive for the team. They reckon the line-up will be the equal of Ferrari's Michael Schumacher - Rubens Barrichello duo and the combination of Ralf Schumacher and Juan Pablo Montoya at Williams. If Mercedes did not believe in themselves, Hubbert would not have got personally involved in the signing of Raikkonen with Peter Sauber, paying the Swiss team 18 million dollars.
The team expects to hit hard next year which is typical of this ambitious group. *"We do not expect to take as long to win as Mercedes,"* said Bernd Pischetsrieder when he announced BMW's return to Formula 1. In the autumn of 1997, his statements had left the press at the Frankfurt Show thinking it was pure arrogance.
But he turned out to be right. The next step is to take the title. Mercedes were world champions in 1998 with Mika Hakkinen at the wheel, after five years. BMW plan to do it quicker than that. But unlike Mercedes, the Bavarian boys have two rivals. They not only have to beat their Stuttgart rivals, they also have to cope with Ferrari and that other German element in the sport, Michael Schumacher, That's some task.

Jacques Villeneuve and BAR: Fourth and final down

by Pierre Durocher
«Journal de Montréal»

The first qualifying season of the year did not go well for BAR, as the two Jordans are fourth and seventh on the grid, while Villeneuve and Panis are eighth and ninth respectively.
Jacques is angry with Juan Pablo Montoya, reckoning the Colombian has not used his mirrors.

The next day, things get much worse. On lap five, Villeneuve runs into the back of Ralf Schumacher at over 250 km/h and his BAR takes off like a plane. It disintegrates against the concrete retaining wall, but luckily the survival cell is up to the job.
However, one of its rear wheels flies through a gap in the catch fencing and a marshal is killed.
Villeneuve is rocked by what has happened and claims Ralf jumped on the brakes, while the German reckons it was Jacques' fault.
Jacques escaped from the accident with back pains, which would stay with him for the next few weeks. To make matters worse, Panis was demoted from fourth to seventh, having overtaken under a yellow flag. These three lost points would cost the team dear at the final reckoning.

Nothing but disappointment

The team has lived through countless disappointments. It turned out to be the BMW-Williams team which was challenging the usual front runners, while the surprise of the year came courtesy of Peter Sauber's team.
BAR-Honda finished the season in sixth place in the Constructors' classification, behind Jordan, the other Honda powered team and that was a major disappointment.

Villeneuve's only consolation in 2001 was the two third place finishes in Spain and Germany. They were the first two podium finishes in the history of the BAR team.
"These two results were down to luck and retirements at the end of the race," acknowledged the sport's most rebellious driver. In 2002, I want to get on the podium because my car is one of the most competitive.

"I want to start winning again. If I don't manage it, then this BAR adventure will have been a bitter failure," added Villeneuve, before going off on his end of season holiday.
In the following synopsis of the year, you will see that everything went wrong for Pollock's brave band of men.

A replica for the launch

Presentation of the new BAR-Honda in London on 25th January.
The press had to make do with staring at a replica, as Villeneuve had just destroyed the real one in testing in Spain. Right from the first time it turned a wheel, Jacques made it clear to the engineers he did not like the car. However, there was a need to appear optimistic at the launch.

"If the team doesn't finish in the top three in the Constructors' Championship, it will be disappointing for everyone," said a good humoured Villeneuve, who had just announced he had split up with fiancee Dannii Minogue.
As far as the arrival of Olivier Panis was concerned, Villeneuve reckoned that he now had a team-mate *"who will wake me up. For the last two years, I've had one who let me go to sleep."*
Villeneuve was in doubt that Panis, an experienced driver, would be quicker than him in the early stages of the season, as the Frenchman had done much more work over the winter.

A disastrous start

Saturday 3rd March, Melbourne, Australia
The first qualifying season of the year did not go well for BAR, as the two Jordans are fourth and seventh on the grid, while Villeneuve and Panis are eighth and ninth respectively.
Jacques is angry with Juan Pablo Montoya, reckoning the Colombian has not used his mirrors.
The next day, things get much worse. On lap five, Villeneuve runs into the back of Ralf Schumacher at over 250 km/h and his BAR takes off like a plane.
It disintegrates against the concrete retaining wall, but luckily the survival cell is up to the job.
However, one of its rear wheels flies through a gap in the catch fencing and a marshal is killed.
Villeneuve is rocked by what has happened and claims Ralf jumped on the brakes, while the German reckons it was Jacques' fault.
Jacques escaped from the accident with back pains, which would stay with him for the next few weeks.
To make matters worse, Panis was demoted from fourth to seventh, having overtaken under a yellow flag. These three lost points

PIERRE DUROCHER
*46 years old, has been a sports journalist for the "Journal de Montreal" since 1975.
He has covered, ice hockey, baseball, Canadian football, boxing, tennis and several Olympic Games. He began following Formula 1 in 1997, the year Jacques Villeneuve won the title. Since then he has concentrated on motorsports (F1 and CART). He loves the job.*

2001 vu du Canada

would cost the team dear at the final reckoning.

Signs of impatience

1st April, Interlagos, Brazil
After another lost weekend in Malaysia, BAR came to Brazil 0 - 5 down on Jordan.
Villeneuve had only completed seven race laps since the start of the season and was already getting impatient. *"It's three years now that the promise of competitiveness has not been achieved. If I seem not to care, it's too hide my impatience."*
Villeneuve qualified 12th, one place behind Panis. JV is not amused.
In the race, Panis finishes a great fourth to score the team's first points.
Unfortunately a mix up during the pit stop prevented him making it to the podium, as the Frenchman had to wait for his team-mate's car to pull out, the two men having mistakenly come in together. Panis' pit stop lasted 1 minute and 47 seconds!

The first podium

29th April, Catalunya, Spain
Finally, at the Spanish Grand Prix, Villeneuve and BAR made a breakthrough to take the first ever podium finish in the history of the team. However, the weekend had got off to a very bad start.
Villeneuve managed to qualify seventh, despite the fact the teams forgot to connect

his brakes and the car was 11 kilos overweight!

lucky podium finish in Hockenheim, when nine of the eleven cars which started ahead of Villeneuve failed to finish the race.
The expected evolutions from Honda never showed up, while the engineers seemed incapable of solving the problems affecting an ill-conceived chassis.
During the summer, Villeneuve summed it up: *"We have been left for dead and we will stay that way"*.
He was not talking through his hat, as the BAR team only picked up one little point (at Monza) from the last five races of the season.
Villeneuve scraped the bottom of the barrel in the United States Grand Prix, qualifying down in 18th spot, behind the Minardi of Fernando Alonso.
His heart was no longer in it. Resigned to his fate, he just wanted this miserable season to come to an end, so that the BAR-Honda 003 could be thrown in the dustbin.
In fact it was a dustbin.
Now, we must wait and see if the next British American Racing vintage will be any better.
"I don't want to hear any more promises. I want results." So said Jacques Villeneuve, totally at the end of his tether.

"Believe me Craig, these hair implants make me much younger!" Jacques Villeneuve in conversation with Craig Pollock. The friends are still on good terms, but results show that friendship is not a guarantee of success.

Making the most of Hakkinen's heart braking retirement on the first lap, he made it to the flag in third place.
Phew! A great weight was lifted off Jacques' shoulders, as he had always wanted to be the first BAR driver to get to the podium.
Strangely, Villeneuve had a bad weekend in Austria, qualifying down in 12th place and messing up a passing move on Eddie Irvine during the race. Panis, on the other hand, showed well and came home in fifth place. *"I would give myself an "E" for my performance,"* was Villeneuve's honest assessment.

A descent into hell

This bad weekend set the tone for the rest of BAR's season. It was a real descent into hell.
The team began to lose ground to the opposition and haemorrhaged performance all the way to Japan, with the exception of a

The light at the end of the tunnel?

by Kunio Shibata
«GPX Press», Tokyo

2001 wo hurikaeru

For several years now, I have been saying the same thing: The passion for F1 in Japan ended a long time ago. The TV viewing figures and the specialist magazine circulations are both dropping, slowly but constantly. However, even though Michael Schumacher was crowned champion long before the Japanese GP, Suzuka attracted a far bigger crowd than in past years. It seems that something is stirring again on the Japanese motor sport scene.

Honda bogs down

Suzuka, on the eve of the final GP of the season. I was dining at the circuit. Gerhard Berger, BMW's sporting director sat opposite me. In a sincere voice, he asked me, *"why isn't Honda getting its act together?"* I gave him a short answer. *"That's just what I would like to know."*
A McLaren-Honda driver in the Nineties, Berger has first hand experience of the qualities of the Honda engineers. At the time, Honda crushed all its rivals and picked up 11 titles between 1986 and 1992. But since their comeback last year, they have never got near their past successes. All they managed was two third places thanks to Jacques Villeneuve, helped by a bit of luck, but not at all by the performance of his BAR-Honda. It is a measly result, while BMW, which returned to F1 at the same time as Honda, won four races, took four poles in 2001. Thanks to BMW and Michelin also, Williams is pretty much the second best team after Ferrari. The difference is huge.
This year, Honda decided to supply two teams; BAR and Jordan. The Japanese engine specialists reckoned that partnering two

teams would give them twice the data to work on. However, Osamu Goto, their former boss is convinced this is incorrect. *"If the partner teams are not competent enough, the data acquired will never be much use."* BMW's head technical man, Dr. Mario Theissen agrees. *"I cannot understand why Honda insists on working with two teams."*
But it seems that Honda is beginning to

understand that there is no benefit nor future in this sort of collaboration. While Honda has denied it several times, the rumours continue to fly that soon, they will opt to go with just one team. Logically, that would be BAR, given that Honda is already involved in the development of its chassis.
The 2001 Honda engine was only a development of the previous year's model. *"It worked well last year and we thought it would still be competitive,"* said one of the engineers. Already, this type of approach does not fit what is known as the "Honda Way." Unlike today, at the time of the V6 turbo and the normally aspirated V10 and V12, they never hesitated to try something new at all costs. This year, not only did they not launch a new engine, there was pre-

cious little development work done on the existing unit. Villeneuve complained that the Honda engine was heavy and gutless. We won't know what its actual power output was, but it is more than likely it was a long way off the figures generated by the BMW, Ferrari and Mercedes units, or even the Ferrari customer engines used by Sauber, that is to say their previous year's engine.
Why was Honda unable to produce the power? *"It was a performance problem rather than a reliability issue,"* said technical director, Kazutoshi Nishizawa. That would imply they looked at several ideas but rejected all of them.
Can Honda be competitive once again? Probably, but not right away. I fear their strategy of choosing teams in the second division could be a major obstacle.

Toyota - a chaotic year

"Drive your dreams" is a Toyota advertising slogan. Accompanying it on Japanese TV were shots of Toyota's F1 car in action and it was shown over and over again. This would have unthinkable a couple of years ago, as Toyota was considered, and still is, as an old-fashioned family firm. Since then, they have radically changed direction and are heading for a younger audience. And in order to attract them F1 was a natural choice.
It is amazing to think that Toyota is complete debt-free. If they want to build a new factory, they just go out and do it, paying cash. In fact their finance department is jokingly referred to as Toyota Bank, because of the healthy state of their coffers. Toyota has already spent around 100 million dollars to expand TMG, Toyota's European F1 base in Cologne. It has grown from 18,000 square metres to 30,000. But for the Japanese company whose turnover is reckoned at over six and a half billion dollars for 2000, this is just pocket money! Currently, the team employs 550 people

KUNIO SHIBATA,
44 years old, he left Japan, giving up his jov in journalism in 1982 to move to Paris and study Politocal Science. He became a freelance producer for Japanese television and havinf always been interested in motor racing, he began covering the Grand Prix for a press agency in 1987 when Satoru Nakajima arrived on the scene. He has written for the specialist Japanese magazine «Grand Prix Xpress» since 1991.

from 27 countries. It is in short, a collection of people who have worked in all spheres of motor sport, from rallying to touring cars, sports cars to motorcycles and of course F1.

At the end of March, at the Paul Ricard circuit, they unveiled their first car, the Toyota AM01, in front of around 350 journalists and then began testing immediately. Unfortunately, it did not get off to a great start. On the second lap, Mika Salo had a big accident, hitting the concrete barrier. Suffering with a back injury, Salo took two months off before driving again. The accident was caused by a broken suspension part.

---

the choice of drivers, which took an age to resolve, showed a deep divide between East and West

One month later, when Salo was still convalescing, TMS suddenly announced it had sacked its technical director, Andre de Cortanz. He had been overseeing the entire project and running the technical department. Other engineers, who worked closely with him, were also shown the door, in a storm of sackings. It put the project in jeopardy. Eiji Nagano, the motorsport director said they had no choice. *"If we had dragged our feet over this decision, if we had waited for other solutions, it would have been too late. It was now or never."*

De Cortanz's appointment had always been viewed with suspicion. It seems that team boss Ove Andersson was actually against this choice, which had been made in Tokyo. Why? Because when Toyota was racing at Le Mans, De Cortanz was the man behind the Peugeot 906 which was beating their machine! It must be a Japanese streak of masochism. Whatever the reason, Tokyo rated their choice.

Unfortunately, De Cortanz is not very good at getting on with other people, wanting to know everything and do everything himself. Nothing was working while he was in charge. If Toyota really could not get over being beaten by Peugeot, it should have employed Jean Todt!

Minardi's Gustav Brunner was poached as the replacement, in the role of chief designer. According to Nagano, *"he is not only technically sound, he is also good at management."*

While waiting for Brunner's car, the AM02 to arrive at the start of 2002, Toyota is still testing with his predecessor's. At Suzuka, Salo lapped in 1.38.02, or 5.5 seconds slower than Michael Schumacher's pole position time. Is this too big a gap, or can it be

closed easily? Naturally the TMG people believe it's the latter. Indeed, given the "green" state of the track, it might be more sensible to compare its time with those on the first day of the grand prix weekend. In that case, Mika Salo would have been 14th just behind Nick Heidfeld, which is quite respectable.

But the TMG bosses are playing it safe. *"For our first season, we will be quite happy if our car just gets through qualifying."*

They are almost bound to achieve this modest ambition. In fact, given their budget and resources, they should be able to mix it with BAR, Jordan and Jaguar.

Now twenty four years old, Takuma has made it to the top level of the sport in just five years!

The main worry might well turn out to be conflict between TMG and Tokyo. The two sides collaborated to dump De Cortanz. But the choice of drivers, which took an age to resolve, showed a deep divide between East and West. TMG insisted they wanted test driver Alan Macnish as the second driver, while Tokyo was not at all keen. Finally, Andersson made his own decision and the board decided to keep quiet.

Alan is no doubt a nice lad. But it strikes me, his capabilities as an F1 driver are limited. I hope this choice, which was far from unanimous, will not make Toyota's first season in F1 even more difficult.

Sato - birth of a real star?

English F3: Takuma Sato, French F3: Ryo Fukuda, German F3: Toshihiro Kaneishi. All three of these young samurai have won their respective championships in 2001. Something that has never been seen before in the history of motorsport.

Thanks to them, the image of Japanese racing drivers has been transformed. Before, they were considered lacking in aggression, speed and communication skills, as they could not speak English. But these three are definitely aggressive - sometimes too aggressive - very quick, and speak perfect English or French.

Brazilians have long considered Japan as a poor country where the people cannot play football. But gradually, Japanese soccer players are moving onto the world stage. The same is happening in motor racing. I

think the youngsters have adopted a new mentality.

Of this trio, Sato has progressed more than the other two, as he will drive for Jordan in F1 next year. Circumstances certainly helped, as he is a Honda protege and the Machiavellian Eddie Jordan has taken him on to aid future negotiations with the Japanese company when it comes to ensuring his engine supply.

I reckon this is the main reason why Sato's contract with the team is a long one, for an inexperienced driver - two years with a two year option.

However, Takuma's talent is undeniable. It is not just his record in the British F3 series, where he scored 12 wins, equalling Ayrton Senna's total, but also his unusual career progression. He started racing very late and never even sat in a kart until he was nineteen!

Born to a well-off family, he was always interested in motor sport. But his father, boss of an important Tokyo law firm, never understood his son's passion. As a substitute, he took up cycling.

At school he set up a club and after two years he won a national schools championship. Then, when he moved on to university, he became the number one at national level. But he still hankered after motor racing. He quit university and enrolled at a Honda racing school.

Sato looks like being the best so far. But will he be on a par with Kimi Raikkonen or Felipe Massa? Is he a future champion? It's too early to tell.

He took first place and that won him finance from Honda for one year and he did not hesitate in heading for England. Now twenty four years old, Takuma has made it to the top level of the sport in just five years! Comparing him with the six Japanese drivers who have completed at least one season of F1, Sato looks like being the best so far. But will he be on a par with Kimi Raikkonen or Felipe Massa? Is he a future champion? It's too early to tell. One thing's for sure, he will not be the last Japanese driver making it into F1.

His presence will no doubt attract other talented drivers who will not think twice about leaving their homeland to try for the big prize. They are on their way.

◁◁ Eddie Jordan and Craig Pollock talk with Kazutoshi Nishizawa, Honda's F1 project leader had to deal with chalk and cheese, while working with these two rival team bosses.

Tyres: fourth consecutive title for Bridgestone

Two titles with Hakkinen and McLaren in 1998 and 1999, followed by two more with Michael Schumacher and Ferrari in 2000 and 2001. The achievement could hardly have been bettered by for the Japanese tyre manufacturer, after five years in Formula 1. However, unlike the previous two seasons, when Bridgestone enjoyed a monopoly, supplying all the teams, after Goodyear's withdrawal, this year, they had a fierce fight on their hands.

Out of Formula 1 since the end of 1984, Michelin's return to the blue riband of motor sport was eagerly awaited. The tyre war was fascinating, but Bridgestone emerged as the clear winner: 13 pole positions to 4, 13 victories to 4 and 9 fastest laps to 8.

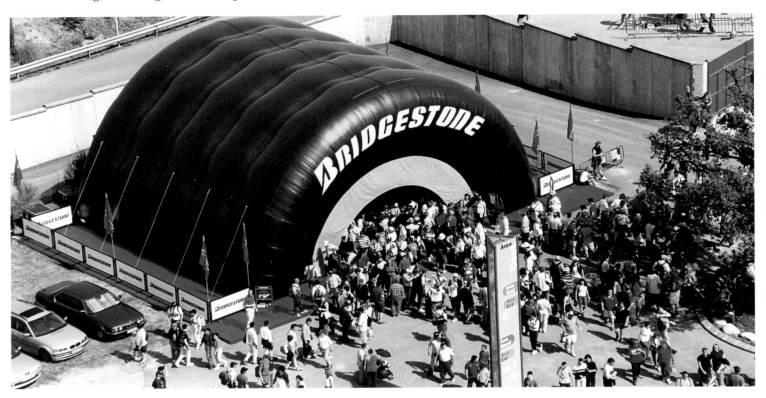

The largest tyre on the track

One of Bridgestone's main aims, since it made its first foray into Formula 1 back in 1997, was to increase its brand awareness in the European markets. Five seasons on, the obvious speaks for itself: four world championship titles won by Ferrari and McLaren-Mercedes have strongly contributed towards achieving that goal. But other key initiatives by the Japanese tyre manufacturerhave also played an important role.

In Formula One racing, Bridgestone does not only claim fame for its successes on the track.

The aggressive advertising campaigns run on-site have not gone unnoticed.

In 1998, the company's second year in grand prix racing, Bridgestone/Firestone Europe's marketing department began to operate an exhibition unit in the public areas at the race tracks hosting the grands prix. It featured a display of road tyres, a shop selling branded "goodies" and more often than not, a Bridgestone-shod F1 show car.

For 2001, Bridgestone decided to up the ante in this area and that has led to the appearance of one of the biggest structures in the commercial zone at the race tracks.

Up to now, the Bridgestone/Firestone area consisted of a conventional tent, covering a surface area of fifty square metres.

Now, not only has the size increased to one hundred eighty square metres, it is also far more visually arresting as it takes the form of a giant inflatable Formula 1 tyre! It is an impressive seven metres high and is home to an F1 show car, giving race fans a close up look at the machines they have come to see race. There is also an F1 simulator ride so that they can get as close to experiencing the sensations felt by the drivers as possible. Naturally, the full range of Bridgestone and Firestone tyres is also on display.

"*With two tyre manufacturers involved in the sport this year, we felt we had to do something special, in order to stand out,*" explained Nicolas Duquesne, the man in charge of F1 Sales Promotion.

"*We felt we should at the very least have the biggest Formula 1 tyre in the paddock! Hence this inflatable tent. We also wanted the public to learn that we make a wide range of tyres suitable for all cars, and also the Battlax range for motorcycles.*"

▷ *The defending world champion, the Ferrari F1 2000, was throughout the year one of the most successful attractions in Bridgestone's inflatable tent.*

Getting the giant tyre set up is not the work of a moment and involves a complicated installation process. "It's the sheer size of it that means it takes time to assemble," says Duquesne.
"Although all we really need is an electric socket as we use four motors to power up the assembly. We start the process on Tuesday morning and we have to finish erecting the main structure by Wednesday evening. On Thursday we tidy everything up and start preparing the presentation side, getting all the give-aways and brochures ready, checking the simulator is fully operational and generally making sure the area reflects Bridgestone's attention to detail."
Some cynics might say that Formula 1 is full of hot air and this is certainly the case when it comes to Bridgestone's giant tyre.

"We cannot allow the tyre to go down over night," confesses Duquesne. "So we have security 24 hours to ensure we don't puncture the atmosphere of perfection! It would not

do if the display began to collapse, so it is constantly monitored." Such a large display is bound to stand out from the crowd and at the Austrian Grand Prix for example, it was located right in the middle of the commercial area with high visibility from all sides, even the air, which is an important advertising tool, when television coverage features aerial footage of the circuit.
The giant tyre was used at eight European Grand Prix this year and generated a lot of interest.
"The spectators have given us a good response and thousand of fans have visited our unit," says Duquesne. "The youngsters particularly enjoy coming along to try the simulator, which features action from all the race tracks on the F1 calendar, allowing them to "drive" around the circuits."

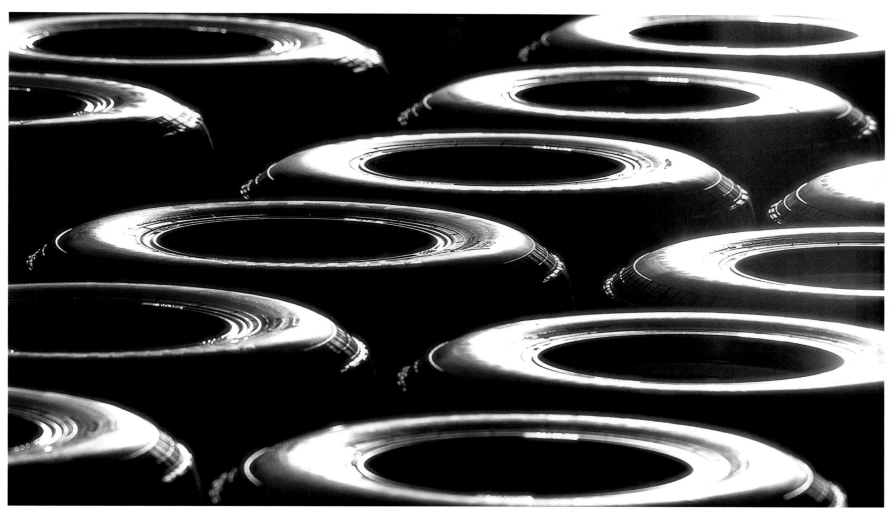

Jean Todt: «*The technical relationship between us is exceptional*»

Bridgestone took its fourth world title this year and for the past two, they have come courtesy of Ferrari and Michael Schumacher. The right time for Scuderia Ferrari's sporting director, Jean Todt, to explain what this back-to-back success means to the Italian team. "It shows we did a good job over the winter and that we were well prepared right from the start of the season," he said. "Having won with four races in hand, speaks for itself. Additionally, the fact that we were up against two competitive teams this year, who fought among themselves for the second and third places, meant we were able to pull out a gap."
"Basically, we did a good job on the chassis and engine side and Bridgestone did the same on the tyre front. An important point in our

success was that all the key people in the team confirmed their future with the Scuderia back in October, to the end of 2004.
This stability on the technical and driver front, as well as our partnership with Bridgestone, meant we could work in a clear and motivated fashion."
The arrival of a rival tyre company changed the tyre situation dramatically, but according to Todt, it did not change the working relationship. "It continued in the same way," he maintained. "Although with a better understanding of the product, we were able to make quicker progress, even in terms of adjusting the car's design in terms of suspension to suit the tyres. The fact that we extended our agreement with Bridgestone to the end of 2004 earlier this

year has given us stability on the technical side, for both ourselves and Bridgestone. The technical relationship between us is exceptional."

As Bridgestone's director of motorsport, Hiroshi Yasukawa, admits, Ferrari encouraged Bridgestone to maintain its advantage over it's tyre rival, a view Todt agrees with. "If in some situations we realised that the tyres were not exactly what we wanted, we pushed them hard to understand how to improve," admitted the Frenchman. "We work together on that and constantly monitor that our tyres

are as good as the rival brand. That's good for Bridgestone because they always have a valid comparison. We have shown that when the tyres are at the top level, we are capable of getting top results. In other words we make strong demands but we reward their work."

Asked to indicate the team's key success factors, Jean Todt gave a straight answer. "It is just the result of hard working groups, between chassis, engine, tyre manufacturer and drivers. As well as the proof that Ferrari has had a very strong package."

The Scuderia has no intention of slowing down.

The 2002 development plans are already well advanced. "We have been working for many months on the 2002 car and engine", he said. "Even though the F1 regulations will remain mostly the same as this year, we will have a new car and, hopefully, improved performances.

We have been developing our relationship since 1999 and we did not hesitate to stay with Bridgestone for many more years."

Bridgestone Motorsport's technical manager, Hisao Suganuma. ▽

Hisao Suganuma: «traction control helping tyres as well as drivers»

At this year's Spanish Grand Prix, a major change to the Formula 1 regulations saw a raft of electronic driver aids making their reappearance on the scene. The FIA felt that freeing up the rules concerning electronic systems was the only way to remove a climate of suspicion that these devices were being used illegally, given that they were proving difficult if not impossible, to detect.

The new systems, particularly launch control, designed to prevent wheelspin as the cars leave the grid, have proved troublesome for some teams.

Although there is no direct link between these systems and the tyres, traction control in particular does have an effect on what happens to the contact patch between car and track.

"Regarding tyre performance, we believed before it was introduced, that traction control would influence it," explains Bridgestone Motorsport's Technical Manager, Hisao Suganuma. "It effectively reduces wheel spin and rear wheel sliding. Therefore this should help reduce the degradation of the rear tyres. When we came to the Spanish GP, it was difficult to know in advance what advantage these new electronic systems would bring."

The advantages of a system which prevents wheelspin and allows the cars to slide less in the corners has obvious benefits for the tyres, which are put under less stress.

"The system did stop the rear sliding," admits Suganuma.

"We believe it helped and our tyre performed very well and part of that success came from the traction control system."

Suzuka: 55 F1 wins for Bridgestone

At this year's French Grand Prix, Bridgestone reached a landmark in its five year history, when a car on Bridgestone tyres won a race for 50th time. The first came courtesy of McLaren-Mercedes and Mika Hakkinen in the 1998 Australian GP. The fiftieth was won by Ferrari and Michael Schumacher, who coincidentally also celebrated his fiftieth grand prix win in France.

"This good result means we are still on the way to our objective, which is to increase our brand awareness," said Hiroshi Yasukawa, Bridgestone's Motorsport Director, after the race. *"The actual number of wins is not what concerns us. The important factor is its effect in terms of the value it brings us. The fact Bridgestone and Michael Schumacher both reached their fifty grand prix wins at the same time is an extra piece of good fortune. Since we came into the sport in 1997 we have gained experience from Formula 1 and enjoyed good results. But there is still a lot to achieve and the fifty wins is just one step on the way."*

At the French Grand Prix, the company confirmed it planned to have a long term future in Formula 1.

"We made this statement because of all the rumours suggesting Bridgestone was planning to withdraw from Formula 1, because of difficulties being experienced in the USA," explained Yasukawa. *"Normally, we would not consider reacting to rumours, but on this occasion the timing was right. That was partly because our President, Mr. Watanabe was in Magny-Cours. He was actually in Europe for the opening of our new factory in Poland. This was the first time he had been to a race since his appointment as President. We felt that Bridgestone had to stress its confidence in our F1 programme. The length of our involvement will depend on the general company situation, but as long as that continues to be*

okay then we will stay in the sport. There is no date set, but we have not yet achieved our objectives."

F1 involvement has benefits in other areas apart from publicity.

"There are the technical issues to be considered," claimed Yasukawa. *"Recently we launched a new ultra high-performance road tyre, the Potenza S-03 PP incorporating close links to Formula 1 technology. F1 cars are among the quickest in the world and our experience in this area helps us produce tyres for normal road cars."*

Yasukawa admitted that reaching the fifty wins landmark in the French GP, on our competitor's home turf added some extra satisfaction to the occasion.

"But now we will have to be very careful at Suzuka, which is a very difficult circuit".

In fact, there was nothing to worry about. By claiming his 53rd career win - his 20th with Bridgestone - Michael Schumacher gave the Japanese tyre manufacturer their 55th F1win. The four-times world champion is full of praise.

"The biggest point is the partnership," he said. *"The relationship we have built since 1999 is, I think, very special.*

One of the key factors of our success is that we work very closely together and try to beat the rest. Formula One is improving all the time. We must therefore continue to work together and move on. I heard that Bridgestone produced 120 different specifications this year. Our aim is to win and I very much look forward to achieving this together."

△
Time to celebrate for Jean Todt and his drivers in Budapest: Ferrari have won both Championships, as they had done in 2000.

ALESI -HÄKKINEN:

201 grands prix for one, 162 for the other. A pretty similar experience, but that's where it ends, because when it comes to results, there is no comparison. One win and two poles for Alesi; 20 wins and two world championship titles for Häkkinen. On the personality side, they have precious little in common either: on the one hand, an explosive Latin temperament, on the other, Scandinavian reserve. One thing however is

Jean Alesi

1989

Jean Alesi makes his debut at the French Grand Prix. Sixteenth on the grid, the young man has an extraordinary race at the wheel of the Tyrrell 018 and finishes 4th. He even ran second from lap 45 to 49, before stopping to change tyres. He finished in the points again in Italy (5th) and Spain (4th) The Frenchman only drove eight races but finished 9th in the Drivers' championship.

1991

Alongside Alain Prost, who was second in the 1990 championship, Alesi again got off to a lightning start, with quickest time in the first day of qualifying in Phoenix. But after that, things did not go well. Sixth in Brazil, he had to wait until the Monaco GP to get on the third step of the podium, repeating that performance in Germany and Portugal. At Spa, he led for nine laps and looked like winning, until the engine let go. His first

1990

At the wheel of the agile high-nose Tyrrell, Alesi had an amazing start to the season. In Phoenix, he was 4th on the grid and made a dream start to lead for the first 34 laps. Passed by Ayrton Senna, he finished second, eight seconds behind the Brazilian. Sixth in Imola, he qualified 3rd in Monaco and finished 2nd one second down on Senna. He was 3rd in the Drivers' classification after four rounds. He would not score for the rest of the season, ending up 9th with 13 points. But he made a good enough impression for Williams and Ferrari to fight over him. He chose the Scuderia. *"Its the realisation of a lifelong dream,"* he said at the mid-season. *"I'm lucky to join Ferrari when it's at the top of its form and also to spend a year as Alain Prost's pupil. I intend winning races next year."*

season in red ended with 7th place and 21 points. *"At the start of the season, we had technical difficulties,"* he admitted. *"After that, the team suffered with political problems. But I don't regret coming to Ferrari. It's the sort of opportunity that doesn't come up too often in a driver's career."*

1992

Prost is replaced by Capelli, but the results are not much better for the Italian squad. Fourth in Brazil, Alesi once again gets onto the podium in third place in Spain and Canada. The Ferrari loses its edge as the season continues and the Frenchman only scored points on three more occasions: 5th in Germany and Japan, 4th in Australia, ending up 7th in the championship on 18 points. Its a long way off his original expectations when he joined the Reds. *"The 92A was never on a par*

▷ *Estoril 1993: Jean Alesi leads Mika Häkkinen*

1989, Paul Ricard Circuit: in between two F3000 races with the Jordan team, Alesi replaces Michele Alboreto at Tyrrell to make his F1 debut.

Eight grands prix later, Phoenix 1990: the Frenchman leads Ayrton Senna.

Monaco 1991: in his first wheel in the Principality, at the wheel of a Ferrari, Alesi finishes 3rd behind Senna and Mansell.

same dream, different destiny

certain. In their own way, both men have left their mark on the modern era of F1. In the case of the Frenchman, it is because of his extraordinary debut and his permanently generous spirit and for the Finn, it is because of the results obtained and the fact he waited seven seasons before settling into his winning ways. Let's take a look at the careers of these two exceptional men.

by Vincent Souchaud

Mika Häkkinen

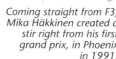

Coming straight from F3, Mika Häkkinen created a stir right from his first grand prix, in Phoenix in 1991.

Suzuka 1993: Häkkinen's first podium, congratulated by team-mate Ayrton Senna, for whom this is his penultimate win.

Estoril 1993: Häkkinen (7) has just shot off the second row to take the lead. But Alesi (27) will pass him at the end of the straight.

1991

Mika Häkkinen was a revelation at his first ever grand prix, the opening round in Phoenix. Driving for Lotus, he qualified 13th. In the race, he got a fright, when the steering wheel came off in his hands, but he managed to keep off the wall. After pitting twice, to ensure the wheel was safely back on, he drove a good race, but retired 20 laps from the flag, when lying 12th. In Brazil, the Finn finished 9th, before going on to score his first points, in his third race in Imola. Starting from the back row, he finished fifth. For the rest of the season, he usually quali-

fied at the back of the grid, but at least he was consistent: 6 finishes, 6 retirements. He ended the year 15th in the championship with 2 points.

1992

His second year with Lotus saw him make giant steps forward, both in qualifying and the race. Starting from the back of the grid for the first half of the season, he gradually moved up the order and was 7th fastest in Portugal and Japan. In the races, he started to score: 6th in Mexico, the second round, 4th in Magny-Cours, 6th at Silverstone, 4th in Hungary, 6th at Spa and 5th in Portugal. Nine finishes from 15 starts and 8th in the championship, just behind Alesi with 11 points.

1993

Having joined McLaren as a test driver, the Finn only drove in the last three grands prix of the season, replacing the sacked Michael Andretti. In Portugal, he made a devastating impact. At the wheel of the McLaren-Ford, he qualified 3rd, ahead of team-mate Ayrton Senna, beating him by 48 thousandths. On the Sunday, he shot off the line, squeezing Senna, which allowed Alesi to take the lead. He went off the track on lap 33, when lying 4th. In Japan, he qualified third again, this time 42 thousandths behind Senna and drove a sensible race to finish third; the first podium of his career. In Adelaide, Häkkinen was 5th on the grid, but had to retire before half distance, when lying 3rd. In the end, he was 15th in the championship, with 4 points. More importantly, with Senna's departure to Williams, he had the opportunity to establish himself at McLaren.

tribute

Spa 1994: the engine on the Ferrari has just broken and a disgusted Alesi sits by the track.

Montreal 1995: luck finally smiles on Jean Alesi. His first win on his 31st birthday.

Used to doing well during seven years with Ferrari and Benetton, Alesi only scored 11 points between 1998 and 2000, with Prost and Sauber.

with the Williams and only rarely up to the level of the McLarens and Benettons. Not only was the chassis impossible to set up, but the engine was cruelly short of power."

1993

After three seasons with McLaren, Gerhard Berger was recruited to help rebuild Ferrari. But Alesi had to wait until Monaco to score his first points for third place. Apart from that, nothing much...On 1st July, Jean Todt joined the Scuderia as Sporting Director. Two months later, the first fruits start to show. In Monza, Alesi qualified third and finished second; his best finish since joining Ferrari, 43 races earlier. In Portugal, he led for 19 laps, before finishing fourth. He closed the season with another 4th in Australia, which helped him to 6th in the championship on 16 points. At the end of the season, the Frenchman said: "We are betting everything on 1994. I am sure the 94 Ferrari will be a success."

1994

It's a promising start: 3rd in qualifying and the race in Brazil, Alesi is then injured in testing at Mugello and misses two grands prix. From June onwards, the results begin to come through. In Canada he was 2nd on the grid, his first front row for the Scuderia and ends up 3rd on the Sunday. At Silverstone, he finishes 2nd after Schumacher is disqualified. Two weeks later at Hockenheim, the two Ferraris of Berger and Alesi monopolise the front row. In the race, Alesi's engine lets go on the first lap, while Berger wins. Reliability is still a concern. In Spa, Alesi runs 2nd until the engine goes again on lap 3. In Monza, he does it on Saturday, taking pole. He leads the race for the opening 14 laps until the gearbox breaks. In Japan, he is on the podium for the 5th time that season, finishing 5th in the championship on 24 points, but he is still chasing his first win.

1995

After coming 5th in the season opener in Brazil, Alesi's hopes are high as he finishes 2nd in Argentina, having led for 8 laps. He then finishes 2nd in Imola. But bad luck is around the corner. He is lying second in Spain until the engine lets go. He collides with Brundle in Monaco when lying third. In Canada, fortune finally smiles on him. Second with 12 laps to go, he inherits the lead when Schumacher runs into electrical problems. It was the total experience: a first win on his birthday, driving a Ferrari with Number 27 on the nose at the Gilles Ville-neuve circuit. Second at Silverstone, bad luck strikes again. In Germany and Hungary the engine blew. In Spa he leads on lap 3 when the suspension breaks. Then, in Monza he leads for 16 laps, when a bearing robs him of a Ferrari triumph on home turf in front of the tifosi. At the European GP at the Nurbur-gring, he leads from lap 13 to 64 until he has to give best to Schumacher. It's his best season: 5th with 42 points. But it is also his last year with Ferrari.

1996

Along with Gerhard Berger, Alesi switches to Benetton-Renault, the reigning world champions, with 11 wins in 1995. But none in 1996! Alesi keeps getting close, climbing onto the podium 8 times: 2nd in Brazil, he leads in Monaco from lap 41 to 59, then retires with broken suspension, handing victory to Olivier Panis. In Monza, he leads from lap 6 to 30, but cannot hold off Schumacher. He finishes 4th in the championship with 47 points, his best total. Just before the French GP, Renault announces it is quitting F1 at the end of 1997.

1994

Teamed with Brundle, the Finn had a difficult start to the season. He put in some brilliant drives. In Imola he managed to finish 3rd and in Monaco, he qualified on the front row for the first time, alongside Schumacher, who was taking his first ever pole. Unfortunately, he went off at the start, then the Peugeot engine broke in Spain, Canada and France. In Silverstone, Mika finished third again. He was suspended for Hungary, having been found guilty of causing the big accident in Germany. He inherited 2nd place in Spa, his best result, after Schumacher

was disqualified. He then finished third in Monza, Estoril and Jerez. This turnaround at the end of the year brought him 4th place in the championship with 26 points, just ahead of Alesi.

1995

The arrival of the Mercedes engine at McLaren did not immediately allow Häkkinen to carry on where he had left off in 1994. After a good start with 4th in Brazil, the Finn was involved in first lap accidents in Argentina and Canada, spun out of second place in Spa and saw his engine break in Spain, Monaco, England, Germany, Hungary and Portugal. He saved his season with two 2nd places in Monza and Suzuka, before suffering a terrible accident in practice for the Australian

GP in Adelaide. 7th on 17 points at the end of the season, he was lucky to be alive.

1996

David Coulthard replaced Mark Blundell alongside the Finn. The McLaren-Mercedes made progress, but still lagged behind Williams, Ferrari and Benetton. He finished 5th in Australia and 4th in Brazil. He was very consistent, with 13 finishes, 11 of them in the points. Three 3rd places at Silverstone, Spa and Monza gave him 5th place in the championship on 31 points. It was a good sign for 1997.

1997

Mika gets off to a reliable start: 3rd in Australia, 4th in Brazil, 5th in Argentina and 6th in Imola. The rest did not go so well: he retired 6 times from 10 starts, was disqualified once and only scored points once, for 3rd place in Hockenheim. But his career was at a turning point. In the Luxembourg GP at the Nurburgring, he took his first ever pole, before retiring once again. 4th in Japan, the Finn won the final race of the season, the European GP at Jerez, ahead of team-mate David Coulthard. Mika is only 6th on 27 points. Coulthard is 3rd with 36, but the best is yet to come.

1998

The McLaren-Mercedes MP4/13 proves competitive out of the box. Häkkinen and Coulthard rack up 12 poles, 9 of them in a row. Mika takes 9 of them and wins 8 times: Australia, Brazil, Spain, Monaco, Austria, Germany, Luxembourg at the Nurburgring and Japan. Three more podiums and two other points finishes round off his season. And of

course, its enough to take the title, after a final duel with Schumacher, which he wins in Suzuka. *"Nothing feels real,"* he said after the race. *"It's too much to take in. After I crossed the line, I drove very slowly to clear my head. I couldn't do it. It was a very hard year, but I liked it a lot. It's mega!"* by 100 points to 86, Mika was world champion.

1999

In pure performance terms, Häkkinen continued where he left off: 11 poles, 5 in a row at the start of the year, then six more between Silverstone and Monza. Reliability was another matter: only 5 wins, in Sao Paulo, Barcelona, Montreal, Budapest and Suzuka, five further podiums, a sixth place and five retirements. And, all season long, a duel at

▷ *1995: the first season with Mercedes power was notable for several retirements and the terrible Adelaide accident.*

1995

1996

▷ *Jerez 1997: Hakkinen wins the European Grand Prix by one second from team-mate David Coulthard to take the first of his twenty F1 victories.*

1997

▷ *Suzuka 1998: five years after taking his first podium at this very circuit, Hakkinen picks up his eighth win of the season to become World Champion.*

1998

◁ *Still Suzuka, this* ▷ *time in 1999: the Finn celebrates his second world championship title.*

1999

▷ *Spa 2000: after an incredible passing move on Michael Schumacher, Mika flies to the flag, to increase his lead in the championship.*

2000

2001

Montreal 2001: Alesi takes 5th place, his best result from 29 Grand Prix start with Prost.

Indianapolis 2001: 200th grand prix for Jean Alesi, at the wheel of a Jordan-Honda. He finished 7th; his 16th finish from 16 races.

1997

Alesi's second Benetton season starts badly. In Australia he misses the pit board telling him to come in to refuel and runs out of petrol, when lying 2nd. From June on, he improves, finishing second in Montreal and Silverstone. In Monza, in front of the tifosi, the Frenchman takes pole, the second of his career and leads for 31 laps from Coulthard's McLaren, before pitting. The Scotsman gets out ahead and takes the win. In the Luxemburg GP, he records the 16th second place finish of his career, his final podium for Benetton, before moving to Sauber. He is again fourth in the drivers' classification with 36 points.

1998

After seven seasons with Ferrari and Benetton, Alesi finds himself with a mid-grid team. The Saubers are rarely capable of fighting with the big boys, but Jean's competitive nature allows him to pull off the odd miracle. In Austria, in the rain, he is second in quali-fying, Sauber's best ever performance. But in the race, he tangles with Fisichella on lap21. Six weeks later, he finishes 3rd at Spa. A disappointing 11th at the end of the season with 9 points.

1999

The second year with Sauber is not as good as the first. All Alesi manages is two 6th places, in Imola and Suzuka, in his last race for the Swiss team, to finish 16th in the championship, his worst finish. He does however manage to put his Sauber on the front row at Magny-Cours, taking to the track right at the start of the session, before the rain.

2000

Moving to Prost, Alesi experiences his worst ever season: 12 retirements and only five finishes, the best being 9th in the European GP. Apart from qualifying 7th in Monaco, there was no respite. And, for the first time in his career, not a single point to his name.

2001

Twelve races and 4 points for Prost, before the divorce, then five races and one point for Jordan. He finished 16 of the 17 races, making him the F1 endurance champion. 14th in the classification with 5 points and his dignity, passion, aggression and skill still intact. ∎

2002: Neither Mika nor Jean

by Didier Braillon, (*L'Equipe*)

Alesi is all smiles, alongside Jarno Trulli as he returns to the Jordan fold, at the 2001 Hugarian Grand Prix. Just as his F1 career seemed to have taken off again, two months later came the news he would be replaced in 2002, by the British F3 champion, Japan's Takuma Sato.

Between the two of them they started 363 grands prix: 162 for Mika Häkkinen and 201 for Jean Alesi. Next year, they will no longer be with us. World Champion in 1998 and 1999, winner of twenty grands prix, the McLaren-Mercedes driver has decided to take a twelve month sabbatical. Having taken just one victory, in Montreal in 1995 for Ferrari, the man who drove for both Prost-Acer and Jordan-Honda has declared the time has come to put an end to his career. Jean Alesi broke the news himself at a Bridgestone press conference in the New Otani Hotel in Tokyo on 10th October, the Wednesday before the final round of the series at Suzuka. This news seemed to have more impact than the McLaren driver's announcement which came on 13th September in the Monza paddock. Häkkinen had actually informed Ron Dennis of the decision back in May at the Monaco race.

"Mika is definitely not giving up racing permanently. Given that he is an important part of our plans for the future, I told him not to get too used to lounging around on a beach in 2002," said the McLaren boss. However, on the morning of the Japanese Grand Prix, the Finn happily posed with assorted items of beach accessories, including a rubber ring and a bucket and spade. But with Kimi Raikkonen stepping in to fill the breach alongside David Coulthard, what chance is there of seeing Mika again in 2003?

It seems that even Häkkinen himself is not sure what the future will bring. He will wait and see if, after a few months, the longing to get behind the wheel returns. If, like Niki Lauda and Alain Prost before him, he attempts a comeback, he will be risking eve-rything he has achieved to date. *"I don't really feel like racing,"* he admitted in Japan. *"When I wake up in the morning, I'm not happy. That's why I had to move on. Doing a good job and enjoying it are two different things."* He certainly did do a good job. Sure, he "only" won two grands prix, but given his

inner turmoil, his bad luck and the frailty of his equipment, it was a worthy season. He also out-qualified his ever improving team-mate nine times out of seventeen. *"The hardest thing was waiting for the right time to announce my decision, once I had taken it,"* he admitted. *"From Monaco to Monza, I had to wait sixteen weeks."*

In 2002, Mika and Erja will be devoted parents, who will then be over a year old. *"His birth certainly changed my priorities and the way I looked at racing,"* revealed the father. *"For the moment, I reckon I'll attend some races next year, to support the team and to see how David and Kimi get on with the championship. Maybe it will drive me mad and I'll think I want to race again! Maybe I will really appreciate the break and won't want to come back."*

The Japanese fans, especially the young girls, showed the patience of Job, waiting for him to emerge from the Suzuka paddock. The Japanese "groupies" reckoned his blonde hair and pale skin were worthy of turning him into a cult figure. F1 will no doubt carry on just fine without Häkkinen, but his departure was as nothing as the sense of shock, tinged with a feeling of guilt, that rocked France

daggers drawn, with Ferrari, first in the hands of Michael Schumacher and then, after the German's Silverstone accident, in the hands of Irvine, who was beaten at the last in Japan, just like his team-mate the previous year. A second title, with 76 points to the Irishman's 74.

2000
The Finn is going for the hat-trick and is again dominant in qualifying, with 3 consecutive poles, but he only has 6 points after 3 races. His four wins, in Spain, Austria, Hungary and Belgium, and seven 2nd places are not enough to stop Michael Schumacher

from taking his third title. The Finn is second on 89 points, beaten at Suzuka, with one race remaining. He ended up 19 points behind the champion.

2001
A season with two sides. There were wins, at Silverstone and Indianapolis, but there were also retirements. Barcelona was typical of these, when he retired on the last lap with the win in the bag. After 7 events he only had 4 points and only nine after 10 grands prix! No poles and 5th place in the championship with 37 points, his worst score since 1997. ■

◁ Häkkinen had a busy time at the 2001 Italian Grand Prix: he announced he was taking a year off and had a big crash at Lesmo in free practice. After dropping out on Sunday, Mika is in pensive mood.

---

when Alesi, the superstar with one win, announced he was on his way.
Married to the former actress, Kumiko Goto, himself a star of several TV commercials, he had returned to Eddie Jordan, with whom he won the 1989 Formula 3000 series. That had been in a Reynard chassis, fitted with a Mugen engine. Since then, Honda, regarded him as one of the family and so it seemed like an act of betrayal and a loss of face, when Jordan took on their own Takuma Sato, who had won the British F3 championship, to replace Jean in 2002.
"I'm retiring. At the moment, I don't know what I'll do, but I won't drive in F1 again," revealed Alesi in Tokyo. At first, he had been confident about next year, but at Indianapolis he started to get wind of what was going on, as his option with the team ran out. There was nothing to be done, even if Honda had wanted to help, except that their decision to put Sato in the car was, "an act of madness." It was an act, aimed at countering any popularity that might swing Toyota's way when they enter the

◁ With Häkkinen taking a sabbatical, the only two world champions in action in 2002 will be Michael Schumacher and Jacques Villeneuve.

sport next year. Was Eddie Jordan scoring political points against the similarly Honda-powered BAR team.

Alesi turned down the offer of a seat with Arrows, which did not really appeal. So, at the age of thirty seven, his career became the victim of market forces rather than any drop off in his performance as a driver. Despite the emotional storms which wrecked his relationship with Prost Grand Prix and sent him to Jordan, his competitive urge and motivation were as strong as ever. As this year's championship came to an end, it was for Alesi an endless round of sad fare-

wells. But the odd little phrase here and there, hinted that maybe this was not quite the end. *"I'm not planning to stay at home all the time, even if I love Kumiko and the kids,"* he said. *"I am not worried about doing something different, as long as it has four wheels and a steering wheel."* He hinted there was something in the pipeline. *"There are all sorts of alternatives, including a proposition from Eddie Jordan. So if I find a role that requires a suit, then I'll wear a suit, but the helmet won't be far away either."* On the 3rd March 2002, in Melbourne, the season will begin without Mika or Jean. Have they gone forever or just a while? ■

◁ Mika with Erja: family life will be his priority in 2002.

John Cooper (1923-2000): The man who powered Formula 1

by Jacques Vassal
«Auto Passion»

Fornula 1 has gone through profound changes in the past fifty years. One major evolution was the switch from front to mid/rear engined cars. That was down to John Cooper, who died at the end of 2000. Here we pay tribute to a visionary.

Mechanic, driver, constructor, tuner and team manager, John Cooper was all of these things, up to his death at the age of 77. In F1 terms, the mid engine concept remains his finest legacy, while he is best remembered by the general public for the Mini-Cooper. Cooper developed the performance version of the Alex Issigonis designed Mini, in close collaboration with BMC.

John's father, Charles Cooper, was born in Paris in 1893, in a family of artists. Born in 1923, John was brought up to the sound of engines in his father's workshop. Charles Cooper had returned to England, starting out as a mechanic with Napier. He then opened his own garage business in Surbiton, to the south of London. He prepared cars to race on the famous Brooklands circuit.

Little John would go and watch the races and from the age of 12, he learned to drive an Austin Seven, specially prepared by his father.

However, John Cooper would become better known as a mechanic and tuner rather than as a driver. He eventually moved on to become a constructor. In 1938, he left Grammar School to work for his father,

served in the Navy during the war and then in the Royal Air Force. In 1946, he set up Cooper as a constructor.

THE RENAISSANCE

It took longer for motor racing to get off the ground again in England, than it did in Italy and France. A 500 cc formula was born, using motorcycle engines. It meant that young impecunious men could race on a budget. Short of funds, Charles and John spotted the opportunity and to publicise their product, John raced in the first few events. Father and son built the

Fiat Topolino. They sawed up two of them, welding the two front ends together, thus producing a chassis with four independently sprung wheels. For reasons of economy, drive came courtesy of a chain and they put the engine behind the driver. It was powered by a single seater 497 cc JAP engine, coupled to a Triumph four speed box. The Mk. 1 made its debut on 26th July 1946 at a Prescott hillclimb. A few weeks later they scored their first class win in Brighton. Just as they had hope, they took orders for twelve cars. In early 1947, they set up the Cooper Car Company Limited.

At this point, a very talented young driver joined forces with Cooper. At the age of 18, Stirling Moss ordered a Cooper-JAP. He won the race at the Easter meeting at Goodwood. This was the first of many on his way to the championship title. Better still, Moss would use the Cooper to tackle an international programme. In 1949, Moss used a new 1000 cc V-twin engined version to race in Formula 2 on the continent, mainly in Italy. At the Lake Garda circuit, he took a sensational 3rd place behind the two litre Ferraris. Apart from Moss's skill at the wheel, it was noticeable that, what the Cooper lacked in power, it made up for with better traction and less weight. In the 1950 Monaco GP, the second ever race in the history of the world championship, it was Harry Schell who dipped his toe in the water with an 1100 cc Cooper-JAP. But the Paris based American, who at 29 was taking part in his first grand prix, was caught up in an accident. After that, Coopers only featured in less important races. It was in one of these, at Cadours on 18th September 1950, that the great French champion, Raymond Sommer was killed at the wheel of a Cooper-JAP. It was rumoured, though never proven, that the steering column had broken. Despite this setback, Cooper progressed and won numerous races in the newly recognised Formula 3 series. The next few models featured an ever increasing number of parts made in-house, such as the suspension and a tubular chassis. With a front engined car, the company enjoyed a successful period in Formula 2.

PLAYING WITH THE BIG BOYS

Early 1952, Formula 1 was suffering from a lack of constructors. So as not to discredit the world championship, FIA decided to open it up to Formula 2 cars, either 2 litre normally aspirated or 500 cc with compressor. Ferrari and Maserati had cars to suit this formula, as did Osca and Gordini. In Germany, AFM used 6 cylinder engines based on the BMW 328. In England, the 4 cylinder 2 litre Alta engine was used by HWM and Connaught, while Cooper chose the Bristol 6 cylinder with hemi heads, itself a copy of the BMW 328. Two Formula 3 drivers, Alan Brown and Eric Brandon had decided to tackle the grands prix. The Coopers built them two cars with tubular chassis and the Bristol engine. It only made 140 horsepower, but

JACQUES VASSAL, Journalist, writer and translator, Jacques Vassal has contributed for over eleven years to Auto Passion magazine. He has worked as a freelance since the start of 2000 for various specialist publications, producing essays, portraits, interviews and retrospectives. picture: Sylvie Foucher

Cadours, 18th September 1950: French champion Raymond Sommer, in his Cooper-JAP, in the race which would cost him his life. (archives Dominique Pascal)

it was inexpensive and strong. At the Easter meeting, on 14th April 1952, the very first Cooper-Bristol, straight out of the factory, was driven by none other than Juan Manuel Fangio. The Argentinian had come to Goodwood to race the BRM V16. But as it was not ready, he jumped into the brand new Cooper and finished 6th in the Chichester Cup. What Brandon and Brown did not know, was that Cooper had built a third car for the 22 year old son of another garage owner.

Mike Hawthorn would soon prove his talent at the wheel, eclipsing his elders. He raced in five grands prix in 1952 and finished 3rd in the British, 4th in Belgium and in Holland. Brown had one points finish (5th in Switzerland) and Brandon did not score. Thanks to the Cooper-Bristol, Hawthorn caught the eye of Enzo Ferrari and joined the Scuderia for 1953.

That year, the Cooper drivers, Alan Brown, Bob Gerard and Ken Wharton failed to score any points. Neither did Moss, who raced a Cooper-Alta in three events. The engines lacked power and the factory lacked funds.

In 1954, a new Formula 1 was introduced, with 2.5 litre normally aspirated or 750 cc with compressor engines. Cooper only managed to field a car in the British GP, with no result.

The factory survived thanks to Formula 3 and sports cars (the Cooper-Jaguar.) Then, in 1955, the little "bobtail" Cooper with an 1100 cc Climax engine signalled a new era, as the Surbiton constructor collaborated with the Coventry engine company,

which, until then had specialised in powering water pumps. But it was with a Bristol engine that Cooper returned to Formula 1 at Aintree for the 1955 British Grand Prix. But this time, the engine was fitted at the rear. Also new on the scene was the driver. A young mechanic from Australia, he was called Jack Brabham. But on that 16th July, he was forced to retire.

Hippodrome de Caen, July 1958: the two Cooper-Climax of the Rob Walker team, with Stirling Moss (winner of this non-championship Grand Prix on car n° 4) and Maurice Trintignant. (archives Dominique Pascal)

AN INCREASE IN POWER

Before triumphing in Formula 1, Cooper first went into Formula 2, where Brabham, Roy Salvadori and Tony Brooks all shone. Engine capacity was 1500 cc. This suited the Climax 4 cylinder. From 1000 cc with overhead cam, it evolved into an 1100 then a 1500 with two overhead cams. In 1957, the Cooper-Climax won loads of F2 races, including the Oulton Park Gold Cup with Jack Brabham. Then Cooper headed for F1 again with 2 litre Climax engines. It only put out 175 hp, but Barabham and Salvadori got the most out of them. In Monaco, Brabham ran 5th and finished 6th because of a fuel problem, but the point for this was only allocated in 1960. Thus it fell to Salvadori to score Cooper's first world championship points in F1, when he came fifth in the British GP at Aintree. The Constructors' Cup began in 1958, a year of great success for Cooper. Along with other manufacturers, Cooper realised that power was not everything: a light driveable car was also essential. Vanwall finally managed to win the championship with a front engined car, but it owed much to the talent of Moss and Brooks, as well as Lewis-Evans. Its streamlined bodywork also helped; the first time a wind tunnel had been used, under the guidance of Frank Costin and Lotus boss Colin Chapman. Of course, Hawthorn took the title that year in a Ferrari Dino 256, still

Monaco, 10th May 1959: after Moss and Trintignant for Rob Walker in 1958, Jack Brabham gives the Cooper team its first win in a world championship Grand Prix. He beats the Ferrari of Tony Brooks. (archives Dominique Pascal)

with engine at the front, helped by a bit of luck. However, it was obvious that the days of the front engined car were numbered. The last win for this configuration came at the 1960 Italian GP (Phil Hill in a Ferrari Dino..) Aston Martin and Scarab were the last constructors to stick with the outdated design, but soon gave up. Ferrari and BRM soon copied the Cooper and Lotus mid/rear engined layout. When the 1500cc F1 category was introduced in 1961, there were no more front engined cars competing in grands prix.

A FUTURISTIC IDEA

Before the war and not forgetting the Benz "Tropfenwagen" seen at Avus in 1923, Ferdinand Porsche was working for Auto Union and pioneered the centrally mounted engine in grand prix cars. From 1934 to '39, the V16 Auto Union and then the V12, had won several races. In 1947, the

Italian industrialist, Piero Dusio created the F1 Cisitalia, a 1500 cc supercharged car with mid/rear mounted engine, designed by Porsche. But lack of funds meant it never raced in a grand prix. A few years later, the Sachs-Gordini from France took up the idea. A prototype was built, but again lack of funds meant it did not race. That is how Cooper, more for reasons of economy than out of a technical vision, became the pioneer of this layout in F1. 1958 got off to a great start for the marque. The entrant Rob Walker, a friend and customer, won the first two races of the season: in Argentina, where the Vanwalls were missing, Stirling Moss drove the 2 litre Cooper-Climax. Fangio was driving at home, in his penultimate race in a Maserati 250 F. he led but had to stop and change tyres. At half distance, Moss took the lead and looked after his tyres to avoid having to pit and thus gave Cooper its first F1 win, with a 2.7 second lead over Musso's Ferrari. The Vanwalls were in Monaco, but it was Maurice Trintignant, who won at the wheel of Walker's Cooper, by twenty seconds from Usso and 39 seconds ahead of Collins. Brabham, in a factory Cooper fitted with a new 2.2 litre Climax, putting out 220 hp came fourth. In Holland, the other factory driver, Roy Salvadori, finished fourth. He had a good season: 3rd in Britain, 2nd in Germany. There would be no further Cooper wins that year, leaving the Vanwalls and the BRMs to a

lesser degree, to challenge the Ferraris. Hawthorn took the title for Ferrari, just ahead of Moss and Brooks in his Vanwall. Behind them came Schell (BRM) and Salvadori (Cooper) equal on 15 points. The Surbiton marque came third in the Constructors' classification, behind Vanwall and Ferrari, but ahead of BRM. Cooper

◁

Reims, 3rd July 1960: the excellent NZ driver and future constructor Bruce McLaren, at the wheel of the second factory Cooper-Climax, finishes 3rd in the Grand Prix de l'ACF.
(archives Dominique Pascal)

was now recognised as a legitimate challenger.

THE CROWNING GLORY

The next two years would see Cooper reach the very top of the F1 tree. In 1959, Coventry-Climax finally produced a 2.5 litre version of its FPF 4 cylinder engine, putting out 240 hp, while the Cooper chassis has evolved into the T 51. Brabham and the young New Zealander, Bruce McLaren were the drivers, sometimes joined by the American Masten Gregory. Salvadori was waiting for the Aston Martin and drove a private Cooper with a Maserati engine. Moss had left Vanwall, stopped off briefly at BRM and then joined the Walker team alongside Trintignant. Cooper was up against the BRM P25 and the Ferrari Dino 256. Brabham was up against Tony Brooks and Stirling Moss. The Australian, who drove hunched over the wheel in an effective if ungainly style, won two grands

prix that year and with several other good finishes, took the title. Cooper took the Constructors' cup with five wins from eight grands prix with 40 points from Ferrari on 32.

At 22 years of age, Bruce McLaren was the youngest ever GP winner in the United States 1959 race. He won the first round of the 1960 series in Argentina, the last year of the 2.5 litre formula. Cooper continued to dominate this year, but it would start to show its limitations. While Ferrari and BRM were persisting with front engine cars, a new challenge was on the way, in the shape of Lotus, who used the same engine, but had far superior suspension. Colin Chapman's team had a more methodical and scientific approach. While the Coopers could be described as mechanics' cars, the Lotus were engineers'. Stirling Moss came fourth in Argentina, setting the fastest lap and he could see the writing was already on the wall. He convinced Rob

△

Reims, 3rd July 1960: John Cooper can celebrate: not only has he beaten the Ferraris, but there are four Coopera in the first four!
(archives Dominique Pascal)

Walker to buy a Lotus 18 and went on to win in Monaco. But Jack Brabham and his Cooper fought back, to win the next five races: Holland, Belgium, France, Britain and Portugal. There was only the Italian even to go. In the absence of the English teams, who boycotted the race over a disagreement about the track layout at Monza, victory went to Phil Hill. Brabham was world champion and Cooper also, for the second consecutive year.

In 1961, the new 1500 cc formula is introduced with a minimum weight of 450 kilos. Ferrari and BRM switched to rear engined cars and Porsche joined in with its old F2 cars. Ferrari was favourite for the title with its new 156, with Lotus as the main challenger. Cooper stagnated through lack of funds and new ideas and only finished 4th out of 5 in the Constructors' classification, easily won by Ferrari. Brabham was the first to use the new V8 Climax, in Germany and Italy, but it was not enough. 1962 was a bad year for Ferrari, with the championship a fight between BRM and Lotus. Graham Hill and his BRM V8 was world champion ahead of Jim Clark and the stunning Lotus 25. Brabham left Cooper to set up his own team. McLaren was still with Cooper but would soon do the same thing, while Cooper opted to collaborate with BMC. The famous Mini-

◁

Monte-Carlo Rally, janvier 1965: the Mini-Cooper S of Makinen-Easter, won this famous event to give John Cooper a morale boosting lift.
(archives Dominique Pascal)

Coopers, in 1000, 1100 and then 1300 cc form put up some great performances in Saloon Car racing and rallies and these results help boost sales of the road cars. The sale of 120,000 of these brought in enough in royalties for Cooper to reinvest in F1. He took on Phil Hill in 1964, but the heart and the budget were no longer in it. Charles died that year and John, who was running the company, had a serious road accident. At least in F3, Jackie Stewart won everything or almost in a Ken Tyrrell entered Cooper-BMC. It helped sell even more Cooper single-seaters.

IN BED WITH MASERATI

In 1965, Cooper was recuperating and he took on a young talented Austrian called Jochen Rindt. Yet again, the results were not great, but the prospects for 1966 looked better. At the end of 1965, Cooper sold his team to the Marks and Spencer millionaire Jonathan Sieff. His links with Maserati allowed for the supply of the Italian three litre V12, putting out 360 horsepower, in preparation for the new Formula 1 which would start in 1966. John Cooper continued to run the team, helped by Roy Salvadori. The Cooper-Maseratis were driven alternately by Jochen Rindt, who came second in Belgium behind Surtees in the Ferrari and the American Ritchie Ginther, who was waiting for the new Honda. They scored a few points. John Cooper stormed out of Ferrari and joined Cooper as from

the French GP. Rob Walker took on a customer Cooper T 86 Maserati V12, which were driven by Jo Siffert, Georges Filipinetti, Guy Ligier and Jo Bonnier. The marque was competitive once again. In Germany, Surtees finished second behind Brabham and Rindt was 3rd. Surtees went one better, to win in Mexico at the end of the year, beating the Brabham-Repco. Cooper was third in the Constructors' behind Brabham and Ferrari. Brabham became the first and only man to win the Drivers' title in his own car. Surtees came second, having won in Belgium in a Ferrari, while Rindt, in a Cooper all year was third. Rindt stayed with Cooper-Maserati for 1967, with Pedro Rodriguez replacing Surtees, who moved to Honda. The Mexican won in his first outing with his new team in South Africa. With several fancied runners dropping out, the local man John Love, who led for a long time in his Cooper-Climax, came second. This would be Cooper's swansong and the Surbiton marque would never win in F1 again. It finished third in the Constructors' classification in 1967.

THE DYING EMBERS

In 1968, the Coopers used the BRM V12, which was more modern and powerful than the Maserati. England's Brian Redman and the Italian Lodovico Scarfiotti, who had left Ferrari, were the new recruits and finished 3rd and 4th in Spain. Brian

Redman was actually driving in the Spa 1000 Kilometres on the day of the Monaco race (he won) and so it was Luciano Bianchi who replaced him in Monaco. He finished 3rd with Scarfiotti 4th again. Sadly Scarfiotti was killed in Germany, tackling a hillclimb event on 8th June. He should have been competing in the Belgian GP the following day. Bianchi finished sixth, while Redman crashed because of a faulty tyre.

The car caught fire and although Redman survived, he was out of action for several weeks. Bianchi raced alone in Holland but was not classified. For the French GP at Rouen, the Coopers were driven by Vic Elford and Johnny Servoz-Gavin, whose car failed before the start. Elford picked up a few precious points to help Cooper to 6th place in the Constructors' classification.

In 1969, with no money and no sponsors, Cooper finally threw in the F1 towel. It's final appearance came courtesy of a private entry for Vic Elford, who drove a 1967 car in Monaco under the Antique Automobile Racing banner! He finished just out of the points in seventh.

John Cooper stayed in business as a Honda and Rover dealer, while still keeping his ties with BMC, then British Leyland. In 1994, the Mini-Cooper was produced once again. It was the final satisfaction for this likeable bon viveur of a man, who was a good servant to the world of motor racing

Reims, 3rd July 1966: It is the first year of the 3 litre Formula 1. Another brilliant New Zealander, Chris Amon, here at Thillois corner, drives the third factory Cooper-Maserati. They were all delayed with vapour-lock. He would finish 8th. Behind him, the Ferrari 312 of Lorenzo Bandini (n° 20) and the private Cooper-Maserati of Guy Ligier (n° 4). (archives Dominique Pascal)

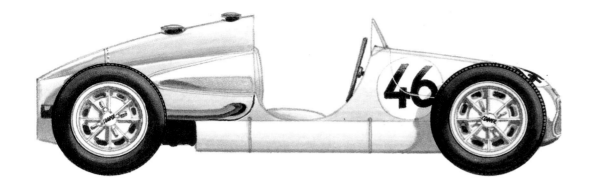

◁

Cooper T9-JAP
Stirling Moss
Lago di Garda (F2)
1949

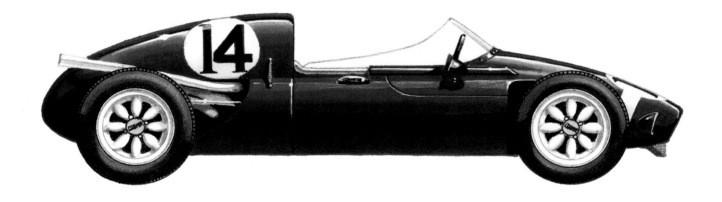

◁

Cooper T20-Bristol
Mike Hawthorn
Grand Prix de Belgique
1952

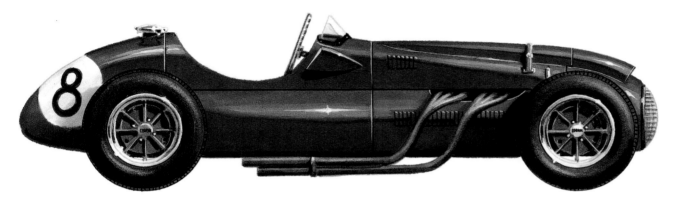

◁

Cooper T43-Climax
(R.C.C. Walker Team)
Stirling Moss
Grand Prix d'Argentine
1958

◁

Cooper T53-Climax
Jack Brabham
Grand Prix de l'A.C.F
1960

◁

Cooper T81-Maserati
John Surtees
Grand Prix du Mexique
1966

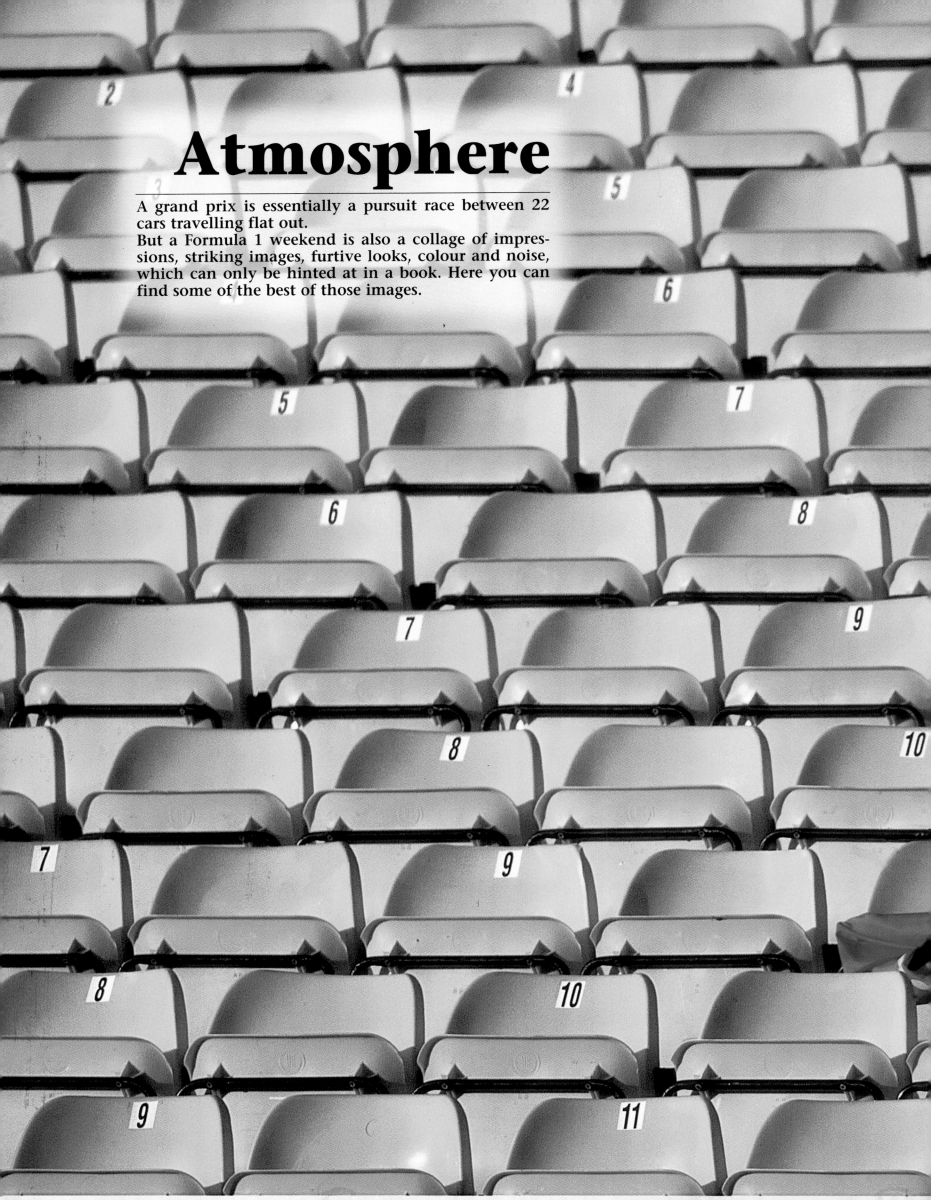

Atmosphere

A grand prix is essentially a pursuit race between 22 cars travelling flat out.

But a Formula 1 weekend is also a collage of impressions, striking images, furtive looks, colour and noise, which can only be hinted at in a book. Here you can find some of the best of those images.

Thanks for being there

Is Formula 1 a macho universe? Absolutely, as it is more than twenty years now since a woman started a grand prix. Luckily, from press officers to groupies, there are still plenty of pretty women in the paddock, to keep the men on their toes.

ATMOSPHERE

All the colours

To a photographer's eye, a grand prix is not just about cars driving round in circles on a Sunday afternoon. When they roam the pits with their lenses, the results are sometimes surprising, often remarkable.

ATMOSPHERE

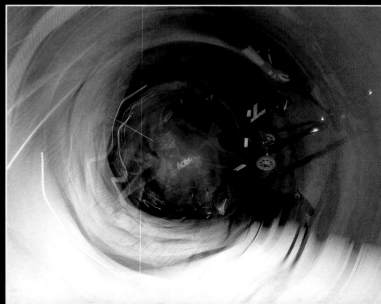

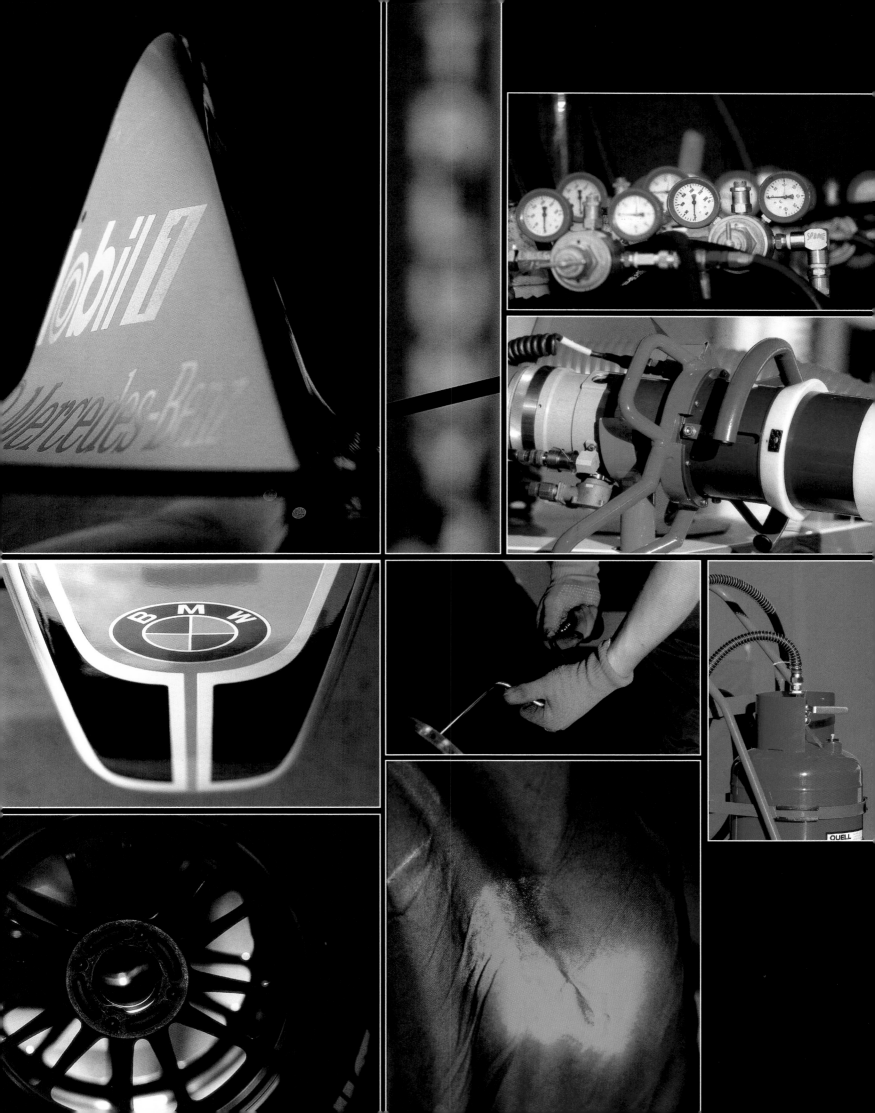

ATMOSPHERE

Yellow suits you so well

Fifth place in the world championship, a few good races, several disappointments, changes of fortune, not to mention changes of driver. All this made up Jordan's 2001 season. It was the same story for many of the other Formula 1 teams.

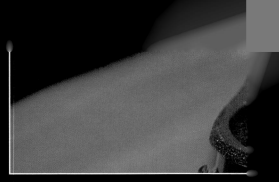

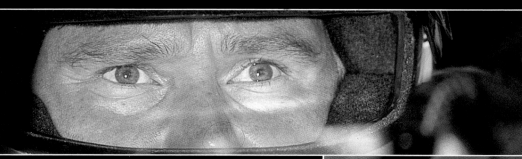

ATMOSPHERE

A steady foot a good eye

From dark looks to the stare of a killer, the drivers are as readily identifiable by their eyes as they are by their crash helmets. Can you recognise them?

(From top to bottom, left to right: Juan Pablo Montoya, Michael Schumacher, Kimi Räikkönen, David Coulthard, Jacques Villeneuve, Eddie Irvine, Nick Heidfeld, Ralf Schumacher, Jean Alesi, Tarso Marques, Mika Häkkinen, Heinz-Harald Frentzen, Ricardo Zonta, Giancarlo Fisichella and Alex Yoong).

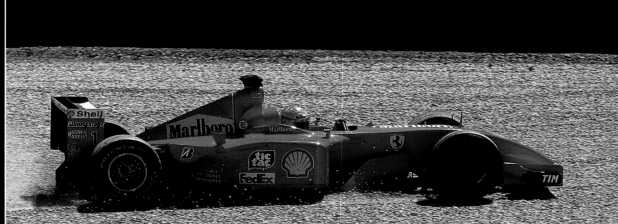

ATMOSPHERE

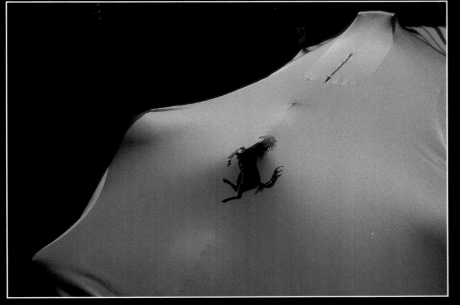

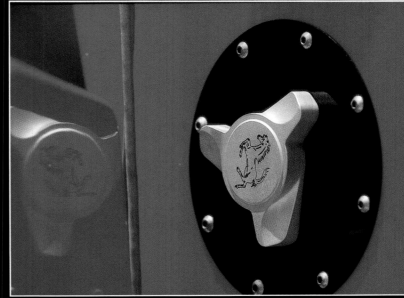

Red with pleasure

The 2001 season was without a doubt, the most extraordinary in the history of Scuderia Ferrari: Drivers's and Constructors titles and a rash of records, all served to make it a carmine year.

ATMOSPHERE

The 17 Grands Prix

There they go! From Melbourne to Suzuka, the Formula 1 circus has hustled around the world, from east to west, north to south, in its usual frenzied fashion. 17 starts, 17 podiums and in between, the 17 grands prix themselves, a theatre of joy, tears and plenty of work. The tale of a season which was painted red.

Schumacher opens his account!

Ferrari did not take long to show that bright red would be the dominant colour this season. In Melbourne the Scuderia cars made the front row of the grid their own.

In the race, David Coulthard was the only one capable of stopping them making a clean sweep of it, sneaking his McLaren into second place. The lesson to be learnt from the first race was clear: those who wanted to match Ferrari's pace would have a lot of work to do. No one ever really managed it.

QANTAS AUSTRALIAN GRAND PRIX
MELBOURNE

Rubens Barrichello seemed to be very comfortable with the 2001 Ferrari. Having been quickest on Friday, he qualified second on the grid.

The Ferraris sweep all before them

The front row sees red

Scuderia Ferrari claimed the front row of the grid as its own, during qualifying in Melbourne.
At the wheel of the same car which he had crashed on Friday (see below,) Michael Schumacher set a time which was out of everyone's reach. "*It's a really nice feeling to start the new season where we left off the old one. We are in any case very confident for the race.*" Rubens Barrichello was second and was equally delighted."*I feel a lot more comfortable in this car than in last year's one. It suits my driving style better. In fact, if I had not lost time in the mor-*ning *session, I think I could have threatened Michael's time.*"
Naturally, there was some disappointment in the McLaren camp. While Mika Hakkinen posted a damage limiting third fastest time, David Coulthard could do no better than sixth. "*We weren't able to set up the car properly today,*" complained the Finn.
Despite this, Hakkinen seemed to be all smiles and relaxed as the season got underway. Friends reckoned that fatherhood, with his first child

Hugo being born at the end of 2000, was a calming influence on the Finn.
That sense of calm certainly did not come from his new car, the MP4/16. On the contrary, it was the cause of much agonising. "*Testing has thrown up quite a few problems,*" admitted the Finn. Indeed the McLaren team had been handicapped by gearbox and engine bothers with several breakages meaning that Mika had been unable to complete a single race distance over the winter!

First day of practice

Barrichello quickest, Schumacher highest!

Michael Schumacher inspects the wreckage of his car after his Friday accident.
"*We are pleased that there have been great steps forward in the area of safety, even if it is always possible to do still better,*" was Jean Todt's analysis later that same day. "*For example, that gravel trap. It was not perfectly flat and that is why the car rolled over. We know the danger an uneven trap presents and we had pointed out the problem to the organisers. They had dealt with it at other places but not this one.*"

There are only a few minutes remaining of Friday's practice. Michael Schumacher is flat out, trying to beat the time set by team-mate Rubens Barrichello, who has been quickest since the morning session. Coming into Turn 6, the German's Ferrari gets out of shape, slips sideways into the gravel trap and rolls over in spectacular fashion.
Everyone holds their breath. But once the car comes to rest, the world champion removes the steering wheel and climbs out of the cockpit uninjured. Once again, the modern F1 cars had proved how incredibly strong they are. "*I was told there were yellow flags at Turn 5,*" he explained later. "*I slowed down, but I didn't see anything, so I accelerated again. Then I saw the flags at Turn 6. I braked a bit too hard, when I was on the limit and the car went into a slide, then it rolled. But I did not hit the wall and there was no impact, just a gentle roll! I am perfectly fine.*"
In Jean Todt's opinion, the fact Schumacher was alright was a minor miracle. "*A few years back, Michael would never have got out of something like that without injury.*"

The new AP04 was presented just prior to free practice.

Alain Prost wants to rock the house

The new Prost-Acer AP04 was only unveiled on the Wednesday before practice in Melbourne, but it had already been testing since 15th January and had actually been going very nicely thank you.

Straight from the crate in Barcelona, the 2001 car had been the previous car's lap times by a massive five seconds!

The testing results seemed to point to a quality piece of kit. In the following week, Jean Alesi often did set some surprising times, be it at Barcelona or Estoril and he was often the quickest driver on any given day.

The French team seemed to have got its act together. "*I think we have come up with a very good and reliable car,*" rejoiced Alain Prost. "*It's nothing special, but it seems to have no weak points. In fact, when everything goes well, our results depend more on what the others do than what we can produce.*"

As far as sponsorship was concerned, there was still plenty of available space with the side pods carrying large Prost logos, which did not bode well on the financial front. "*Obviously we are going to have to keep an eye on our expenditure,*" continued Prost. "*As our car is reliable,*

it should cost us less to run in testing, but Pedro De La Rosa's defection poses us a few problems."

The Spaniard had signed a deal as test driver, bringing with him a crock of gold from Spanish oil company Repsol. But the week before the Australian Grand Prix, he ducked out of the deal, preferring to go for a similar testing role with Jaguar. "*This business gives us a headache,*" admitted an angry Prost. "*Because we have not been looking for another third driver. And also because we will miss the money that we had expected to receive. I will be taking the matter to court.*"

△ After a disastrous year with Minardi, Gaston Mazzacane moved to Prost in 2001. It was to be no better, as he only lasted four grands prix before being replaced by Luciano Burti.

Happy as a kid at Christmas

Jean Alesi seems as happy as a lad who has just been given his first train set. "*Everyone is talking about my second childhood. But old age is a tag stuck on me by the press,*" he suggested on the day of the AP04 launch.

Jean Alesi laughs, bubbling with enthusiasm and explains yet again why he can't wait for the first day of practice. "*I am happy, because I know that this season I'll be able to fight. Sometimes, before the start of a season, you worry about reliability and sometimes you know it's going to be hell. But not this time.*"

Jean reckoned he had already tamed the AP04. "*I can't adapt my driving style to a car. I need to be able to attack without holding back. That's no problem with the AP04. Without wishing to sound pretentious, you could put anyone in this car, Schumacher included, and I am sure I would beat him. I am really excited about being able to show everyone how fantastic this car is.*"

However, on Saturday, Jean of Avignon showed absolutely nothing with a 14thfastest time. "*We had difficulties in setting up the car on this rather unique track,*" he explained. "*The car goes from being well balanced to bad with just the slightest change. The car can definitely do better.*"

Kimi Raikkonen was one of the rookies in Melbourne, along with Juan Pablo Montoya, Enrique Bernoldi and Fernando Alonso. The Sauber man came out of it rather well, as he qualified 13th, just three places behind Nick Heidfeld. Not a bad debut.

STARTING GRID

M. SCHUMACHER 1'26"892	-1-	R. BARRICHELLO 1'27"263
Mika HÄKKINEN 1'27"461	-2-	H.-H. FRENTZEN 1'27"658
Ralf SCHUMACHER 1'27"719	-3-	David COULTHARD 1'28"010
Jarno TRULLI 1'28"377	-4-	Jacques VILLENEUVE 1'28"435
Olivier PANIS 1'28"518	-5-	Nick HEIDFELD 1'28"615
J. P. MONTOYA 1'28"738	-6-	Eddie IRVINE 1'28"965
Kimi RÄIKKÖNEN 1'28"993	-7-	Jean ALESI 1'29"893
Jos VERSTAPPEN 1'29"934	-8-	Jenson BUTTON 1'30"035
Giancarlo FISICHELLA 1'30"209	-9-	Enrique BERNOLDI 1'30"520
Fernando ALONSO 1'30"657	-10-	Gaston MAZZACANE 1'30"798
Luciano BURTI 1'30"978	-11-	Tarso MARQUES 1'33"228

In Australia, as in so many other countries, Ferrari is the most popular team with the crowds. While the drivers refrained from celebrating on the podium, the fans nevertheless showed their pleasure at Michael Schumacher's win.

The first start of a new season and although David Coulthard tried to move up from his sixth place on the grid, he found his path blocked.

The first corner was pretty tight in Melbourne with a hard fight for third place. Having messed up the start from second on the grid, Rubens Barrichello finds himself behind Heinz-Harald Frentzen.

Mika Hakkinen poses for the traditional photo-portrait at the start of the season. In the first grand prix, the Finn was the only man who seemed capable of giving Michael Schumacher a run for his money. It seemed that yet again the year would turn into the usual tussle between Ferrari and McLaren. "In 2001, we will not be on the defensive, we will be attacking," maintained McLaren Managing Director, Martin Whitmarsh. "We are going to win back the title we lost in 2000." To this end, the team's Technical Director, Adrian Newey came up with a completely new car, the MP4/16. For the first time since 1998, the car was not an evolution of the previous year's. "As the technical regulations changed for this year, we started from a clean sheet of paper," he explained.

The Scuderia gets off to a good start

The 2001 season got off to a pretty good start for Scuderia Ferrari. Michael Schumacher won at a canter in Melbourne, while Mika Hakkinen, his presumed rival for the title, was forced to retire.

Leading from the start, the German pulled out a lead over the Finn, a tenth of a second at a time, until the McLaren man retired on lap 26 with broken suspension. "I don't know what happened, but I hit the guardrail quite hard," commented Hakkinen. "I went to the medical centre to be checked out, but everything is okay. I think we could have won today."

With the main threat out of the way, Schumacher backed off to take his fifth consecutive win, ahead of David Coulthard. "I eased up towards the end, because we had not done many race distances and I wasn't sure how reliable the car was," recounted the world champion.

Rubens Barrichello finished third, so that the Scuderia ended the first race with both its cars on the podium. "I messed up the start," explained the Brazilian. "Then, when I was passing Frentzen, we touched and that damaged my steering. I did what I could but it was hard to turn the car. Towards the end, Ross (Brawn, Ferrari's Technical Director) told me to slow down because of an oil pressure problem."

Drama on lap five

The horror sequence: coming up behind Ralf Schumacher too quickly, Jacques Villeneuve's BAR takes off and crashes into the catch fencing. The driver got out unharmed, but a marshal was fatally injured by a wheel off the BAR.

"I am happy to have scored six points today, but this result is meaningless compared with what happened today." In this single sentence, David Coulthard summed up the feelings of all the drivers at the end of the Australian Grand Prix.

There was no question of celebration after the accident involving Jacques Villeneuve and Ralf Schumacher on lap 5. Flat out down the main straight, the BAR drove into the back of the Williams and took off, flying into the concrete wall at the side of the track. It was a very violent impact, but somehow, both drivers emerged unscathed.

Unfortunately, that was not the case for one of the trackside marshals, Graham Beveridge, who was behind the concrete wall, just opposite a hole in the catch fencing, designed so that marshals and drivers could get through. By some incredibly

unlucky twist of fate, one of the rear wheels off Villeneuve's car passed through the gap and hit Beveridge at full speed. The 52 year old was taken to Melbourne's Alfred Hospital and died shortly after being admitted. Seven other people, spectators, were slightly injured.

The Safety Car was immediately brought out after the accident, so that the track could be cleared of the debris left from what had been a truly horrific crash.

After the race, neither Jacques Villeneuve nor Ralf Schumacher could really explain why the accident had happened. "Ralf was much slower than me," said the Canadian. "I tried to pass him on the right, then to the left, but he braked and we touched." "I think Jacques was being over optimistic," was the German's view of the incident. "I was holding my line, I braked as late as I had done the previous lap

and I felt a huge impact at the rear before I saw the BAR fly over my head."

After the race, the podium ceremony was a sombre affair and no champagne was sprayed. "We have to find ways of improving safety for those people who are here to look after ours," said Michael Schumacher.

The race organisers announced they would be making plans to look after the family of the deceased. The Australian Grand Prix sadly demonstrated there is still plenty to do to improve safety at the races. "We will study the question of marshals' safety," maintained Williams Technical Director Patrick Head. "It might be that there is no need for people to be put at risk simply to give the drivers flag signals, if it can be done by some system using lights." A study of this option was put into place with the idea of giving it a trial run in 2002.

Fantastic people

Marshals are fantastic people. From the early hours of the morning to the end of the races, they spend their days at the side of the track, often soaked to the skin or burnt under a blistering sun. They are the only element of the huge organisation that goes into a grand prix that offer their services free of charge. They do it for the love of motorsport.

In real terms, they see little of the actual racing, or at least less than they would sitting on the sofa at home in front of the television. Never mind, they enjoy it; being close to the action and providing a ser-

vice. Whether they are first-aiders, firemen or flag marshals their roles are indispensable to the organisation of a successful meeting. By its very nature, their job, standing at the side of the track, is dangerous, but none of them think of the risks as they take up their positions.

And yet, after the previous year's accident at Monza, where a fire marshal was killed by a wheel off a Jordan, the same macabre scenario was played out again in Melbourne. Two dead in the space of six months, two fatalities too many proved that there

was still a lot to do to protect these people forgotten by progress in the area of safety.

The FIA has done so much to improve the safety of the cars that drivers now walk away from accidents which would certainly have been fatal just a few years ago. This means that other dangerous elements tend to get forgotten. The Melbourne incident forced the FIA to take a fresh look at the safety of those standing at the side of the track. In that respect at least, the deaths of marshals at Monza and Melbourne were not totally in vain.

Under the microscope!

All eyes were on Juan Pablo Montoya for the Colombian's first grand prix. If Frank Williams had dumped the wonder-child Jenson Button in favour of the South American, he must have had good reason.

In the United States, he won the Indycar championship and the Indy 500, just like Jacques Villeneuve. It was an impressive calling card.

However, in Melbourne, Juan Pablo was "only" eleventh on the grid, while his team-mate was fifth. The Colombian was tuning himself in slowly.

QANTAS AUSTRALIAN GRAND PRIX

QANTAS AUSTRALIAN GRAND PRIX

△ Yippee! The BAR mechanics (inset) applaud Olivier Panis' fourth place finish in his first grand prix for the British team. A few hours later they would not be so happy.

▷ Juan Pablo Montoya discovers his new world. "At the moment, I am still learning," he claimed. "On the driving side, the F1 cars are easier to drive than the American Champcars. They have so many driver aids that it's not too hard!" A provocative remark if ever there was one.

A good start for the Jordan team. Heinz-Harald Frentzen qualified fourth on the grid and picked up two points after Panis was disqualified. The duel between BAR and Jordan to be the best Honda-powered team was already underway.

▽

Olivier Panis loses his points

Two years is a long time in Formula 1 and Olivier Panis had not finished in the points since Germany in 1999. In Melbourne, he came home fourth, but in the end he didn't get to keep his points, losing them a few hours after the race. A protest from the Sauber team saw him penalised 25 seconds. As he had a 22.093 seconds lead over seventh placed Kimi Raikkonen, he was classified behind him and thus out of the points.

The Sauber crew had noticed that the man from Grenoble had overtaken under yellow flags and protested his result. Called before the Stewards, Panis denied the offence, but the officials were having none of it, penalising him 25 seconds, as they reckoned this was the total time he would have lost if he had been called in during the race for a ten second stop-go penalty, which is the standard punishment for overtaking under yellow flags.

Obviously, the BAR driver was not best pleased on Sunday night. "It's all nonsense! I never saw those flags, because if I had, I wouldn't have passed. That Nick Heidfeld really ruined my weekend as he had already messed up my qualifying lap on Saturday."

Both Saubers in the points

That's what you call starting with all guns blazing! With two cars in the points, the Sauber team had won its bet, gambling on picking up as many points as possible in the early part of the year, making the most of the C20's reliability and profiting from the failures of those less well prepared.

At the end of this grand prix and thanks to Panis' disqualification (see above,) Nick Heidfeld picked up the three points for fourth place, having brilliantly fought off the advances of Heinz-Harald Frentzen in the closing stages. "Finally a race which means I can forget my 2000 season," rejoiced the young German.

A glass in his hand, sitting quietly behind the Sauber pit, he was evidently enjoying his moment of glory. "I was able to get a good pace and even at the end of the race, when Heinz-Harald Frentzen was pushing me, I was still able to attack and stay calm."

For his part, Kimi Raikkonen had finished seventh, an exceptionally consistent and confident drive for a 21 year old, taking part in his first grand prix. He seemed unperturbed by it all. "I know it was my first grand prix, but it's nothing to get too excited about," he replied to those who were surprised at his cool approach. "I just drove my best. I did not get a very good start, but after that I found my rhythm. I had a bit of understeer at the start, but the balance gradually improved."

Three hours after the end of the race, the Finn moved up a place, after Panis was disqualified. Scoring points in one's first grand prix is a rare occurrence, although the likes of Alain Prost and Jacques Villeneuve had done it in the past.

Will Kimi Raikkonen follow in their footsteps? Everyone in Finland believes it, including his parents Matti and Paula, who were in Melbourne to watch the young prodigy's debut. Matti had started both his kids karting at the age of eight; a strategy which seemed to be paying off. While Kimi was starting in F1, his elder brother Rami was leading the Finnish Group N Rally Championship.

PRACTICE TIMES

No	Driver	Car/Engine/Chassis	Practice Friday	Pos.	Practice Saturday	Pos.	Qualifying	Pos.	Warm-up	Pos.
1.	M. Schumacher	Ferrari/F2001/208	1'29"284	3°	1'27"561	2°	1'26"892	1°	1'30"839	6°
2.	Rubens Barrichello	Ferrari/F2001/209	1'28"965	1°	1'29"945	13°	1'27"263	2°	1'31"450	9°
3.	Mika Häkkinen	McLaren/Mercedes/MP4-16/3	1'29"799	5°	1'27"775	3°	1'27"461	3°	1'30"152	2°
4.	David Coulthard	McLaren/Mercedes/MP4-16/1	1'29"324	4°	1'27"540	1°	1'28"010	6°	1'30"099	1°
5.	R. Schumacher	Williams/BMW/FW23/3	1'30"277	8°	1'28"666	6°	1'27"719	5°	1'32"687	15°
6.	Juan Pablo Montoya	Williams/BMW/FW23/2	1'31"721	15°	1'29"184	12°	1'28"738	11°	1'30"559	4°
7.	Giancarlo Fisichella	Benetton/Renault/B201/3	1'32"475	16°	1'30"549	16°	1'30"209	17°	1'34"572	21°
8.	Jenson Button	Benetton/Renault/B201/1	1'33"403	21°	1'30"893	19°	1'30"035	16°	1'34"554	20°
9.	Olivier Panis	BAR/Honda/003/2	1'31"166	10°	1'28"677	7°	1'28"518	9°	1'30"584	5°
10.	Jacques Villeneuve	BAR/Honda/003/3	1'31"559	12°	1'28"962	11°	1'28"435	8°	1'32"108	14°
11.	Heinz-Harald Frentzen	Jordan/Honda/EJ11/4	1'30"802	8°	1'27"940	4°	1'27"658	4°	1'31"566	10°
12.	Jarno Trulli	Jordan/Honda/EJ11/3	1'29"267	2°	1'28"193	5°	1'28"377	7°	1'31"811	12°
14.	Jos Verstappen	Arrows/Asiatech/A22/3	1'31"669	14°	1'31"590	20°	1'29"934	15°	1'30"396	3°
15.	Enrique Bernoldi	Arrows/Asiatech/A22/2	1'33"203	20°	1'30"782	18°	1'30"520	18°	1'32"106	13°
16.	Nick Heidfeld	Sauber/Petronas/C20/3	1'30"345	7°	1'28"895	10°	1'28"615	10°	1'30"966	11°
17.	Kimi Räikkönen	Sauber/Petronas/C20/2	1'31"453	11°	1'28"851	8°	1'28"993	13°	1'31"665	11°
18.	Eddie Irvine	Jaguar/R2-3	1'31"573	13°	1'28"861	9°	1'28"965	12°	1'31"061	8°
19.	Luciano Burti	Jaguar/R2-2	1'33"011	18°	1'30"578	17°	1'30"978	21°	1'33"772	18°
20.	Tarso Marques	Minardi/European/PS01/2	1'36"463	22°	1'34"491	22°	1'33"228	22°	1'35"514	22°
21.	Fernando Alonso	Minardi/European/PS01/1	1'32"587	17°	1'30"360	15°	1'30"657	19°	1'33"717	16°
22.	Jean Alesi	Prost/Acer/AP04/3	1'31"089	9°	1'29"981	14°	1'29"893	14°	1'34"421	19°
23.	Gaston Mazzacane	Prost/Acer/AP04/2	1'33"153	19°	1'34"431	21°	1'30"798	20°	1'33"747	17°

MAXIMUM SPEEDS

No	Driver	P1 Qualifs	Pos	P1 Race	Pos	P2 Qualifs	Pos	P2 Race	Pos	Finish Qualifs	Pos	Finish Race	Pos	Trap Qualifs	Pos	Trap Race	Pos
1.	M. Schumacher	283,5	6°	281,3	6°	294,1	11°	292,6	17°	296,0	10°	292,6	9°	309,4	11°	306,6	7°
2.	R. Barrichello	283,6	5°	281,6	4°	291,0	16°	291,4	19°	293,5	16°	291,9	10°	305,6	15°	305,2	12°
3.	M. Häkkinen	285,1	3°	281,3	5°	296,2	6°	294,7	11°	296,8	6°	293,7	6°	309,7	10°	308,2	6°
4.	D. Coulthard	283,6	4°	282,7	2°	298,7	5°	297,3	4°	295,7	3°	295,5	4°	311,3	4°	310,6	3°
5.	R. Schumacher	288,0	1°	273,5	16°	299,8	2°	293,8	15°	301,0	2°	287,3	18°	312,9	2°	304,9	13°
6.	J.-P. Montoya	286,6	2°	285,4	1°	301,3	1°	302,5	1°	302,5	1°	299,8	2°	313,7	1°	312,7	1°
7.	G. Fisichella	274,8	21°	272,3	17°	288,1	21°	285,1	22°	287,9	22°	282,4	21°	302,6	21°	297,1	18°
8.	J. Button	276,8	19°	271,9	18°	288,0	22°	287,3	21°	290,6	18°	283,8	20°	303,7	19°	296,8	19°
9.	O. Panis	281,9	11°	279,2	9°	293,4	12°	295,6	8°	295,5	12°	294,3	5°	309,9	8°	304,2	14°
10.	J. Villeneuve	281,6	12°	269,0	20°	294,4	10°	294,1	13°	295,5	5°	290,7	15°	309,8	9°	295,0	20°
11.	H.-H. Frentzen	282,0	9°	281,7	3°	291,2	15°	298,4	6°	294,1	13°	301,2	1°	305,2	16°	309,0	4°
12.	J. Trulli	282,1	10°	276,7	12°	292,6	14°	291,8	18°	293,8	15°	291,1	13°	308,3	12°	305,5	11°
14.	J. Verstappen	282,4	8°	278,2	10°	292,5	5°	296,0	9°	296,0	9°	291,8	11°	311,7	3°	308,4	5°
15.	E. Bernoldi	280,9	13°	270,5	19°	295,0	9°	298,8	2°	296,1	4°	293,0	8°	307,5	13°	299,4	17°
16.	N. Heidfeld	277,2	18°	279,4	8°	288,8	19°	293,0	16°	291,1	17°	293,4	7°	303,0	20°	306,2	9°
17.	K. Räikkönen	280,8	15°	277,9	11°	288,9	18°	294,1	14°	290,5	19°	291,0	14°	304,1	18°	305,8	10°
18.	E. Irvine	280,2	16°	274,6	15°	295,0	8°	296,1	7°	295,6	11°	291,7	12°	310,8	6°	306,2	8°
19.	L. Burti	277,7	17°	276,7	13°	292,8	13°	295,4	9°	293,9	14°	290,4	16°	306,7	14°	303,0	15°
20.	T. Marques	272,0	22°	263,0	21°	288,5	20°	288,3	20°	288,6	21°	284,7	19°	299,7	22°	287,0	21°
21.	F. Alonso	276,7	20°	275,0	14°	289,8	17°	294,4	12°	290,0	20°	288,5	17°	304,6	17°	301,4	16°
22.	J. Alesi	282,6	7°	279,7	7°	297,9	3°	298,8	4°	297,6	3°	294,8	4°	310,8	7°	310,7	2°
23.	G. Mazzacane	280,8	14°	217,0	22°	295,2	10°	295,2	10°	296,2	7°	-	-	311,0	5°	220,9	22°

CLASSIFICATION & RETIREMENTS

Pos	Driver	Team	Time
1.	M. Schumacher	Ferrari	1:38:26.533
2.	Coulthard	McLaren Mercedes	+1.717
3.	Barrichello	Ferrari	+ 33.491
4.	Panis	BAR Honda	+ 62.050
5.	Heidfeld	Sauber Petronas	+ 71.479
6.	Frentzen	Jordan Honda	+ 72.807
7.	Räikkönen	Sauber Petronas	+ 84.143
8.	Burti	Jaguar	+ 1 lap
9.	Verstappen	Arrows Asiatech	+ 1 lap
10.	Alesi	Prost Acer	+ 1 lap
11.	Irvine	Jaguar	+ 1 lap
12.	Alonso	Minardi	+ 2 laps
13.	Fisichella	Benetton Renault	+ 3 laps

Lap	Driver	Team	Reason
1	Mazzacane	Prost Acer	brakes
3	Bernoldi	Arrows Asiatech	off
4	Marques	Minardi	engine
5	Villeneuve	BAR Honda	accident
5	R. Schumacher	Williams BMW	accident
26	Häkkinen	McLaren Mercedes	suspension
39	Trulli	Jordan Honda	engine
41	Montoya	Williams BMW	engine

All results : © 2001 Fédération Internationale de l'Automobile, 2 Ch. Blandonnet, 1215 Genève 15, Suisse

FASTEST LAPS

Driver	Time	Lap
1. M. Schumacher	1'28"214	34
	216,414 km/h	
2. Coulthard	1'28"838	40
3. Barrichello	1'29"060	33
4. Montoya	1'29"606	40
5. Häkkinen	1'29"612	25
6. Panis	1'30"199	36
7. Räikkönen	1'30"229	35
8. Frentzen	1'30"266	35
9. Heidfeld	1'30"317	35
10. Trulli	1'30"432	29
11. Burti	1'30"903	31
12. Alesi	1'31"030	31
13. Irvine	1'31"267	29
14. Verstappen	1'31"999	56
15. Button	1'32"001	24
16. Alonso	1'32"043	56
17. Fisichella	1'32"407	23
18. R. Schumacher	1'34"406	3
19. Villeneuve	1'34"432	3
20. Bernoldi	1'36"689	2
21. Marques	1'38"249	2

PIT STOPS

Driver	Time	Lap	Stop n°
1. Verstappen	28"519	14	1
2. Button	30"061	18	1
3. Fisichella	30"358	26	1
4. Alonso	28"632	32	1
5. Button	30"919	32	2
6. Trulli	32"295	33	1
7. Alesi	29"025	35	1
8. Räikkönen	29"246	36	1
9. Burti	30"202	36	1
10. M. Schumacher	28"717	37	1
11. Heidfeld	28"247	37	1
12. Frentzen	28"142	37	1
13. Verstappen	29"084	38	2
14. Barrichello	28"658	39	1
15. Irvine	28"852	39	1
16. Panis	28"763	40	1
17. Coulthard	28"516	41	1
18. Alonso	29"170	41	2
19. Irvine	32"568	50	2
20. Fisichella	25"972	50	2

THE CIRCUIT

FIRST ROUND

QANTAS AUSTRALIAN GRAND PRIX, MELBOURNE

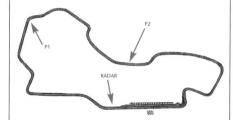

Date :	March 4, 2001
Length :	5303 meters
Distance :	58 laps, 307.574 km
Weather :	cloudy, 23°

Best result for a driver running Bridgestone tyre:

M. Schumacher, Ferrari, winner

CHAMPIONSHIP

(after one round)

Drivers :
1. M. Schumacher 10
2. D. Coulthard 6
3. R. Barrichello 4
4. N. Heidfeld 3
5. H.-H. Frentzen 2
6. K. Räikkönen 1

Constructors :
1. Ferrari 14
2. McLaren Mercedes 6
3. Sauber Petronas 4
4. Jordan Honda 2

RACE SUMMARY

- Michael Schumacher gets the best start, while Barrichello gets it wrong.
- On lap 3, Barrichello attacks and passes Frentzen, who spins but keeps going.
- Villeneuve crashes heavily into the back of Ralf Schumacher's Williams on lap 5. The Safety Car is brought out.
- The race restarts 10 laps later, with Michael Schumacher leading Hakkinen.
- Button gets a 10 second penalty because his mechanics did not clear the grid in time at the start.
- At half distance, Michael Schumacher has a 9.7 second lead over Barrichello, 11.4 on Coulthard and 22.8 on Trulli.
- Coulthard catches out Barrichello, who is baulked by Alonso.
- The pit stops mean Coulthard is momentarily in the lead, but he finishes second.

How to read the graphs shown below :
The "Lap by Lap" shows the position of every driver on every race lap, with the race laps shown horizontally and the positions vertically. For example, on lap 38, David Coulthard was leading from Rubens Barrichello and Michael Schumacher.
The table of "Leading Gaps" is based on the lap by lap information, but only for some selected drivers (for ease of understanding.) It adds in the gaps between these drivers. The line marked "0" represents the winner's average speed. In general, this starts at a slower speed than its eventual average speed, because of the weight of fuel carried on board the car. Then, it goes above the average, before dropping again during the refuelling pit stops. This graph therefore allows one to see at any given time the number of seconds (vertically) separating the drivers on every lap (horizontally.) Below, one can see that David Coulthard (black line) is clearly closing on Michael Schumacher (red line) towards the end of the race.

LAP CHART

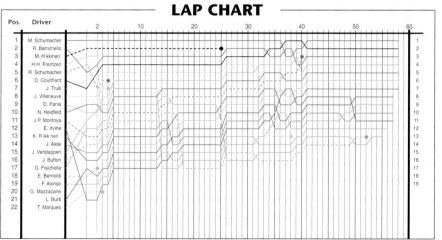

GAPS ON THE LEADER BOARD

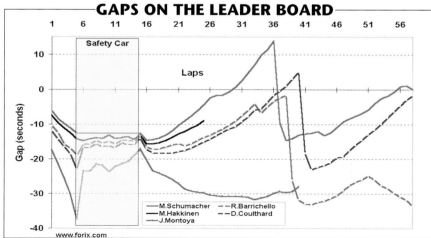

www.forix.com

A hellish race

Driving a Formula 1 car in the rain is not easy. But it becomes virtually impossible to keep it on the road in a storm.
In Sepang, a tropical downpour hit the track just after the start of the race. All the drivers went off the track at least once and even the arrival of the Safety Car to neutralise the race did not help matters as the F1 cars proved unable to keep up with a Mercedes AMG!
Once the track dried up, the Ferraris scored a one-two finish. They had come from a long way back as a mistake in labelling their tyres meant they lost over a minute in the pits.

PETRONAS MALAYSIAN GRAND PRIX
KUALA LUMPUR

Ralf Schumacher on the second row.

The Bridgestone-Michelin battle takes shape

Twice on Saturday, Ralf Schumacher put his name at the top of the time sheet in the qualifying session for the Malaysian Grand Prix. Twice, he got his BMW powered Williams ahead of the Ferraris. But in the end, Michael Schumacher and then Rubens Barrichello managed to demote him. Even so, a place on the second row was unexpected so early in the season.

The Williams chassis was no doubt one of the better creations of the year and the 2001 BMW engine was equally proficient. All the same, Ralf Schumacher's performance that day owed a great deal to his Michelin tyres.

"Honestly, I didn't think the car would be this quick today," said the world champion's little brother. "But the people at Michelin have done a great job and this is the result. The tyres are already working a lot better here than in Australia a fortnight ago."

Was Michelin about to challenge the established order? The oldies who had been around in F1 twenty years ago remembered the good old days when the French firm first upset the Goodyear applecart with the introduction of the radial racing tyre.

Ralf Schumacher's Malaysian performance was a clear sign that a tyre war was well and truly engaged, even if the Clermont-Ferrand manufacturer was only tackling its second grand prix. In Paris, back on 5th February, when the marque revealed its Formula 1 programme, there was no talk of winning races in the first year.

However, Bridgestone still monopolised the front row. The Japanese manufacturer had welcomed the arrival of Michelin, as it guaranteed more publicity and was seen as a positive move. The duel between the two companies had certainly generated plenty of column inches in the press.

So would Ferrari or McLaren consider giving the Michelins a try? Pierre Dupasquier, the French company's motor sport boss had a humorous take on the question. "We are open to everything," he offered with a big grin. "Even secret tests. Back in the Seventies, Enzo Ferrari had wanted to hold a secret test with our tyres, to see how they compared to the Goodyears. We went to Fiorano, with the tyres hidden in a removal van. Ferrari did the test,... and signed with us!" Contracts were less binding in those days.

STARTING GRID

M. SCHUMACHER 1'35"220	-1-	R. BARRICHELLO 1'35"319
R. SCHUMACHER 1'35"511	-2-	Mika HÄKKINEN 1'36"040
Jarno TRULLI 1'36"180	-3-	J. P. MONTOYA 1'36"218
Jacques VILLENEUVE 1'36"397	-4-	David COULTHARD 1'36"417
H.-H. FRENTZEN 1'36"578	-5-	Olivier PANIS 1'36"681
Nick HEIDFELD 1'36"913	-6-	Eddie IRVINE 1'37"140
Jean ALESI 1'37"406	-7-	Kimi RÄIKKÖNEN 1'37"728
Luciano BURTI 1'38"035	-8-	G. FISICHELLA 1'38"086
Jenson BUTTON 1'38"258	-9-	Jos VERSTAPPEN 1'38"509
Gaston MAZZACANE 1'39"006	-10-	Tarso MARQUES 1'39"714
Fernando ALONSO 1'40"249	-11-	Enrique BERNOLDI (disqualified)

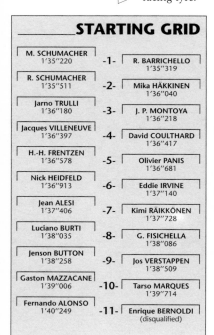

A mad third lap

Lap two. With the race only just underway, Michael Schumacher already seems in control. *"At the end of the second lap, I thought the race was already over,"* he admitted.

But it was at that precise moment that the German went off the track, caught out by the start of a downpour which had not yet hit the entire circuit. Just behind him, a helpless Rubens Barrichello followed him off the track. *"It was incredible,"* recounted the Brazilian. *"I saw Michael go off, but there was absolutely nothing I could do. My car went straight on and I had to let it go. If I had tried something, I ran the risk of running into Michael."*

The two Ferraris managed to get going again and returned to the pits, Barrichello ahead of Schumacher, to fit rain tyres. However, Rubens was given one dry weather tyre at the front, for reasons the Scuderia could not explain. Naturally, the Brazilian refused to drive off until the mechanics found the missing wheel! Michael Schumacher was thus forced to wait his turn in the queue. It was a comedy moment which lasted 12 seconds; an eternity by F1 standards. *"I was going half mad behind Rubens,"* admitted Schumacher. *"I could not see exactly what was going on and I was screaming in my helmet for them to push him out the way, as I thought Rubens had just stalled."*

The two Scuderia cars were not the only ones to be caught out by the rain.

Between laps three and five, apart from the Ferraris, Enrique Bernoldi, Jacques Villeneuve, Nick Heidfeld, Giancarlo Fisichella, Jarno Trulli (who was leading at the time,) David Coulthard, Jean Alesi, Juan Pablo Montoya, Jenson Button and Fernando Alonso all went off. Even after fitting rain tyres, Barrichello went off a further three times, showing just how much water was covering the Sepang track.

Race Control then brought out the Safety Car to get everyone in line, but still the cars spun off. *"Even at 100 km/h behind the Safety Car, I was still aquaplaning and there were huge puddles everywhere,"* said David Coulthard, who was leading at the time. *"At times, it was impossible to follow the Safety Car. It was going quicker than us!"*

The Safety Car saved the day for the two Ferraris, as it allowed them to make up the lost minute after the pit stop fiasco and they were able to rejoin the pack.

The race was underway again on lap ten, as the Safety Car pulled in. The worst of the storm had passed and the track was already beginning to dry.

That played into the hands of the Ferraris, who had taken the risk of fitting intermediate tyres, ideal for damp conditions. The gamble paid off.

The Regenmeister strikes again

The race had begun, looking like a comfortable procession for the two Ferraris, Michael Schumacher ahead of Rubens Barrichello.

When the red lights went out, Michael Schumacher made a great start, while brother Ralf managed to get his BMW-Williams ahead of the Brazilian's Ferrari. He tried to block him, but the two cars touched and the Williams spun off.

"I know Ralf was ahead," said Rubens Barrichello after the race. *But he didn't leave me any room. When a driver is on the outside, he absolutely must leave enough room for the other car, because otherwise it's bound to end in a crash."*

The two Ferraris then took off in the distance, before a typically tropical storm hit the Sepang track (see above.) Once the race was underway again, Michael Schumacher put on another display. Overtaking on the left, the right, running five seconds a lap quicker than anyone, dealing with up to three cars a lap, he moved up from 11th to first place in just six laps! It was a demonstration that it will go down in history. It also stuck in the throat of some of his rivals. After the race, a number of voices were raised in complaint, claiming the Ferraris had used some form of traction control to go that quickly in the wet. *"The Ferraris are vastly superior to anything else. We have rarely seen that in F1,"* affirmed Alain Prost. These doubts only disappeared at the Spanish Grand Prix, when electronic aids were once again allowed in the sport.

△
The turning point of the race: Michael Schumacher has just fitted rain tyres and comes out of the pit lane just ahead of the Safety Car, despite being delayed by the mix up with tyres on his team-mate's car. A few seconds more and he would have found himself a lap down on the leaders, with little hope of catching up.

◁
On the left, the Champagne, on the right the trophy. And in the middle, the man who already looked favourite for the title.

"And again!" Having been hit up the rear in Australia, it was the same story for Ralf Schumacher. He got going again, to finish fifth.

▽◁
"Whoops! I think it was the right hand lane!" Giancarlo Fisichella gets it wrong and causes confusion on the parade lap. A second parade lap is needed and the Italian will start right from the back.
▽

▷ Having qualified badly, David Coulthard made the most of the intervention of the elements to temporarily take the lead. He finished in third place, behind the Ferrari duo.

▷ Jarno Trulli qualified fifth and led briefly before heading for the gravel trap. He finished eighth.

Frentzen fires both barrels

Heinz-Harald Frentzen finished the Australian Grand Prix in fifth place, just behind Nick Heidfeld. At the end of the race, the Jordan driver did all he could to pass the Sauber, without managing it. A few days later on his official Internet site, Frentzen openly accused the Swiss team of using traction control, which was of course, illegal. *"I don't know if traction control comes as an option with the Ferrari engine,"* said an ironic Heinz-Harald. *But every time Nick (Heidfeld) accelerated out of a corner, I could hear his engine stutter as though it had a misfire."* This is a standard side effect of traction control. *"I am not saying Sauber cheated,"* insisted Frentzen at Sepang. *"In the German press, notably "Bild,"*

Nick was accused of cheating. That's not what I said. All I am saying is that the drivers with Ferrari engines had something which allowed them to exit the corners better. But I am sure it's a legal system," he concluded, with a grin which said it all. That upset Michael Schumacher. *"Making these remarks is completely stupid,"* boomed the world champion. *"The season has got off to a good start and here we have an individual making stupid remarks, which the press are quick to seize on. Now he denies it. What does that mean? We work very hard. Ferrari spends a fortune to race, Nick drove very well and this guy should look more to what he is doing rather than look for excuses."*

WEEKEND GOSSIP

• **Villeneuve was not scared**

Seen on television, Jacques Villeneuve's accident in the Australian Grand Prix was one of the most terrifying in recent years. However, the man himself claimed he had not been scared at all: *"when I saw the television pictures, I was shocked,"* admitted the Canadian. *"From the cockpit it was a big accident, but from outside it looked worse. Usually, when you crash, you see more or less where you are going to hit. But in this instance, as the car was travelling backwards, I wasn't aware of anything. I didn't know when the impact was coming or if I was going to finish upside down or the right way up. So I really wasn't frightened."*

• **EM.TV sells to Kirch**

EM.TV, the company which owns half of Bernie Ecclestone's SLEC holdings, the company which owns the F1 television rights, was in big trouble. On the Frankfurt Stock Exchange its shares had dropped from 112 Euros to 6 in one year. Short of funds, EM.TV negotiated the sale of its part of SLEC to the German Kirch media group for 550 million dollars. A year ago, EM.TV had paid almost double that amount, one billion dollars.

• **A bad move**

For the Malaysian Grand Prix organisers, moving the race from October to March did not constitute a stroke of genius. Despite a major advertising campaign in the city of Kuala Lumpur, they found it incredibly difficult to sell grandstand tickets for the race, given it was taking place just five months after the previous year's event. It was all the more embarrassing then, that they had put up an extra 15,000 seats at the first corner, whose line had been modifed.

A deluge on the track and feverish activity in the pit lane. Jos Verstappen comes in to join a Jordan. ▷▷

When it comes to hotels, Malaysia how to do things in style. Here is the famous Sunway Lagoon with an artificial wave machine and a rope bridge over a precipice. ▽

Four little laps and then they're off

Sauber and BAR

Malaysia is almost a home race for the Sauber team. Their Ferrari engines are re-badged Petronas, the name of Malaysia's national oil company and the cars are painted in its colours. When they pulled up onto the grid, the crowd reserved a huge ovation for Nick Heidfeld and Kimi Raikkonen.
Unfortunately, it did not bring them much luck in the race. Kimi Raikkonen broke down with gearbox problems, before he had got to the first

corner, while Nick Heidfeld was out on lap 4, having spun off on a puddle. *"I tried to keep the car moving, but it just dug its wheels in and I was stuck."*
The two BAR's of Olivier Panis and Jacques Villeneuve did not fare much better. The Frenchman's engine exploded, while the Canadian went off the track. The grand prix had lasted just four laps for these two teams.

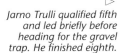

PRACTICE TIMES

No	Driver	Car/Engine/Chassis	Practice Friday	Pos.	Practice Saturday	Pos.	Qualifying	Pos.	Warm-up	Pos.
1.	Michael Schumacher	Ferrari/F2001/208	1'38''929	2°	1'36''548	4°	1'35''220	1°	1'52''316	7°
2.	Rubens Barrichello	Ferrari/F2001/206	1'38''931	3°	1'36''188	1°	1'35''319	2°	1'49''763	1°
3.	Mika Häkkinen	McLaren/Mercedes/MP4/16/3	1'39''861	6°	1'36''519	3°	1'36''040	4°	1'57''064	13°
4.	David Coulthard	McLaren/Mercedes/MP4/16/1	1'39''300	4°	1'36''814	5°	1'36''417	8°	1'50''846	2°
5.	Ralf Schumacher	Williams/BMW/FW23/3	1'40''617	10°	1'36''475	2°	1'35''511	3°	1'55''109	11°
6.	Juan Pablo Montoya	Williams/BMW/FW23/2	2'13''188	22°	1'37''502	13°	1'36''218	6°	1'55''278	12°
7.	Giancarlo Fisichella	Benetton/Renault/B201/3	1'41''375	21°	1'38''548	16°	1'38''086	16°	1'58''656	17°
8.	Jenson Button	Benetton/RenaultB201/1	1'42''214	17°	1'38''712	17°	1'38''258	17°	2'07''047	22°
9.	Olivier Panis	BAR/Honda/003/2	1'40''229	9°	1'37''391	9°	1'36''681	10°	1'53''470	9°
10.	Jacques Villeneuve	BAR/Honda/003/3	1'41''003	11°	1'37''463	12°	1'36''397	7°	1'53''482	10°
11.	Heinz-Harald Frentzen	Jordan/Honda/EJ11/4	1'40''197	7°	1'37''030	6°	1'36''578	9°	1'52''061	6°
12.	Jarno Trulli	Jordan/Honda/EJ11/3	1'38''846	1°	1'37''231	7°	1'36''180	5°	1'51''046	3°
14.	Jos Verstappen	Arrows/Asiatech/A22/1	1'41''794	15°	1'39''401	19°	1'38''509	18°	1'51''508	5°
15.	Enrique Bernoldi	Arrows/Asiatech/A22/3	1'42''514	18°	1'38''958	18°	-	-	2'01''630	19°
16.	Nick Heidfeld	Sauber/Petronas/C20/2	1'41''027	12°	1'37''459	11°	1'36''913	11°	1'53''352	8°
17.	Kimi Räikkönen	Sauber/Petronas/C20/1	1'41''592	14°	1'37''428	10°	1'37''728	14°	1'51''265	4°
18.	Eddie Irvine	Jaguar/R-2/2	1'39''520	5°	1'37''360	8°	1'37''140	12°	1'58''322	9°
19.	Luciano Burti	Jaguar/R-2/3	1'40''211	8°	1'37''636	14°	1'38''035	15°	2'01''120	18°
20.	Tarso Marques	Minardi/European/PS01/2	1'42''872	20°	1'40''171	22°	1'39''714	20°	2'04''349	21°
21.	Fernando Alonso	Minardi/European/PS01/1	1'43''107	21°	1'39''956	21°	1'40''249	21°	2'01''771	20°
22.	Jean Alesi	Prost/Acer/AP04/3	1'41''834	16°	1'38''130	15°	1'37''406	13°	1'57''832	14°
23.	Gaston Mazzacane	Prost/Acer/AP04/4	1'42''563	19°	1'39''651	20°	1'39''006	19°	1'58''416	16°

MAXIMUM SPEEDS

No	Driver	P1 Qualifs	Pos	P1 Race	Pos	P2 Qualifs	Pos	P2 Race	Pos	Finish Qualifs	Pos	Finish Race	Pos	Trap Qualifs	Pos	Trap Race	Pos
1.	M. Schumacher	299,1	1°	289,9	11°	150,5	10°	148,8	1°	269,3	4°	262,2	13°	303,4	11°	304,7	10°
2.	R. Barrichello	296,9	9°	292,2	7°	152,0	5°	144,0	10°	268,1	9°	260,9	15°	303,3	12°	305,6	8°
3.	M. Häkkinen	300,5	4°	294,5	4°	146,6	21°	145,7	3°	267,1	13°	264,9	6°	307,6	4°	311,2	3°
4.	D. Coulthard	301,9	3°	291,8	8°	143,1	22°	141,0	16°	268,9	5°	262,5	12°	308,2	3°	307,9	5°
5.	R. Schumacher	307,7	1°	299,2	1°	125,0	6°	146,4	2°	273,6	2°	268,3	1°	313,2	1°	313,1	2°
6.	J. P. Montoya	305,4	2°	295,6	2°	150,4	11°	142,2	14°	274,5	4°	266,7	3°	311,6	2°	299,4	15°
7.	G. Fisichella	289,5	21°	280,7	19°	153,0	1°	139,4	21°	260,2	22°	252,1	21°	296,2	22°	294,8	18°
8.	J. Button	290,6	17°	280,1	20°	152,4	3°	144,1	9°	260,3	21°	256,3	20°	296,3	21°	296,2	16°
9.	O. Panis	297,0	8°	283,5	18°	152,0	4°	139,6	20°	268,2	8°	262,5	11°	304,3	9°	287,4	19°
10.	J. Villeneuve	298,2	6°	289,1	12°	148,7	17°	140,4	17°	269,4	3°	263,9	8°	305,4	6°	296,1	17°
11.	H.-H. Frentzen	295,7	11°	290,8	9°	151,4	7°	145,5	5°	268,3	6°	264,2	7°	300,2	17°	305,9	6°
12.	J. Trulli	295,4	14°	293,4	5°	150,6	9°	145,7	4°	267,1	11°	265,2	4°	301,9	15°	308,7	4°
14.	J. Verstappen	295,4	15°	295,5	3°	150,2	12°	145,4	6°	267,3	10°	267,5	2°	304,4	8°	313,6	1°
15.	E. Bernoldi	295,5	13°	285,1	17°	150,0	13°	141,7	15°	267,1	12°	265,0	5°	304,7	7°	256,4	21°
16.	N. Heidfeld	290,3	18°	287,6	14°	149,3	15°	139,9	18°	262,9	18°	258,1	19°	296,7	20°	301,5	12°
17.	K. Räikkönen	290,1	19°	-	-	147,0	20°	-	-	261,6	20°	-	-	297,4	19°	-	-
18.	E. Irvine	297,8	7°	292,2	6°	152,8	2°	139,8	19°	268,3	7°	263,2	10°	306,2	5°	285,9	20°
19.	L. Burti	295,9	10°	290,2	10°	149,4	14°	142,4	13°	266,2	16°	263,6	9°	300,9	16°	305,7	7°
20.	T. Marques	289,0	22°	279,3	21°	148,5	18°	145,0	7°	263,8	17°	261,3	14°	302,5	14°	302,3	11°
21.	F. Alonso	290,0	20°	288,6	13°	147,2	19°	142,6	12°	262,0	19°	259,5	17°	299,1	18°	305,5	9°
22.	J. Alesi	295,5	12°	286,3	15°	149,1	16°	144,2	8°	266,9	22°	260,4	16°	302,8	13°	301,5	13°
23.	G. Mazzacane	294,7	16°	285,7	16°	151,0	8°	143,3	11°	266,8	15°	258,8	18°	304,1	10°	299,9	14°

CLASSIFICATION & RETIREMENTS

Pos	Driver	Team	Time
1.	M. Schum.	Ferrari	1:47:34.801
2.	Barrichello	Ferrari	+23.660
3.	Coulthard	McLaren Mercedes	+ 28.555
4.	Frentzen	Jordan Honda	+46.543
5.	R. Schum.	Williams BMW	+ 48.233
6.	Häkkinen	McLaren Mercedes	+ 48.606
7.	Verstappen	Arrows Asiatech	+81.560
8.	Trulli	Jordan Honda	+ 1 lap
9.	Alesi	Prost Acer	+ 1 lap
10.	Burti	Jaguar Racing	+ 1 lap
11.	Button	Benetton Renault	+ 2 laps
12.	Mazzacane	Prost Acer	+ 2 laps
13.	Alonso	European Minardi	+ 3 laps
14.	Marques	European Minardi	+ 4 laps

Lap	Drivers	Team	Reason
1	Räikkönen	Sauber Petronas	transmission
2	Panis	BAR Honda	engine
4	Irvine	Jaguar Racing	off
4	Montoya	Williams BMW	off
4	Bernoldi	Arrows Asiatech	off
4	Heidfeld	Sauber Petronas	off
4	Villeneuve	BAR Honda	off
32	Fisichella	Benetton Renault	fuel pressure

FASTEST LAPS

	Driver	Time	Lap
1.	Häkkinen	1'40''962 197,646 km/h	48
2.	R. Schum.	1'41''503	54
3.	M. Schum.	1'41''833	2
4.	Barrichello	1'42''037	2
5.	Frentzen	1'42''119	50
6.	Coulthard	1'42''839	47
7.	Verstappen	1'43''029	55
8.	Villeneuve	1'43''470	2
9.	Trulli	1'43''559	52
10.	Burti	1'43''697	52
11.	Alesi	1'43''853	53
12.	Montoya	1'43''926	2
13.	Mazzacane	1'43''991	53
14.	Button	1'44''891	52
15.	Heidfeld	1'45''328	2
16.	Alonso	1'45''585	50
17.	Marques	1'46''016	50
18.	Fisichella	1'46''989	2
19.	Bernoldi	1'47''294	2
20.	Irvine	1'51''532	2
21.	Panis		0

All results :
© 2001 Fédération Internationale de l'Automobile, 2, Ch. Blandonnet, 1215 Genève 15, Suisse

LAP CHART

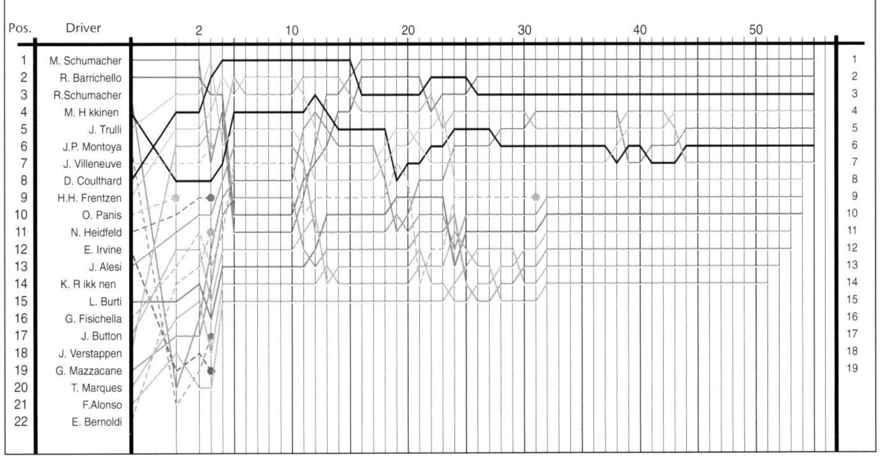
Pos.
Driver
M. Schumacher
R. Barrichello
R.Schumacher
M. H kkinen
J. Trulli
J.P. Montoya
J. Villeneuve
D. Coulthard
H.H. Frentzen
O. Panis
N. Heidfeld
E. Irvine
J. Alesi
K. R ikk nen
L. Burti
G. Fisichella
J. Button
J. Verstappen
G. Mazzacane
T. Marques
F.Alonso
E. Bernoldi

PIT STOPS

	Driver	Time	Lap	Stop n°
1.	Alonso	39''001	2	1
2.	Fisichella	43''577	3	1
3.	Button	59''284	3	1
4.	Burti	1'06''372	3	1
5.	Marques	1'03''839	3	1
6.	Alonso	1'00''158	3	2
7.	Coulthard	41''086	4	1
8.	Frentzen	42''702	4	1
9.	Barrichello	1'45''847	4	1
10.	M. Schumacher	1'56''461	4	1
11.	Verstappen	47''236	4	1
12.	Trulli	50''046	4	1
13.	Häkkinen	44''016	4	1
14.	Alesi	45''491	4	1
15.	R. Schumacher	1'06''195	4	1
16.	Mazzacane	50''040	4	1
17.	Häkkinen	33''462	18	2
18.	R. Schumacher	36''772	18	2
19.	Alonso	36''712	18	3
20.	Fisichella	41''128	20	2
21.	Barrichello	40''343	21	2
22.	Frentzen	35''394	21	2
23.	Verstappen	34''323	22	2
24.	Trulli	33''459	23	2
25.	Burti	45''131	23	2
26.	Alesi	35''348	23	2
27.	Button	38''802	23	2
28.	Mazzacane	46''699	24	2
29.	Coulthard	35''080	25	2
30.	M. Schumacher	39''158	30	2
31.	Marques	58''899	28	2
32.	Alonso	36''444	31	4
33.	Mazzacane	38''753	34	3
34.	R. Schumacher	34''925	38	3
35.	Trulli	35''076	39	3
36.	Häkkinen	34''383	40	3
37.	Barrichello	34''462	41	3
38.	Alonso	36''593	40	5
39.	Verstappen	33''263	43	3

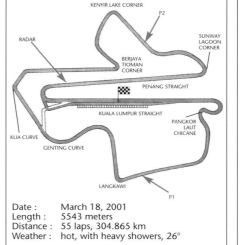

THE CIRCUIT

SECOND ROUND

PETRONAS MALAYSIAN GRAND PRIX, KUALA LUMPUR

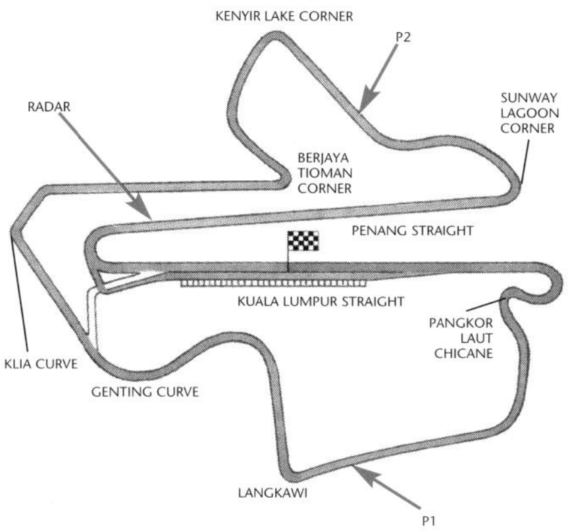
KENYIR LAKE CORNER
P2
RADAR
SUNWAY LAGOON CORNER
BERJAYA TIOMAN CORNER
PENANG STRAIGHT
KUALA LUMPUR STRAIGHT
PANGKOR LAUT CHICANE
KLIA CURVE
GENTING CURVE
LANGKAWI
P1

Date : March 18, 2001
Length : 5543 meters
Distance : 55 laps, 304.865 km
Weather : hot, with heavy showers, 26°

BRIDGESTONE

Best result for a driver running Bridgestone tyre:

Michael Schumacher, Ferrari, winner

CHAMPIONSHIP

(after two rounds)

Drivers :

1. M. Schumacher 20
2. D. Coulthard 10
   R. Barrichello 10
4. H.-H. Frentzen 5
5. N. Heidfeld 3
6. R. Schumacher 2
7. K. Räikkönen...................................1
   M. Häkkinen 1

Constructors :

1. Ferrari...30
2. McLaren Mercedes 11
3. Jordan Honda 5
4. Sauber Petronas..............................4
5. Williams BMW 2

RACE SUMMARY

- Even before the start, Fisichella tries to line up on the wrong place on the grid. A second start procedure takes place. Montoya starts from the pit lane, having stalled his race car.
- Michael Schumacher makes the best start, while behind him, Barrichello and Ralf Schumacher collide.
- The rain starts to fall at the end of lap 2. It turns into a storm which, in the space of a few seconds, triggers off an amazing series of spins. Everyone pits and the Safety Car comes out.
- Chaos in the Ferrari garage: one of Barrichello's tyres is a dry weather one. Michael Schumacher has to queue while the problem is solved.
- The rain stops and the Safety Car comes in on lap 10.
- Only the Ferrari drivers have fitted intermediate tyres and they make the most of the drying track to take the top places on lap 16. They are lapping around five seconds quicker than the pack.
- After the planned pit stops, the track is completely dry. Michael Schumacher cruises to his second win of the season..

GAPS ON THE LEADER BOARD

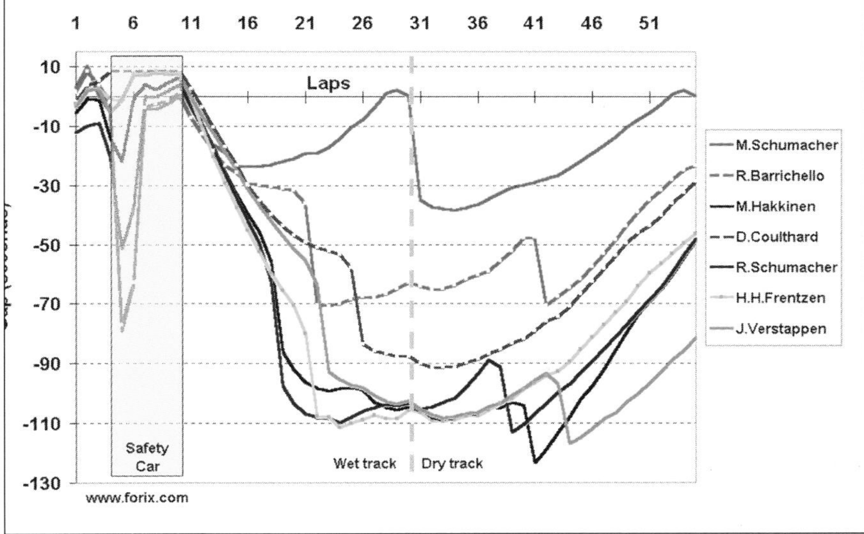
1 6 11 16 21 26 31 36 41 46 51
Laps
10
-10
-30
-50
-70
-90
-110
-130
M.Schumacher
R.Barrichello
M.Hakkinen
D.Coulthard
R.Schumacher
H.H.Frentzen
J.Verstappen
Safety Car
Wet track
Dry track
www.forix.com

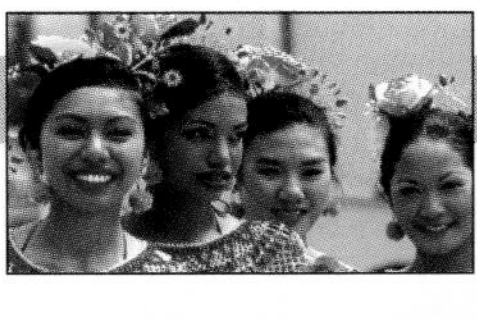

David barges through

What a race! The Brazilian Grand Prix turned out to be one of the most exciting races of the season.

What with a storm and several crashes, it was action packed and David Coulthard managed to move his McLaren up from fifth on the grid, right past Michael Schumacher to take his first win of the season.

It was a major achievement, in that the Scotsman charged past the German in the rain, an environment where the world champion is usually unbeatable.

GRANDE PRÊMIO DO BRASIL
INTERLAGOS

Third pole in three races for Michael Schumacher

Michael versus Ralf: a first

STARTING GRID

R. SCHUMACHER 1'14"090	-1-	M. SCHUMACHER 1'13"780	
J. P. MONTOYA 1'14"165	-2-	Mika HÄKKINEN 1'14"122	
R. BARRICHELLO 1'14"191	-3-	David COULTHARD 1'14"178	
H.-H. FRENTZEN 1'14"633	-4-	Jarno TRULLI 1'14"630	
Kimi RÄIKKÖNEN 1'14"924	-5-	Nick HEIDFELD 1'14"810	
Jacques VILLENEUVE 1'15"182	-6-	Olivier PANIS 1'15"046	
Luciano BURTI 1'15"371	-7-	Eddie IRVINE 1'15"192	
Enrique BERNOLDI 1'15"657	-8-	Jean ALESI 1'15"437	
G. FISICHELLA 1'16"175	-9-	Jos VERSTAPPEN 1'15"704	
Jenson BUTTON 1'16"229	-10-	Fernando ALONSO 1'16"184	
Tarso MARQUES 1'16"784	-11-	G. MAZZACANE 1'16"520	

It had never happened before: for the start of a grand prix, two brothers would be heading off for the first corner side by side, as in Interlagos, the two Schumacher brothers monopolised the front row of the grid. However, the fight looked a bit unequal. Michael, six years older than his brother, would be starting from the clean side of the track, while Ralf lined up on the dirty side. *"Of course, I am not ideally placed for the start,"* confirmed Ralf. *"But if I get off the line well, we will see. If I get away in the lead, I can assure you I will be hard to pass."*

Mind you, he would still have to try and take the lead, something his brother was not prepared to contemplate. *"I think that, back in Germany, our parents will find the start very entertaining,"* admitted Michael with a smile. *"Ralf and I trust one another completely. We will be hard but fair. We know one another too well to crash into one another."* Their last duel of this kind dated back to their karting days, ten years earlier on the Kerpen track near Cologne, where they cut their racing teeth. *"I was in front and Michael was trying to pass me,"* recalled Ralf. *"It was raining very hard and then he got so close, that his brake pedal got caught in my exhaust and we both crashed off the track."*

While Michael was not too surprised to find himself on pole for the seventh consecutive time, the performance of his little brother was somewhat unexpected. Especially as he admitted his Williams FW23 was not easy to drive. *"It was well balanced, but very nervous and difficult to drive. It's difficult to put together the perfect lap in these conditions,"* confirmed Ralf.

The German owed in part his second place to the power of his BMW engine. On Saturday, Ralf was the quickest down the straight, hitting 318 km/h against 308 for Michael.

Ralf Schumacher qualified well, but started badly and he was hit hard from behind. It was the third race in a row that had ended in this way for the younger Schumacher.

The Interlagos track is one of the most popular with the photographers. However, Sao Paulo (inset) is not the most photogenic city in South America.

David Coulthard swims through in Interlagos

David Coulthard more at home in the wet than Michael Schumacher? There was something surreal about this.

"*I don't know if it's the best win of my career. Maybe, but anyway, I really loved today!*" Coming off the podium, David Coulthard was still in seventh heaven. Thanks to this win, the Scotsman had for the first time managed to beat Michael Schumacher fair and square in the wet.

This was no mean achievement and David Coulthard was rather proud of it.

"*We got off to a very bad start this season,*" he claimed. "*But the guys back in the factory have worked like mad to improve the car. Today, we can see that their efforts are beginning to pay off. It's a huge relief.*"

In fact, the Scotsman's win owed a great deal to a gamble on the grid, which was to set up the car for the wet. "*We knew it was definitely going to rain during the second part of the race and we went for intermediate settings. In the early stages, I had to fight to keep up with the leaders. I was praying for the rain to come. A couple of drops fell on the second lap, but it was almost nothing. The team was watching the sky and kept telling me it was on its way and that it would not be too much longer, but it seemed to take for ever.*" When the storm finally did hit, around lap 45, the Scotsman McLaren proved unbeatable. "*In the rain, it was really fantastic,*" continued Coulthard. "*When I caught up with Michael (Schumacher) I couldn't see anything. In these conditions, you have to trust whoever is in front. I dived down the inside at the first corner and I passed him.*" From then on, Michael Schumacher only ever saw the back of the McLaren, unable to match its pace. Given the German's undoubted talent in the rain, this surprised many. After the race, the man himself did not offer much of an explanation and seemed rather put out. "*I am not happy, but that's to be expected,*" said the world champion. "*The car wasn't working the way I would have liked and there was nothing I could do against David today. We had not really opted for rain settings like the McLarens. We went for a sort of compromise which did not work properly right from the start. I also went off the track quite a few times, which isn't normal.*"

With this first win of the season, David Coulthard was now only six points behind Michael Schumacher. It was enough to give the Scotsman wings. "*I know we have some improvements coming for our car for the next race in Imola. We will do our best. As for myself, I feel in top form, life is good and everything is fine. That's the main thing.*"

At the start, Mika Hakkinen, who qualified third, stalls on the grid. Luckily the others manage to avoid him.

An unusual podium in Interlagos, with David Coulthard presiding over Michael Schumacher and Nick Heidfeld.

Third place for Nick Heidfeld

A podium for Sauber

On Sunday during the podium ceremony, the sound system at the circuit played a Samba. David Coulthard could not resist dancing to the beat. He was not alone. Down beneath him, despite the constraints of wearing fire suits in the hot weather, the Sauber mechanics danced a Conga. They had also been overcome by the tropical beat, thanks mainly to the fact their driver was up there above them in third place.

For his part, Peter Sauber is too restrained to indulge in these sorts of antics, but he was in party mood nevertheless. "*This is an extraordinary day for us,*" he exulted. "*At the start of the season, I had said we would not be capable of getting on the podium. But there we are, I was wrong!*" A huge smile accompanied this last remark. The man from Zurich was so happy, he even forgot to light his cigar. He had good reason. In Interlagos, the C20s were always running in the points or thereabouts. Although, at the flag, Nick Heidfeld got to the podium in thanks partly

to some retirements, the performance of the Saubers was nevertheless impressive. "*On full tanks, having opted for a one stop strategy, Nick was quicker than Heinz-Harald Frentzen in the Jordan, which is a very positive sign for the future,*" was Peter Sauber's analysis of the situation.

o

Luciano Burti is all aflame! Thrilled at the idea of racing in front of his home crowd, the local boy's Jaguar would not go the distance, for the first time this season. He qualified 14th and retired on lap 21.

GRANDE PRÊMIO DO BRASIL

Montoya pulls off the passing move of the year!

Here I come! At the main straight, Juan Pablo Montoya muscles in on Michael Schumacher. A daring move.

▷

The pits stops are the worst moments of the weekend for the mechanics. It's very stressful and it shows.

After Mika Hakkinen stalled on the grid, the marshals were unable to shift his McLaren, so the Safety Car was brought out for a single lap.

Once the track was clear, the race was on again. At the start of lap three, Juan Pablo Montoya pulled off a bravura move to get past Michael Schumacher, under braking for the first corner. *"He had more top speed than me,"* reckoned the Ferrari driver. *"I braked late, but he must have braked even later. He pushed me a bit, we touched, but I have no complaints about him and I congratulate him. It was a great move."*

One of the reasons Frank Williams had signed up the Colombian was his aggressive driving style and with this move, he showed he feared no one.

"The fact I led a grand prix means nothing," he admitted two weeks later in Imola. *Everyone is surprised I managed to pass Michael. But I don't intend treating one driver differently to the rest, just because he's called Schumacher."* Juan Pablo's charge ended on lap 39, when he came up to pass Jos Verstappen in the Arrows. The Dutchman appeared to forget to

break for the *"Subido do Lago"* corner and speared the leading Williams. *"I did not know he was leading and he braked very early,"* pleaded Jos. *"I'm really sorry!"*

Crashing cameras

The Interlagos circuit is beginning to show its age. Even if all the buildings were constructed in 1990 when the track was renovated, the humidity had taken an early toll on the structures.

On Friday morning, just a few minutes before the end of free practice, a video camera fitted on runners about the pits, crashed to the floor just outside the Jaguar garage. No one was hurt, but it fell just inches away from team boss Bobby Rahal. The frame holding it to the rail had rusted away and looked like coming down too. It was one of many signs that the entire circuit needed a good overhaul. *"There are races here every weekend of the year,"* explained a marshal. *But apart from the Grand Prix weekend, the authorities don't spend a cent on the place."*

WEEKEND GOSSIP

• **Three timely points for Panis**

After a season as McLaren's test driver, Olivier Panis was in fine form. In Brazil, he picked up his first points of the season (having lost the ones he scored in Australia,) by finishing fourth, despite a bad start to the race. Qualified behind Mika Hakkinen, he was held up by the Finn's McLaren at the start and came round at the end of the first lap in thirteenth spot. He attacked like mad, overtaking in rapid succession, Alesi, Raikkonen, Heidfeld, Frentzen and Trulli, to emerge third after 26 laps! He eventually finished fourth, three places ahead of Jacques Villeneuve.

• **Schumi not buying Sauber**

The rumour had been picked up by several specialist magazines. Michael Schumacher was apparently on the verge of buying shares in the Sauber team, with a view to eventually becoming its new owner, in the style of Alain Prost. In Sepang, the German's manager, Willi Weber, had done nothing to deny the story, even adding that he too quite liked the idea of buying into Sauber.

On Thursday however, Schumacher categorically denied the idea. *"I don't know who started this rumour, but it's completely illogical. I really don't see myself as a team boss. When I finally stop racing, I don't know what I'll do, but I don't think it will be connected with F1."*

• **New surface**

Year after year, the drivers point an accusing finger at the terribly bumpy surface of the Interlagos track. In 2000, the vibrations caused by its irregular surface had caused the rear wings to snap on the Saubers. That year, the organisers had layed down a new surface, which had failed to smooth out the bumps. For 2001, they tried yet again, resurfacing the main straight and this time it was a little bit more successful.

Nevertheless, the long term future of the Brazilian Grand Prix was still in doubt. The violent nature of the city of Sao Paulo had impacted on the teams, with several mechanics robbed in their cars near the circuit.

▷

Fourth place for Olivier Panis brought the Frenchman his first points of the year.

▷

Buildings crammed everywhere, roads blocked with traffic from morning to night, awful pollution: welcome to Sao Paulo The Magnificent, a city that takes time to reveal its charms.

▽

PRACTICE TIMES

No	Driver	Car/Engine/Chassis	Practice Friday	Pos.	Practice Saturday	Pos.	Qualifying	Pos.	Warm-up	Pos.
1.	Michael Schumacher	Ferrari/F2001/208	1'16"598	3°	1'14"652	5°	1'13"780	1°	1'15"971	1°
2.	Rubens Barrichello	Ferrari/F2001/206	1'16"994	7°	1'14"895	7°	1'14"191	6°	1'16"145	2°
3.	Mika Häkkinen	McLaren/Mercedes/MP4/16/3	1'16"882	5°	1'14"108	2°	1'14"122	3°	1'16"308	3°
4.	David Coulthard	McLaren/Mercedes/MP4/16/1	1'15"220	1°	1'14"182	3°	1'14"178	5°	1'16"679	6°
5.	Ralf Schumacher	Williams/BMW/FW23/3	1'16"929	6°	1'14"282	4°	1'14"090	2°	1'16"375	4°
6.	Juan Pablo Montoya	Williams/BMW/FW23/2	1'16"851	4°	1'13"963	1°	1'14"165	4°	1'17"008	8°
7.	Giancarlo Fisichella	Benetton/Renault/B201/3	1'18"096	17°	1'16"439	20°	1'16"175	18°	1'18"773	20°
8.	Jenson Button	Benetton/Renault/B201/1	1'19"585	22°	1'16"411	19°	1'16"229	20°	1'20"008	22°
9.	Olivier Panis	BAR/Honda/003/3	1'17"432	12°	1'15"039	9°	1'15"046	11°	1'16"711	7°
10.	Jacques Villeneuve	BAR/Honda/003/4	1'17"455	13°	1'16"135	16°	1'15"182	12°	1'17"405	12°
11.	Heinz-Harald Frentzen	Jordan/Honda/EJ11/4	1'17"072	8°	1'14"837	6°	1'14"633	8°	1'17"138	10°
12.	Jarno Trulli	Jordan/Honda/EJ11/3	1'16"224	2°	1'15"163	11°	1'14"630	7°	1'16"449	5°
14.	Jos Verstappen	Arrows/Asiatech/A22/1	1'17"792	16°	1'15"972	15°	1'15"704	17°	1'18"074	18°
15.	Enrique Bernoldi	Arrows/Asiatech/A22/4	1'18"233	19°	1'16"160	17°	1'15"657	16°	1'18"460	19°
16.	Nick Heidfeld	Sauber/Petronas/C20/3	1'17"102	9°	1'15"096	10°	1'14"810	9°	1'17"135	9°
17.	Kimi Räikkönen	Sauber/Petronas/C20/1	1'17"712	15°	1'15"031	8°	1'14"924	10°	1'17"213	11°
18.	Eddie Irvine	Jaguar/R-2/4	1'17"295	10°	1'15"409	12°	1'15"192	13°	1'17"420	13°
19.	Luciano Burti	Jaguar/R-2/3	1'17"430	11°	1'15"470	13°	1'15"371	14°	1'17"674	14°
20.	Tarso Marques	Minardi/European/PS01/2	1'19"005	21°	1'18"212	22°	1'16"784	22°	1'19"126	21°
21.	Fernando Alonso	Minardi/European/PS01/3	1'18"222	18°	1'16"602	21°	1'16"184	19°	1'18"016	17°
22.	Jean Alesi	Prost/Acer/AP04/4	1'17"518	14°	1'15"735	14°	1'15"437	15°	1'17"728	16°
23.	Gaston Mazzacane	Prost/Acer/AP04/4	1'18"269	20°	1'16"347	18°	1'16"520	21°	1'17"681	15°

MAXIMUM SPEEDS

No	Driver	P1 Qualifs	Pos	P1 Race	Pos	P2 Qualifs	Pos	P2 Race	Pos	Finish Qualifs	Pos	Finish Race	Pos	Trap Qualifs	Pos	Trap Race	Pos
1.	M. Schumacher	306,1	8°	305,6	15°	260,0	1°	247,9	4°	309,3	6°	316,8	6°	308,8	8°	313,7	1°
2.	R. Barrichello	307,0	6°	308,0	9°	257,4	4°	228,3	21°	306,6	14°	311,0	15°	309,8	7°	306,9	10°
3.	M. Häkkinen	305,8	10°	-		253,9	10°	-		306,5	16°	-		307,9	9°	-	
4.	D. Coulthard	309,7	4°	310,0	5°	258,5	2°	247,1	5°	310,4	5°	316,4	8°	311,8	3°	312,5	2°
5.	R. Schumacher	311,9	1°	312,5	2°	257,1	5°	254,5	1°	312,5	3°	321,1	3°	314,3	1°	311,8	4°
6.	J. P. Montoya	311,4	2°	312,5	3°	258,4	3°	248,0	3°	311,5	4°	318,4	5°	311,5	4°	308,5	7°
7.	G. Fisichella	301,5	19°	302,6	18°	249,2	18°	242,6	12°	307,3	11°	309,0	18°	306,7	12°	299,1	17°
8.	J. Button	298,5	22°	295,0	21°	248,1	19°	236,7	17°	299,5	22°	306,7	21°	302,4	19°	299,6	16°
9.	O. Panis	306,7	7°	308,0	8°	253,8	11°	246,7	6°	308,1	10°	322,2	1°	305,0	17°	309,5	5°
10.	J. Villeneuve	305,6	13°	311,1	4°	251,6	14°	245,9	8°	309,1	7°	319,0	4°	305,5	16°	302,7	15°
11.	H.-H. Frentzen	305,6	12°	305,6	14°	253,4	12°	243,9	10°	305,6	18°	308,5	19°	305,7	14°	304,9	11°
12.	J. Trulli	305,6	12°	305,7	11°	256,3	6°	244,5	9°	306,9	12°	308,3	20°	307,3	11°	304,3	12°
14.	J. Verstappen	310,0	3°	309,7	6°	252,2	13°	240,6	16°	314,4	1°	316,4	7°	313,8	2°	303,0	13°
15.	E. Bernoldi	308,2	5°	305,0	16°	245,7	20°	232,7	20°	312,7	2°	321,7	2°	300,0	21°	285,1	21°
16.	N. Heidfeld	299,8	21°	306,1	10°	255,1	8°	242,8	11°	301,2	21°	310,4	16°	302,3	20°	308,9	6°
17.	K. Räikkönen	300,0	20°	305,4	13°	256,0	7°	248,6	2°	302,6	20°	311,5	14°	304,1	18°	307,6	8°
18.	E. Irvine	305,8	9°	305,6	13°	254,4	9°	246,0	7°	308,3	8°	312,5	11°	310,5	6°	302,9	14°
19.	L. Burti	302,9	17°	314,5	1°	250,6	16°	241,9	13°	305,1	19°	312,2	12°	306,9	12°	298,6	18°
20.	T. Marques	304,3	14°	302,0	19°	243,9	22°	234,2	19°	306,7	13°	310,2	17°	305,6	15°	296,5	20°
21.	F. Alonso	303,7	15°	301,7	20°	245,3	21°	236,4	18°	306,4	17°	312,5	10°	299,4	22°	298,3	19°
22.	J. Alesi	305,7	11°	304,9	17°	251,3	15°	241,8	14°	308,3	9°	312,0	13°	310,7	5°	307,4	9°
23.	G. Mazzacane	303,6	16°	309,3	7°	249,5	17°	240,9	15°	306,5	15°	314,0	9°	307,8	10°	312,3	3°

CLASSIFICATION & RETIREMENTS

Pos	Driver	Team	Time
1.	Coulthard.	McLaren Mercedes	1:39:00.834
2.	M. Schum.	Ferrari	+ 16.164
3.	Heidfeld	Sauber Petronas	+ 1 lap
4.	Panis	BAR Honda	+ 1 lap
5.	Trulli	Jordan Honda	+ 1 lap
6.	Fisichella	Benetton Renault	+ 1 lap
7.	Villeneuve	BAR Honda	+ 1 lap
8.	Alesi	Prost Acer	+ 1 lap
9.	Marques	European Minardi	+ 3 laps
10.	Button	Benetton Renault	+ 7 laps

Lap	Driver	Team	Reason
0	Häkkinen	McLaren Mercedes	clutch
3	Barrichello	Ferrari	accident
16	Bernoldi	Arrows Asiatech	hydraulic
26	Alonso	European Minardi	electronics
31	Burti	Jaguar Racing	engine
39	Verstappen	Arrows Asiatech	accident
39	Montoya	Williams BMW	accident
53	Irvine	Jaguar Racing	engine stalled
55	R. Schum.	Williams BMW	accident
55	Mazzacane	Prost Acer	clutch
56	Räikkönen	Sauber Petronas	spin
64	Frentzen	Jordan Honda	engine

All results: © 2001 Fédération Internationale de l'Automobile, 2 Ch. Blandonnet, 1215 Genève 15, Suisse

FASTEST LAPS

	Driver	Time	Lap
1.	R. Schum.	1'15"693 204,938 km/h	38
2.	Coulthard	1'16"498	44
3.	M. Schum.	1'16"545	44
4.	Montoya	1'16"593	31
5.	Panis	1'16"732	44
6.	Villeneuve	1'17"106	41
7.	Irvine	1'17"132	43
8.	Frentzen	1'17"522	41
9.	Alesi	1'17"609	43
10.	Trulli	1'17"632	41
11.	Räikkönen	1'17"816	33
12.	Fisichella	1'17"830	41
13.	Heidfeld	1'18"064	42
14.	Mazzacane	1'18"176	23
15.	Burti	1'18"759	29
16.	Verstappen	1'18"875	26
17.	Bernoldi	1'19"449	12
18.	Marques	1'19"734	34
19.	Alonso	1'19"765	16
20.	Button	1'19"846	38
21.	Barrichello	1'58"705	2

PIT STOPS

	Driver	Time	Lap	Stop n°
1.	R. Schumacher	5'14"156	3	1
2.	Irvine	36"410	6	1
3.	Villeneuve	39"017	12	1
4.	Alesi	50"027	24	1
5.	M. Schumacher	35"052	25	1
6.	Mazzacane	37"611	25	1
7.	Panis	35"152	28	1
8.	Button	6'42"403	28	1
9.	Räikkönen	37"490	37	1
10.	Heidfeld	39"439	38	1
11.	Marques	38"960	38	1
12.	Coulthard	36"183	40	1
13.	Fisichella	38"585	42	1
14.	Villeneuve	35"954	42	2
15.	Frentzen	36"342	43	1
16.	Trulli	38"541	44	1
17.	Alesi	38"731	44	2
18.	R. Schumacher	38"161	41	2
19.	Fisichella	37"590	44	2
20.	Villeneuve	1'17"408	44	3
21.	Panis	1'47"355	45	2
22.	Button	38"088	39	2
23.	Frentzen	42"140	45	2
24.	Trulli	48"657	45	2
25.	Heidfeld	40"410	45	2
26.	Marques	37"716	44	2
27.	M. Schumacher	35"002	46	2
28.	Mazzacane	38"609	46	2
29.	R. Schumacher	42"272	42	3
30.	Irvine	39"408	46	2
31.	Räikkönen	35"278	46	2
32.	Coulthard	33"037	47	2
33.	R. Schumacher	52"722	48	4

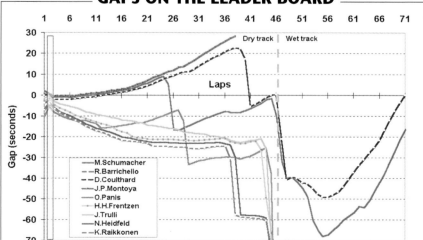

BRIDGESTONE

Best result for a driver running Bridgestone tyres:

D.Coulthard, McLaren Mercedes, winner

CHAMPIONSHIP

(after three rounds)

Drivers :
1. M. Schumacher 26
2. D. Coulthard 20
3. R. Barrichello 10
4. N. Heidfeld 7
5. H.-H. Frentzen 5
6. O. Panis 3
7. R. Schumacher 2
   J. Trulli 2
9. K. Räikkönen 1
   M. Häkkinen 1
   G. Fischella 1

Constructors :
1. Ferrari 36
2. McLaren Mercedes 21
3. Sauber Petronas 8
4. Jordan Honda 7
5. BAR Honda 3
6. Williams BMW 2
7. Benetton Renault 1

THE CIRCUIT

THIRD ROUND

GRANDE PRÊMIO DO BRASIL, INTERLAGOS

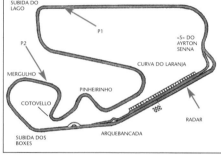

Date : April 1, 2001
Length : 4309 meters
Distance : 71 laps, 305.909 km
Weather : hot and raining, 28°

RACE SUMMARY

- Hakkinen is left on the grid at the start. Michael Schumacher makes a perfect start. Ralf Schumacher does not.

- The Safety Car come out for one lap, while Hakkinen's car is cleared away.

- At the start of lap 3, Montoya attacks Michael Schumacher and passes him with a daring move. Further back, Barrichello runs into the back of Ralf Schumacher, for the second grand prix in a row.

- Montoya does not really manage to pull out an advantage over Michael Schumacher, but he keeps the lead until lap 25, when Michael Schumacher makes a pit stop.

- On lap 38, Montoya is still leading when he is hit from behind by Verstappen, whom he has just lapped.

- Coulthard is now in the lead and refuels.

- It starts to rain on lap 45. Panis was unable to benefit from the fact he was already in the pits and has to stop again for rain tyres.

- When Coulthard fits rain tyres, he rejoins the track just ahead of Michael Schumacher.

- Frentzen retires on lap 64, allowing Heidfeld onto the podium. Out in front, Coulthard wins from Michael Schumacher.

LAP CHART

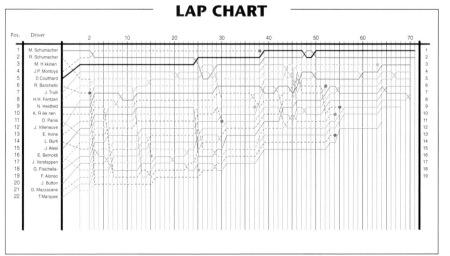

GAPS ON THE LEADER BOARD

That's number one!

The San Marino Grand Prix was totally dominated by one man and one machine: Ralf Schumacher and his BMW powered Williams with its Michelin tyres.
All rivals had to admit this was an unbeatable combination on the day. Having been knocked out of the first three grands prix, hit from behind, the young German made amends in style at Imola. It was a case of sweet revenge in the blue and white camp.

RAN PRÊMIO WARSTEINER DI SAN MARINO
IMOLA

Friday morning: Ralf Schumacher's Williams sports an amusing "Keep Your Distance" on its rear wing. It was an allusion to the fact he had been hit from behind in the last three races. Williams certainly managed to retain their sense of humour.

The Imola circuit seen from a helicopter. A home to F1 since 1980, the Emilian circuit had traditionally signalled the start of the European part of the season.

A pensive Mika Hakkinen. He might have been back on the front row at Imola, but it could not make up for the early season disappointments.

McLaren forget their manners

"I am so sorry to have disappointed the Italian fans. Ahem! I won't do it again." David Coulthard was in a teasing mood after qualifying and with good reason. He had just had one over on the tifosi by out-qualifying the Ferraris on their home track, a few dozen kilometres from the Maranello factory.

In the other McLaren, Mika Hakkinen had also snubbed the home team, putting his car on the front row of the grid in what had been a total triumph for McLaren. "I am really very confident about the rest of the season," affirmed Hakkinen, a large smile playing on his lips. "If you look at how hard we had to fight in the first few grands prix, it's really fantastic to be back in front. Everyone in the team has worked very hard." David Coulthard confirmed this. "Last night, our mechanics worked until four in the morning to change the settings we had yesterday," explained the Scotsman. "This morning, it still wasn't right, so we changed everything again. The guys are working like mad." Which in the end paid off. "I think the championship is far from lost," continued Hakkinen. "I am 25 points behind Michael Schumacher, but I am experienced. I know there is

still a long way to go, so I am not too worried."

The Ferrari drivers were the ones who were concerned, even if they hid their anxiety behind a technical explanation, based on the fact the Scuderia had opted to qualify and race on the harder of the two tyre types supplied by Bridgestone, while McLaren had gone for the softer compound. "I am happier to start from the second row on the right tyres, than on the front row with tyres which will not go the distance," said Schumacher, apparently trying to persuade himself that fourth on the grid was okay. "I am not worried about the race, but I am a bit disappointed for our fans. But I can assure them that it will be an interesting race tomorrow. The situation is not as bad as it seems."

In Brazil, where Schumacher was beaten in the wet by Coulthard, he described his car as strange. At a Fiorano test, the following week, a few days of rain had allowed the team to recreate the Sao Paulo conditions, discovering a genuine problem, which they had sorted in time for Imola, which had thus reassured the Scuderia.

STARTING GRID

David COULTHARD 1'23"054	-1-	Mika HÄKKINEN 1'23"282
Ralf SCHUMACHER 1'23"357	-2-	M. SCHUMACHER 1'23"593
Jarno TRULLI 1'23"658	-3-	R. BARRICHELLO 1'23"786
J. P. MONTOYA 1'24"141	-4-	Olivier PANIS 1'24"213
Heinz-H. FRENTZEN 1'24"436	-5-	Kimi RAIKKONEN 1'24"671
Jacques VILLENEUVE 1'24"769	-6-	Nick HEIDFELD 1'25"007
Eddie IRVINE 1'25"392	-7-	Jean ALESI 1'25"411
Luciano BURTI 1'25"572	-8-	Enrique BERNOLDI 1'25"872
Jos VERSTAPPEN 1'26"062	-9-	Fernando ALONSO 1'26"855
Giancarlo FISICHELLA 1'26"902	-10-	Gaston MAZZACANE 1'27"750
Jenson BUTTON 1'27"758	-11-	Tarso MARQUES 1'28"281

A first for Ralf, BMW and Michelin

He led cleanly from start to finish. Ralf Schumacher's win in the San Marino Grand Prix was totally dominant.

The German led all the way from lights out to chequered flag, to claim not only the first win of his career, but also the first for BMW and Michelin since these two marques made their return to Formula 1.

It had therefore taken the Clermont-Ferrand company just four races to emerge victorious, a fact underlined by Ralf Schumacher after the race. *"The Michelin tyres are really fantastic, especially in race conditions like those we experienced today,"* he declared. *"What Michelin has achieved in such a short space of time is remarkable. But the car was also very well balanced and the engine ran faultlessly."*

In fact, the day went off like a dream for the world champion's little brother. He made the best start off the second row and got past the two McLarens on the run down to the first corner. From then, he won as he pleased. He built up a lead lap by lap, until it settled down to around ten seconds at half distance. *"I couldn't believe it when I found myself leading at the first corner,"* he said. *"It was all going so well that the race seemed to last a long time. I started to think about the*

possibility of winning about 14 laps from the end. I told myself it was too early and I put it out of my mind until there were just three laps to go. Those three laps lasted an eternity!"*

Of course, the first person to congratulate Ralf, as he stepped out of the car, was his brother Michael. *"Michael said to me, "well done, it was the right moment"... This win is very nice, but I still feel very calm. It hasn't sunk in yet, but I can tell you we will be partying tonight."*

In the paddock, the entire Michelin crew posed for a family photo, with a delighted Pierre Dupasquier in the middle. *"In the snow yesterday, when it was only 4 degrees, it was not going too well. But, when it's fine everything works perfectly,"* joked the French company's competitions boss. *"We have known since Brazil that we are competitive, but as recently as two months ago, we would not have dared dream of winning our fourth race. It was a brave decision for Michelin to return to F1 and this victory shows it was the right thing to do."*

It seemed as though this first win for the Williams-BMW-Michelin was going to be the first of many. *"Everyone worked very hard at Williams and it's beginning to pay off,"* concluded Ralf Schumacher. *"And it's just a start. We have a lot of new developments, so we will see."*

David Coulthard was powerless

David Coulthard had been hoping to rack up a second consecutive Imola win. Starting from pole, he found himself powerless against the Ralf Schumacher locomotive. *"I got too much wheelspin at the start and Ralf made the most of it to get past me,"* recounted the Scotsman. *"After that, I tried to hang onto him, but there was nothing I could do. He was just too quick. In fact, he was so quick in the early stages, I began to think he was on a five stop strategy! But as the laps went by, I realised he wasn't going to stop any more often than us and that the race was lost."*

On top of that, the McLaren man had a few problems with the balance of his car. *"The tyres were not consistent and I was having a job hanging onto the car. From that point of view, this was the toughest race of the season so far. I think that, all things considered, I am lucky to come away with six*

points."* In the other McLaren, Mika Hakkinen finished fourth. He also messed up his start and spent much of the race stuck behind Jarno Trulli, who had got past him at the first corner.

△
It's a win. BMW Technical Director, Mario Theissen, Ralf Schumacher and Williams Technical Director, Patrick Head pose with the team.

◁◁
The spectacle of the start grid seen from a helicopter: the last moments of calm before the storm.

◁
"Well done little brother!" Michael Schumacher, who retired on lap 25, comes to congratulate Ralf.

The start. Coming up to the former corner of Tamburello, Ralf Schumacher is already in the lead. No one would come to trouble him on the way to the flag.

An arty shot of Michael Schumacher. It was not really a good weekend for him in Imola.

Jarno Trulli qualified fifth and finished fifth for the second consecutive time. His team-mate, Heinz-Harald Frentzen picked up the single point for sixth place. The start of the season was going quite well for Jordan.

Everything went wrong for Michael Schumacher: the world champion had even been overtaken by Jacques Villeneuve, before retiring.

It was not really a good weekend for Rubens Barrichello in Imola. Sixth on the grid, he somehow managed to salvage something for himself and the Scuderia, finishing on the third step of the podium.

WEEKEND GOSSIP

• F1 forgeries

On the Friday before the race, the Italian police discovered an illegal printing press, churning out forged tickets for the San Marino Grand Prix. Based in the south of the country in Salerno, the printers had apparently produced thousands of counterfeit tickets. The organisers stepped up security checks at the gates in an effort to stop people getting in with the fakes.

• The Canadian blames himself

Once again, Jacques Villeneuve was beaten in qualifying by his team-mate Olivier Panis. However, the Canadian was not prepared to blame his car. The Frenchman was simply quicker. "I am not in crisis, I am just cross with myself," commented Jacques Villeneuve after the qualifying session.

• Parallel championship

Bernie Ecclestone and all the team owners met on the Friday. Nothing much came out of it. The teams simply confirmed that the interests of all were coming together: major manufacturers, teams, sponsors and the Kirch Group (owners of 75% of Bernie Ecclestone's company.) They would all be trying to work more closely together to assure the future of Formula 1 and fight off the threat from the car companies, who had announced they were prepared to set up an alternative championship to Formula 1, starting in 2008.

"That way leads nowhere!" Kimi Raikkonen gets it wrong at the exit to Tosa corner and would end up against the concrete wall.

A sad day for the tifosi

A good mood ran through the grandstands just prior to the start. Even though the Ferraris were not that well placed on the grid, with Michael Schumacher fourth and Rubens Barrichello sixth, the Italian press had decided to go with the Scuderia drivers' excuse for this setback. In other words, their poor qualifying performance was down to having chosen a type of tyre which would come good for them in the race.

But right from the start, they would be forced to recant. While Ralf Schumacher made the perfect start, his brother Michael was overwhelmed by Jarno Trulli. The world champion therefore came round at the end of the first lap in fifth place, before giving best to Juan Pablo Montoya, then Olivier Panis and Rubens Barrichello on lap four. It seemed as though his F2001 was not at its best. "*I had a sudden problem with the gearbox,*" explained Schumacher after the race. "*But, in any case, this was not my weekend. It was a difficult race and it all ended with a problem which we have not really identified yet. But it has something to do with the bodywork around the left front wheel.*" It was a problem that Michael Schumacher had apparently already encounterd in practice for the Australian Grand Prix.

Not only had the German retired, but this San Marino Grand Prix drew him to the conclusion that the opposition had now caught up with Ferrari in terms of performance. "*We cannot win every time,*" he continued. "*But let's say that our rivals have closed the gap to us. We still have work to do this season.*"

Rubens Barrichello saved the bacon for the Scuderia with third place. "*I messed up my start,*" admitted the Brazilian. "*My car was very quick, but on this track it really is impossible to overtake.*"

In Imola, Michael Schumacher had to console himself with the fact victory went to his little brother. "*It's the first time in F1 that two brothers win grands prix. I think our parents can be proud of us.*"

However, as far as the crowd at Imola was concerned, the wrong Schumacher had won. Thankfully, "their" Schumacher still led the world championship classification; equal on points with David Coulthard. It was some small comfort when the time came to pack up and head for home.

PRACTICE TIMES

No	Driver	Car/Engine/Chassis	Practice Friday	Pos.	Practice Saturday	Pos.	Qualifying	Pos.	Warm-up	Pos.
1.	Michael Schumacher	Ferrari/F2001/208	1'25"096	1°	1'30"737	1°	1'23"593	4°	1'26"948	6°
2.	Rubens Barrichello	Ferrari/F2001/206	1'25"372	2°	1'31"003	2°	1'23"786	6°	1'26"941	5°
3.	Mika Häkkinen	McLaren/Mercedes/MP4/16/3	1'26"341	4°	1'34"036	10°	1'23"282	2°	1'26"836	3°
4.	David Coulthard	McLaren/Mercedes/MP4/16/5	1'27"132	11°	1'31"536	3°	1'23"054	1°	1'26"440	1°
5.	Ralf Schumacher	Williams/BMW/FW23/3	1'25"829	3°	1'33"025	7°	1'23"357	3°	1'26"727	2°
6.	Juan Pablo Montoya	Williams/BMW/FW23/2	1'39"812	22°	1'34"548	12°	1'24"141	7°	1'28"142	13°
7.	Giancarlo Fisichella	Benetton/Renault/B201/3	1'28"322	15°	1'39"214	20°	1'26"902	19°	1'29"623	20°
8.	Jenson Button	Benetton/Renault/B201/5	1'28"902	17°	1'38"306	19°	1'27"758	21°	1'29"593	19°
9.	Olivier Panis	BAR/Honda/003/3	1'26"535	5°	1'33"071	8°	1'24"213	8°	1'27"534	9°
10.	Jacques Villeneuve	BAR/Honda/003/5	1'26"739	8°	1'34"789	13°	1'24"769	11°	1'28"035	12°
11.	Heinz-Harald Frentzen	Jordan/Honda/EJ11/4	1'27"406	13°	1'32"164	5°	1'24"436	9°	1'26"954	7°
12.	Jarno Trulli	Jordan/Honda/EJ11/5	1'26"923	9°	1'36"046	16°	1'23"658	5°	1'27"575	10°
14.	Jos Verstappen	Arrows/Asiatech/A22/6	1'29"750	21°	1'34"948	14°	1'26"062	17°	1'27"728	11°
15.	Enrique Bernoldi	Arrows/Asiatech/A22/3	1'29"273	19°	1'33"884	9°	1'25"872	16°	1'28"639	15°
16.	Nick Heidfeld	Sauber/Petronas/C20/3	1'27"142	12°	1'32"392	6°	1'25"007	12°	1'26"929	4°
17.	Kimi Räikkönen	Sauber/Petronas/C20/1	1'26"552	6°	1'31"726	4°	1'24"671	10°	1'27"492	8°
18.	Eddie Irvine	Jaguar/R-2/4	1'26"599	7°	1'41"711	21°	1'25"392	13°	1'28"655	16°
19.	Luciano Burti	Jaguar/R-2/3	1'26"933	10°	-	22°	1'25"572	15°	1'30"030	21°
20.	Tarso Marques	Minardi/European/PS01/4	1'29"589	20°	1'36"671	18°	1'28"281	22°	1'29"480	18°
21.	Fernando Alonso	Minardi/European/PS01/1	1'28"931	18°	1'36"058	17°	1'26"855	18°	1'30"150	22°
22.	Jean Alesi	Prost/Acer/AP04/3	1'27"437	14°	1'34"531	11°	1'25"411	14°	1'29"347	17°
23.	Gaston Mazzacane	Prost/Acer/AP04/4	1'28"586	16°	1'35"056	15°	1'27"750	20°	1'28"404	14°

MAXIMUM SPEEDS

No	Driver	P1 Qualifs	Pos	P1 Race	Pos	P2 Qualifs	Pos	P2 Race	Pos	Finish Qualifs	Pos	Finish Race	Pos	Trap Qualifs	Pos	Trap Race	Pos
1.	M. Schumacher	298,7	3°	290,5	9°	229,7	5°	220,1	15°	176,4	7°	167,9	12°	305,6	1°	306,5	11°
2.	R. Barrichello	295,8	7°	289,6	14°	230,4	3°	225,1	3°	176,5	5°	170,5	5°	299,3	7°	305,6	13°
3.	M. Häkkinen	296,7	5°	292,8	4°	227,8	11°	221,9	10°	174,9	9°	169,7	9°	298,0	10°	308,3	5°
4.	D. Coulthard	293,0	14°	293,0	3°	230,3	4°	223,5	7°	178,1	3°	170,4	7°	297,3	13°	309,6	3°
5.	R. Schumacher	299,7	2°	296,9	2°	232,6	2°	226,4	1°	172,8	14°	171,2	3°	304,6	2°	312,3	1°
6.	J. P. Montoya	300,7	1°	297,8	1°	232,7	1°	225,0	4°	173,7	11°	170,5	4°	302,0	4°	311,4	2°
7.	G. Fisichella	288,8	21°	281,8	21°	222,1	17°	219,7	19°	170,9	18°	167,5	14°	291,5	21°	300,9	19°
8.	J. Button	288,0	22°	283,2	19°	221,3	22°	219,5	16°	167,7	21°	166,0	19°	291,1	22°	299,5	20°
9.	O. Panis	295,6	8°	290,4	10°	227,7	6°	217,8	20°	176,6	4°	169,1	10°	298,8	8°	307,3	10°
10.	J. Villeneuve	295,5	9°	290,4	10°	227,7	12°	217,8	18°	175,7	8°	169,1	11°	297,6	11°	307,9	7°
11.	H.-H. Frentzen	295,4	10°	292,5	5°	227,4	13°	218,7	18°	172,3	15°	166,1	17°	297,6	12°	307,9	7°
12.	J. Trulli	295,2	11°	289,3	16°	227,3	14°	223,2	8°	180,2	1°	172,9	2°	297,8	11°	304,1	17°
14.	J. Verstappen	296,5	6°	290,2	11°	226,9	15°	220,2	13°	173,3	12°	168,5	11°	302,0	3°	304,0	18°
15.	E. Bernoldi	297,1	4°	290,6	8°	228,8	8°	223,5	6°	176,5	6°	173,4	1°	300,1	6°	307,7	8°
16.	N. Heidfeld	292,5	17°	289,6	15°	228,8	7°	221,0	14°	174,1	10°	170,0	8°	294,5	17°	307,3	9°
17.	K. Räikkönen	294,6	12°	292,7	5°	228,1	10°	222,7	9°	178,9	2°	166,0	20°	293,3	20°	308,2	6°
18.	E. Irvine	292,8	15°	290,0	13°	228,6	9°	224,0	5°	173,3	13°	170,5	6°	293,7	19°	304,8	16°
19.	L. Burti	291,4	18°	287,1	17°	224,5	18°	219,0	17°	170,1	19°	166,1	18°	295,8	16°	304,9	15°
20.	T. Marques	291,1	19°	281,3	22°	222,5	20°	214,6	21°	166,3	22°	163,5	21°	296,6	15°	298,9	21°
21.	F. Alonso	290,2	20°	282,3	20°	224,5	18°	214,4	22°	171,8	16°	162,7	22°	294,1	18°	297,7	22°
22.	J. Alesi	294,1	13°	291,5	7°	226,8	16°	225,7	2°	171,7	17°	167,8	13°	298,4	9°	305,8	12°
23.	G. Mazzacane	292,6	16°	290,2	12°	225,0	17°	221,2	12°	169,5	20°	166,4	16°	296,8	14°	305,2	14°

CLASSIFICATION & RETIREMENTS

Pos	Driver	Team	Time
1.	R. Schum.	Williams BMW	1:30:44.817
2.	Coulthard	McLaren Mercedes	+ 4.352
3.	Barrichello	Ferrari	+ 34.766
4.	Häkkinen	McLaren Mercedes	+ 36.315
5.	Trulli	Jordan Honda	+ 85.558
6.	Frentzen	Jordan Honda	+ 1 lap
7.	Heidfeld	Sauber Petronas	+ 1 lap
8.	Panis	BAR Honda	+ 1 lap
9.	Alesi	Prost Acer	+ 1 lap
10.	Bernoldi	Arrows Asiatech	+ 2 laps
11.	Burti	Jaguar Racing	+ 2 laps
12.	Button	Benetton Renault	+ 2 laps

Lap	Driver	Team	Reason
6	Alonso	European Minardi	off
7	Verstappen	Arrows	exhaust
18	Räikkönen	Sauber Petronas	steering wheel
25	M. Schum.	Ferrari	left front wheel
29	Mazzacane	Prost Acer	engine
31	Villeneuve	BAR Honda	engine
32	Fisichella	Benetton Renault	engine
43	Irvine	Jaguar Racing	engine
49	Montoya	Williams BMW	clutch
51	Marques	European Minardi	engine

All results : © 2001 Fédération Internationale de l'Automobile, 2, Ch. Blandonnet, 1215 Genève 15, Suisse

FASTEST LAPS

	Driver	Time	Lap
1.	R. Schum.	1'25"524	27
		207,646 km/h	
2.	Coulthard	1'25"569	44
3.	Barrichello	1'26"117	46
4.	Häkkinen	1'26"308	61
5.	Montoya	1'26"385	46
6.	M. Schum.	1'27"229	21
7.	Frentzen	1'27"243	36
8.	Heidfeld	1'27"350	57
9.	Trulli	1'27"358	20
10.	Panis	1'27"582	47
11.	Villeneuve	1'27"614	27
12.	Irvine	1'27"854	28
13.	Burti	1'27"932	29
14.	Alesi	1'28"369	44
15.	Räikkönen	1'28"604	17
16.	Mazzacane	1'28"954	21
17.	Bernoldi	1'28"956	37
18.	Button	1'29"096	38
19.	Fisichella	1'29"644	14
20.	Verstappen	1'30"403	4
21.	Alonso	1'31"671	4
22.	Marques	1'31"725	38

PIT STOPS

	Drivers	Time	Lap	Stop n°
1.	Button	24"424	19	1
2.	Button	26"268	20	2
3.	Alesi	27"582	21	1
4.	Fisichella	25"640	21	1
5.	Bernoldi	26"850	21	1
6.	Marques	27"136	21	1
7.	M. Schumacher	32"616	23	1
8.	Trulli	25"932	24	1
9.	Heidfeld	26"922	25	1
10.	Mazzacane	31"225	25	1
11.	Frentzen	24"814	26	1
12.	Montoya	26"273	27	1
13.	Panis	27"719	27	1
14.	Coulthard	25"239	28	1
15.	R. Schumacher	24"687	29	1
16.	Häkkinen	24"764	29	1
17.	Villeneuve	25"550	29	1
18.	Irvine	29"358	31	1
19.	Barrichello	24"449	32	1
20.	Burti	29"611	32	1
21.	Button	25"900	39	3
22.	Bernoldi	27"844	41	2
23.	Marques	26"927	40	2
24.	Trulli	26"021	43	2
25.	Frentzen	25"488	44	2
26.	Coulthard	24"324	45	2

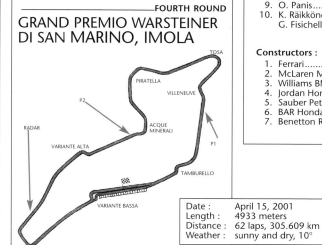

BRIDGESTONE

Best result for a driver running Bridgestone tyre:

D. Coulthard, McLaren Mercedes, second

CHAMPIONSHIP

(after four rounds)

Drivers :

1. M. Schumacher	26
D. Coulthard	26
3. R. Barrichello	14
4. R. Schumacher	12
5. N. Heidfeld	7
6. H.-H. Frentzen	6
7. M. Häkkinen	4
J. Trulli	4
9. O. Panis	3
10. K. Räikkönen	1
G. Fisichella	1

Constructors :

1. Ferrari	40
2. McLaren Mercedes	30
3. Williams BMW	12
4. Jordan Honda	10
5. Sauber Petronas	8
6. BAR Honda	3
7. Benetton Renault	1

THE CIRCUIT

FOURTH ROUND

GRAN PREMIO WARSTEINER DI SAN MARINO, IMOLA

Date :	April 15, 2001
Length :	4933 meters
Distance :	62 laps, 305.609 km
Weather :	sunny and dry, 10°

RACE SUMMARY

- Ralf Schumacher makes the best start and leads through the first corner, having overwhelmed the two McLarens, which had started from the front row of the grid.

- Trulli also makes a great start and splits the two McLarens.

- Nothing is going right for Michael Schumacher, who is passed first by Panis and then by Barrichello.

- By lap 10, Ralf Schumacher has a 1.4 second lead over Coulthard and 14 seconds over the Trulli-Hakkinen tandem, which leads Montoya.

- On lap 223, Michael Schumacher cruises slowly into the pits with a puncture. The German continues, but retires on lap 25.

- The pit stops start on lap 27, with Montoya the first to come in. Once back on track, the Colombian passes Trulli on the outside at Tamburello!

- On lap 40, Ralf Schumacher has a ten second lead over his pursuers.

- Around lap 45, the second run of pit stops begins. Montoya loses over a minute with a hose problem. He stalls as he leaves, but retires in the pits a couple of laps later.

- The Williams team show Ralf Schumacher the pit board with the word "pump" on it. The German is not in trouble however and takes the first grand prix win of his career, ahead of Coulthard and Barrichello.

LAP CHART

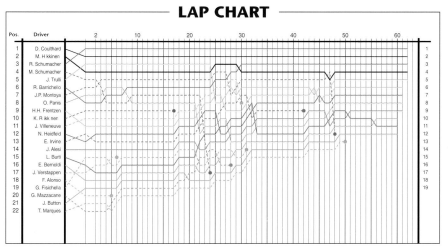

GAPS ON THE LEADER BOARD

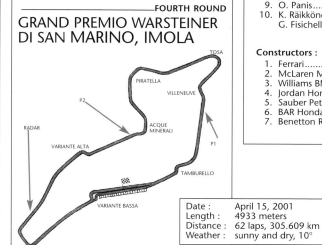

Poor Mika!

After a calamitous start to the season, with only a modest fourth place at Imola offering meagre consolation, Mika Hakkinen was hoping to get back to his winning ways at the Barcelona circuit. The plan looked to be working, as he was comfortably in the lead as he began the final lap. But then, his mount failed him yet again. He tried his best to coax it to the finish line, but in vain. With a heavy heart, Mika hitched a ride back to the pits, on the side pod of the only MP4/16 still running, that of his team-mate David Coulthard.

Michael Schumacher inherited the win, but it was hardly a glorious victory for the German.

GRAN PRÊMIO MARLBORO DE ESPAÑA
BARCELONE

Return of the rivals

Eddie Irvine leaves the pits. In Barcelona, Bobby Rahal (below) decided to replace Luciano Burti with Pedro De La Rosa. It didn't bring a change in fortunes.

There it was then; a Michael Schumacher - Mika Hakkinen front row. We hadn't seen that for some time and it revived happy memories. While Schumacher had enjoyed a brilliant start to the season, to lead the points table jointly with David Coulthard, for the Finn, the 2001 season had not been a happy affair. Therefore, Barcelona marked a return to the glory days of 1998, 1999 and 2000 and the duels between these two F1 rivals.

For Michael Schumacher, this was also the moment to show

that hsi Ferrari F2001 was still the car to beat, even if problems at the past two grands prix might have made one think otherwise. *"What problems?"* challenged the world champion. *"People say to me that Ferrari is going down, but I honestly haven't seen the slope. The fact is that here we are, exactly where we want to be, out in front. We have worked hard to be here and that's it."*

Schumacher did his time halfway through the session and it was so much quicker than anyone else's, it really looked as though he wouldn't be threatened. Except perhaps by Hakkinen, who was fighting back and qualified just 85 thousandths of a second slower than the Ferrari driver. And he did it without traction control. *"I disconnected the system, which helped me a bit,"* confirmed the Finn. *"If you have a little problem in a corner, you can sometimes compensate by playing*

with the throttle, which you can't do if the traction control is operating. But I am disappointed not to be on pole. It all came down to Turn 5, where the back of the car stepped out a bit."

Mika Hakkinen was back in business after a disastrous start to the season (after four grands prix, he was only seventh in the championship, with four points.) The revival had come at just the right time. *"It's given my confidence a boost,"* he confirmed. *"Especially here, where I have won for the past three years and where I have some excellent memories. I think this will help a lot for the race."*

Behind the two old rivals, David Coulthard qualified third and Rubens Barrichello was fourth. Ralf Schumacher, the winner in Imola was only fifth. It seemed that, in qualifying at least, his tyres were not working that well on this circuit.

STARTING GRID

M. SCHUMACHER 1'18"201	-1-	Mika HÄKKINEN 1'18"286
David COULTHARD 1'18"635	-2-	R. BARRICHELLO 1'18"674
Ralf SCHUMACHER 1'19"016	-3-	Jarno TRULLI 1'19"093
Jacques VILLENEUVE 1'19"122	-4-	Heinz-H. FRENTZEN 1'19"150
Kimi RÄIKKÖNEN 1'19"229	-5-	Nick HEIDFELD 1'19"232
Olivier PANIS 1'19"479	-6-	J. P. MONTOYA 1'19"660
Eddie IRVINE 1'20"326	-7-	Luciano BURTI 1'20"585
Jean ALESI 1'20"601	-8-	Enrique BERNOLDI 1'20"696
Jos VERSTAPPEN 1'20"737	-9-	Fernando ALONSO 1'21"037
Giancarlo FISICHELLA 1'21"065	-10-	Pedro De la Rosa 1'21"338
Jenson BUTTON 1'21"916	-11-	Tarso MARQUES 1'22"522

To the general surprise of everyone in the Prost team, its new recruit, Luciano Burti, qualified ahead of his team-mate Jean Alesi no less in Barcelona. "Everything is going very well with the team," remarked the Brazilian after qualifying. I immediately felt welcome and it's very relaxed, which no doubt contributed to my performance. We struggled a bit to get the right settings, because of the wind down the main straight, but overall, I'm not unhappy."

The same could not be said for Jean Alesi. "Nothing good came out of this qualifying session," complained the Frenchman. "It's a real shame, because we could do better on a track which we know so well. From now on, it's clear: as long as we don't have the new parts we are waiting for, then things won't get better."

Jacques gets BAR's first podium

Jacques Villeneuve was pretty pumped up when he arrived in Barcelona. *"Guys, it can't go on like this,"* he had warned when he arrived on Thursday. *"This is now the fifth grand prix of the season and I haven't scored a single point. On top of that, Olivier (Panis, his co-driver) is ahead of me in qualifying. It's not working."*

For the whole weekend, the Canadian never stopped pushing his race engineers, starting with his faithful sidekick, Jock Clear. *"Jacques was very angry this weekend,"* admitted the Englishman after the race. *"On Saturday, after qualifying, he gave us a hard time when we made a mistake with his brakes. He*

didn't hold back from telling the press it was our fault. He really put us under a lot of pressure." At least it produced something as the Canadian finished the Spanish Grand Prix in third place.

He therefore climbed onto the podium for the first time since 1998. It was also the first podium in the history of the BAR team and the first for engine supplier Honda, since its return to Formula 1 in 2000. *"It's fantastic,"* reckoned Villeneuve after the race. *"Everyone in the team has really worked hard over the past three years and this podium is just the boost that everyone needed. But there was no way I could do any better as the car was very difficult to drive today."*

One lap too many

What an incredible end to a race! The situation was suddenly turned on its head. Just as he was starting the last of the 65 laps of the Spanish Grand Prix, Mika Hakkinen's McLaren had a 42.5 second lead over Michael Schumacher. The Finn was winning by a country mile in Formula 1 terms. Surely nothing stood between him and victory.

Nothing except his own car as things turned out. In the chicane after the straight, right at the start of the final lap Hakkinen's MP-4/16 lost momentum. In the press office and of course in the McLaren pit, everyone held their breath. The Finn continued, but he was slowing all the time. A few hundred metres further on, at Turn 7, he parked his smoking and spitting car on the grass. It was over. *"I can't believe it,"* exclaimed Hakkinen, back in his garage. *"When it happened, everything was going so well. I was so confident in my car, it was unreal. I think it was a clutch problem, because I couldn't get any gear, no matter which one I tried. As I was on an uphill section, there was nothing I could do to bring the car home."*

That is how a surprised Michael Schumacher found himself climbing to the top step of the podium, even though, for the last twenty laps, he had been fighting his Ferrari which was not on particularly good form. *"To be honest, when I went past Mika's car, I was really upset for him,"* commented the German driver. *"He had done better than us in the two pit stops, he had driven a great race, without mistakes and our fight reminded me of the good old days. It was a real shock, seeing him stopped just a few hundred metres from the flag."*

For his part, Schumacher had his problems too. Having led from the start for the first 43 laps of the race, the German lost a lot of ground after his second refuelling stop, because his last set of tyres were causing a worrying vibration.

A first for Juan Pablo

Another beneficiary of the misfortunes which befell Mika Hakkinen was Juan Pablo Montoya, who finished second at the wheel of his Williams-BMW. So, much to his great surprise, the Colombian picked up his first ever F1 points in fine style. *"I've had quite a bit of bad luck since the start of the season,"* he commented. *"And I am very happy that this bad run has ended with a rather lucky second place. My car wasn't perfect today, but it was working better than in qualifying."*

An excellent start by the Williams driver had a lot to do with it, as he went from eleventh place on the grid to sixth, by the end of the opening lap. All that without traction control. *"I had switched off the launch control, as it wasn't working very well on our car,"* explained Montoya. *"Yes, I made a pretty good start, even though I touched a Sauber at the first corner. After that, I concentrated on not making any mistakes when I saw Ralf had gone off. The car was a bit vicious in some corners."*

 Michael Schumacher profited from Mika Hakkinen's misfortune to win. That's motor racing sometimes.

An unusual podium: while Michael Schumacher is well used to standing on the top step, it was the first time this season that we had seen Juan Pablo Montoya and Jacques Villeneuve put in an appearance.

A pensive Olivier Panis. Having got the better of Jacques Villeneuve since the start of the season, the man from Grenoble finished out of the points, while the Canadian made it to the podium.

 **GRAN PREMIO MARLBORO DE ESPAÑA**

Zoom in on Jenson Button. Just as at Imola, two weeks earlier and as would happen in Austria two weeks later, in Catalunya, the Englishman qualified in the penultimate 21st spot on the grid.
The Benetton team had not got off to a bad start to the season, it was completely catastrophic. In Barcelona, poor Jenson was not helped by a painful shoulder which had bothered him since the Malaysian Grand Prix. In fact, he needed pain-killing injections prior to qualifying.

GRAN PREMIO MARLBORO DE ESPAÑA

Disbelief in the McLaren camp. The breakdown which hit Mika Hakkinen on the final lap of the race, turned a party into a rainy day. On the left, Ron Dennis and his driver don't know what to say after the race. On the right, Erja Hakkinen and the team have just realised what has happened to Mika.
▽

The curse of the final lap

All the drivers are well acquainted with the old adage that to finish first, first you have to finish and it's not over until you take the chequered flag. Mika Hakkinen had time to reflect on that in Barcelona, as his McLaren-Mercedes let him down on the very last lap of the Spanish Grand Prix, when the win was in the bag. Lotus team owner Colin Chapman maintained that the perfect race car was the one which fell apart the moment it crossed the finish line. In Barcelona, the McLaren team came close to demonstrating this idea to perfection, if only this had not happened four kilometres short of the race total of 307.

These things have happened before in F1. On 2nd June 1991 in Montreal, Nigel Mansell retired just two kilometres from the flag, after he waved too early to the crowd and stalled his Williams-Renault!

At Monaco, in 1982, Riccardo Patrese spun on the very last lap, handing the lead to Didier Pironi, whose Ferrari then ran out of fuel a few seconds later. That left Andrea de Cesaris in front, but just at that moment, he retired his Alfa-Romeo at Casino Square with a blown engine.

Usually, these things happen about once every ten years. It was just unlucky for Hakkinen that fate decreed it would be his turn in Barcelona. Knowing that he thus entered the pages of the F1 history book was no doubt of absolutely no consolation to him.

And traction control is back

Bernie Ecclestone produced his own version of the Oscars, by dishing out Formula 1 "Bernies." The first ever recipients were Sid Watkins, Jenson Button, Michael Schumacher and Murray Walker.
▽

Accusations of cheating aimed at some teams were now a thing of the past. Wins were no longer to be accompanied by suspicion. In order to act against the climate of uncertainty as regards the legality of the cars, the FIA had decided to once again allow the use of electronic devices such as traction and launch control. Why? Because the systems were so sophisticated, the sport's governing body had been unable to detect them when used illegally.

From now on, drivers would be able to floor the throttle without any worries. The electronics on the car would do the rest and would ensure the rear wheels would not tie themselves in knots. It would be a great comfort in the wet, but it would also level things out between the very good drivers and the average ones. On top of that, it would now be impossible to mess up the start by getting too much wheelspin. In principle, from Barcelona, all starts would be perfect and with no whiff of tyre smoke.

Unless of course the system was not working properly. Which is exactly what happened in Barcelona on David Coulthard's car and would happen again at several grands prix, especially in the McLaren and Jordan camps. The rule changes affected three areas: traction control, the standing start and completely automatic gearchanges. As far as the engine was concerned, the teams now played with the ignition, the injection and the throttle opening to control how much power was applied under acceleration.

A race of missed opportunities

Tarso Marques in action. In Barcelona, the Brazilian qualified last, which was nearly always the case throughout his season.
▷▽

21st lap. Ralf Schumacher, fourth at the time, spins off into the gravel.
▽

Given the problems encountered by Michael Schumacher and Mika Hakkinen, two drivers, Ralf Schumacher and David Coulthard might have taken up the running, but for problems of their own.

The German, a winner two weeks earlier in Imola, was running fourth when he went off the track on lap 21. *"To be honest, I'm not really sure what happened. The car was going quite well and the race looked like being a good one after two difficult days. The brakes were working fine, when suddenly the car went sideways. It slid into the gravel and got stuck. A shame."*

Michelin's competitions boss Pierre Dupasquier regretted the incident. *"Given what happened later, I can't help thinking that Ralf could have lucked in to the win today,"* was his analysis of what might have been.

David Coulthard had started third and could no doubt have won, if his car had not stalled on the grid before the parade lap, forcing him to start from the back of the pack. Caught up in an accident at the first corner, he was forced to pit to change the front wing. He then had a long afternoon charging through the field, to take fifth place.

PRACTICE TIMES

No	Driver	Car/Engine/Chassis	Practice Friday	Pos.	Practice Saturday	Pos.	Qualifying	Pos.	Warm-up	Pos.
1.	Michael Schumacher	Ferrari/F2001/210	1'20"880	5°	1'18"634	1°	1'18"201	1°	1'21"211	4°
2.	Ruben Barrichello	Ferrari/F2001/206	1'20"823	3°	1'18"674	2°	1'18"674	4°	1'20"680	1°
3.	Mika Häkkinen	McLaren/Mercedes/MP4/16/4	1'20"894	6°	1'19"281	8°	1'18"286	2°	1'20"901	2°
4.	David Coulthard	McLaren/Mercedes/MP4/16/5	1'20"107	1°	1'18"686	3°	1'18"635	3°	1'21"148	3°
5.	Ralf Schumacher	Williams/BMW/FW23/5	1'21"259	8°	1'19"406	9°	1'19"016	5°	1'21"886	7°
6.	Juan Pablo Montoya	Williams/BMW/FW23/2	1'22"020	13°	1'20"202	12°	1'19"660	12°	1'22"558	11°
7.	Giancarlo Fisichella	Benetton/Renault/B201/3	1'22"971	18°	1'21"404	18°	1'21"065	19°	1'24"468	20°
8.	Jenson Button	Benetton/Renault/B201/5	1'23"201	19°	1'21"804	20°	1'21"916	21°	1'23"754	15°
9.	Olivier Panis	BAR/Honda/003/6	1'20"826	4°	1'19"253	7°	1'19"479	11°	1'21"558	5°
10.	Jaques Villeneuve	BAR/Honda/003/5	1'21"401	9°	1'19"577	10°	1'19"122	7°	1'22"120	9°
11.	Heinz-Harald Frentzen	Jordan/Honda/EJ11/4	1'22"221	14°	1'19"903	11°	1'19"150	8°	1'21"558	6°
12.	Jarno Trulli	Jordan/Honda/EJ11/5	1'21"647	10°	1'19"186	6°	1'19"093	6°	1'21"929	8°
14.	Jos Verstappen	Arrows/Asiatech/A22/6	1'22"962	17°	1'21"069	16°	1'20"737	17°	1'23"240	13°
15.	Enrique Bernoldi	Arrows/Asiatech/A22/3	1'22"888	16°	1'20"997	15°	1'20"696	16°	1'24"138	18°
16.	Nick Heidfeld	Sauber/Petronas/C20/5	1'21"808	12°	1'19"010	5°	1'19"232	10°	1'22"343	10°
17.	Kimi Räikkönen	Sauber/Petronas/C20/1	1'21"786	11°	1'18"765	4°	1'19"229	9°	1'22"864	12°
18.	Eddie Irvine	Jaguar/R-2/4	1'20"615	2°	1'21"289	17°	1'20"326	13°	1'23"294	14°
19.	Pedro de la Rosa	Jaguar/R-2/3	1'21"184	7°	1'22"296	21°	1'21"338	20°	1'23"847	17°
20.	Tarso Marques	Minardi/European/PS01/4	1'25"540	22°	1'24"371	22°	1'22"522	22°	1'24"924	22°
21.	Fernando Alonso	Minardi/European/PS01/1	1'23"801	20°	1'21"493	19°	1'21"037	18°	1'24"361	19°
22.	Jean Alesi	Prost/Acer/AP04/5	1'22"843	15°	1'20"741	13°	1'20"601	15°	1'23"794	16°
23.	Luciano Burti	Prost/Acer/AP04/4	1'23"885	21°	1'20"801	14°	1'20"585	14°	1'24"633	21°

MAXIMUM SPEEDS

No	Driver	P1 Qualifs	Pos	P1 Race	Pos	P2 Qualifs	Pos	P2 Race	Pos	Finish Qualifs	Pos	Finish Race	Pos	Trap Qualifs	Pos	Trap Race	Pos
1	M.Schumacher	290,1	5°	282,4	2°	303,7	4°	298,5	8°	286,4	5°	280,3	4°	313,7	9°	311,0	14°
2	R. Barrichello	294,5	1°	278,1	6°	304,3	2°	298,6	6°	288,0	3°	278,7	8°	314,1	6°	307,6	19°
3	Mika Häkkinen	291,4	2°	281,9	3°	301,4	5°	300,1	4°	287,3	4°	281,0	3°	313,1	10°	320,7	1°
4	David Coulthard	290,2	4°	280,0	4°	300,5	7°	301,7	3°	283,9	13°	280,0	6°	311,1	13°	318,7	2°
5	R.Schumacher	290,8	3°	278,4	5°	304,2	3°	302,0	2°	289,0	2°	283,8	1°	318,0	2°	317,1	5°
6	J. P. Montoya	285,7	15°	272,7	11°	305,6	1°	302,7	1°	290,1	1°	282,2	2°	321,5	1°	318,2	4°
7	G. Fisichella	285,7	16°	260,7	19°	292,4	20°	289,5	21°	277,7	20°	271,0	21°	307,6	19°	305,1	20°
8	Jenson Button	281,2	19°	270,9	13°	290,1	22°	289,5	20°	275,3	21°	271,3	20°	304,9	21°	304,8	21°
9	Olivier Panis	286,0	14°	271,6	12°	301,0	6°	296,9	11°	284,1	11°	280,3	5°	314,5	5°	316,9	6°
10	J. Villeneuve	284,4	17°	269,3	15°	300,5	9°	298,5	7°	285,9	6°	278,4	11°	315,1	3°	313,4	8°
11	H.-H. Frentzen	287,8	11°	260,5	20°	299,7	11°	297,1	9°	284,8	8°	275,0	17°	310,7	16°	313,4	9°
12	Jarno Trulli	290,0	6°	277,3	7°	299,8	10°	296,3	15°	283,0	15°	276,4	15°	311,0	14°	312,5	10°
14	Jos Verstappen	287,9	10°	269,6	14°	297,6	16°	298,6	5°	281,6	17°	278,9	7°	310,7	15°	318,4	3°
15	E. Bernoldi	282,0	18°	266,0	16°	299,7	12°	292,7	19°	283,1	14°	275,0	19°	310,2	17°	308,3	18°
16	Nick Heidfeld	287,0	12°	274,5	9°	298,8	14°	296,9	12°	284,5	9°	278,4	12°	312,1	12°	312,2	11°
17	Kimi Räikkönen	288,6	9°	283,1	1°	300,5	8°	297,0	10°	285,8	7°	278,7	9°	314,8	4°	311,5	13°
18	Eddie Irvine	286,9	13°	275,7	8°	297,6	18°	296,8	13°	282,6	16°	278,4	10°	313,8	7°	309,9	15°
19	P. de la Rosa	279,2	20°	257,3	22°	296,2	19°	295,3	17°	278,7	19°	275,2	16°	307,5	20°	314,9	7°
20	Tarso Marques	275,7	21°	258,9	21°	291,1	21°	288,7	20°	274,0	22°	267,9	22°	303,6	22°	303,2	22°
21	F. Alonso	273,9	22°	263,7	18°	298,0	15°	293,0	18°	280,1	18°	275,0	18°	308,5	18°	309,1	17°
22	Jean Alesi	289,2	8°	273,0	10°	299,0	13°	295,9	16°	284,2	10°	276,7	14°	313,7	8°	309,2	16°
23	L. Burti	289,5	7°	264,8	17°	297,6	17°	296,3	14°	283,9	12°	278,2	13°	312,2	11°	312,0	12°

CLASSIFICATION & RETIREMENTS

Pos	Driver	Team	Time
1.	M. Schum.	Ferrari	1:31:03.305
2.	Montoya	Williams BMW	+ 40.738
3.	Villeneuve	BAR Honda	+ 49.626
4.	Trulli	Jordan Honda	+ 51.253
5.	Coulthard	McLaren Mercedes	+51.616
6.	Heidfeld	Sauber Petronas	+61.893
7.	Panis	BAR Honda	+ 64.977
8.	Räikkönen	Sauber Petronas	+ 79.808
9.	Häkkinen	McLaren Mercedes	DNF/engine
10.	Alesi	Prost Acer	+ 1 lap
11.	Burti	Prost Acer	+ 1 lap
12.	Verstappen	Arrows Asiatech	+ 2 laps
13.	Alonso	European Minardi	+ 2 laps
14.	Fisichella	Benetton Renault	+ 2 laps
15.	Button	Benetton Renault	+ 3 laps
16.	Marques	European Minardi	+ 3 laps

Lap	Driver	Team	Reason
6	Frentzen	Jordan-Honda	accident
6	de la Rosa	Jaguar Racing	accident
9	Bernoldi	Arrows Asiatech	fuel pressure
21	R. Schum.	Williams BMW	spin
49	Irvine	Jaguar Racing	engine
50	Barrichello	Ferrari	rear suspension broken

FASTEST LAPS

Driver	Time	Lap
1. M. Schum.	1'21"151 209,831 km/h	25
2. Häkkinen	1'21"368	49
3. Barrichello	1'21"720	27
4. Coulthard	1'22"091	41
5. R. Schum.	1'22"362	19
6. Panis	1'22"475	26
7. Villeneuve	1'22"513	22
8. Irvine	1'22"568	23
9. Heidfeld	1'22"738	26
10. Montoya	1'22"841	39
11. Räikkönen	1'23"049	40
12. Trulli	1'23"087	24
13. Alesi	1'23"668	20
14. Burti	1'23"794	23
15. Verstappen	1'23"965	17
16. Alonso	1'24"423	37
17. Bernoldi	1'24"740	4
18. Fisichella	1'25"298	14
19. Button	1'25"406	57
20. Marques	1'25"791	16
21. de la Rosa	1'25"932	3
22. Frentzen	1'26"158	3

All results : © 2001 Fédération Internationale de l'Automobile, 2, Ch. Blandonnet, 1215 Genève 15, Suisse

PIT STOPS

	Drivers	Time	Lap	Stop n°
1.	Bernoldi	35"653	1	1
2.	Coulthard	38"373	1	1
3.	Alonso	33"030	16	1
4.	Button	44"060	17	1
5.	Marques	33"593	18	1
6.	Verstappen	32"580	19	1
7.	Trulli	31"928	21	1
8.	Montoya	30"231	21	1
9.	M. Schumacher	30"745	23	1
10.	Villeneuve	31"350	23	1
11.	Räikkönen	30"892	23	1
12.	Alesi	33"048	23	1
13.	Fisichella	37"655	23	1
14.	Heidfeld	29"561	24	1
15.	Irvine	32"352	24	1
16.	Panis	43"931	24	1
17.	Burti	32"304	24	1
18.	Barrichello	30"957	25	1
19.	Häkkinen	31"157	27	1
20.	Coulthard	30"748	28	2
21.	Räikkönen	32"454	38	2
22.	Heidfeld	32"204	39	2
23.	Verstappen	33"259	39	2
24.	Trulli	32"143	40	2
25.	Alonso	32"901	39	2
26.	Montoya	32"362	41	2
27.	Villeneuve	31"844	41	2
28.	Fisichella	31"631	40	2
29.	M. Schumacher	31"194	43	2
30.	Marques	33"061	41	2
31.	Button	38"215	41	2
32.	Panis	31"275	43	2
33.	Barrichello	31"764	44	2
34.	Coulthard	30"185	44	3
35.	Irvine	31"366	45	2
36.	Burti	31"174	47	2
37.	Barrichello	29"205	48	3
38.	Häkkinen	30"433	50	2
39.	Alesi	29"695	50	2

BRIDGESTONE

Best result for a driver running Bridgestone tyre:

Michael Schumacher, Ferrari, winner

CHAMPIONSHIP

(after five rounds)

Drivers :

1. M. Schumacher 36
2. D. Coulthard 28
3. R. Barrichello 14
4. R. Schumacher 12
5. N. Heidfeld 8
6. J. Trulli 7
7. H.-H. Frentzen 6
   J. P. Montoya 6
9. M. Häkkinen 4
   J. Villeneuve 4
11. O. Panis 3
12. K. Räikkönen 1
    G. Fisichella 1

Constructors :

1. Ferrari 50
2. McLaren Mercedes 32
3. Williams BMW 18
4. Jordan Honda 13
5. Sauber Petronas..............................9
6. BAR Honda 7
7. Benetton Renault 1

THE CIRCUIT

FIFTH ROUND

GRAN PREMIO MARLBORO DE ESPAÑA, CATALUNYA

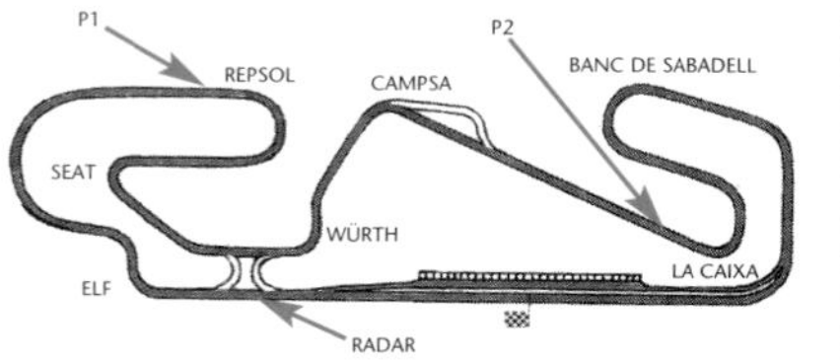

P1
P2
REPSOL
CAMPSA
BANC DE SABADELL
SEAT
WÜRTH
ELF
LA CAIXA
RADAR

Date :	April 29, 2001
Length :	4730 meters
Distance :	65 laps, 307.323 km
Weather :	cloudy and dry, 7°

RACE SUMMARY

- Coulthard's McLaren refuses to budge at the start of the formation lap. The Scotsman is forced to start from the back of the grid.
- Michael Schumacher makes the best start ahead of Hakkinen. At the back, Couthard collides with another car and has to pit for a new nose. It's not his day.
- On lap 12, Montoya passes Trulli during the pits stops, both drivers having come in at the same time.
- On lap 21, Montoya passes Trulli in the pit stops, both men having come in at the same time.
- On lap 24, Panis refuels and loses a lot of time because of a computer problem.
- Still in the lead, Michael Schumacher pits for the second time on lap 43.
- In second place, Hakkinen steps up the pace and refuels seven laps later. He rejoins in the lead.
- Hakkinen seems to have the race in the bag, but he slows and stops on the final lap. Michael Schumacher takes the win.

LAP CHART

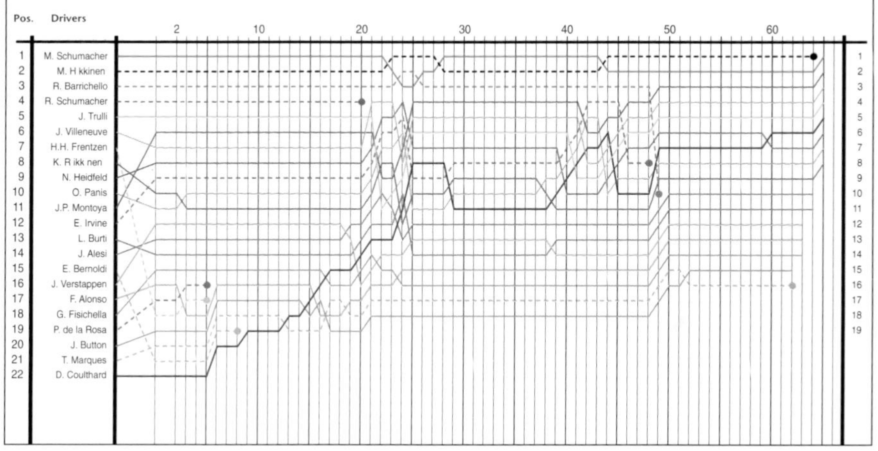

Pos.
Drivers
2
10
20
30
40
50
60
M. Schumacher
M. H kkinen
R. Barrichello
R. Schumacher
J. Trulli
J. Villeneuve
H.H. Frentzen
K. R ikk nen
N. Heidfeld
O. Panis
J.P. Montoya
E. Irvine
L. Burti
J. Alesi
E. Bernoldi
J. Verstappen
F. Alonso
G. Fisichella
P. de la Rosa
J. Button
T. Marques
D. Coulthard

GAPS ON THE LEADER BOARD

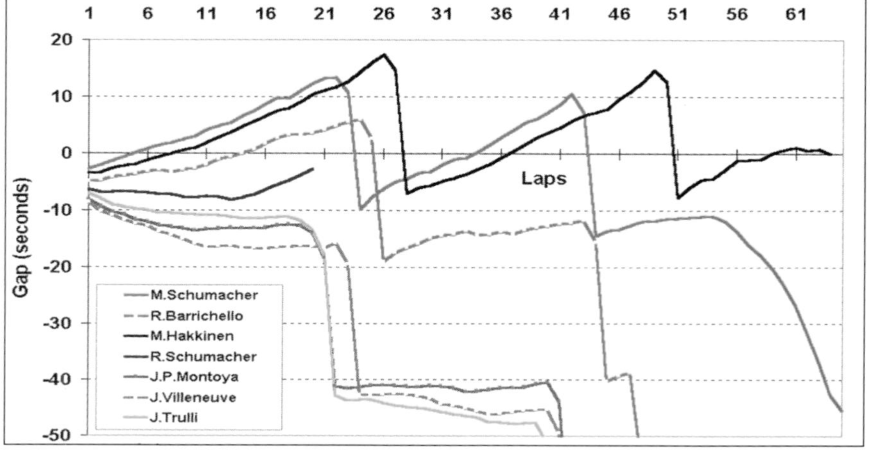

1
6
11
16
21
26
31
36
41
46
51
56
61
Laps
Gap (seconds)
20
10
0
-10
-20
-30
-40
-50
M.Schumacher
R.Barrichello
M.Hakkinen
R.Schumacher
J.P.Montoya
J.Villeneuve
J.Trulli

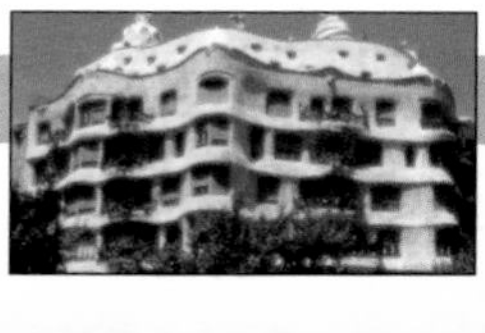

Seven to one for David Coulthard

What a race! Four cars stalled on the grid, the Safety Car called out, a merciless duel between Juan Pablo Montoya and Michael Schumacher, which ended with both of them in the gravel, then David Coulthard taking the lead during the pit stops: the Austrian Grand Prix was hard fought from the first to the last lap.

Starting from seventh place on the grid, the Scotsman made the most of problems afflicting the others to take his second victory of the season.

GROSSER A1 PREIS VON ÖSTERREICH
SPIELBERG

"Whoops!" Michael Schumacher, giving it everything in qualifying, goes off into the gravel to avoid Jos Verstappen's Arrows. It was a harmless excursion, as he still ended up on pole.

The splendour that is Zeltweg. In the month of May, the surrounding hills were still topped with snow, adding to the beauty of the Austrian countryside.

In Zeltweg, Eddie Irvine qualified thirteenth for the fourth time in a row. The Jaguar team still had a lot of work to do to get onto the road to success.

STARTING GRID

M. SCHUMACHER 1'09"562	-1-	J. P. MONTOYA 1'09"686	
Ralf SCHUMACHER 1'09"789	-2-	R. BARRICHELLO 1'09"789	
Jarno TRULLI 1'10"202	-3-	Nick HEIDFELD 1'10"211	
David COULTHARD 1'10"331	-4-	Mika HÄKKINEN 1'10"331	
Kimi RÄIKKÖNEN 1'10"396	-5-	Olivier PANIS 1'10"435	
H.-H. FRENTZEN 1'10"923	-6-	Jacques VILLENEUVE 1'11"058	
Eddie IRVINE 1'11"632	-7-	Pedro De la Rosa 1'11"752	
Enrique BERNOLDI 1'11"823	-8-	Jos VERSTAPPEN 1'12"187	
Luciano BURTI 1'12"206	-9-	Fernando ALONSO 1'12"640	
Giancarlo FISICHELLA 1'12"644	-10-	Jean ALESI 1'12"910	
Jenson BUTTON 1'13"459	-11-	Tarso MARQUES 1'13"585	

A Ferrari in front, the Williams wait in ambush

Juan Pablo Montoya alongside him, Ralf Schumacher right behind: Michael Schumacher was not in the most comfortable of positions at the start of the Austrian Grand Prix, except that he was on pole.

The Ferrari driver was surrounded by the two Williams-BMW, which could make the most of their Michelin tyres to gain the upper hand. "We made a lot of improvements to the car in testing, last week in Valencia, but we are still a good second off the McLarens," reckoned Ralf Schumacher after qualifying. "That's why I'm very surprised that we are a few tenths ahead of them here. But it's always difficult to find the limit of the car on this track. I don't know what will happen in the race, but we should be quite competitive. Especially in the second half of the race, when there will be more rubber on the track."

Naturally, Ralf was a bit disappointed to be out-qualified by Juan Pablo Montoya.

"It's always tough to be beaten by your team-mate, but never mind, it happens sometimes. I'm not surprised. In Brazil, Juan Pablo showed everyone he can be very quick."

Juan Pablo himself was surprised at his performance. "Given how the morning session went, I didn't think I could get on the front row, ahead of the McLarens," admitted the Colombian. "I think the track was quickest in the middle of the session and that's exactly when I went out. But, I have to say things are getting better for us. Normally, Friday is always difficult, but not this time. We were able to really work on our set up." On Saturday, Michael Schumacher spent quite a bit of time working out exactly at what point his tyres were at their best. "I wasn't sure if it was best to go for one or two quick laps today. I tried a bit of everything," admitted the world champion. The second ploy might have worked for him, except that Jos Verstappen spun right in front of

him. "I was going very quickly at that point and when I saw Jos sliding, I thought I could go straight past. But his car came back onto the track, I had to swerve and that sent me into the gravel. It was nothing serious and I immediately worked out where his car was heading."

With the McLaren drivers being a long way back, the world champion could afford to be confident. "But I am not ruling out their chances of winning," offered Schumacher. They usually make good starts and could easily be fourth or fifth on the first lap and move up from there. I am sure they will sort out their problems before the race." He didn't know how right he would be.

A crazy race in Zeltweg

Against all expectations, the sixth round of the 2001 championship finally turned to the advantage of David Coulthard and his McLaren, even though he started from seventh on the grid after a disastrous qualifying session. *"Last night, I dreamed I won the race, after emerging from the wreckage of a first corner crash,"* said the Scotsman after the race. *"I could never have imagined that things would happen the way they did, with the Williams holding up the Ferraris."*

Having made a bad start, Michael Schumacher did indeed lose the advantage of pole position, to find himself stuck behind the two Williams-BMWs during the opening laps. *"From where I was, I could see it was obvious something was going to go off between Montoya and Michael (Schumacher,)* continued Coulthard. *It was not a question of if it was going to happen, but of where and when."* The Scotsman was right. On lap 16,

the Williams took the Ferrari with it into the gravel. Michael Schumacher was now sixth, having to pass Olivier Panis and Kimi Raikkonen before getting back to the leaders. Making the most of the pit stops, Coulthard took the lead on lap 47, never to relinquish it all the way to the chequered flag. *"From where I was starting on the grid, I had taken on a heavy fuel load, so that way we could be flexible when it came to race strategy, according to how the race developed,"* explained the McLaren man. *"Luckily the Safety Car was brought out in the early stages and that meant I could save fuel."* Staying out on the track for longer than Rubens Barrichello, Coulthard emerged from the pit lane in the lead with just 24 laps remaining. *"I was flat out for all the race,"* he concluded. *"It was great fun. That what grands prix should be like. Our car was not very easy to drive today and I had to be very careful, but it's a fantastic result."*

Three points eventually

The Sauber team lived through an amazing day in Austria. Qualified sixth and ninth, the two Swiss cars had every chance of picking up some points in the Austrian Grand Prix. However, at the start, half their chances went out the window, when Nick Heidfeld was left stranded on the grid. For his part, Kimi Raikkonen was valiantly defending the team colours. Eighth at the end of the opening lap, he managed to climb as high as third by lap 24, before finishing fourth, passed only by Michael Schumacher. It was an excellent result, confirmed only four hours after the end of the race. This was because the BAR team had protested Raikkonen for having overtaken Luciano Burti under yellow flags. The Austrian Stewards finally rejected the protest.

The three points that came with this result pushed the Sauber equipe over the total of 100 Formula 1 points. In the Constructors' classification, the Swiss team was now fifth, just one little point behind the Jordan-Honda team.

Launch control fails take-off

The return of launch control, authorised since the last Spanish Grand Prix, had not been a trouble free experience. In Barcelona, Heinz-Harald Frentzen and David Coulthard completely botched their starts because of a failure of their systems.

In Austria, when most people reckoned these problems had been consigned to the past, no less than four cars were left glued to the grid when the red lights went out: the two Jordan-Hondas, Nick Heidfeld's Sauber and Mika Hakkinen's McLaren. It was a cruel blow for this quartet of drivers. *"It's terribly disappointing,"* admitted Mika Hakkinen, before skulking out of the circuit. *"I don't know what happened. Maybe it was a technical problem, maybe it was my fault. We will have to see. But, of course, my chances of winning the world championship are even less likely now."*

In the Jordan camp, neither car got off the line. Heinz-Harald Frentzen's problem was a broken gearbox, whereas in Jarno Trulli's case the culprit was a stalled engine. Once on his way, the Italian was black flagged for having failed to stop at a red light at the pit lane exit.

Nick Heidfeld's Sauber had an electrical problem. He eventually got going, one lap behind the field and was classified ninth.

Michael Schumacher was not immune to electrical gremlins. *"The car did not get off the line the way it should have done and when I realised something was up, I had to make a manual start. It cost me a lot of time,"* explained the world champion. *"I am*

convinced we will sort these problems. These systems are still quite new and so these problems are understandable."

Williams debacle

Having made impeccable starts than to a well adjusted launch control system, the two Williams led the charge for the first part of the race.

However, on lap eleven, Ralf Schumacher, who was lying second, was forced to retire after losing pressure in his braking system. *"The brake pedal got progressively longer and longer and in the end, I had no brakes at all,"* explained Ralf.

Out in front, Juan Pablo Montoya was doing his best to fight off the advances of Michael Schumacher, the Colombian also suffering from minor brake problems. He lost the lead on lap 16, going off into the gravel trying to ward off an attack from the Ferrari. *"It was just a racing accident,"* reckoned Montoya. *"Michael braked late, me too. I locked the wheels and the car went sideways."*

Schumacher did not agree with the Colombian's version of events. *"Normally, I enjoy this sort of fight, but not this time. I think Juan Pablo was not looking where he was going. He was just looking to see where I was to make sure I went off with him. It was stupid."*

Rejoining seventh, Juan Pablo Montoya finally retired on lap 42 with hydraulic problems.

△
I''ve won! David Coulthard came from a long way back to take a victory which put him back in the hunt for the world championship. Below: the podium.

There was such chaos on the starting grid that the Safety Car was immediately brought out to calm things down. At that time, the two Williams led the two Ferraris.

◁

Lap 16: Juan Pablo Montoya tries to fight off Michael Schumacher at the top of the hill at the second corner. A slightly optimistic braking ended in the gravel for the Colombian.

 **GROSSER A1 PREIS VON ÖSTERREICH**

Jarno Trulli at work in the Styrian hills. In Zeltweg, the Italian was one of the victims of the latest plague; faulty launch control. Starting last behind everyone, the Italian was finally disqualified and shown the black flag for ignoring the red light at the pit lane exit.

GROSSER A1 PREIS VON ÖSTERREICH

paddock

▷△
An exciting off for Jos Verstappen during Friday's practice. Nevertheless, the Dutchman had a good Austrian Grand Prix, finishing sixth to score his only point of the season.

▷
Having been outpaced by Jacques Villeneuve in Spain, Olivier Panis regained the upper hand in Austria. The Frenchman qualified two places ahead of his team-mate and scored two points, while the Canadian finished eighth.

The magnificent Zeltweg track seen from the air.
▷▽

After his off-track excursion on Saturday, Michael Schumacher was back in the gravel trap on Sunday!
▽

WEEKEND GOSSIP

• Ron confirms equal status

Ron Dennis denied favouring Mika Hakkinen, as the English press had been claiming for several weeks. "Of course I was affected by what happened in 1995 in Australia, when I had to go and see Mika in hospital," admitted the McLaren boss. "Who would not be affected by something like that? But that doesn't mean I favour him. I treat both my drivers in exactly the same way in all circumstances."

• Death of Paul Morgan

Paul Morgan, the Managing Director of Ilmor Engineering (the company which produces the Mercedes Formula 1 engines) died on the Saturday of this event in a light aircraft crash. The single engined plane he was flying crashed on landing at an English airfield. His tragic death badly affected his Swiss partner Mario Illien, who founded Ilmor with Paul Morgan. (Ilmor taking its name from their two names.)

• A Moscow Grand Prix

It now seemed certain that a grand prix would be organised in Moscow. In Zeltweg, the Austrians were worried about their event disappearing from the calendar, given that one race would have to go to make way for Moscow. Bernie Ecclestone held a press conference in Austria on Friday to explain that the track would be built on the island of Nagatino, in Moscow itself. Work would start immediately, with a budget of 170 million Swiss Francs financed by the city.

• A new flying palace for Schumi

Michael Schumacher had just bought a new private jet; a latest generation Falcon 2000, which can carry up to 19 people at 900 km/h. The cost: 24 million Euros. Rather more modestly, his brother Ralf was renting a Hawker Horizon when he needed it.

• Black mood at Benetton

The Benetton team is not happy. In Zeltweg on Friday, its two cars ended practice at the bottom of the time sheet, behind the Minardis! The team blamed the new engine for all its woes, with its 111 degree V angle. But the French engine constructor made the team fit a Supertec engine in the Benetton chassis the week after the race, to prove to the team that its chassis was far from perfect. A nice friendly atmosphere then!

• Di Montezemolo a minister?

Silvio Berlusconi had tried to entice Luca di Montezemolo to join his government as minister of sport or minister of external affairs. "It was all supposed to be secret until Sunday night," said a surprised Montezemolo in Zeltweg. "It's true I thought about it." A few days later, he turned down the offer.

Rubens' dream flies away

Lap 71 of the race. On the pit wall, Jean Todt is getting agitated. He can be seen frantically pressing buttons and speaking at length. He is talking to both his drivers and asking Rubens Barrichello, who is preparing to finish second, to let Michael Schumacher, who is just behind, pass him. For the Brazilian, who led for 31 of these 71 laps of the Austrian Grand Prix, the dream of victory disappeared a long time ago.

Finally, at the exit to the last corner on the last lap, just a few metres from the flag, that "Rubinho" slowed down and let Schumacher through. *"I waited for the last corner, because it is not easy to drive flat out, concentrating on all the controls in front of you, while at the same time, thinking about your contract, what it says and what obliges me to let Michael pass,"* explained Barrichello after the race. *"All that while having to listen to Jean Todt, who asked me several times to give up my position....it really wasn't easy!"*

When Eddie Irvine drove for Ferrari, from 1996 to 1999, the Irishman adopted the philosophical approach in these situations. He knew what it meant to drive for Ferrari and he was there more to pick up a nice salary, rather than to win races. Rubens Barrichello preferred to adopt a more sporting philosophy. He had already been asked to help Michael in the past, but only towards the end of the championship. It never had happened as early as this in Austria, when he was still in with a chance of the title. *"I am very disappointed,"* concluded the little Brazilian. *"Having said that, I cannot explain it in public. I spoke too much in Malaysia and that gave me some bother. I have to speak to the team so that I can say what I feel."*

As far as Schumacher was concer-ned, the matter was straight-forward. *"After Mika retired, one could easily*

Jean Todt on the pit wall

see which driver McLaren was going to favour. We have to concentrate on that. Imagine that I miss out on the title for just two points at the end of the season. It would be absurd. There is too much pressure and money in Formula 1 to contemplate it. Team orders have always been part of F1 and McLaren apply them too."

PRACTICE TIMES

No	Driver	Car/Engine/Chassis	Practice Friday	Pos.	Practice Saturday	Pos.	Qualifying	Pos.	Warm-up	Pos.
1.	Michael Schumacher	Ferrari/F2001/210	1'11"647	5°	1'10"039	2°	1'09"562	1°	1'12"790	5°
2.	Rubens Barrichello	Ferrari/F2001/206	1'11"401	3°	1'10"103	3°	1'09"786	4°	1'12"331	4°
3.	Mika Häkkinen	McLaren/Mercedes/MP4/16/4	1'11"272	2°	1'10"148	4°	1'10"342	8°	1'11"647	1°
4.	David Coulthard	McLaren/Mercedes/MP4/16/5	1'11"245	1°	1'10"010	1°	1'10"331	7°	1'11"765	2°
5.	Ralf Schumacher	Williams/BMW/FW23/5	1'11"555	4°	1'10"397	6°	1'09"769	3°	1'13"549	15°
6.	Juan Pablo Montoya	Williams/BMW/FW23/4	1'12"299	11°	1'10"391	5°	1'09"686	2°	1'13"558	16°
7.	Giancarlo Fisichella	Benetton/Renault/B201/3	1'14"833	21°	1'13"345	19°	1'12"644	19°	1'15"662	21°
8.	Jenson Button	Benetton/Renault/B201/5	1'15"570	22°	1'13"969	22°	1'13"459	21°	1'15"692	22°
9.	Olivier Panis	BAR/Honda/003/6	1'12"259	9°	1'11"351	11°	1'10"435	10°	1'13"221	11°
10.	Jacques Villeneuve	BAR/Honda/003/5	1'12"290	10°	1'10"935	10°	1'11"058	12°	1'13"012	8°
11.	Heinz-Harald Frentzen	Jordan/Honda/EJ11/6	1'11"977	7°	1'10"434	7°	1'10"923	11°	1'11"800	3°
12.	Jarno Trulli	Jordan/Honda/EJ11/5	1'12"555	13°	1'10"751	8°	1'10"202	5°	1'12"993	6°
14.	Jos Verstappen	Arrows/Asiatech/A22/6	1'12"705	14°	1'11"831	14°	1'12"187	16°	1'13"548	14°
15.	Enrique Bernoldi	Arrows/Asiatech/A22/3	1'12"853	16°	1'12"029	16°	1'11"823	15°	1'13"543	13°
16.	Nick Heidfeld	Sauber/Petronas/C20/5	1'11"776	6°	1'10"863	9°	1'10"211	6°	1'13"201	10°
17.	Kimi Räikkönen	Sauber/Petronas/C20/6	1'12"189	8°	1'11"382	12°	1'10"396	9°	1'13"005	7°
18.	Eddie Irvine	Jaguar/R-2/4	1'12"346	12°	1'11"543	13°	1'11"632	13°	1'13"406	12°
19.	Pedro de la Rosa	Jaguar/R-2/3	1'12"847	15°	1'11"994	15°	1'11"752	14°	1'13"149	9°
20.	Tarso Marques	Minardi/European/PS01/4	1'14"314	19°	1'13"968	20°	1'13"585	22°	1'15"265	19°
21.	Fernando Alonso	Minardi/European/PS01/3	1'14"523	20°	1'13"333	18°	1'12"640	18°	1'14"745	18°
22.	Jean Alesi	Prost/Acer/AP04/6	1'13"288	18°	1'13"485	21°	1'12"910	20°	1'14"611	17°
23.	Luciano Burti	Prost/Acer/AP04/4	1'13"169	17°	1'12"714	17°	1'12"206	17°	1'15"487	20°

MAXIMUM SPEEDS

No	Driver	P1 Qualifs	Pos	P1 Race	Pos	P2 Qualifs	Pos	P2 Race	Pos	Finish Qualifs	Pos	Finish Race	Pos	Trap Qualifs	Pos	Trap Race	Pos
1.	M. Schumacher	305,7	7°	308,0	7°	210,8	2°	202,5	5°	278,9	5°	275,6	5°	302,0	5°	306,9	2°
2.	R. Barrichello	307,5	4°	310,2	1°	206,6	10°	203,8	3°	282,5	3°	277,2	2°	303,2	4°	304,9	5°
3.	M. Häkkinen	302,5	15°	269,1	20°	208,8	6°	154,3	21°	276,7	12°			296,8	15°	184,9	21°
4.	D. Coulthard	304,3	12°	308,7	5°	208,5	6°	207,1	1°	276,9	10°	275,6	6°	297,9	12°	303,6	8°
5.	R. Schumacher	311,2	1°	302,4	15°	206,1	11°	196,6	13°	283,4	2°	271,0	14°	305,2	2°	296,6	17°
6.	J. P. Montoya	310,1	2°	309,1	3°	212,3	1°	200,7	8°	283,9	1°	280,5	1°	305,5	1°	308,4	1°
7.	G. Fisichella	296,9	20°	298,7	18°	198,4	21°	180,9	20°	269,1	20°	197,7	20°	293,4	20°	273,6	20°
8.	J. Button	294,9	21°	297,8	18°	198,7	20°	194,7	17°	268,8	21°	266,8	17°	291,1	21°	296,8	16°
9.	O. Panis	307,6	3°	306,0	10°	206,6	9°	200,5	9°	276,7	11°	275,4	7°	300,9	9°	300,2	12°
10.	J. Villeneuve	300,3	17°	309,5	2°	205,2	12°	198,9	11°	276,0	13°	274,8	9°	296,7	16°	306,1	3°
11.	H.-H. Frentzen	305,6	8°	-		209,7	8°	-		275,3	16°			301,7	7°	-	
12.	J. Trulli	305,9	6°	306,2	9°	208,4	7°	195,5	14°	277,8	7°	271,3	13°	301,0	8°	298,4	15°
14.	J. Verstappen	306,7	5°	309,0	4°	201,4	13°	200,4	10°	280,1	4°	275,7	4°	303,3	3°	303,8	7°
15.	E. Bernoldi	305,6	9°	308,3	6°	200,3	19°	195,5	15°	277,1	9°	273,4	11°	301,8	6°	298,4	14°
16.	N. Heidfeld	302,7	14°	306,7	8°	209,9	3°	203,7	4°	278,7	6°	275,0	8°	297,1	14°	305,3	4°
17.	K. Räikkönen	302,4	16°	305,2	11°	209,6	4°	204,2	2°	277,2	8°	277,1	3°	296,5	17°	304,1	6°
18.	E. Irvine	300,1	18°	302,6	14°	200,7	15°	201,2	6°	273,9	18°	274,4	10°	296,4	18°	302,4	9°
19.	P. de la Rosa	303,3	13°	304,3	12°	201,3	14°	192,7	18°	276,0	14°	271,6	12°	298,0	11°	300,9	11°
20.	T. Marques	291,1	22°	296,7	19°	200,6	16°	186,7	19°	267,1	22°	264,9	19°	289,9	22°	293,1	18°
21.	F. Alonso	298,4	19°	298,2	17°	200,4	18°	195,4	16°	271,2	19°	266,2	18°	294,3	19°	292,8	19°
22.	J. Alesi	305,0	10°	301,0	16°	196,1	22°	198,3	12°	275,8	15°	270,5	16°	297,3	13°	299,5	13°
23.	L. Burti	304,9	11°	304,3	13°	200,5	17°	201,2	7°	274,5	17°	270,8	15°	298,7	10°	302,3	10°

CLASSIFICATION & RETIREMENTS

Pos	Driver	Team	Time
1.	Coulthard	McLaren Mercedes	1:27:45.927
2.	M. Schum.	Ferrari	+ 2.191
3.	Barrichello	Ferrari	+ 2.528
4.	Räikkönen	Sauber Petronas	+ 41.594
5.	Panis	BAR Honda	+ 53.776
6.	Verstappen	Arrows Asiatech	+ 1 lap
7.	Irvine	Jaguar Racing	+ 1 lap
8.	Villeneuve	BAR Honda	+ 1 lap
9.	Heidfeld	Sauber Petronas	+ 2 laps
10.	Alesi	Prost Acer	+ 2 laps
11.	Burti	Prost Acer	+ 2 laps

Lap	Driver	Team	Reason
0	Frentzen	Jordan Honda	gearbox at the start
0	Häkkinen	McLaren Mercedes	electronics
4	Fisichella	Benetton Renault	engine
11	R. Schum.	Williams BMW	brakes
15	Trulli	Jordan Honda	balck flag
18	Bernoldi	Arrows Asiatech	hydraulic
26	Marques	European Minardi	gearbox
39	Alonso	European Minardi	clutch
42	Montoya	Williams BMW	hydraulic
49	de la Rosa	Jaguar Racing	transmission
61	Button	Benetton Renault	oil leak

All results : © 2001 Fédération Internationale de l'Automobile, 2 Ch. Blandonnet, 1215 Genève 15, Suisse

FASTEST LAPS

Driver	Time	Lap
1. Coulthard	1'10"843	48
	219,832 km/h	
2. Barrichello	1'11"009	68
3. M. Schum.	1'11"030	69
4. Montoya	1'11"140	40
5. Räikkönen	1'11"284	70
6. Heidfeld	1'11"388	69
7. Villeneuve	1'11"718	70
8. Irvine	1'12"088	69
9. Panis	1'12"204	39
10. Verstappen	1'12"423	36
11. Burti	1'12"642	69
12. Alesi	1'13"130	41
13. Button	1'13"498	38
14. Bernoldi	1'13"587	15
15. R. Schum.	1'13"888	7
16. de la Rosa	1'13"978	35
17. Trulli	1'14"082	12
18. Alonso	1'14"432	36
19. Marques	1'15"212	25
20. Fisichella	1'58"438	2

PIT STOPS

Drivers	Time	Lap	Stop n°

NO TIMING INFORMATION AVAILABLE DUE TO A TECHNICAL FAULT

Best result for a driver running Bridgestone tyre:

David Coulthard, McLaren Mercedes, winner

THE CIRCUIT

SIXTH ROUND

GROSSER A1 PREIS A1 VON ÖSTERREICH, SPIELBERG

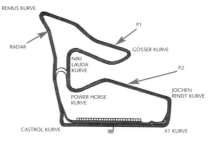

Date : May 13, 2001
Length : 4326 meters
Distance : 71 laps, 307.146 km
Weather : dry and sunny, 23°

CHAMPIONSHIP

(after six rounds)

Drivers :

1. M. Schumacher 42
2. D. Coulthard 38
3. R. Barrichello 18
4. R. Schumacher 12
5. N. Heidfeld 8
6. J. Trulli 7
7. J. P. Montoya 6
   H.-H. Frentzen 6
9. O. Panis 5
10. J. Villeneuve 4
    M. Häkkinen 4
    K. Räikkönen 4
13. J. Verstappen 1
    G. Fisichella 1

Constructors :

1. Ferrari............................60
2. McLaren Mercedes 42
3. Williams BMW 18
4. Jordan Honda.................13
5. Sauber Petronas.............12
6. BAR Honda......................9
7. Benetton-Renault 1
   Arrows Asiatech 1

RACE SUMMARY

- Four cars are stuck on the grid at the start: Trulli, Frentzen, Heidfeld and Hakkinen.
- The two Williams fly off into the lead, Montoya in front.
- Hakkinen finally gets going from the pits, three laps down.
- The Safety Car is kept out until lap 4 so that the grid can be cleared.
- Verstappen passes Irvine and Coulthard. He was on a three stop strategy.
- On lap 6, Montoya has a 1.3 second lead over Ralf Schumacher, 2.3 seconds over Michael Schumacher, 2.9 on Barrichello and 3.1 on Verstappen.
- Ralf Schumacher retires on lap 10. Villeneuve attacks Irvine and goes off.
- Montoya eases up in the lead. On lap 14, his lead over Michael Schumacher is down to just 0.3 seconds and 0.6 on Barrichello.
- On lap 15, Michael Schumacher manages to pass Montoya after a good scrap between the two men. Barrichello makes the most of the fact they touch, to take the lead. At the

same time, Trulli is black flagged for having ignored the red light at the end of the pit lane.

- Incredibly, Barrichello in the lead, comes under attack from Verstappen, until the Dutchman makes his last stop on lap 23.
- * Lap 25 and Michael Schumacher passes Panis for fourth place.
- Lap 30 sees Barrichello with a 2.5 second lead over Coulthard, 5.5 seconds ahead of Michael Schumacher and 8.2 seconds on Raikkonen, whom the German passed on lap 28.
- When Barrichello makes his second stop, Coulthard ups the pace. Three laps later, the Scotsman refuels and takes the lead.
- Barrichello lets Michael Schumacher pass at the exit to the final corner of the race. The Brazilian does not seem to pleased at having to give up his position.

LAP CHART

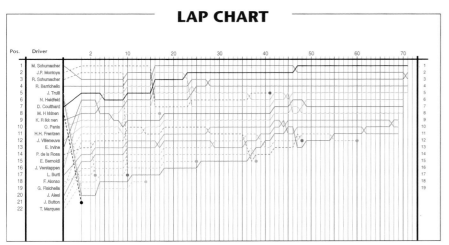

GAPS ON THE LEADER BOARD

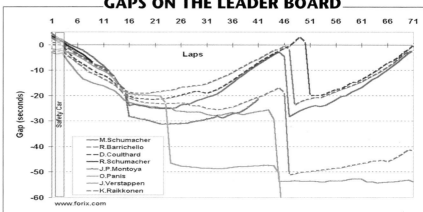

Simply the best

In Monaco, Michael Schumacher took his fourth win from seven races so far that season. It was also his fifth triumph in the Principality and the fifth time he spent Sunday night sitting alongside the Prince at the Gala Dinner. No wonder his mechanics carried him shoulder high in front of the podium!

The only conclusion to be drawn that day, was that Michael Schumacher was going to walk away with the 2001 title, simply because he had no worthy rivals. While the Williams-BMW definitely had the pace, they still lacked a little bit of reliability, needed to win on a regular basis.

As for this year's MP4/16, it was often capable of keeping up with the Ferrari, but not for long. In the seven races held so far, Mika Hakkinen had only seen the chequered flag twice, bringing home a total of just four miserable championship points. This awful run of bad luck would not come to an end in Monaco either.

Therefore, the only hope that someone could challenge Michael Schumacher rested on David Coulthard's shoulders. In Monaco, he spent more than half the race stuck behind a modest Arrows, which raised doubts about the Scotsman's abilities, even among his most ardent supporters.

GRAND PRIX DE MONACO
MONTE-CARLO

David Coulthard excelled himself to take his second pole position of the season in Monaco. At the time, he did not know that, hot on the heels of his Austrian win, this qualifying session would be the high-point of his season. After that, the Scotsman would never see pole again, nor would he win another race.

"Is there room at the back?" Michael Schumacher is glued to the barriers in his attempt to squeeze the last thousandths of a second out of his car. It is part of the amazing spectacle on offer each year in the Principality. As a matter of fact, there was room at the back, even though it looks impossible. But it was not enough to give the German pole.

Having spend most of the season to date qualifying on the back two rows, Giancarlo Fisichella managed to put his Benetton in the top half of the Monaco grid. Nice work.

Second pole for the Scotsman

David Coulthard wins the first round between the barriers

In Monaco each year, the qualifying session resolves itself as a sort of battle of the barriers. The drivers have to find the quickest racing line, making use of every inch of the track, which involves kissing the barriers, but without actually hitting them.

Michael Schumacher is very good at this little game. Having won the Monaco Grand Prix on four occasions prior to 2001, the German has the talent to match the very specialist demands of this circuit. On the Saturday of the meeting, one of his engineers admitted that Michael had really given it his all to try and get on pole. However, while he held on to the Number One position for a good third of the qualifying session, he saw the prized slot snaffled from him by David Coulthard, who really wanted it that day. *"I had made a mistake at*

the Swimming Pool section on Thursday," he said. "It affected my *confidence a bit, because you really cannot afford to hit the barriers here. Since then, I've been building up speed gradually and it's coming."*

His final qualifying lap certainly showed that his mount was well adapted to the track. *"Looking at the split times, I knew the potential was there. All I had to do was put the sectors together. On my last quick lap, I knew it was a good one and I just made sure I made no mistakes in the final section. Which means I might have been able to go a little bit quicker."*

The Scotsman was certainly pleased with his performance. *"Yes, I'm happy, because, of all the circuits, the Monaco one is the toughest from a technical point of view. Finding the right moment to go out on the track, with the right set-up, with no traffic and without making any mistakes, requires a bit of magic."*

Michael Schumacher, second on the day, simply could not find the right formula. *"My quickest lap wasn't perfect,"* admitted the German. *"When I got to the Portier corner, it felt as though someone had moved the barriers closer together! It was a strange feeling, because the track was really too narrow!"*

On an upward spiral after his win in Austria, two weeks earlier, David Coulthard was in just the right

mood to add the Monaco Grand Prix to his record book. *"I am a lot more experienced than in the past and I intend driving a faultless race. I know Michael and Mika are hoping I will make a mistake, but I'm touching wood. Everyone makes mistakes. The trick is not to make any at the vital moment."*

Minardi attacks Toyota

The Minardi team was taking to court its former Technical Director Gustav Brunner and the Toyota team, due to make its F1 debut in 2002.

Three weeks before this grand prix, despite a contract binding him to Minardi, the Austrian engineer had quit the Italian team to immediately join the Toyota project. According to Minardi owner, Paul Stoddart, this defection cost him the signature of a major sponsor. He was therefore asking for several million dollars in damages and interest from Brunner. This action was supported by Ron Dennis, who declared himself angry to see that Toyota was "buying everything in Formula 1." *"It is high time that something is done to stop these predatory actions,"* boomed Stoddart. *"They are paying vast amounts to buy four or five people from each team, who join them with their brains and laptops bursting with information."*

Reassuring tests

After a near disaster in Austria, when no less than four cars were left stuck on the grid at the start, the FIA decided to authorise driver to practice their starts on the grid. These test runs took place at the end of each of the two half sessions in Monaco and the teams were very pleased with the ruling. *"Being allowed to*

practice our starts is an excellent idea," agreed Ferrari Technical Director Ross Brawn. *"Until now, people practised the starts at the exit to the pit lane, in very different conditions to those you find on the real start grid. This time, I think it should be possible to avoid the sort of problems we saw in Austria."*

Monaco, the jewel of the Mediterranean, poses in all its glory. It is a scene which generates extreme feelings. The Formula 1 folk either love it or hate it. There is no middle path.

Mika Hakkinen threads his way through the yachts and the terraces of Monaco. Running into traffic on his quick laps, the Finn eventually qualified third.

Two more years at Ferrari for Schumacher

It was not exactly the most burning question of the hour, but one more mystery was put to rest on 22nd May. Scuderia Ferrari announced that it had extended its agreement with Michael Schumacher to the end of the 2004 season.

The world champion's previous contract tied him to the team to the end of 2002 and so this extension finally put an end to some pretty far fetched rumours. It was said that Toyota, due to join the F1 club in 2002, had offered the German driver a blank cheque to join them from 2003. Incredible though it might seem, the story went that Schumacher could fill in his own figure on the cheque book stub, according to what he felt he was worth!

Having kicked off in 1996, it now seemed that the collaboration between the triple world champion and the Ferrari team was set to last, in principle, for at least nine years. Almost a record in the history of motor sport - a record equalled in fact by Mika Hakkinen, tied to his McLaren team in 2001 for a similar period, although the Finn only took part in the final few races in 1993.

However, after 2004, what the German driver had in mind was not clear. But on that 22nd May, he did make it clear that, come the end of this latest extension to his contract, he would no doubt bring his driving career to an end. This declaration went against previous statements suggesting he would keep going "at least until the age of 40," which would see him through to 2009.

Ferrari also announced an extension to Rubens Barrichello's contract, for one year only, to the end of 2002. This was perhaps more surprising. After the last grand prix, in Austria, where he had to move over to let Schumacher through, the Brazilian had made his bitterness clear, in a very public fashion. There was thus plenty of speculation that he would seek employment elsewhere for the following year. For its part, the Scuderia was reckoned to be chasing the services of the young Sauber driver, Kimi Raikkonen.

But, having previously said he would only consider staying with Ferrari if he could sign a contract for the next three years, Rubens Barrichello backed down and accepted the role of understudy for one more season. It was no doubt the least unattractive offer which had come his way.

"What are these things then?" Jo Bauer, FIA Technical Delegate measures and questions... In Monaco, in the constant battle to find more downforce, Arrows and Jordan had both turned up with an additional mid-wing. It was banned on Thursday night.

STARTING GRID

M. SCHUMACHER 1'17"631	-1-	David COULTHARD 1'17"430
R. BARRICHELLO 1'17"856	-2-	Mika HÄKKINEN 1'17"749
Eddie IRVINE 1'18"432	-3-	Ralf SCHUMACHER 1'18"029
Jarno TRULLI 1'18"921	-4-	J. P. MONTOYA 1'18"751
Giancarlo FISICHELLA 1'19"220	-5-	Jacques VILLENEUVE 1'19"086
Olivier PANIS 1'19"294	-6-	Jean ALESI 1'19"245
Pedro De la Rosa 1'20"033	-7-	Heinz-H. FRENTZEN 1'19"316
Nick HEIDFELD 1'20"261	-8-	Kimi RAIKKONEN 1'20"081
Fernando ALONSO 1'20"788	-9-	Jenson BUTTON 1'20"342
Enrique BERNOLDI 1'21"336	-10-	Jos VERSTAPPEN 1'20"823
Tarso MARQUES 1'22"201	-11-	Luciano BURTI 1'21"771

▷△ Michael Schumacher wins in the Principality for the fifth time

The start. With David Coulthard out of the way, Michael Schumacher takes the lead. The only time he would see his rivals would be in his mirrors.

△ After the effort comes the reward. Rubinho is also carried in triumph by his mechanics, after coming second.

"In the end it was an easy win"

"It was quite an easy drive!" After the race, Michael Schumacher admitted he has not had to fight too hard for his fourth win of the season. In fact, the only battle he fought throughout the 78 laps of the Monaco Grand Prix was with himself, as he worked hard to maintain his concentration. "I got on the radio and asked Ross (Brawn, Ferrari Technical Director) a whole lot of questions about the position of other drivers. He told me to concentrate as he didn't want another Indianapolis. (Last year, Schumacher had spun when losing concentration.) He told me his heart wasn't up to it. I told him not to worry and that I would take care of his heart."

A little conversation which shows that the German had no real worries during his pleasant Sunday afternoon drive. "Someone asked me why I didn't jump for joy on the podium," he added. "To be honest, I wasn't that excited. There was nothing special about this win. Nothing much happened during the race, or at least nothing worth jumping on the podium for. It's always nice to win in Monaco, as it is special, but this time it was quite easy. Right from Thursday I found a good set up, I had a bit of luck and here I am."

Thanks to traction control, some drivers predicted that the Monaco track would be easier to deal with than usual. Michael Schumacher did not agree. "It was still physically tiring," he continued. We were lapping quite quickly. As traction control means you can go quicker, in some ways it can be more tiring."

With this, his fourth win of the season, Michael Schumacher could tackle the next part of the season in a calm state of mind. Especially as his main rivals, the McLaren drivers, had once again run into reliability problems. "It would be wrong to think we can now rest on our laurels," affirmed Ferrari's Sporting Director Jean Todt on Sunday night. "Michael's lead is not as big as that. Everyone in the team knows that, in order to maintain our level of performance we have to continue working hard." The Scuderia would move to Magny-Cours the day after the Monaco Grand Prix, for a week's testing to prepare for the French Grand Prix. And, from Saturday, all the equipment would be loaded onto a flight for the next race in Montreal, the Canadian Grand Prix.

Barrichello second in pain

Michael Schumacher's team-mate, Rubens Barrichello, finished second, but in contrast to the other Ferrari driver, the Brazilian did not have an easy time, in agony with cramps in his right leg for most of the race. "The pain started around the ninth or tenth lap," he explained. "I started to have terrible cramps in my foot. Something must have broken in the cockpit, because the accelerator pedal started to vibrate like mad. I asked Ross (Brawn) what I should do and he told me to drink a lot from my bottle."

Around lap 18, "Rubinho" could hardly feel his right foot and started to lose two seconds a lap to Schumacher. "It was the worst moment. At the exit to Casino square, I would press on the pedal, but it was like a dentist had put my foot to sleep. I tried to move my toes and bit by bit, it got better. I asked God to help me make it to the finish, because the car was really fantastic. Probably the best I have ever driven in my career."

▷ A Ferrari one-two ahead of a Jaguar. Eddie Irvine makes the most of what would be his only podium of the season.

▷▷ Michael Schumacher was in a league of his own in Monaco. That was often the case this season.

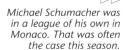

David Coulthard's chances had gone even before the start.

"*Someone who is stuck behind Bernoldi for 43 laps cannot claim to be a championship contender.*" Or another version: "*Bernoldi should have moved over. After all, he was fighting for last place and David is in the running for the title.*" These are just two phrases which were flying around the paddock after the race, as people argued about the Coulthard "affair." Everyone had an opinion; either indignant or ironic.

Having qualified on pole, the Scotsman's fate was sealed when, yet again, he ran into bother with the launch control on his McLaren. It had already cost him dear in Spain and had eliminated Mika Hakkinen two weeks earlier in Austria.

In Monaco, Coulthard stalled on the grid at the start of the formation lap and was therefore forced to start from the back of the grid. His climb through the field did not last long. Having dealt with Tarso Marques' Minardi on lap 4, the McLaren man then came up behind the Arrows of Fernando Alonso. He only got by when the Brazilian stopped to refuel on lap 43!

It was not for want of trying. Several times he pulled alongside the Arrows, at the climb up the Avenue d'Ostende or on the descent to Mirabeau. When this tandem was passed by the leaders, the Scotsman tried to tuck in behind. Each time, Bernoldi resisted and Coulthard had to dive onto the brakes.

Had he been too timid or did the Brazilian block

Jaguar's only podium of the season comes at just the right time

Jaguar's only podium finish of the season was as unexpected as Jean Alesi's sixth place. Both of them naturally made the most of retirements ahead of them, but they still deserve the credit for getting to the flag.

After the race, Eddie Irvine took it in a calm and humorous fashion. Two years with the Jaguar team had not changed him. "*As we are not currently negotiating my 2002 salary at the moment, I have to admit that any progress we made today was more to do with the car than with the driver. In fact, we had a new aerodynamic package here which has completely transformed the R2. In four years with Ferrari, I have never experienced such a major step forward. We were quick all weekend and I hope we can maintain that momentum in Canada.*"

The Irishman reckoned there were still several problems to sort out before he could entertain thoughts of winning. "*We still have a lot to do to reach the level of those at the front,*" he admitted. "*The car is still very difficult to drive, because of a problem we have had with it since last year. Having said that, I am very happy with this result. After all, two Ferraris and a Jaguar; that's what Formula 1 should be about, isn't it?*"

A champion in trouble

him unfairly? The general opinion was that if Michael Schumacher had been in the McLaren man's shoes, he would have got by with a forceful manoeuvre. It was hard to imagine him spending 40 laps behind an Arrows.

Not surprisingly, McLaren boss Ron Dennis leaned towards the blocking theory. Along with Mercedes motor sport chief Norbert Haug, he went to pay a visit to the young Brazilian to express his displeasure. "*It's not right to hold up a driver who is in the hunt for the title when you are defending 13th place,*" boomed Ron. "*In a year's time no one will remember Bernoldi. He knows it and he was just doing his best to get his car on television for as long as possible, to please his sponsors.*"

Tom Walkinshaw, the fiery Arrows owner, was not impressed that Dennis and Haug had come calling on his driver. "*What are they getting involved with?*" he said angrily. "*All Enrique did was defend his position. David Coulthard's first problem was stalling on the grid.*"

At least the Scottish driver was not as aggressive as his boss when he met Bernoldi, no doubt because he knew he had not performed brilliantly. "*I thought he might make a risky move and that we would both end up in the barrier,*" explained Coulthard.

One thing was certain: by losing eight more points to Michael Schumacher in the championship, Couthard's chances of taking the title were slipping from his grasp.

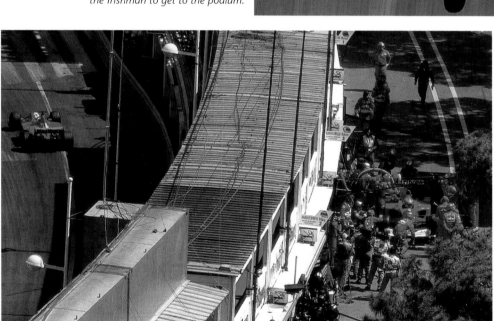

Eddie Irvine in action. The Jaguar was no doubt one of the prettiest cars of the 2001 season (as long as you like the colour green!) In Monaco, the new aerodynamic package developed by the team helped the Irishman to get to the podium.

The gap Michael Schumacher pulled out over Rubens Barrichello is clear to see. While the former is refuelling in the pits, the latter is still tackling the Swimming Pool section.

Juan Pablo Montoya flies between the Monaco barriers. The Colombian had already raced in the Principality in his Formula 3000 days. In F1, he was an early victim of the difficult track, going out as early as lap three.

After finishing on the podium in Spain, Jacques Villeneuve succeeded in coming home fourth in the Monaco Grand Prix, thus picking up three more points. He still put his team under pressure, affirming that he wanted to leave if "it did not finish third in the constructors' classification." Good for morale!

Jean Alesi at work, braking for the Grand Hotel corner. Sixth place was waiting for him at the end of the day.

A fireman in the Monaco pit lane. It is very narrow and cannot be widened until a new pits complex is built along the harbour front.

A big impact with heavy consequences. Heinz-Harald Frentzen hits the barrier on lap 50. Eddie Jordan later claimed the accident was caused by his driver being unfit, which would lead to their separation two months later.

The champagne flows at Prost

Sixth place for Jean Alesi

Nothing like it had been seen at Prost for several years, or almost. Half an hour after the race, the motorhome awning was the scene of a champagne fight with most of the blue shirts soaked through in the stuff.

Jean Alesi's sixth place was the cause of this euphoria. For the French team, this was its first point since the 1999 European Grand Prix. It was a point which showed that the AP04 had made some progress, but it could have been two points if Jean Alesi had not needed to make an unscheduled stop nine laps from the end. *"It was terrible,"* he recalled. *"In the tunnel, I suddenly felt a vibration at the rear. It was either a puncture or broken suspension. I warned the pits and Alain told me to come in immediately. They changed the wheel and I was off again, but it was agonising."*

The French driver reckoned this was a new beginning for the Prost team. *"This point makes me so happy and I feel our adventure is getting off to a new start today. Formula 1 is like football: it's not over until it's over. And the Prost team is not over I tell you."*

Shall we discuss this matter again in Hockenheim?

WEEKEND GOSSIP

• Villeneuve about to leave

Jacques Villeneuve announced that he was still not sure about staying with the BAR team in 2002. In fact, his contract with the British based squad expired at the end of 2001 and the Canadian declared in Monaco that he would only stay put if it finished in the top three in the Constructors' Championship. There was still rather a lot of work to do, because at the time, BAR was only in sixth place on nine points. Jacques also admitted he was suffering with bad back pains. It seemed he might have jogged a vertebra as a result of his accident in the Australian Grand Prix, which caused the pain, that got much worse every time he hit a bump. *"It even hurts when I go over the kerbs,"* he said.

• Jaguar decides to stay put

The Jaguar team had planned to build a new ultra-modern factory near Silverstone circuit, but it had abandoned the idea.

• Farewell to Gabriele Rumi and Vittorio Brambilla

Two bastions of Italian motorsport died over the Monegasque weekend. They were Gabriele Rumi, former co-owner of the Minardi team and Vittorio Brambilla. The 63 year old former F1 driver was remembered for his impetuous character and driving talent. Brambilla never really got his hands on a competitive car during his 74 grands prix career. Nevertheless, he secured one pole position and one win, in 1975. On that day, he was so happy to have won that he raised both arms as he crossed the finish line, promptly losing control and crashing into the guard rail!

• Jarno at the GPDA

During the traditional meeting of the GPDA (Grand Prix Drivers Association) on the Friday of Monaco, Jarno Trulli was elected as one of the directors, alongside Michael Schumacher and David Coulthard.

PRACTICE TIMES

No	Driver	Car/Engine/Chassis	Practice Friday	Pos.	Practice Saturday	Pos.	Qualifying	Pos.	Warm-up	Pos.
1.	Michael Schumacher	Ferrari/F2001/211	1'20"316	2°	1'18"456	2°	1'17"430	2°	1'21"650	3°
2.	Rubens Barrichello	Ferrari/F2001/206	1'20"959	4°	1'19"651	8°	1'17"856	4°	1'22"502	4°
3.	Mika Häkkinen	McLaren/Mercedes/MP4/16/4	1'19"853	1°	1'18"282	1°	1'17"749	3°	1'21"017	2°
4.	David Coulthard	McLaren/Mercedes/MP4/16/5	1'21"091	6°	1'19"031	4°	1'17"430	1°	1'20"944	1°
5.	Ralf Schumacher	Williams/BMW/FW23/5	1'20"938	3°	1'18"725	3°	1'18"029	5°	1'22"650	6°
6.	Juan Pablo Montoya	Williams/BMW/FW23/2	1'22"035	10°	1'19"603	7°	1'18"751	7°	1'23"590	12°
7.	Giancarlo Fisichella	Benetton/Renault/B201/6	1'22"214	11°	1'20"591	13°	1'19"220	10°	1'23"407	10°
8.	Jenson Button	Benetton/Renault/B201/5	1'24"026	17°	1'21"316	14°	1'20"342	17°	1'24"137	18°
9.	Olivier Panis	BAR/Honda/003/6	1'23"662	16°	1'20"528	12°	1'19"294	12°	1'23"595	13°
10.	Jacques Villeneuve	BAR/Honda/003/4	1'22"010	9°	1'20"397	11°	1'19"086	9°	1'23"747	14°
11.	Heinz-Harald Frentzen	Jordan/Honda/EJ11/6	1'21"505	7°	1'20"064	10°	1'19"316	13°	1'22"566	5°
12.	Jarno Trulli	Jordan/Honda/EJ11/5	1'21"048	5°	1'19"307	6°	1'18"921	8°	1'23"574	11°
14.	Jos Verstappen	Arrows/Asiatech/A22/6	1'23"409	15°	1'21"827	17°	1'20"823	19°	1'23"066	8°
15.	Enrique Bernoldi	Arrows/Asiatech/A22/3	1'24"015	18°	1'22"024	18°	1'21"336	20°	1'25"328	20°
16.	Nick Heidfeld	Sauber/Petronas/C20/5	1'22"807	14°	1'22"207	19°	1'20"261	16°	1'23"842	15°
17.	Kimi Räikkönen	Sauber/Petronas/C20/6	1'22"800	13°	1'21"621	15°	1'20"081	15°	1'24"042	16°
18.	Eddie Irvine	Jaguar/R-2/4	1'22"302	12°	1'19"081	5°	1'18"432	6°	1'22"816	7°
19.	Pedro de la Rosa	Jaguar/R-2/6	1'27"316	22°	1'22"316	20°	1'20"033	14°	1'23"200	9°
20.	Tarso Marques	Minardi/European/PS01/4	1'25"920	20°	1'23"313	21°	1'22"201	22°	1'26"365	22°
21.	Fernando Alonso	Minardi/European/PS01/3	1'26"393	21°	1'21"670	16°	1'20"788	18°	1'24"941	19°
22.	Jean Alesi	Prost/Acer/AP04/6	1'21"935	8°	1'20"020	9°	1'19"245	11°	1'24"046	17°
23.	Luciano Burti	Prost/Acer/AP04/5	1'24"857	19°	1'25"795	22°	1'21"771	21°	1'25"938	21°

MAXIMUM SPEEDS

No	Driver	P1 Qualifs	Pos	P1 Race	Pos	P2 Qualifs	Pos	P2 Race	Pos	Finish Qualifs	Pos	Finish Race	Pos	Trap Qualifs	Pos	Trap Race	Pos
1.	M. Schumacher	213,5	6°	205,5	4°	211,3	2°	198,2	4°	267,9	3°	262,0	7°	292,5	4°	288,2	7°
2.	R. Barrichello	214,3	4°	199,6	13°	208,8	4°	201,3	2°	267,7	4°	262,9	2°	293,3	2°	287,7	10°
3.	M. Häkkinen	213,6	5°	195,8	19°	211,1	3°	196,6	9°	264,5	10°	255,8	19°	288,3	10°	284,0	16°
4.	D. Coulthard	216,0	1°	205,9	2°	211,5	1°	202,0	1°	265,2	8°	262,4	6°	290,8	8°	291,4	2°
5.	R. Schumacher	214,6	3°	204,9	6°	205,6	8°	194,8	11°	273,0	1°	265,9	1°	299,1	2°	294,0	1°
6.	J. P. Montoya	209,5	13°	175,9	21°	206,6	6°	187,5	17°	272,5	2°	262,7	3°	299,5	1°	277,7	20°
7.	G. Fisichella	205,9	17°	200,2	12°	200,0	20°	191,4	14°	259,0	19°	258,3	16°	286,3	18°	286,1	14°
8.	J. Button	202,4	19°	202,1	10°	205,7	5°	196,9	8°	258,4	21°	259,9	15°	285,2	20°	288,8	6°
9.	O. Panis	215,5	2°	194,9	20°	204,9	12°	180,4	21°	264,0	12°	255,2	21°	290,2	9°	273,9	21°
10.	J. Villeneuve	206,8	16°	199,0	16°	207,3	5°	197,0	7°	262,4	15°	262,5	5°	287,0	16°	289,1	5°
11.	H.-H. Frentzen	211,3	10°	199,0	15°	201,3	18°	192,1	13°	260,8	18°	259,9	14°	285,6	19°	287,7	9°
12.	J. Trulli	212,8	7°	199,1	14°	203,5	10°	190,6	15°	264,0	11°	257,7	17°	286,3	17°	283,4	17°
14.	J. Verstappen	210,9	11°	205,1	5°	202,6	16°	197,1	6°	263,2	13°	260,4	9°	287,8	13°	287,6	11°
15.	E. Bernoldi	202,1	21°	202,4	8°	201,1	19°	193,5	12°	263,0	14°	260,1	13°	287,6	14°	287,8	8°
16.	N. Heidfeld	207,9	15°	165,9	22°	205,2	11°			262,0	16°			287,2	15°		
17.	K. Räikkönen	212,4	9°	207,5	1°	205,6	9°	197,8	5°	261,2	17°	260,3	10°	288,3	12°	287,6	12°
18.	E. Irvine	209,5	12°	204,0	7°	203,6	14°	196,0	10°	266,2	6°	262,6	4°	291,4	3°	291,0	3°
19.	P. de la Rosa	209,2	14°	201,4	9°	193,5	22°	180,6	20°	264,7	9°	260,1	12°	288,3	11°	286,9	13°
20.	T. Marques	194,4	22°	197,9	18°	199,4	21°	184,2	19°	256,5	22°	255,5	20°	283,6	22°	279,7	19°
21.	F. Alonso	202,2	20°	197,9	17°	203,6	15°	188,3	16°	258,8	20°	256,5	18°	285,1	21°	283,3	18°
22.	J. Alesi	212,6	8°	205,9	3°	204,6	13°	198,7	3°	266,7	5°	261,9	8°	291,9	5°	290,4	4°
23.	L. Burti	205,6	18°	201,0	11°	201,3	17°	187,5	18°	265,3	7°	260,2	11°	291,8	6°	284,8	15°

CLASSIFICATION & RETIREMENTS

Pos	Driver	Team	Time
1.	M.Schum.	Ferrari	1:47:22.561
2.	Barrichello	Ferrari	+ 0.431
3.	Irvine	Jaguar Racing	+ 30.698
4.	Villeneuve	BAR Honda	+ 32.454
5.	Coulthard	McLaren Mercedes	+ 1 lap
6.	Alesi	Prost Acer	+ 1 lap
7.	Button	Benetton Renault	+ 1 lap
8.	Verstappen	Arrows Asiatech	+ 1 lap
9.	Bernoldi	Arrows Asiatech	+ 2 laps
10.	Räikkönen	Sauber Petronas	+ 5 laps

Lap	Driver	Team	Reason
1	Heidfeld	Sauber Petronas	accident
3	Montoya	Williams BMW	accident
14	Panis	Bar Honda	direction
16	Häkkinen	McLaren Mercedes	suspension
19	de la Rosa	Jaguar Racing	hydraulics
25	Burti	Prost Acer	brakes
31	Trulli	Jordan Honda	hydraulics
44	Fisichella	Benetton Renault	accident
50	Frentzen	Jordan Honda	accident
55	Alonso	European Minardi	gearbox
57	Marques	European Minardi	transmission
58	R. Schum.	Williams BMW	engine

FASTEST LAP

	Driver	Time	Lap
1.	Coulthard	1'19"424	68
		152,749 km/h	
2.	M. Schum.	1'19"770	50
3.	Barrichello	1'20"329	57
4.	Villeneuve	1'20"417	75
5.	Irvine	1'20"681	76
6.	Räikkönen	1'20"705	60
7.	Frentzen	1'20"810	46
8.	R. Schum.	1'20"975	47
9.	Alesi	1'21"151	73
10.	Button	1'21"580	65
11.	Fisichella	1'21"646	37
12.	Häkkinen	1'21"682	12
13.	Verstappen	1'21"732	74
14.	Bernoldi	1'22"053	75
15.	Trulli	1'22"345	30
16.	Alonso	1'22"956	28
17.	de la Rosa	1'23"483	18
18.	Burti	1'24"206	18
19.	Marques	1'24"570	33
20.	Panis	1'24"719	10
21.	Montoya	1'25"773	2

PIT STOPS

	Drivers	Time	Lap	Stop n°
1.	Burti	32"992	3	1
2.	Panis	34"328	12	1
3.	Panis	11'04"407	13	2
4.	Häkkinen	55"054	14	1
5.	Räikkönen	5'05"935	15	1
6.	Verstappen	1'01"864	42	1
7.	Bernoldi	33"124	43	1
8.	Marques	32"431	44	1
9.	Alonso	31"164	47	1
10.	Button	29"632	49	1
11.	Alesi	29"573	51	1
12.	M. Schumacher	28"112	55	1
13.	Villeneuve	28"243	56	1
14.	Barrichello	27"676	60	1
15.	Irvine	27"986	60	1
16.	Räikkönen	29"787	58	2
17.	Coulthard	26"954	65	1
18.	Alesi	28"610	69	2

BRIDGESTONE

Best result for a driver running Bridgestone tyre:
Michael Schumacher, Ferrari, 1:47:22.561

THE CIRCUIT

SEVENTH ROUND

GRAND PRIX DE MONACO, MONTE CARLO

Date : May 27, 2001
Length : 3370 meters
Distance : 78 laps, 262.860 km
Weather : warm and sunny, 22°

CHAMPIONSHIP

(after seven rounds)

Drivers :
1. M. Schumacher 52
2. D. Coulthard 40
3. R. Barrichello 24
4. R. Schumacher 12
5. N. Heidfeld 8
6. J. Villeneuve 7
   J. Trulli 7
8. J. P. Montoya 6
   H.-H. Frentzen 6
10. O. Panis 5
11. E. Irvine 4
    K. Räikkönen 4
    M. Häkkinen 4
14. J. Verstappen 1
    J. Alesi 1
    G. Fisichella 1

Constructors :
1. Ferrari 76
2. McLaren Mercedes 44
3. Williams BMW 18
4. Jordan Honda 13
5. BAR Honda 12
   Sauber Petronas 12
7. Jaguar Racing 4
8. Arrows Asiatech 1
   Prost Acer 1
   Benetton Renault 1

RACE SUMMARY

- David Coulthard stalls at the start of the formation lap. As he does not manage to get going until all the others have passed, he is forced to start from the back of the grid.

- Michael Schumacher gets away cleanly, ahead of Hakkinen and Barrichello.

- Lap 3 and Montoya crashes out at the swimming pool.

- Coulthard comes up behind Bernoldi, but cannot get by. He will have to wait until the Arrows refuels and will even be lapped by Michael Schumacher.

- Hakkinen runs into bother and has to pit. He rejoins 16th before retiring.

- On lap 25, Michael Schumacher leads his team-mate Barrichello by 14 seconds. He has a lead of 25.2 seconds over Ralf Schumacher, 29.3 seconds on Irvine and 34.7 seconds on Trulli and Villeneuve.

- Lap 50 and Frentzen crashes heavily at the port chicane. A hydraulic failure seems to be the cause of the accident, but later the Jordan team claims it might have been driver failure.

- The pit stops do not change the order.

- Lap 58 and Irvine passes Ralf Schumacher, who retires shortly afterwards in the pits.

- Coulthard has climbed up to sixth and pits very late, on lap 66.

- In fifth place, Alesi stops eight laps from the flag to change tyres. Coulthard thus moves up to fifth, demoting Alesi to sixth.

- Michael Schumacher completes his Sunday stroll to win, with Barrichello making it a Ferrari one-two and Irvine a surprising third. Bernoldi, the unwitting hero of the afternoon is ninth and second to last.

All results : © 2001 Fédération Internationale de l'Automobile, 2, Ch. Blandonnet, 1215 Genève 15, Suisse

LAP CHART

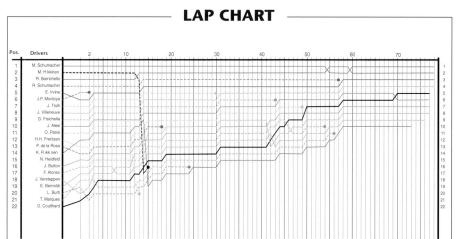

GAPS ON THE LEADER BOARD

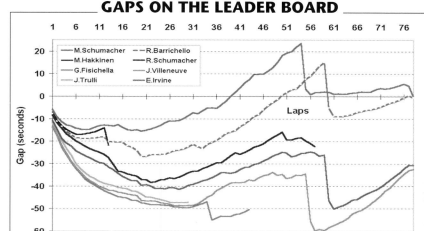

Ralf does it again

In Montreal, Ralf Schumacher took his second win of the season, after first tasting victory in San Marino.

Having started from second on the grid, the youngest of the Schumacher brothers had to spend most of the race behind the elder one. Even though his car seemed much quicker than the Ferrari, he was only able to get the upper hand during the pit stops. It was a result that pleased everyone : Ralf, happy with the win, Michael, second, pleased to see his little brother on top and his main title rival, David Coulthard, slip a further six points behind in the championship. The Scotsman had been forced to retire with engine problems.

GRAND PRIX AIR CANADA
MONTRÉAL

Heinz-Harald Frentzen only drove on the Friday in Montreal. On Saturday morning, the German was replaced by Jordan's test driver, Ricardo Zonta. In Monaco, Frentzen had a crash which had left him with severe headaches. On Friday, "HH" had yet another accident which reawakened his migraine and dizziness. Overnight, he therefore decided to head back home to Monaco for some medical tests.

Giancarlo Fisischella adores Montreal. The two previous years, he had finished on the podium. Not this time. After showing signs of improvement in Monaco, the Benetton had plunged back down the order and the Italian was only 18th.

The Schumi brothers share the front row

Michael versus Ralf: the revenge!

Crescent Street during the grand prix weekend. It has an atmosphere which is unique on the Formula 1 calendar.

The hairpin on the magnificent island circuit of Montreal.

Were the McLarens going to lose ground to the Ferraris? In Montreal at least, the qualifying session was entirely dominated by Michael Schumacher. Right from his first flying lap, the German set a time which took him straight to the top of the time sheet. With over half a second advantage over his pursuers, Schumacher looked as though he was going to be tough to beat in the race.

The surprise came from his brother Ralf, who hoisted his BMW-Williams to second place, especially astonishing as free practice had not gone well for him. "I really don't know how we managed to improve the car this much," said an amazed Ralf after the session. "When I saw my time, the team asked me how I did it and I couldn't tell them! Since yesterday, we have had difficulty adapting our chassis to the tyres, but during the lunch-break we made a few changes to the set up and it seems to have done the job. On top of that, it's at least ten degrees hotter than this morning, which helped us a lot."

It was the second time this season, the first being in Brazil, that the two Schumacher brothers would line up alongside one another on the front row of the grid.

Twenty minutes or so before the end of the session, the session had to be stopped on two separate occasions, when first Rubens Barrichello and then Nick Heidfeld hit the famous "Welcome to Quebec" wall opposite the pits.

With only 1 minute and 35 seconds remaining when the track was opened again, there was not much chance of anyone improving their times. Six cars took to the track, but only David Coulthard managed to go quicker, moving up from fourth to third place. "I am very disappointed not to be on the front row," commented the Scotsman. "The car can definitely do better." Jacques Villeneuve was another disappointed driver; unhappy to be ninth, while team-mate Olivier Panis was sixth.

STARTING GRID

Left	Row	Right
M. SCHUMACHER 1'15"782	-1-	Ralf SCHUMACHER 1'16"297
David COULTHARD 1'16"423	-2-	Jarno TRULLI 1'16"459
R. BARRICHELLO 1'16"760	-3-	Olivier PANIS 1'16"771
Kimi RÄIKKÖNEN 1'16"875	-4-	Mika HÄKKINEN 1'16"979
Jacques VILLENEUVE 1'17"035	-5-	J. P. MONTOYA 1'17"123
Nick HEIDFELD 1'17"165	-6-	Ricardo ZONTA 1'17"328
Jos VERSTAPPEN 1'17"903	-7-	Pedro De la Rosa 1'18"015
Eddie IRVINE 1'18"016	-8-	Jean ALESI 1'18"178
Enrique BERNOLDI 1'18"575	-9-	Giancarlo FISICHELLA 1'18"622
Luciano BURTI 1'18"753	-10-	Jenson BUTTON 1'19"033
Tarso MARQUES 1'20"690	-11-	Fernando ALONSO (Déclassé)

Ralf dominates Michael

What a duel! The two Schumacher brothers put on a great chasing display which eventually went in favour of Ralf, who took his second grand prix win after San Marino at the wheel of his BMW-Williams.

Michael Schumacher was quickest away at the start in his Ferrari, leading his brother through the first corner. As the laps went by, the Ferrari man tried to pull out a lead, but the Williams appeared to have no trouble sticking with him. *"I wondered why Michael was so slow,"* commented the younger Schumacher when it was all over. *"I thought he was trying to look after his brakes, because I could keep up with him very easily. In fact, instead of him pulling away, it was the two of us who built a gap over the rest of the pack."*

When Juan Pablo Montoya and Rubens Barrichello went off the track, the Safety Car came out on lap 20. Once the race was underway again, Michael Schumacher worked at building up a two second lead, which took Ralf Schumacher a few laps to claw back. *"For some reason, my tyres seemed to pick up rubber while following the Safety Car,"* reckoned the day's eventual winner. *"It took a long time for them to get clean again."*

On lap 35, Ralf mounted his first serious attack on his brother, under braking for the final chicane. From then on, the younger Schumacher was visibly quicker and often poked the nose of his Williams alongside the Ferrari, but without any success. *"I couldn't really get past,"* he continued. *"I warned the pits I was going to wait for the stops, because I knew we would be pitting later. We had really taken on a lot of fuel and I knew I had a good chance of taking the lead after the stops. There was no need to take any risks before then."*

When Michael Schumacher rumbled down the pit lane on lap 46, the Williams driver stepped up the pace and built up enough of an advantage to emerge in the lead after his own stop on lap 51. It was game over. *"I tried to push before Ralf stopped,"* admitted Michael. *"But with a heavy fuel load on board, there was nothing I could do."*

With the Ferrari gradually dropping back towards the end of the race, Ralf Schumacher was never bothered again and he cruised to the second win of his career, much to the delight of Edouard Michelin, present in Montreal and genuinely moved to see his tyres win. The podium was filled with joie de vivre: Ralf was happy with his victory and Michael was delighted with six more points in his championship bag. *"If I have to lose, then it might as well be to Ralf. At least it keeps it in the family!"* joked the world champion.

Eddie Jordan denounces espionage

On Wednesday, the Montreal circuit is traditionally open to the public free of charge. Fans could walk freely down the pit lane and see the cars undergoing final preparations in the hands of the mechanics.

This year, the custom was cancelled and the public was not allowed in the circuit. According to the organisers, the teams kept nearly all their equipment and cars hidden away in the back of the garages, behind screens and no one could as much as catch a glimpse of a piece of bodywork. It has to be said that in 2000, even Minardi had hidden everything from view!

This was a situation which upset the locals and criticism was aimed at the teams. *"You should not accuse the teams of improper behaviour,"* counter-attacked Eddie Jordan. *"We did not initiate this situation. It's the photographers. These days we get sent detailed photos of all the other cars and that's not right. We invest millions for months, to develop new parts. The other teams photograph them and copy them in a couple of days. That's not right. We simply have to protect ourselves against this situation. I have even been sent another team's complete race sheet, with fuel consumption and engine revs. The photo was taken from the Paddock Club, above the pits, over the shoulder of an engineer. With the latest cameras, it's just become crazy."*

According to Jordan, photographers should obey some sort of code of honour. *"It could work. Whenever we've adopted some sort of code in Formula 1, it has been respected."*

Finally the podium!

Mika Hakkinen's 2001 season did not match his talent. That could be seen from the fact that his visit to the podium in Montreal was the first of the season after eight grands prix.

Even then, it was only the third rung, which is not really enough for someone who was world champion in 1998 and 1999. *"Of course, it's not quite good enough, but I'm happy all the same. As I started from eighth on the grid, I could not really hope for more than a podium today."* The Finn had not been too happy with his car and therefore played second fiddle to the Schumacher brothers. *"I'm just happy there aren't three of them,"* he said after the race.

△ *Ralf Schumacher in action. The German built his victory during the pit stops. Quite something, beating Ferrari on strategy!*

△ *The start: Michael Schumacher hangs onto the advantage of pole position.*

It was definitely not Jacques Villeneuve's weekend. After a troubled practice, the Canadian was forced to retire on lap 35 with transmission problems.
▽

A great day for the Sauber team, with
one of its drivers, Kimi Raikkonen in
fourth place. Passed by Jos Verstappen
on the opening lap, the young Finn
was then hit from behind by Ricardo
Zonta's Jordan. "I was very lucky not
to go off the track," he admitted after
the race. Slightly damaged, his
Sauber C20 lost some of its edge, which
allowed Mika Hakkinen to get past.

GRAND PRIX AIR CANADA

Villeneuve and Montoya trade insults

This Canadian Grand Prix was the backdrop to an extraordinary row between Juan Pablo Montoya and Jacques Villeneuve.

On Friday, the Canadian was the victim of an accident when he was tapped from behind by the Colombian and the BAR driver publically complained that he had been blocked on several occasions by the Williams man.

At the end of the afternoon, during a drivers' briefing, the two men had a violent row, even grabbing one another by the collar. Jacques Villeneuve told the Colombian that if he continued in this fashion, he would kill someone, Montoya replied that at least he had not killed anyone yet; a reference to the incident in Melbourne when a wheel off Villeneuve's car had caused the death of a track marshal. It was at this point that the Canadian grabbed the Williams driver by the collar. Race Director, Charlie Whiting, had to intervene in order to separate them. They were both warned they would be suspended if they did anything stupid in the race.

Two points more for the Prost team and a festival of smoke to celebrate the fact. In Montreal, Jean Alesi finished fifth, scoring points for the second consecutive time. At the time he didn't know it would also be the last.

"But when will they move this ruddy wall?" The famous "Quebec Wall," thus named because of the advertising it carries to entice tourists, found some new victims this year, including Rubens Barrichello and Nick Heidfeld during the qualifying session. In the race, his team-mate Kimi Raikkonen picked up three more points for the Swiss team.

Pedro De La Rosa during a pit stop, seen from an unusual angle. In Montreal, the Spaniard scored his first point of the season by finishing sixth.

Schumacher supports Bernoldi

At the Monaco Grand Prix, two weeks earlier, the Brazilian driver Enrique Bernoldi had been called all the names under the sun by Ron Dennis and Norbert Haug. In Montreal, the Arrows driver gave his own point of view: *"When I got out of the car, I was tired,"* he recalled. *"That's quite normal after 76 laps of the Monaco track. Ron and Norbert came bearing down on me in the parc ferme to shout at me. I couldn't understand a word of what they were saying, because, from my point of view, I had only done my job. I didn't block anyone and concentrated on my driving. I think I did what I had to do."* It was an opinion supported by Michael Schumacher, who described the Brazilian's driving as *"absolutely correct."* David Coulthard however, still maintained that his adversary had driven *"like an imbecile,"* zigzagging across the track several times. *"He should not have done that. It's against the rules which we have established between ourselves,"* reckoned the McLaren man.

The Newey affair shakes the paddock

In Montreal, Adrian Newey, the most sought after technical brain in the paddock, was at the centre of a scandal which could have made for a good film script. It all began on the Friday before the Canadian Grand Prix weekend. That morning, Jaguar issued a press release stating that Adrian Newey, McLaren's technical director, had just signed a contract to join them in August 2002.

A few minutes later, McLaren issued a three line comment stating that Newey would continue working for them after the expiry of his present agreement. McLaren then backed this up with a longer statement which maintained that the engineer had extended his contract for a further three years. *"I regret the speculation caused by my discussions with Bobby Rahal,"* added Newey. *"I came very close to working with him and it was a very difficult decision. I am very sorry for any embarrassment caused to my friends at Jaguar and McLaren because of this situation."*

Embarrassment was a euphemism. In the Jaguar camp, Bobby Rahal was absolutely furious. According to him, Adrian Newey had actually signed a binding contract, for a salary of six million Euros a year; a good deal more than many of the drivers could lay claim to earn. Bobby Rahal knew Adrian Newey well, from their days together in the Indycar championship. *"I have been speaking to Adrian about it ever since I came into F1,"* explained Rahal. *"Our friendship was based on trust, which has been seriously damaged today. Jaguar firmly intends to pursue this matter in the courts to have the contract signed by Adrian respected."*

On Thursday, the London High Court found in favour of the green team. According to its injunction, McLaren no longer had the right to employ Adrian Newey after his current contract expired on 31st July 2002. Jaguar had won the first round of what promised to be a long legal battle. However, if Newey was forced to work for Jaguar against his will, chances were his work would not be very good. Bobby Rahal knew that and so his action was aimed at getting the maximum in damages rather than really expecting the collaboration of a man who had already betrayed him.

McLaren replied to the injunction, specifying it only applied to 12th June. On the 13th, the two parties, Jaguar and McLaren, announced they had reached an amicable settlement along with apologies from Newey aimed at Jaguar. It was the epilogue to a strange story which had seen Newey manage to upset both his boss, Ron Dennis and his friend, Bobby Rahal.

The event of the week for Montreal society was of course the opening, just prior to the grand prix weekend, of "Newtown," the trendy bar-restaurant-disco which Jacques Villeneuve (Villeneuve = Newtown in English) had opened in Montreal's Crescent Street. It was packed out throughout the weekend, much to the delight of the owner.

PRACTICE TIMES

No	Driver	Car/Engine/Chassis	Practice Friday	Pos.	Practice Saturday	Pos.	Qualifying	Pos.	Warm-up	Pos.
1.	Michael Schumacher	Ferrari/F2001/210	1'19"166	11°	1'16"200	1°	1'15"782	1°	1'18"663	6°
2.	Rubens Barrichello	Ferrari/F2001/212	1'18"570	4°	1'16"986	4°	1'16"760	5°	1'19"201	8°
3.	Mika Häkkinen	McLaren/Mercedes/MP4/16/5	1'17"672	1°	1'16"828	3°	1'16"979	8°	1'18"650	5°
4.	David Coulthard	McLaren/Mercedes/MP4/16/6	1'18"086	2°	1'16"707	2°	1'16"423	3°	1'18"540	2°
5.	Ralf Schumacher	Williams/BMW/FW23/5	1'18"641	6°	1'17"521	8°	1'16"297	2°	1'19"536	10°
6.	Juan Pablo Montoya	Williams/BMW/FW23/6	1'18"639	5°	1'18"216	14°	1'17"123	10°	1'19"372	9°
7.	Giancarlo Fisichella	Benetton/Renault/B201/6	1'20"364	15°	1'19"347	19°	1'18"622	18°	1'21"344	20°
8.	Jenson Button	Benetton/Renault/B201/5	1'22"766	21°	1'19"213	18°	1'19"033	20°	1'21"114	19°
9.	Olivier Panis	BAR/Honda/003/6	1'19"102	10°	1'17"284	7°	1'16"771	6°	1'18"512	1°
10.	Jacques Villeneuve	BAR/Honda/003/7	1'21"916	19°	1'17"937	11°	1'17"035	9°	1'19"572	11°
11.	Ricardo Zonta	Jordan/Honda/EJ11/6	1'19"057	9°	1'18"595	15°	1'17"328	12°	1'18"545	3°
12.	Jarno Trulli	Jordan/Honda/EJ11/4	1'18"990	8°	1'17"618	9°	1'16"459	4°	1'18"875	7°
14.	Jos Verstappen	Arrows/Asiatech/A22/6	1'20"561	16°	1'18"030	13°	1'17"903	13°	1'19"775	12°
15.	Enrique Bernoldi	Arrows/Asiatech/A22/3	1'21"259	17°	1'18"649	16°	1'18"575	17°	1'20"059	15°
16.	Nick Heidfeld	Sauber/Petronas/C20/3	1'18"967	7°	1'17"103	5°	1'17"165	11°	1'20"062	16°
17.	Kimi Räikkönen	Sauber/Petronas/C20/6	1'19"427	13°	1'17"144	6°	1'16"875	7°	1'19"876	13°
18.	Eddie Irvine	Jaguar/R-2/4	1'18"508	3°	1'17"982	12°	1'18"016	15°	1'18"594	4°
19.	Pedro de la Rosa	Jaguar/R-2/6	1'19"707	14°	1'17"774	10°	1'18"015	14°	1'20"012	14°
20.	Tarso Marques	Minardi/European/PS01/4	1'25"415	22°	1'21"013	22°	1'20"690	21°	1'21"415	21°
21.	Fernando Alonso	Minardi/European/PS01/3	1'22"206	20°	1'20"549	21°	-	-	1'21"071	18°
22.	Jean Alesi	Prost/Acer/AP04/6	1'19"209	12°	1'18"935	17°	1'18"178	16°	1'20"943	17°
23.	Luciano Burti	Prost/Acer/AP04/5	1'21"280	18°	1'19"693	20°	1'18"753	19°	1'21"563	22°

MAXIMUM SPEEDS

No	Driver	P1 Qualifs	Pos	P1 Race	Pos	P2 Qualifs	Pos	P2 Race	Pos	Finish Qualifs	Pos	Finish Race	Pos	Trap Qualifs	Pos	Trap Race	Pos
1.	M. Schumacher	270,5	1°	264,3	3°	298,0	2°	293,3	10°	294,1	4°	291,1	13°	323,9	5°	326,6	13°
2.	R. Barrichello	269,0	2°	268,1	1°	294,5	8°	296,0	4°	294,1	3°	296,1	3°	323,2	7°	330,0	6°
3.	M. Häkkinen	268,9	4°	267,8	2°	293,8	11°	298,1	3°	294,0	5°	293,7	5°	318,4	21°	330,5	4°
4.	D. Coulthard	268,2	5°	253,9	15°	294,5	7°	290,7	17°	292,8	7°	288,3	17°	321,8	10°	320,0	19°
5.	R. Schumacher	267,5	7°	262,7	5°	298,2	1°	298,8	1°	295,4	1°	297,1	2°	321,5	11°	333,8	1°
6.	J. P. Montoya	268,9	3°	256,4	12°	295,6	4°	298,5	2°	294,7	2°	298,0	1°	323,6	6°	333,7	2°
7.	G. Fisichella	261,5	19°	216,3	22°	292,0	17°	283,0	22°	289,7	17°	-	-	321,5	12°	312,7	22°
8.	J. Button	259,6	20°	252,6	16°	287,9	20°	284,5	21°	286,1	21°	282,7	21°	318,9	18°	319,3	21°
9.	O. Panis	265,7	10°	248,8	17°	294,9	5°	292,6	14°	292,4	9°	291,8	9°	323,9	4°	325,3	15°
10.	J. Villeneuve	265,2	12°	258,0	11°	292,1	15°	291,1	16°	292,1	10°	291,7	10°	322,0	9°	328,3	8°
11.	R. Zonta	265,6	11°	260,6	8°	294,4	9°	295,1	6°	292,6	8°	293,9	4°	324,1	3°	328,3	9°
12.	J. Trulli	268,2	6°	262,0	6°	294,1	10°	293,0	12°	291,8	12°	291,4	11°	320,9	15°	325,3	16°
14.	J. Verstappen	263,8	18°	259,2	10°	291,4	18°	293,6	9°	291,0	13°	293,6	6°	319,6	16°	327,2	12°
15.	E. Bernoldi	264,9	14°	255,3	13°	290,1	19°	293,2	11°	288,9	19°	291,4	12°	321,2	13°	330,5	3°
16.	N. Heidfeld	266,4	8°	216,4	21°	294,6	6°	287,6	19°	292,1	11°	287,6	18°	322,7	8°	325,1	17°
17.	K. Räikkönen	264,9	13°	254,7	14°	296,2	3°	294,8	7°	292,8	6°	292,8	7°	324,4	2°	328,1	10°
18.	E. Irvine	263,9	16°	219,4	20°	292,7	13°	292,7	13°	290,7	14°	290,6	14°	324,7	1°	324,3	18°
19.	P. de la Rosa	264,4	15°	260,4	9°	292,2	14°	295,2	5°	289,8	16°	292,6	8°	317,6	22°	330,1	5°
20.	T. Marques	259,2	21°	247,5	18°	286,8	22°	285,0	20°	284,7	22°	283,6	20°	318,7	20°	319,5	20°
21.	F. Alonso	256,9	22°	244,5	19°	287,3	21°	288,3	18°	287,0	20°	286,0	19°	321,1	14°	329,3	7°
22.	J. Alesi	266,0	9°	263,5	4°	292,1	16°	293,7	8°	290,1	15°	289,4	15°	319,5	17°	327,6	11°
23.	L. Burti	263,8	17°	261,6	7°	293,3	12°	292,3	15°	289,0	18°	288,9	16°	318,8	19°	326,4	14°

PIT STOPS

	Drivers	Time	Lap	Stop n°
1.	J. Button	32"909	7	1
2.	E. Bernoldi	41"123	9	1
3.	J. Button	45"431	9	2
4.	T. Marques	30"938	21	1
5.	J. Verstappen	30"059	23	1
6.	P. de la Rosa	30"815	30	1
7.	L. Burti	32"582	33	1
8.	O. Panis	37"999	36	1
9.	R. Zonta	36"266	36	1
10.	O. Panis	4'08"708	37	2
11.	J. Trulli	32"359	38	1
12.	K. Räikkönen	30"336	39	1
13.	J. Alesi	32"517	41	1
14.	D. Coulthard	30"514	42	1
15.	M. Schumacher	29"609	46	1
16.	J. Verstappen	29"772	47	2
17.	T. Marques	31"095	47	2
18.	M. Häkkinen	30"484	49	1
19.	R. Schumacher	29"038	51	1
20.	P. de la Rosa	29"494	52	2

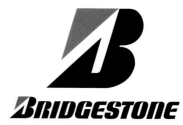

BRIDGESTONE

Best result for a driver running Bridgestone tyre:

Michael Schumacher, Ferrari, second

CHAMPIONSHIP

(after eight rounds)

Drivers :

1. M. Schumacher 58
2. D. Coulthard 40
3. R. Barrichello 24
4. R. Schumacher 22
5. M. Häkkinen 8
   N. Heidfeld.....................................8
7. J. Villeneuve....................................7
   J. Trulli 7
   N. Räikkönen 7
10. J. P. Montoya 6
    H.-H. Frentzen 6
12. O. Panis...5
13. E. Irvine 4
14. J. Alesi...3
15. G. Fisichella 1
    J. Verstappen 1

Constructors :

1. Ferrari..82
2. McLaren Mercedes 48
3. Williams BMW..............................28
4. Sauber Petronas............................15
5. Jordan Honda 13
6. BAR Honda 12
7. Jaguar Racing 5
8. Prost Acer 3
9. Benetton Renault............................1
   Arrows Asiatech 1

THE CIRCUIT

EIGHTH ROUND

GRAND PRIX AIR CANADA, MONTREAL

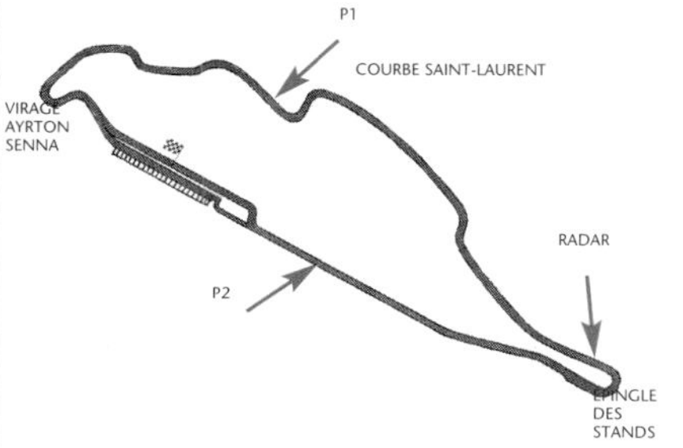

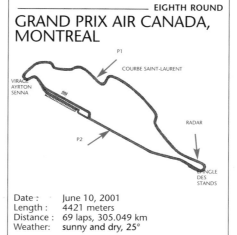

Date : June 10, 2001
Length : 4421 meters
Distance : 69 laps, 305.049 km
Weather: sunny and dry, 25°

CLASSIFICATION & RETIREMENTS

Pos	Driver	Team	Time
1.	R. Schum.	Williams BMW	1:34:31.522
2.	M. Schum.	Ferrari	+ 20.235
3.	Häkkinen	McLaren Mercedes	+ 40.672
4.	Räikkönen	Sauber Petronas	+ 68.115
5.	Alesi	Prost Acer	+ 70.435
6.	de la Rosa	Jaguar Racing	+ 1 lap
7.	Zonta	Jordan Honda	+1 lap
8.	Burti	Prost Acer	+ 1 lap
9.	Marques	European Minardi	+ 3 laps
10.	Verstappen	Arrows Asiatech	DNF
11.	Trulli	Jordan Honda	DNF

Lap	Driver	Team	Reason
1	Fisichella	Benetton Renault	collision
2	Irvine	Jaguar Racing	collision with Heidfeld
2	Heidfeld	Sauber Petronas	collision with Irvine
8	Alonso	European Minardi	transmission
18	Button	Benetton Renault	foil leak
20	Barrichello	Ferrari	off
20	Montoya	Williams BMW	off
25	Bernoldi	Arrows Asiatech	engine
35	Villeneuve	BAR Honda	transmission
38	Panis	BAR Honda	brakes
55	Coulthard	McLaren Mercedes	engine
64	Trulli	Jordan Honda	brakes hydraulics
66	Verstappen	Arrows Asiatech	off

FASTEST LAPS

	Driver	Time	Lap
1.	R. Schum.	1'17"205 206,147 km/h	50
2.	Häkkinen	1'18"148	45
3.	M. Schum.	1'18"176	48
4.	de la Rosa	1'19"006	50
5.	Verstappen	1'19"257	59
6.	Räikkönen	1'19"309	63
7.	Alesi	1'19"328	59
8.	Trulli	1'19"414	29
9.	Barrichello	1'19"722	13
10.	Coulthard	1'19"745	32
11.	Villeneuve	1'19"782	30
12.	Burti	1'19"841	60
13.	Panis	1'19"856	30
14.	Zonta	1'20"078	38
15.	Montoya	1'20"159	18
16.	Bernoldi	1'20"767	11
17.	Button	1'21"124	11
18.	Marques	1'22"312	19
19.	Alonso	1'22"413	4

All results : © 2001 Fédération International de l'Automobile, 2, Ch. Blandonnet, 1215 Genève 15, Suisse

RACE SUMMARY

- As the lights go out, Michael Schumacher leads brother Ralf, Coulthard, Trulli and Barrichello.
- Barrichello steams past Trulli and then Coulthard on lap 3.
- Going like a train, Barrichello sets a race fastest lap on lap 4. He attacks second placed Ralf Schumacher, spins and continues in 16th place.
- The gap between the two brothers grows to 2.4 seconds on lap 25, before dropping to 0.6 seconds on lap 34.
- On lap 20, Montoya hits the barriers and Barrichello goes off trying to avoid him. The Safety Car is brought out until lap 23.
- Ralf Schumacher sets race fastest times on laps 26, 27, 29, 30 and 31.
- Villeneuve retires on lap 35. Ralf Schumacher attacks his brother for the first time, but cannot pass.
- The gap between the two leaders is under 0.3 seconds from lap 35 to 42, with Ralf all over the back of the Ferrari.
- On lap 39, Ralf Schumacher is baulked by his brother.
- Michael Schumacher pits on lap 46. Ralf steps up the pace, putting in several race fastest laps, until he pits on lap 51.
- After his stop, Ralf Schumacher takes the lead.
- Coulthard's engine explodes on lap 56. Ralf Schumacher now leads his brother by 9.2 seconds.
- Ralf Schumacher takes his second win of the season ahead of his brother.

LAP CHART

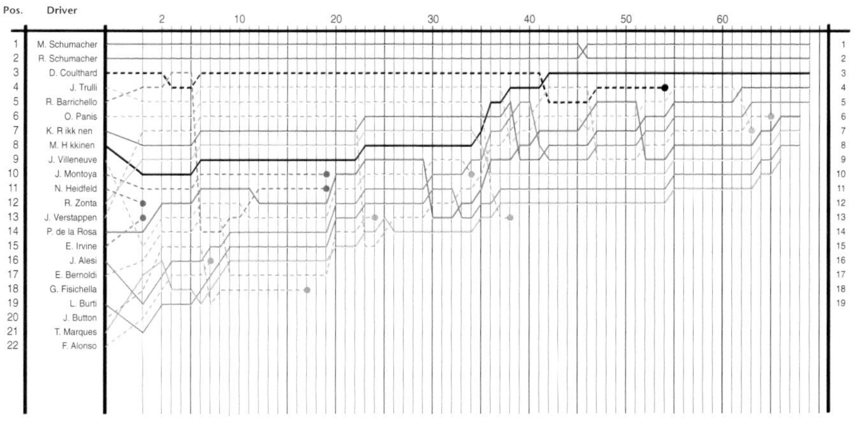

GAPS ON THE LEADER BOARD

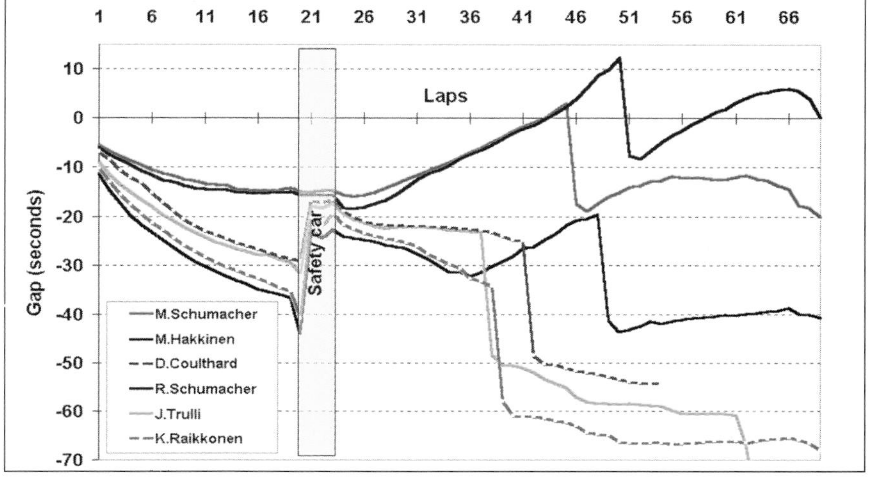

Brothers at war

Just as in Canada, two weeks earlier, Michael and Ralf Schumacher had qualified on the front row for this the European Grand Prix.

However, at the start (photo,) things did not go as smoothly as in Montreal. Having got away well, it seemed as though Ralf would take the lead, but for the fact he was viciously pushed towards the wall by Michael. It was a move which would keep the German media busy for a while to come.

Nothing daunted, the younger man kept on pushing, but it all fizzled out when he was given a ten second stop-go penalty for crossing the white line as he left the pits. It was a benign mistake, followed by a severe penalty and the race was handed to Ferrari on a plate. Much to the delight of the crowd.

WARSTEINER GRAND PRIX OF EUROPE
NÜRBURGRING

The two Schumachers in front again!

"Very kind of you Ralf. Let me win this world championship and then we will see." The two Schumacher brothers still seemed to get on very well in the paddocks.

▷

Bridgestone had invented "the biggest tyre in the paddock" this season. It was in the public area and was a showcase for the manufacturer to display its wares. It was a huge success.

▷▽

Frentzen (8th) and Trulli (7th) on the grid for Jordan. Not bad, but neither man would make it to the chequered flag.

▽

The BMW-Williams are in fine form. On Saturday morning, during free practice, the two blue and white cars set the fastest times in the session. In the afternoon qualifying hour, only Michael Schumacher was capable of spoiling the party and preventing an all Williams front row.

In fact, the Ferrari driver was surprised he had managed to do it. *"This morning when I saw the time begins to drop, I never thought I could get pole position. In fact, I hadn't had enough time to try running on new tyres, because of a hydraulic problem and we had no idea what to expect. Actually, we had made a lot more progress than we expected."*

In second place, Ralf Schumacher admitted he never thought pole would have been within his grasp. *"I realised the Ferraris were going quicker and quicker on old tyres. When I saw Rubens (Barrichello) set a super time, I knew Michael could do it. Actually, I'm quite surprised we are so well placed compared with the Bridgestone runners. What's more, I wasn't able to improve at the end of the session. Usually, the track is quicker then, but that was not the case today because of the dirt some drivers had kicked onto the track. I have the impression some of them do it deliberately after their quick lap to spoil it for the others."*

On this circuit, it seemed that the Michelin tyres worked better the higher the temperature. The Williams drivers were therefore both praying for hot and sunny weather on Sunday, so they could shine in the race.

Juan Pablo Montoya was third on the grid and had every intention of picking up some points. So far this season, with eight races gone, the Colombian had only made it to the finish in the Spanish Grand Prix. *"I'd really like to finish this race for a change,"* he admitted. *"I have encountered too many problems this season, not all of them my fault. It's time for a change."*

Ralf to 2004

As had been rumoured for some while, the Nurburgring was the setting for Williams to announce it had just renewed its contract with Ralf Schumacher until the end of 2004. The young German was therefore going to spend another three years with the Anglo-German squad, in the hope of picking up a world championship title. His contract would therefore expire at the same as his brother Michael's would end with Ferrari.

The title was the avowed aim of the team, which had already won two grands prix this year (in San Marino and Canada.) Certainly the team looked to be heading up the order. Ralf and Williams were banking on Michelin tyres. If the Clermont-Ferrand manufacturer still did not supply one of the two top teams, this relationship would become a privileged one.

Mika will not help David

In the McLaren camp, it seemed that the management was now prepared to help David Coulthard to the detriment of Mika Hakkinen.

Ron Dennis admitted that if Mika was leading David in the race, he would intervene and ask him to let the Scotsman pass. Up until now, the English team boss had repeated that he did not go in for this sort of thing and that he would always let his drivers sort it out on the track. David Coulthard, who had already helped out his team-mate in the past, could legitimately hope that Mika Hakkinen would repay the compliment this season. The Finn only had eight championship points to his name.

But while the McLaren management was ready to back Coulthard, Hakkinen did not seem too well disposed to follow any instructions to give up his position. *"If I find myself leading the grand prix on Sunday, I will continue driving flat out to try and win,"* he declared. Very disappointed not to have won a single grand prix this season, as a result of a run of bad luck which would not release its grip, the Finn seemed determined to cause dissent in the camp. *"I must win,"* he continued. *"That's what I am paid to do and that is what the team expects of me. I fight for myself, to win the championship and I come to every circuit with the aim of winning."*

As far as the Finn was concerned, the start of the second half of the 2001 season was too early in the year to bury his chances. *"The situation is very complicated,"* he admitted. *"I understand how difficult it is. But if my situation has not improved in the next four grands prix, then things will be different and I will then be able to consider helping David."*

STARTING GRID

M. SCHUMACHER 1'14"960	-1-	R. SCHUMACHER 1'15"226	
J. P. MONTOYA 1'15"490	-2-	R. BARRICHELLO 1'15"622	
David COULTHARD 1'15"717	-3-	Mika HÄKKINEN 1'15"776	
Jarno TRULLI 1'16"138	-4-	H.-H. FRENTZEN 1'16"376	
Kimi RAIKKONEN 1'16"402	-5-	Nick HEIDFELD 1'16"438	
Jacques VILLENEUVE 1'16"439	-6-	Eddie IRVINE 1'16"588	
Olivier PANIS 1'16"872	-7-	Jean ALESI 1'17"251	
G. FISICHELLA 1'17"378	-8-	Pedro De la ROSA 1'17"627	
Luciano BURTI 1'18"113	-9-	Enrique BERNOLDI 1'18"151	
Jos VERSTAPPEN 1'18"262	-10-	Jenson BUTTON 1'18"626	
Fernando ALONSO 1'18"630	-11-	Tarso MARQUES 1'18"689	

Schumi Majestic!

It is no longer the McLarens pushing him to greater heights, but the Williams. At the Nurburgring, Michael Schumacher took yet another win, this time in the European Grand Prix. But he was made to fight for it all the way by the ever improving BMW-Williams duo of his brother Ralf and the Colombian, Juan Pablo Montoya.

It all began at the beginning. Michael Schumacher had to "squeeze" his little brother into the wall to keep the advantage of pole position. *"I didn't know what strategy Ralf was on, but I knew we were planning to stop twice,"* explained the Ferrari man after the race. *"There was therefore no question of letting him get ahead. When I saw him coming up the inside, I had to use the rules to the maximum; that is to say I moved over once to retake the line. Unfortunately, it was the only thing to do."*

Once the race was underway, the younger Schumacher lost no time in sticking to his brother's coat tails. *"I was controlling the situation pretty well,"* reckoned the eventual winner. *"I only had one worrying moment, at the hairpin, because I braked too late. I left a bit of room, but I had no reason to make life easy for Ralf. I like fighting with him, because we will always leave just enough room so that the other one can continue. And, in the end, it doesn't really matter which one of us wins."*

Once Ralf Schumacher was out of the running because of his penalty (see below), Michael just had to maintain his advantage over Juan Pablo Montoya, who, by then, was a good ten seconds down. *"On my first set of tyres, my car was not very*

well balanced," was his analysis of the situation. *"I asked for a few changes to the set-up to be made during my first pit stop and after that, everything was much better. I think that, under normal circumstances, I would never really have been challenged by Ralf."*

With a 24 point lead in the championship over David Coulthard, who no longer seemed to be on top form, the rest of Michael Schumacher's season

looked to be a calm one. *"It seems to me that Williams are now are main rivals,"* concluded the German.

A 10 second penalty for Ralf

A too severe punishment

Lap 28. The duel had been raging for a good ten laps as Michael Schumacher prepared to make pit stops at the same time. It was a dubious call from the Williams strategists, who might have done better to leave their man out for a few extra laps to try and build up a lead.

As is generally the case, the Ferrari mechanics proved the most efficient, Michael got going before Ralf. But as the Williams man headed out to the track, he moved just a touch too much to the side and got his two lefthand side wheels on the white line which separates the pit lane from the track. Although illegal, it was an unintentional mistake,

which didn't gain him any advantage, but the Stewards obviously deemed it a hanging offence. Instead of fining the Williams man, they gave him a ten second stop-go penalty. It was a stiff penalty which robbed Ralf Schumacher of his chances of securing a good result. Having made the penalty stop, he found himself behind Rubens Barrichello and David Coulthard. *"I have to accept this penalty,"* regretted the German driver after the race, *"but it's hard to take. I was looking in my mirrors to see if anyone was approaching and naturally, I concentrated more on the traffic than on the position of the white line!"*

After the race, Michael Schumacher shared the general opinion that the penalty was too harsh. *"Of course, I would need to see the video footage to get a clear idea, but according to what I've been told, Ralf only barely touched the line. Okay, it is forbidden in the rules, but I think the penalty should fit the crime. One should decide if it was a deliberate fault or a simple mistake."*

The reigning world champion admitted that allowing some latitude to the Stewards in applying various sanctions would leave the door open to various interpretations and charges of favouritism. However, the end result was that the Stewards' decision robbed everyone of a great tussle between

the two brothers.

Michael was the first to regret this aspect of the incident. *"Of course, I would have liked my fight with Ralf to last to the end of the race,"* he concluded. *"It would have meant David Coulthard would not have finished on the podium!"*

As far as Michael Schumacher was concerned, David Coulthard was still his main rival for the world championship title. However, at the Nurburgring, the two silver arrows never really hit the target.

△

"Take that!" The much talked about move, seen from a helicopter: at the start, Michael squeezed Ralf into the pit wall.

◁

"Of course, it's a BMW, but no one will notice..." Michael Schumacher broke down on the warm-up lap and only just got back to the pits in time.

He got a big fright!

Michael Schumacher had a major scare even before the race had got underway. Doing a reconnaissance lap in the T-car, before forming up on the grid, the car broke down at the back of the circuit. *"It was the worst place to happen, the furthest point from the pits,"* he recounted. *"I was wondering how I would get back before the pit lane closed. It was a strange feeling with all one's hopes disappearing in a moment. Then I saw a scooter, but there was no key in it. Then someone turned up and handed me the key. I told myself there must have been enough time to get back, but I didn't even have time to look at my watch to check!"* In fact, there was enough time, thanks to a BMW scooter! You can't always be choosy.

◁◁

He's won and what's more, in front of his adoring fans. It was well worth a patented Michael Schumacher jump for joy.

 **WARSTEINER GRAND PRIX OF EUROPE**

Reflections on Juan Pablo Montoya's helmet. The Colombian qualified in third place at the Nurburgring, just behind Ralf Schumacher. In the race, he set the fastest lap for the first time this season and finished second. Bit by bit, he was getting the hang of Formula 1 and the Williams team. It would not be too much longer before he also had the measure of his team-mate.

WARSTEINER GRAND PRIX OF EUROPE

Asiatech quits Arrows

A great aerial shot of the Nurburgring circuit with 142,000 seats for 142,000 fans of the Schumacher brothers.

Rumours had been doing the rounds for a few days that Asiatech was planning a change for the following year.

Based on the 2000 season Peugeot V10, still developed at Peugeot Sport's Velizy headquarters, the Asiatech engine had been powering the Arrows cars since the start of the season, with mixed fortunes. Asiatech was basically a Japanese firm, created by the son of the man who founded the Sony Corporation and they had bought the rights to the French engine.

Unhappy about aspects of its collaboration with Arrows, Asiatech had decided to stop supplying the English team, come the end of the year.

Arrows boss, Tom Walkinshaw, was not worried, claiming he had at least three other irons in the engine fire for the following season - apparently these included Cosworth and Ferrari. For its part, Asiatech was planning to invest and buy shares in Alain Prost's team, as well as supplying him with its V10. For the French team, this would constitute an amazing return to Peugeot power. In fact, a few weeks later, Asiatech ended up announcing that they would be joining forces with Minardi. And they call that progress?

Ron Dennis with Adrian Newey on the pit wall. After the scandal in Canada, the two men were back together again, even if something was forever amiss in their relationship. With a third and a sixth place, it was another disastrous weekend for the silver arrows.

WEEKEND GOSSIP

• The Scuderia goes green

Ferrari rolled into the Nurburgring paddock with a new "ecologically friendly" Media motorhome. It sported the Mobius logo, the symbol indicating that materials used in construction were recyclable. Indeed, 95% of the bus had been made from recycled material, from the office furniture to the sides of the awning. *"Even the glue used in the assembly is environmentally friendly,"* boasted the Ferrari folk.

• A two litre Formula 1?

The FIA was considering a reduction in engine size for Formula 1 (the current rules being for three litre power plants) in order to reduce the speed of the cars. BMW's motorsport boss, Mario Theissen, thought this was an absurd notion. *"Without a doubt, this would be the most expensive way of slowing down the cars,"* he explained. *"On top of that, it would only slow the cars down on the straights, when most accidents have nothing to do with top speed."* Mercedes-Benz's Norbert Haug was of the same opinion.

• Jacques stays

Jacques Villeneuve looked set to spend at least another year with the BAR team. The Canadian's contract contained a performance clause, which allowed him to leave the team if it did not finish third in the Constructors' Championship. But the Canadian had not the slightest intention of playing this card. *"I feel comfortable with this team,"* he said in justification of his position. *"For the moment, it is making progress. But the nearer we get to the top, the harder it becomes to make the final step forward."*

• An accidental accident

The Italian judges had shut down the inquiry they had instigated into the death of the fire marshal, Paolo Gislimberti at the 2000 Italian Grand Prix. The magistrates concluded that his death was the result of a series of accidental incidents. The trajectory taken by the wheel was described as "unusual," while the unfortunate fire marshal had actually left his safety post a few seconds before the moment of impact, and was then hit with the full force of the wheel.

The Schumi effect continues to boom

Refuelling in the Jaguar pit. Eddie Irvine qualified 12th at the Nurburgring and just missed out on scoring points, coming home seventh.

The effect of the "Schumi-boom" with red and blue the dominant colour in the grandstands.

The organisers of the European Grand Prix were delighted: the 142,000 grandstand seats available for race day had all been sold out the week prior to the event. *"We always sell out, but never as early as this,"* said an enthusiastic Walter Kafitz, the Nurburgring circuit boss. Kafitz put this phenomenon down to the success of the two Schumacher brothers, which had been given a further boost by their one-two finish, a fortnight earlier in Montreal. *"It's definitely the "double Schumi boom" which has caught the imagination of the fans."*

The circuit had undergone extensive modifications for the 2001 grand prix; the first time extensive work had been carried out since 1984. This resulted in the teams having new garages to work in, at a cost of 30 million D Marks, which represented about one tenth of the Grand Prix's annual budget.

PRACTICE TIMES

No	Driver	Car/Engine/Chassis	Practice Friday	Pos.	Practice Saturday	Pos.	Qualifying	Pos.	Warm-up	Pos.
1.	Michael Schumacher	Ferrari/F2001/206	1'17"507	4°	1'16"308	6°	1'14"960	1°	1'18"371	2°
2.	Rubens Barrichello	Ferrari/F2001/210	1'17"665	5°	1'15"855	3°	1'15"622	4°	1'18"209	1°
3.	Mika Häkkinen	McLaren/Mercedes/MP4/16/7	1'16"408	1°	1'16"038	4°	1'15"776	6°	1'19"164	8°
4.	David Coulthard	McLaren/Mercedes/MP4/16/6	1'16"579	2°	1'16"237	5°	1'15"717	5°	1'18"674	5°
5.	Ralf Schumacher	Williams/BMW/FW23/5	1'17"355	3°	1'15"355	1°	1'15"226	2°	1'18"392	3°
6.	Juan Pablo Montoya	Williams/BMW/FW23/6	1'17"737	6°	1'15"749	2°	1'15"490	3°	1'18"843	6°
7.	Giancarlo Fisichella	Benetton/Renault/B201/6	1'19"339	14°	1'17"785	16°	1'17"378	15°	1'21"766	22°
8.	Jenson Button	Benetton/Renault/B201/5	1'19"978	18°	1'18"674	20°	1'18"626	20°	1'21"423	21°
9.	Olivier Panis	BAR/Honda/003/6	1'18"410	10°	1'16"625	9°	1'16"872	13°	1'19"808	12°
10.	Jacques Villeneuve	BAR/Honda/003/7	1'18"434	12°	1'17"006	12°	1'16"439	11°	1'20"320	17°
11.	Heinz-Harald Frentzen	Jordan/Honda/EJ11/6	1'19"988	19°	1'16"407	8°	1'16"376	8°	1'19"917	14°
12.	Jarno Trulli	Jordan/Honda/EJ11/5	1'18"133	7°	1'16"385	7°	1'16"138	7°	1'19"002	7°
14.	Jos Verstappen	Arrows/Asiatech/A22/6	1'19"640	16°	1'18"123	19°	1'18"262	19°	1'20"115	16°
15.	Enrique Bernoldi	Arrows/Asiatech/A22/3	1'19"822	17°	1'17"686	14°	1'18"151	18°	1'20"098	15°
16.	Nick Heidfeld	Sauber/Petronas/C20/5	1'18"196	8°	1'16"941	11°	1'16"438	10°	1'19"732	9°
17.	Kimi Räikkönen	Sauber/Petronas/C20/6	1'18"413	11°	1'16"852	10°	1'16"402	9°	1'19"787	10°
18.	Eddie Irvine	Jaguar/R-2/4	1'19"503	15°	1'17"609	13°	1'16"588	12°	1'18"466	4°
19.	Pedro de la Rosa	Jaguar/R-2/6	1'18"473	13°	1'18"048	18°	1'17"627	16°	1'19"796	11°
20.	Tarso Marques	Minardi/European/PS01/4	1'21"129	22°	1'20"208	22°	1'18"689	22°	1'20"988	19°
21.	Fernando Alonso	Minardi/European/PS01/3	1'20"183	21°	1'19"164	21°	1'18"630	21°	1'21"367	20°
22.	Jean Alesi	Prost/Acer/AP04/5	1'18"352	9°	1'17"839	17°	1'17"251	14°	1'19"854	13°
23.	Luciano Burti	Prost/Acer/AP04/6	1'20"094	20°	1'17"688	15°	1'18"113	17°	1'20"608	18°

MAXIMUM SPEEDS

No	Driver	P1 Qualifs	Pos	P1 Race	Pos	P2 Qualifs	Pos	P2 Race	Pos	Finish Qualifs	Pos	Finish Race	Pos	Trap Qualifs	Pos	Trap Race	Pos
1.	M. Schumacher	287,0	6°	284,0	8°	228,4	7°	221,3	9°	286,4	5°	302.0	7°	302,0	7°	304,2	9°
2.	R. Barrichello	288,0	3°	283,8	11°	229,8	4°	223,7	5°	288,0	3°	302.2	6°	302,2	6°	302,1	15°
3.	M. Häkkinen	285,6	12°	281,9	17°	232,0	1°	222,0	7°	287,3	4°	297.0	18°	297,0	18°	301,2	17°
4.	D. Coulthard	287,6	4°	283,9	10°	228,7	5°	222,5	6°	283,9	13°	301.3	8°	301,3	8°	301,6	16°
5.	R. Schumacher	293,5	1°	290,8	1°	229,9	3°	227,5	2°	289,0	2°	308.7	1°	308,7	1°	309,1	1°
6.	J. P. Montoya	292,6	2°	289,4	2°	231,0	2°	228,7	1°	290,1	1°	306.7	2°	306,7	2°	308,0	3°
7.	G. Fisichella	281,8	19°	278,0	20°	224,6	15°	218,2	18°	277,7	20°	293.7	22°	293,7	22°	297,6	22°
8.	J. Button	281,0	20°	278,6	19°	222,7	19°	217,8	19°	275,3	21°	294.8	21°	294,8	21°	299,0	19°
9.	O. Panis	283,3	16°	277,9	21°	226,8	10°	213,8	21°	284,1	11°	298.6	15°	298,6	15°	298,2	20°
10.	J. Villeneuve	286,0	9°	283,6	14°	226,5	13°	218,9	17°	285,9	6°	303.0	3°	303,0	3°	305,4	7°
11.	H.-H. Frentzen	285,7	11°	283,7	12°	226,9	9°	220,2	13°	284,8	8°	300.5	11°	300,5	11°	303,2	12°
12.	J. Trulli	284,3	15°	283,7	13°	228,3	8°	219,0	15°	283,0	15°	298.1	16°	298,1	16°	302,8	13°
14.	J. Verstappen	286,3	8°	283,3	15°	224,4	16°	219,8	14°	281,6	17°	300.7	9°	300,7	9°	303,7	10°
15.	E. Bernoldi	286,6	7°	285,5	6°	226,7	12°	220,5	12°	283,1	14°	302.8	4°	302,8	4°	304,8	8°
16.	N. Heidfeld	282,2	18°	282,5	16°	226,7	11°	216,0	20°	284,5	9°	297.4	17°	297,4	17°	302,4	14°
17.	K. Räikkönen	283,1	17°	283,9	9°	228,5	6°	219,0	16°	285,8	7°	299.7	13°	299,7	13°	303,5	11°
18.	E. Irvine	284,7	14°	287,3	3°	226,4	14°	226,7	3°	282,6	16°	298.8	14°	298,8	14°	305,9	6°
19.	P. de la Rosa	284,8	13°	285,9	5°	223,3	18°	225,9	4°	278,7	19°	300.5	10°	300,5	10°	309,1	2°
20.	T. Marques	280,0	22°	276,6	22°	220,2	22°	211,1	22°	274,0	22°	296.7	19°	296,7	19°	298,0	21°
21.	F. Alonso	280,5	21°	280,3	18°	220,5	21°	220,9	11°	280,1	18°	295.8	20°	295,8	20°	301,2	18°
22.	J. Alesi	287,1	5°	285,1	7°	223,3	17°	221,2	10°	284,2	10°	302.4	5°	302,4	5°	306,5	4°
23.	L. Burti	285,9	10°	286,4	4°	222,3	20°	221,6	8°	283,9	12°	300.2	12°	300,2	12°	306,3	5°

CLASSIFICATION & RETIREMENTS

Pos	Driver	Team	Time
1.	M. Schum.	Ferrari	1:29:42.724
2.	Montoya	Williams BMW	+ 4.217
3.	Coulthard	McLaren Mercedes	+ 24.993
4.	Barrichello	Ferrari	+ 33.345
5.	R. Schum.	Williams BMW	+ 45.495
6.	Häkkinen	McLaren Mercedes	+ 64.868
7.	Irvine	Jaguar Racing	+ 66.198
8.	de la Rosa	Jaguar Racing	+ 1 lap
9.	Villeneuve	BAR Honda	+ 1 lap
10.	Räikkönen	Sauber Petronas	+ 1 lap
11.	Fisichella	Benetton Renault	+ 1 lap
12.	Burti	Prost Acer	+ 2 laps
13.	Button	Benetton Renault	+ 2 laps
14.	Alonso	European Minardi	+ 2 laps
15.	Alesi	Prost Acer	off

Lap	Driver	Team	Reason
8	Marques	European Minardi	electrics
24	Panis	BAR Honda	gearbox
30	Bernoldi	Arrows Asiatech	gearbox
45	Trulli	Jordan Honda	hydraulic
49	Frentzen	Jordan Honda	traction control
55	Heidfeld	Sauber Petronas	transmission
59	Verstappen	Arrows Asiatech	engine

FASTEST LAPS

	Driver	Time	Lap
1.	Montoya	1'18"354	27
		209,326 km/h	
2.	R. Schum.	1'18"498	54
3.	Barrichello	1'18"537	59
4.	M. Schum.	1'18"612	49
5.	Irvine	1'18"674	34
6.	Coulthard	1'18"883	63
7.	Burti	1'19"105	57
8.	Häkkinen	1'19"273	65
9.	Trulli	1'19"484	32
10.	de la Rosa	1'19"737	65
11.	Villeneuve	1'19"797	65
12.	Frentzen	1'19"892	31
13.	Alesi	1'20"049	48
14.	Button	1'20"069	25
15.	Räikkönen	1'20"498	34
16.	Fisichella	1'20"729	26
17.	Alonso	1'20"937	29
18.	Heidfeld	1'20"976	53
19.	Verstappen	1'21"154	23
20.	Bernoldi	1'21"188	25
21.	Panis	1'21"314	23
22.	Marques	1'23"778	4

All results :
© 2001 Fédération Internationale de l'Automobile, 2, Ch. Blandonnet, 1215 Genève 15, Suisse

PIT STOPS

	Driver	Time	Lap	Stop n°
1.	Burti	38"692	12	1
2.	Fisichella	32"283	21	1
3.	Bernoldi	43"799	23	1
4.	Button	33"287	23	1
5.	Alonso	40"847	25	1
6.	Verstappen	36"805	26	1
7.	M. Schumacher	32"688	28	1
8.	R. Schumacher	33"906	28	1
9.	Montoya	33"608	29	1
10.	Frentzen	34"001	29	1
11.	Trulli	33"227	30	1
12.	Räikkönen	35"928	32	1
13.	Häkkinen	36"581	33	1
14.	Heidfeld	35"344	33	1
15.	Irvine	36"665	37	1
16.	Coulthard	34"890	38	1
17.	R. Schumacher	35"009	39	2
18.	Alesi	33"429	42	1
19.	Fisichella	33"809	42	2
20.	Villeneuve	33"659	43	1
21.	Barrichello	35"751	44	1
22.	Button	33"784	43	2
23.	de la Rosa	33"490	44	1
24.	Verstappen	33"874	46	2
25.	Alonso	34"423	46	2
26.	M. Schumacher	31"983	50	2
27.	Montoya	32"721	50	2
28.	Burti	32"161	49	2
29.	R. Schumacher	33"224	52	2

BRIDGESTONE

Best result for a driver running Bridgestone tyre:

Michael Schumacher, Ferrari, winner

THE CIRCUIT

NINTH ROUND

WARSTEINER GRAND PRIX OF EUROPE, NÜRBURGRING

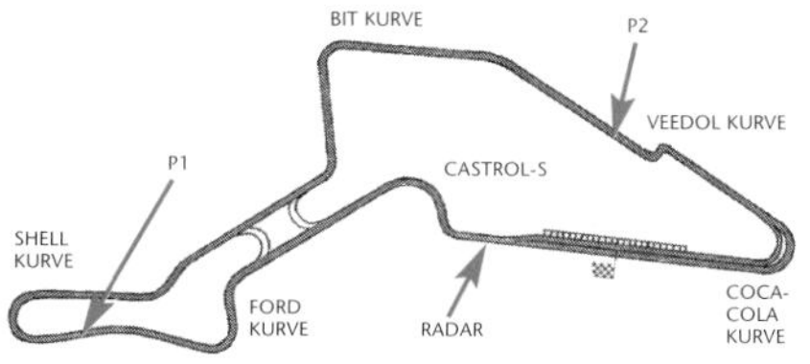

Date : June 24, 2001
Length : 4556 meters
Distance : 67 laps, 305.235 km
Weather : sunny, 23°

CHAMPIONSHIP

(after nine rounds)

Drivers :

1. M. Schumacher 68
2. D. Coulthard 44
3. R. Barrichello 26
4. R. Schumacher 25
5. J. P. Montoya 12
6. M. Häkkinen 9
7. N. Heidfeld 8
8. J. Trulli 7
   N. Räikkönen 7
   J. Villeneuve 7
11. H.-H. Frentzen 6
12. O. Panis 5
13. E. Irvine 4
14. J. Alesi 3
15. J. Verstappen 1
    G. Fisichella 1
    P. de la Rosa 1

Constructors :

1. Ferrari 94
2. McLaren Mercedes 53
3. Williams BMW 37
4. Sauber Petronas 15
5. Jordan Honda 13
6. BAR Honda 12
7. Jaguar Racing 5
8. Prost Acer 3
9. Arrows Asiatech 1
   Benetton Renault 1

RACE SUMMARY

- Ralf Schumacher seems to get off the grid better than Michael. However, the elder brother moves to the right, squeezing Ralf towards the concrete wall. The younger man has to lift slightly and is second.
- At the end of the opening lap, Michael leads Ralf by 1.4 seconds, with a 2.6 second advantage over Montoya and 3.3 seconds over Coulthard.
- Between laps 9 and 11, the gap between the two brothers is 3.4 seconds. After that, the Williams starts to make ground on the Ferrari and sets several race fastest laps.
- On lap 23, the gap between them stabilises at 0.3 seconds. Ralf is all over the back of the Ferrari but cannot pass. Montoya makes the most of it to close on the lead duo. By lap 30, he is just 4.1 seconds behind the lead Ferrari.
- The three leaders refuel between laps 28 and 29, but the order remains unchanged.
- On lap 38, there's an upset. Ralf has to pit for a 10 second stop-go penalty, for having crossed the white line separating the pit lane from the track after his pit stop. The duel between the brothers is thus at an end.
- Michael Schumacher makes his second stop on lap 50, at the same time as Montoya.
- Ralf Schumacher makes his third stop for his second refuelling on lap 52. Coulthard, who only stops once, thus moves into third place.

LAP CHART

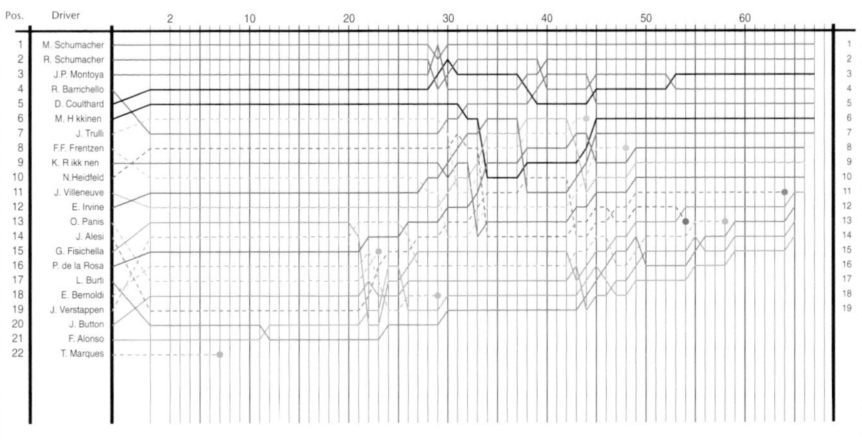

GAPS ON THE LEADER BOARD

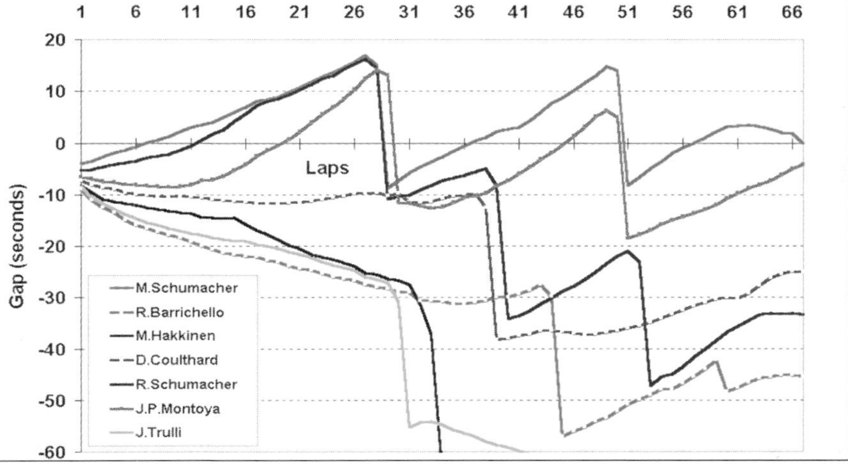

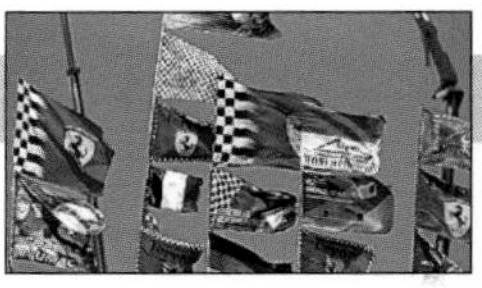

The half century

Even though he had lost out in the battle for pole position, to the benefit of his brother Ralf, Michael Schumacher won the French Grand Prix with a performance worthy of the Maestro.

The victory brought with it a sense of relief, as he now had a 31 point lead over the chasing pack in pursuit of the world championship title. It was a major advantage, given there were only seven more rounds to go this season. The German had plenty of reason to feel confident, given that no other driver appeared to be emerging as a serious rival. Indeed, in the McLaren camp, the problems had come thick and fast in Magny-Cours, with Mika Hakkinen not even making it past the start and David Coulthard finishing a long way back.

MOBIL 1 GRAND PRIX DE FRANCE
MAGNY-COURS

His first pole on his 26th birthday

Happy Birthday Ralf

A first! In Magny-Cours, Ralf Schumacher claimed his very first pole position in a career which, up to this weekend, had numbered 76 grands prix.

It was also the first pole position for Michelin since returning to the discipline at the start of the season. *"This pole is all the more fantastic because we didn't believe it possible,"* admitted Pierre Dupasquier, the French company's competition boss. *"Looking at this morning's lap times, we thought the Ferraris would be untouchable and we would have to settle for second place. We were more than pleasantly surprised by the final result!"*

That result was a close run thing, with the younger Schumacher ending up just one miniscule hundredth of a second ahead of his Ferrari-mounted brother. *"This is an incredible result for the team,"* admitted Ralf. *"But for me, it's just nice. The most important thing is the race."* The youngster set his time fairly early on in the session and he stayed on top to the end of the hour. *"The track had got a bit slower towards the end. I don't think I could have done better."*

It was boiling hot at the French track. The track temperature hit the 46 degree mark at the end of the session. That is no doubt what helped the Michelin tyres and BMW-Williams to take pole position.

Bridgestone stays

As had been widely expected, the Bridgestone tyre company had decided to prolong its presence in Formula 1.

Present on Sunday in Magny-Cours was Shigeo Watanabe, the Managing Director of the Japanese marque. He explained that Bridgestone's arrival in Formula 1 "had allowed the brand to increase its global visibility to an incredible degree.

"In the future, even more car and tyre companies will be involved in F1 and that will see the sport, one of the most popular in the world, become even more important," he underlined. *"Bridgestone will maintain its involvement in Formula 1 for as long as possible."*

Ralf was celebrating his 26th birthday on the Saturday and this pole was a nice present, even if his brother had not given it to him. *"Nobody has given me a present yet today, not even Michael,"* added Ralf. *"But for sure, after this pole, I don't need one."*

At the start of the previous weekend's European Grand Prix, Michael Schumacher had rather squeezed his brother Ralf towards the concrete barrier.

Taking the number one slot, this time it was the younger man's turn to threaten his brother with the same treatment. *"This time, it will be different to last week,"* joked Ralf. *"I'm in front and Michael might have to back off."*

Alongside him in the press conference, Michael just smiled at the thought of the first corner. *"If Ralf does to me what I did to him last weekend, then of course I won't be happy. But that's racing."*

First (and only) pole position for Ralf △ Schumacher in Magny-Cours.

The sparks were flying between Eddie △▷ Jordan and his driver Heinz-Harald Frentzen. The boss reckoned the German was not putting enough effort into his work behind the wheel.

No sign of improvement at Benetton. Jenson Button qualified 17th. ▷

STARTING GRID

R. SCHUMACHER 1'12"989	-1-	M. SCHUMACHER 1'12"999
David COULTHARD 1'13"186	-2-	Mika HÄKKINEN 1'13"268
Jarno TRULLI 1'13"310	-3-	J. P. MONTOYA 1'13"625
H.-H. FRENTZEN 1'13"815	-4-	R. BARRICHELLO 1'13"867
Nick HEIDFELD 1'14"095	-5-	Jacques VILLENEUVE 1'14"096
Olivier PANIS 1'14"181	-6-	Eddie IRVINE 1'14"441
Kimi RAIKKONEN 1'14"536	-7-	Pedro De la Rosa 1'15'020
Luciano BURTI 1'15"072	-8-	G. FISICHELLA 1'15"220
Jenson BUTTON 1'15"420	-9-	Jos VERSTAPPEN 1'15"707
Jean ALESI 1'15"774	-10-	Enrique BERNOLDI 1'15"828
Fernando ALONSO 1'16"039	-11-	Tarso MARQUES 1'6"500

Michael Schumacher, ever nearer the stars

Michael Schumacher is alway pretty demonstrative on the podium. But in Magny-Cours, his first place in the French Grand Prix seemed to give him even more pleasure than usual. *"I really enjoyed this win!"* he confirmed during the post race press conference. *"It was a very tough race, but great fun. It's my fiftieth win and that's an important number. My brother and my teammate were both on the podium with me and I have increased my lead in the championship. Everything is fine. It was a very exciting race for me."*

The fans massed in the Magny-Cours grandstands might not have shared this opinion. Because the long awaited battle between the two Schumacher brothers never materialised. *"I did not get a very good start,"* continued Michael. *"I had a problem with the clutch and David (Coulthard) nearly got past me. We arrived at the first corner side by side and I expected it to stay that way to the hairpin, but he backed off straight away. That was lucky, because I knew I had to stay ahead of him. I don't know how the race would have turned out if I had ended up behind him."*

Ralf thus took the lead ahead of Michael, but the elder brother got by during the pit stops. That meant the race was pretty much over by lap 24, with the Ferrari man simply having to maintain his advantage from then on. *"My second set of tyres was very good and I was really flying through the corners. After that, I then had a few problems again on my third set."*

These problems were not enough to prevent the world champion from claiming his fiftieth win, which edged him ever closer to Alain Prost's all-time record of 51 victories. *"People often misunderstand what these records mean to me. My main objective is to win the world championship and not look at the statistics. I am delighted to have fifty wins, but it is not my main aim. It does mean something, but it is of only secondary importance."*

In third place, Rubens Barrichello ensured it was a good day for Ferrari. *"I am very surprised to have made it to the podium,"* admitted the Brazilian. *"I had some big problems during qualifying, but then everything seemed to have come good for the race."*

With ten grands prix completed, Michael Schumacher found himself leading the championship with a 31 point advantage over his nearest rival, David Coulthard. Ralf Schumacher was next up, a further 16 points behind. Despite this handy lead, the Ferrari driver refused to talk in terms of another title. *"Unfortunately, I am too much of a realist to get excited. There are still 70 points available. There is no reason to celebrate until it is mathematically impossible for me to lose."*

Ralf Schumacher is tyred out

This French Grand Prix highlighted more than any other this year, the significance of the tyre war. As the chassis designers were only too keen to point out, it is much easier to find a second per lap by changing a tyre compound than it is by trying to fine tune the balance of a chassis. But it is equally easy to lose time because of unsuitable tyres. In 2001, the drivers would often refer to the difference in performance levels in the sets of tyres fitted at pit stops, in order to explain their variable form during a race.

In Magny-Cours, Ralf Schumacher cited this problem. Having started from pole position, the younger Schumi led the race for 23 laps, right up to the first pit stops.

At that moment, his mechanics had a problem fitting his right rear wheel, which cost him enough time to find himself in second place, behind his brother Michael. *"In any case, even if I had kept the lead at that point, it would have been difficult for me to stop Michael getting by. I was slower on my second and third sets of tyres,"* he explained after the race. *"Ralf definitely said his car was difficult to drive on his second set of tyres and we will look into it,"* said Michelin competition boss Pierre Dupasquier. *"We are not* in the habit of producing faulty tyres, but you only need one of the four tyres to have a problem for the car's handling to deteriorate. In theory, all our tyres are the same, made in batches, but you never know. We will analyse all the data."*

Nevertheless, the race was lost for Ralf Schumacher and the French tyre company, having to settle for second place, a little over ten seconds behind the world champion's Ferrari.

△
Michael Schumacher and his mechanics were visibly delighted with this victory.

Rubens Barrichello finished third, making it a good day for the Scuderia.
▽◁

Another win as Michael Schumacher takes the flag.
▽

Jarno Trulli flat out on three wheels. The Italian did a good job: qualified fifth, he finished fifth.

McLaren trips over the rug again

Funereal expressions, black looks and angry words: the McLaren garage was not a good place to be after the race. David Coulthard had salvaged something by finishing fourth, but this was a poor reward for a team more used to picking up one-two finishes.

Just as in Brazil, Spain, Austria and Monaco, the McLarens got off on the wrong foot, even before the start was underway. Mika Hakkinen was left stranded on the grid as the field tore off on its formation lap. "It was a gearbox problem and nothing to do with the launch control," explained the team.

For David Coulthard, things were not going too badly until the pit stops. But, as he veered off the track to head for the pits, he did not press the pit lane speed limiter button quickly enough. He claimed he was distracted by his engineer talking to him on the radio. That meant he was given a ten second stop-go penalty for speeding in the pit lane, which dropped him back behind Rubens Barrichello. *"It's a real shame, because this penalty literally ruined my race,"* complained the Scotsman. *"I was very close to Rubens (Barrichello) towards the end, but it was impossible to get past him."*

Fourth place was the best he could do. Lagging behind Michael Schumacher by 31 points, his grasp on the championship was slipping still further away. *"It's difficult but not impossible,"* he concluded optimistically. Hope springs eternal...

"Steady!" David Coulthard holds a slide. Fourth place awaited him, at the end of a difficult weekend for the silver arrows.

WEEKEND GOSSIP

• **Newey's millions**

A few more details were coming out about the Adrian Newey - Jaguar affair. The Anglo-American company had offered the McLaren designer the not inconsiderable sum of 210 million dollars over three years to bring the entire McLaren technical staff with him. It was an incredible amount of money which showed how dramatic the situation really was. If the deal had gone through, McLaren would have lost its entire technical workforce overnight. An unlikely scenario to say the least.

• **Big crowds**

The French Grand Prix drew a crowd of 120,717 on race day and 260,816 over the whole weekend.

• **No clouds hovering over the Schumachers**

The day after the European Grand Prix, which had been the scene of an on-track confrontation between the Schumacher brothers, the German tabloid newspaper "Bild" claimed a scoop, dedicating a whole page to an alleged feud between the two men. It maintained that relations had sunk so low that the brothers were refusing to communicate and that a state of war now existed between them. In Magny-Cours, Michael Schumacher was keen to deny this story, which had gathered momentum over the weekend. *"People don't want to hear what Ralf said. They would rather create a scandal,"* pleaded the world champion. *"For sure, at the Nurburgring, Ralf was very angry about his ten second penalty, which he felt was totally unjust. That's the only reason Ralf was in a bad mood and it's true he was not too happy with what I did to him at the start. That's normal and I haven't liked it when others have done it to me. When you are behind, you are always the one who gets angry. When you are in front everything is OK. That's how it is. Ralf and I spoke about it and there is no problem between us over that start. We work for different teams and we must both make the most of whatever opportunities we have."* The Ferrari driver repeated that his relationship with his brother would never change, even if Ralf would get between him and the title. *"I am a hundred percent certain that we will always get on well. As you know, I have reached a lot of my objectives in my career and I would be very happy if Ralf had the same success. Even if I would be the one to suffer because of it."*

• **Villeneuve in Graham Hill's footsteps**

Jacques Villeneuve could one day take part in the Le Mans 24 Hours, thus following in the footsteps of the late Graham Hill, the only driver to have won the F1 World Championship, the Indianapolis 500 Miles and the Le Mans 24 Hours.

• **Two-wheeled technical director**

Patrick Head made an eye-catching appearance in the paddock on Thursday morning in Magny-Cours. Dressed in leather jacket and jeans with a 70s style scarf wrapped around his neck, the Williams technical director is a confirmed motorcycle nut. As every year, he had spent two days travelling down to the circuit with some friends, on a Harley Davidson.

results

PRACTICE TIMES

No	Driver	Car/Engine/Chassis	Practice Friday	Pos.	Practice Saturday	Pos.	Qualifying	Pos.	Warm-up	Pos.
1.	Michael Schumacher	Ferrari/F2001/210	1'15"810	7°	1'13"729	1°	1'12"999	2°	1'15"429	2°
2.	Rubens Barrichello	Ferrari/F2001/206	1'16"325	10°	1'14"515	6°	1'13"867	8°	1'15"676	3°
3.	Mika Häkkinen	McLaren/Mercedes/MP4/16/7	1'15"372	4°	1'14"295	4°	1'13"268	4°	1'15"428	1°
4.	David Coulthard	McLaren/Mercedes/MP4/16/6	1'14"935	1°	1'13"972	3°	1'13"186	3°	1'15"780	4°
5.	Ralf Schumacher	Williams/BMW/FW23/5	1'15"537	5°	1'13"953	2°	1'12"989	1°	1'17"605	17°
6.	Juan Pablo Montoya	Williams/BMW/FW23/6	1'15"582	6°	1'14"652	7°	1'13"625	6°	1'16"735	11°
7.	Giancarlo Fisichella	Benetton/Renault/B201/6	1'17"566	20°	1'15"873	18°	1'15"220	16°	1'18"084	19°
8.	Jenson Button	Benetton/Renault/B201/5	1'17"172	17°	1'16"129	19°	1'15"420	17°	1'18"431	20°
9.	Olivier Panis	BAR/Honda/003/6	1'16"364	11°	1'15"122	13°	1'14"181	11°	1'16"184	7°
10.	Jacques Villeneuve	BAR/Honda/003/7	1'15"224	3°	1'15"061	12°	1'14"096	10°	1'17"073	14°
11.	Heinz-Harald Frentzen	Jordan/Honda/EJ11/4	1'16"868	13°	1'14"992	11°	1'13"815	7°	1'16"925	13°
12.	Jarno Trulli	Jordan/Honda/EJ11/5	1'16"187	9°	1'14"482	5°	1'13"310	5°	1'15"980	5°
14.	Jos Verstappen	Arrows/Asiatech/A22/6	1'17"285	18°	1'15"829	16°	1'15"707	18°	1'17"120	15°
15.	Enrique Bernoldi	Arrows/Asiatech/A22/3	1'17"527	19°	1'16"177	20°	1'15"828	20°	1'16"777	12°
16.	Nick Heidfeld	Sauber/Petronas/C20/5	1'17"011	15°	1'14"652	8°	1'14"095	9°	1'16"559	9°
17.	Kimi Räikkönen	Sauber/Petronas/C20/6	1'16"906	14°	1'14"872	10°	1'14"536	13°	1'16"136	6°
18.	Eddie Irvine	Jaguar/R-2/4	1'15"133	2°	1'14"824	9°	1'14"441	12°	1'16"567	10°
19.	Pedo de la Rosa	Jaguar/R-2/6	1'16"140	8°	1'15"602	14°	1'15"020	14°	1'16"426	8°
20.	Tarso Marques	Minardi/European/PS01/4	1'18"372	22°	1'17"156	22°	1'16"500	22°	1'21"295	22°
21.	Fernando Alonso	Minardi/European/PS01/3	1'17"866	21°	1'17"135	21°	1'16"039	21°	1'19"986	21°
22.	Jean Alesi	Prost/Acer/AP04/6	1'17"088	16°	1'15"750	15°	1'15"774	19°	1'17"945	18°
23.	Luciano Burti	Prost/Acer/AP04/5	1'16"455	12°	1'15"846	17°	1'15"072	15°	1'17"443	16°

MAXIMUM SPEEDS

No	Driver	P1 Qualifs	Pos	P1 Race	Pos	P2 Qualifs	Pos	P2 Race	Pos	Finish Qualifs	Pos	Finish Race	Pos	Trap Qualifs	Pos	Trap Race	Pos
1.	M. Schumacher	304,3	3°	306,6	11°	297,3	3°	278,3	8°	-	-	-	-	138,1	12°	131,3	12°
2.	R. Barrichello	300,6	5°	306,9	10°	277,6	8°	280,2	4°	-	-	-	-	141,8	3°	133,7	5°
3.	M. Häkkinen	300,3	9°	-	-	277,4	10°	-	-	-	-	-	-	137,2	15°	-	-
4.	D. Coulthard	300,4	8°	309,9	4°	278,9	4°	280,1	5°	-	-	-	-	140,2	6°	132,0	8°
5.	R. Schumacher	307,3	2°	309,1	6°	283,7	1°	282,2	2°	-	-	-	-	141,1	4°	131,4	11°
6.	J. P. Montoya	308,5	1°	311,2	1°	283,3	2°	284,8	1°	-	-	-	-	136,1	17°	132,4	6°
7.	G. Fisichella	293,8	22°	306,2	14°	272,4	20°	277,4	12°	-	-	-	-	134,6	20°	132,4	7°
8.	J. Button	294,6	20°	305,1	17°	272,9	19°	276,5	17°	-	-	-	-	135,6	18°	134,9	3°
9.	O. Panis	300,2	10°	309,0	7°	277,0	12°	277,7	10°	-	-	-	-	137,8	13°	131,7	9°
10.	J. Villeneuve	299,4	13°	306,5	13°	275,9	14°	275,7	18°	-	-	-	-	137,2	14°	126,7	1°
11.	H.-H. Frentzen	298,9	17°	304,6	18°	277,9	6°	278,3	9°	-	-	-	-	135,4	19°	126,6	20°
12.	J. Trulli	299,1	16°	306,0	15°	277,2	11°	277,1	14°	-	-	-	-	138,8	9°	128,0	17°
14.	J. Verstappen	299,3	14°	310,1	3°	273,3	18°	277,4	11°	-	-	-	-	138,1	11°	131,3	13°
15.	E. Bernoldi	298,0	18°	307,6	8°	274,1	17°	276,9	12°	-	-	-	-	136,8	16°	129,2	14°
16.	N. Heidfeld	299,5	12°	306,6	12°	275,8	15°	276,7	16°	-	-	-	-	138,5	10°	131,7	10°
17.	K. Räikkönen	299,1	15°	309,1	5°	276,3	13°	279,6	7°	-	-	-	-	139,0	8°	129,0	15°
18.	E. Irvine	300,0	11°	307,5	9°	278,6	5°	279,7	6°	-	-	-	-	141,9	2°	134,5	4°
19.	P. de la Rosa	300,6	6°	311,0	2°	277,7	7°	280,9	3°	-	-	-	-	140,8	5°	135,7	1°
20.	T. Marques	294,0	21°	299,9	21°	272,1	22°	273,6	20°	-	-	-	-	133,4	22°	125,9	21°
21.	F. Alonso	296,3	19°	300,1	20°	272,3	21°	272,5	21°	-	-	-	-	139,1	7°	126,7	19°
22.	J. Alesi	300,4	7°	302,0	19°	275,2	16°	274,7	19°	-	-	-	-	133,6	21°	129,0	16°
23.	L. Burti	301,9	4°	305,2	16°	277,4	9°	277,2	13°	-	-	-	-	143,0	1°	135,4	2°

CLASSIFICATION & RETIREMENTS

Pos	Driver	Team	Time
1.	M. Schum.	Ferrari	1:33:35.636
2.	R. Schum.	Williams BMW	+ 10.399
3.	Barrichello	Ferrari	+ 16.381
4.	Coulthard	McLaren Mercedes	+ 17.106
5.	Trulli	Jordan Honda	+ 68.285
6.	Heidfeld	Sauber Petronas	+ 1 lap
7.	Räikkönen	Sauber Petronas	+ 1 lap
8.	Frentzen	Jordan Honda	+ 1 lap
9.	Panis	BAR Honda	+ 1 lap
10.	Burti	Prost Acer	+ 1 lap
11.	Fisichella	Benetton Renault	+ 1 lap
12.	Alesi	Prost Acer	+ 2 laps
13.	Verstappen	Arrows Asiatech	+ 2 laps
14.	de la Rosa	Jaguar Racing	+ 2 laps
15.	Marques	European Minardi	+ 3 laps
16.	Button	Benetton Renault	spin
17.	Alonso	European Minardi	engine

Lap	Driver	Team	Reason
0	Häkkinen	McLaren Mercedes	gearbox
6	Villeneuve	BAR Honda	engine
18	Bernoldi	Arrows Asiatech	engine
53	Montoya	Williams BMW	engine
55	Irvine	Jaguar Racing	valve problem

FASTEST LAPS

	Driver	Time	Lap
1.	Coulthard	1'16"088	53
		201,130 km/h	
2.	Barrichello	1'16"181	23
3.	M. Schum.	1'16"286	27
4.	Montoya	1'16"355	34
5.	R. Schum.	1'16"585	18
6.	Irvine	1'17"304	23
7.	Räikkönen	1'17"311	8
8.	Trulli	1'17"369	29
9.	de la Rosa	1'17"508	67
10.	Heidfeld	1'17"538	23
11.	Frentzen	1'17"540	20
12.	Fisichella	1'17"968	26
13.	Villeneuve	1'18"181	4
14.	Panis	1'18"250	68
15.	Burti	1'18"253	50
16.	Button	1'18"359	25
17.	Verstappen	1'18"662	47
18.	Alesi	1'18"817	14
19.	Bernoldi	1'19"181	13
20.	Alonso	1'19"199	62
21.	Marques	1'19"608	54

All results : © 2001 Fédération Internationale de l'Automobile, 2, Ch. Blandonnet, 1215 Genève 15, Suisse

PIT STOPS

	Driver	Time	Lap	Stop n°
1.	Räikkönen	27"236	15	1
2.	Button	26"162	19	1
3.	Fisichella	24"324	20	1
4.	Barrichello	23"585	21	1
5.	Heidfeld	25"983	21	1
6.	Alesi	25"312	22	1
7.	Panis	24"669	23	1
8.	R. Schum.	26"987	24	1
9.	Frentzen	33"610	24	1
10.	M. Schum.	24"167	25	1
11.	Trulli	25"915	25	1
12.	Burti	25"920	25	1
13.	Verstappen	47"249	25	1
14.	Coulthard	25"951	26	1
15.	Marques	27"287	26	1
16.	Irvine	25"938	27	1
17.	de la Rosa	24"712	28	1
18.	Montoya	25"998	30	1
19.	Coulthard	26"880	32	2
20.	Alonso	29"282	36	1
21.	Barrichello	24"747	36	2
22.	Räikkönen	27"375	40	2
23.	Heidfeld	27"435	42	2
24.	de la Rosa	27"237	43	2
25.	R. Schum.	25"412	44	2
26.	Fisichella	26"796	44	2
27.	Button	37"551	44	2
28.	Verstappen	26"028	45	2
29.	Panis	26"294	45	2
30.	M. Schum.	27"370	45	2
31.	Frentzen	25"460	46	2
32.	Trulli	25"172	47	2
33.	Alesi	25"344	47	2
34.	Burti	26"035	48	2
35.	Irvine	26"660	48	2
36.	Montoya	25"459	50	2
37.	Marques	25"603	50	2
38.	Coulthard	24"232	51	3
39.	Barrichello	24"262	54	3

BRIDGESTONE

Best result for a driver running Bridgestone tyre:

Michael Schumacher, Ferrari, winner

CHAMPIONSHIP

(after ten rounds)

Drivers :

1. M. Schumacher 78
2. D. Coulthard 47
3. R. Schumacher 31
4. R. Barrichello 30
5. J. P. Montoya 12
6. N. Heidfeld.......................................9
   M. Häkkinen 9
   J. Trulli 9
9. N. Räikkönen 7
   J. Villeneuve...................................7
11. H.-H. Frentzen 6
12. O. Panis..5
13. E. Irvine 4
14. J. Alesi...3
15. P. de la Rosa...................................1
    G. Fisichella 1
    J. Verstappen 1

Constructors :

1. Ferrari..108
2. McLaren Mercedes 56
3. Williams BMW 43
4. Sauber Petronas............................16
5. Jordan Honda 15
6. BAR Honda 12
7. Jaguar Racing 5
8. Prost Acer.......................................3
9. Arrows Asiatech 1
9. Benetton Renault............................1

THE CIRCUIT

TENTH ROUND

GRAND PRIX MOBIL 1 DE FRANCE, MAGNY-COURS

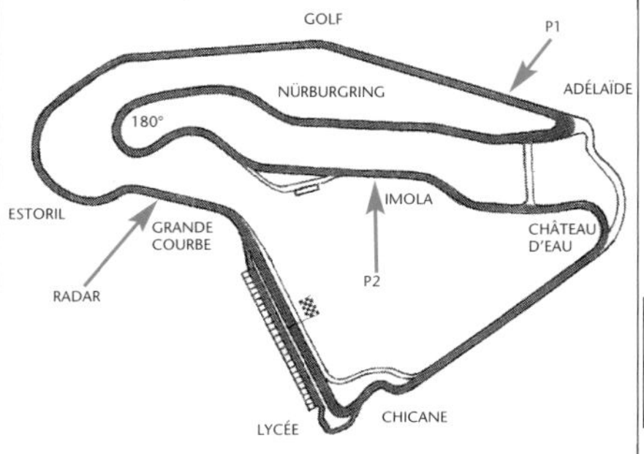
GOLF
P1
NÜRBURGRING
ADÉLAIDE
180°
ESTORIL
IMOLA
GRANDE COURBE
CHÂTEAU D'EAU
P2
RADAR
CHICANE
LYCÉE

Date : July 1, 2001
Length : 4251 meters
Distance : 72 laps, 305.886 km
Weather : hot and sunny, 27°

RACE SUMMARY

- Hakkinen is stuck on the grid as the cars leave for the formation lap. As usual in other words!
- Ralf Schumacher maintains his pole advantage at the start. He is followed by Michael Schumacher, Coulthard and Montoya.
- The leader tries to build a gap but cannot. After 19 laps his lead is only 1.727 seconds!
- The first round of refuelling stops begins, but Ralf's takes 3 seconds longer than planned on lap 24.
- Michael stops next time round and emerges in the lead.
- Lap 32: Coulthard gets a 10 second penalty for speeding in the pit lane.

LAP CHART

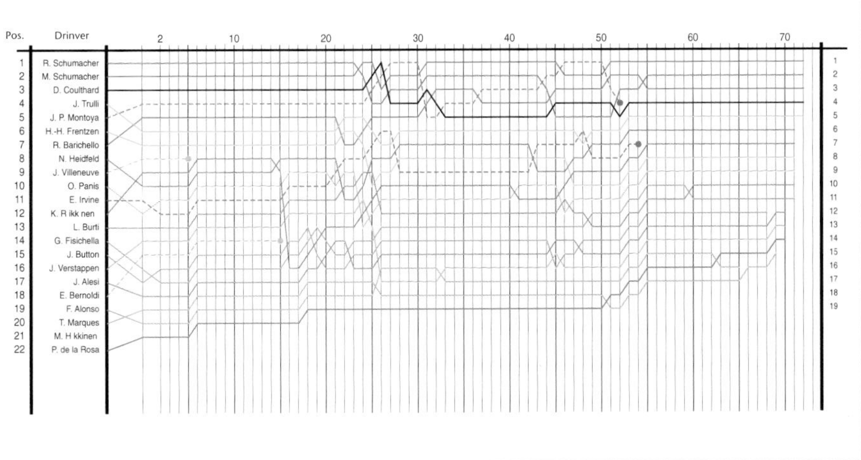
Pos.
Drinver
2 10 20 30 40 50 60 70
R. Schumacher
M. Schumacher
D. Coulthard
J. Trulli
J. P. Montoya
H.-H. Frentzen
R. Barichello
N. Heidfeld
J. Villeneuve
O. Panis
E. Irvine
L. Burti
G. Fisichella
J. Button
J. Verstappen
J. Alesi
E. Bernoldi
F. Alonso
T. Marques
P. de la Rosa

GAPS ON THE LEADER BOARD

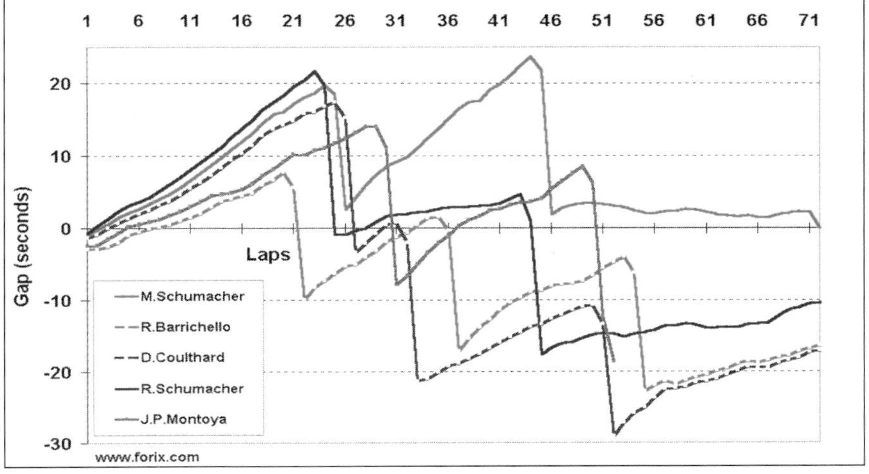
1 6 11 16 21 26 31 36 41 46 51 56 61 66 71
20
10
0
-10
-20
-30
Gap (seconds)
Laps
M.Schumacher
R.Barrichello
D.Coulthard
R.Schumacher
J.P.Montoya
www.forix.com

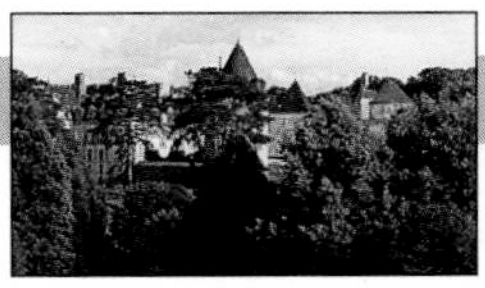

Ghosts laid to rest!

The Finn had not won a single race this year. At last he managed it and finally overcame his woodoo by dominating the British Grand Prix in fine style.

It was not an easy one. He had to fight for it and even had to pull off the not inconsiderable feat of overtaking Michael Schumacher. In the other McLaren, David Coulthard got it all wrong, colliding with Jarno Trulli. For someone who was in the running for the title, it was not the time to suffer from brain fade.

**FOSTER'S BRITISH GRAND PRIX
SILVERSTONE**

David Coulthard fights with the elements at Silverstone, during Friday's practice. It was a good day for the silver arrows, as they set the two best times, with almost a one second advantage over the rest of the pack. But on Saturday, it would be a different story.

▷

"If that's the case, I'm sulking!" At Silverstone, Jacques Villeneuve qualified behind his team-mate Olivier Panis, in twelfth place.

▷▽

And yet another pole for Michael Schumacher. It was already the eighth in a season which looked like being a record breaker.

▽

King Michael back on pole

Michael Schumacher wanted to write his name on the motor sport book of fame right from this weekend. At Silverstone, a win in the British Grand Prix would have been the 51st victory of his career, which would have brought him level with the record set by Alain Prost in 1993.

A victory would also have been the best way to celebrate the fiftieth anniversary of the first Ferrari win in Formula 1, which took place at this very same Silverstone circuit on 14th July 1951. Indeed, an example of the car that won that day, was on display in the paddock. It belongs to a certain Bernie Ecclestone.

Michael Schumacher insisted he paid little attention to these historic considerations. The only thing that mattered to him was winning the 2001 world championship, which he had been chasing since the Australian Grand Prix and now looked to be his for the taking. At Silverstone, he opened his account by taking pole, although it

was not the easiest of his career. *"Today was both really interesting and difficult,"* he commented. *"When we all went out on the track, there was only half an hour to go, so it was all a bit rushed."*

Adding to the confusion, the timing screens decided to play up and the sector times disappeared from view for a few minutes. *"We did not have a lot to go on in terms of dry set up for qualifying, as it had rained all morning,"* continued the world champion. *"On top of that, the monitors weren't working and we didn't know if we were fast or slow at any particular point. It all made for an exciting time."*

Nevertheless, the German did manage to pack in four runs, which was not the case for everyone. Behind him the two McLarens looked menacing, with Mika Hakkinen back on the front row, for the *first time since the Spanish Grand Prix.* *"I'm only giving away eight hundredths to Michael, which is quite satisfying,"* reckoned the Finn.

STARTING GRID

M. SCHUMACHER 1'20"447	-1-	Mika HÄKKINEN 1'20"529
David COULTHARD 1'20"927	-2-	Jarno TRULLI 1'20"930
H.-H. FRENTZEN 1'21"217	-3-	R. BARRICHELLO 1'21"715
Kimi RAIKKONEN 1'22"023	-4-	J. P. MONTOYA 1'22"219
Nick HEIDFELD 1'22"223	-5-	R. SCHUMACHER 1'22"283
Olivier PANIS 1'22"316	-6-	Jacques VILLENEUVE 1'22"916
Pedro De la Rosa 1'23"273	-7-	Jean ALESI 1'23"392
Eddie IRVINE 1'23"439	-8-	Luciano BURTI 1'23"735
Jos VERSTAPPEN 1'24"067	-9-	Jenson BUTTON 1'24"123
G. FISICHELLA 1'24"275	-10-	Enrique BERNOLDI 1'24"606
Fernando ALONSO 1'24"792	-11-	

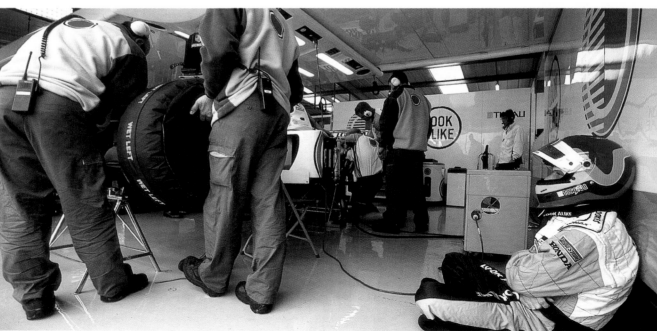

Mika finally shakes off his bad luck

Problems with the suspension, the gearbox, the launch control or electronics: Mika Hakkinen had gone through every fault in the book so far this season.

Back in April, in Barcelona, the Finn had dominated the race, until his car packed up on the very last lap, handing victory to Michael Schumacher. In Magny-Cours, two weeks before this race, he had qualified on the second row, but his car decided to stay parked on the grid. The monkey just wouldn't get off his back.

At Silverstone, the Finn finally put an end to this awful run, winning the British Grand Prix fair and square. He started second, behind Michael Schumacher and got past the German on lap five, no easy feat in itself. The Ferrari ran a tiny bit wide at Copse and the McLaren made the most of it to draw alongside down the next straight. *"It was very important for me to pass Michael early in the race,"* explained Hakkinen after the race. *"If I had been stuck behind him, it would have been very difficult for me to build up the lead I needed to make my two pit stops, because I guessed the Ferraris would only stop once. Having said that, I was surprised at how easily I got past Michael. I don't know if he made a mistake, but I was able to get alongside him. I was ready to give him room to get through the next few corners side by side, but he backed off. I guess he doesn't need to fight with me at the moment."*

Once in the lead, the Finn managed to pull out a respectable gap over his pursuer, setting fastest lap after fastest lap. By flag fall, even though he had made one more stop than the Ferrari, Mika won with a 33 second lead over Michael. It was only on the last lap that Hakkinen backed off. Was that because he remembered retiring within sight of the flag in the Spanish Grand Prix? *"I never thought about it for a moment....well....er..,.Of course I thought about it,"* he continued with a laugh. *"During the last lap, I was convinced something was going to break and I slowed down a lot. Luckily, nothing happened."*

A first win of the year seemed to please the Finn enormously. *"Pleasure? The word isn't strong enough,"* he maintained. *"It is impossible for me to explain why this race was so important for me. I have always wanted to win at Silverstone and I had never done it before. So today is fantastic."*

Despite the euphoria, Hakkinen refused to be too optimistic about the rest of the season. *"Let's see how we go in Hockenheim,"* he concluded. *"I think we have now found a good balance on the car. Of course, I would like to win a few more grands prix this year."*

△
"Hi Thierry!" Mika Hakkinen says hello to our photographer at the end of the race.

◁
Mika Hakkinen was happy as Larry on the Silverstone podium. Rumours of imminent retirement were already doing the rounds, but this win seemed to quash them.

It's the wrong McLaren

David Coulthard knew it and he repeated it all through practice: if he was to stay in contention for the world title, he absolutely had to win the British Grand Prix and start to make up the gap to Michael Schumacher.

He failed to do it. A McLaren did indeed win at Silverstone, but it was the wrong one. David Coulthard saw his race turn sour at the first corner. Having started third, he collided with Jarno Trulli's Jordan, slid wide and rejoined last. His right rear suspension was damaged and he was forced to retire two laps later. *"I was ahead of Trulli and even if I was on the outside line, I reckon he should have left me enough room to get past,"* complained the Scotsman, once back in the garage.

It was a strange explanation, given that it is usually the car holding the outside line which has to make room for the other. Jarno Trulli was particularly disappointed. *"I am really upset,"* lamented the Italian. *"Everything was going so well this weekend, that I was aiming for a podium finish. I don't know if David didn't see me or if he was deliberately trying to push me off, but he closed the door. I braked, even though usually you don't brake at all in that corner, but there was no way of avoiding him."*

Nick Heidfeld takes to the track. He would pick up a point and his team-mate would score two.

◁▽

David Coulthard walks back to the pits after retiring. Could someone claiming to be fighting for the title really afford to tangle with Trulli?

▽

Second and unhappy to be so

Michael Schumacher seemed distinctly downbeat after the race. Not only did he fail to win the British Grand Prix, he also allowed himself to be overtaken by Mika Hakkinen and Juan Pablo Montoya! As he stepped off the podium, he was asked if he had been in bother or whether he had let Hakkinen by, as the Finn did not constitute a threat in championship terms. With an exasperated sigh he replied: *"Of course, it's obvious, I parked at the side of the track and waved him through."*

Michael Schumacher's bad mood was down to his car that day, which had obviously not lived up to expectations. *"The car today wasn't at all as good as yesterday,"* he complained. *"It was very difficult to drive and we will have to look into the reasons for that with the engineers. Of course, it was heavier in the race than during qualifying, by about 100 kilos, because of the fuel load, but most of all, it was badly balanced and too slow."*

Unlike most of the other teams, Ferrari had not done much testing at Silverstone prior to the grand prix, doing most of its running at Fiorano. *"Maybe that's why we weren't on the pace,"* suggested the world champion. *"On top of that, I had a couple of worrying moments on patches of oil and I almost lost control of the car."* Overtaken by Mika Hakkinen and then Juan Pablo Montoya, the German finally finished second. *"Juan Pablo passed me down the straight. We all know the Williams are very quick in a straight line and I came out of the previous corner a bit too slowly."*

He might have "only" come second, but combined with David Coulthard's retirement, it was still enough for the Ferrari man to take out a serious option on a fourth world title. *"Of course, these six points are very important for the championship. But until it's decided, I will keep on fighting hard. We have to stay concentrated."*

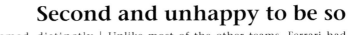

FOSTER'S BRITISH GRAND PRIX

Who would have thought an Arrows pit stop could be so graphic? At Silverstone, the orange cars were still off the pace in qualifying, lining up 17th and 20th on the grid. However, they both finished the race, in 10th and 14th places.

FOSTER'S BRITISH GRAND PRIX

Silverstone finally looks to the future

The 2000 edition of the British Grand Prix had turned to farce. Rain had lashed Silverstone for two weeks prior to the race, held in April. The car parks were under water, the cars got stuck and spectators were told not to come on Saturday and the same message was put out on race day.

That day there were the usual endless traffic jams and several thousand fans had to listen to the race on their car radios, even though they were within sight of the circuit. They got their money back, but the event was tainted with mud and muck.

The fiasco nearly spelt the end of the British Grand Prix. *"We can't let something like this happen,"* warned FIA Vice President Promotional Affairs and the sport's commercial rights holder, Bernie Ecclestone. *"Countries like Russia, China, South Africa and the Arab Emirates all want to stage events. We can only race in the best venues."*

Formula 1's boss did not feel Silverstone, in its current form, was part of that group. *"This circuit is like an old Victorian building, whose owners occasionally paper over the cracks, year after year."* Completely out-classed by the facilities at such places as Sepang and Indianapolis, the English circuit had finally decided to launch a programme of major improvements. *"Things are moving forward,"* confirmed Ecclestone. *"It was about time, as without that, England would have lost its grand prix!"*

Silverstone thus planned to spend 130 million Euros to turn the Northamptonshire facility into "the world's motorsport capital," with a museum, cinemas, driving schools and so forth.

A new motorway link was already under construction near the track, which it was hoped, would finally put an end to the legendary traffic jams. It had not materialised this year and the queues were as bad as ever. Park and Ride facilities had been put in place, but the bus ride wasn't cheap at 75 Euros per person. It was enough to make you want to stay at home.

A further three points for the Sauber team

The Saubers continued to surprise the F1 establishment. Discretely and without making waves, the Swiss team was piling up the points, establishing itself in fourth place in the Constructors' classification.

Thanks to finishing fifth and sixth at Silverstone, the Sauber-Petronas C20 had now amassed 19 points, ahead of vastly better funded squads, which had the benefit of support from major motor manufacturers, such as Jordan, BAR, Jaguar and Benetton. This situation was proof that the Sauber boys had finally got the hang of developing their car during the course of the season. In the past, the team was always accused of being unable to improve its car over the year. Once the engineers had drawn the car, they tended to immediately switch their attention to the following year's challenger.

However, this year for a change, a major effort was made to fine tune the C20. At Silverstone, given that more fast circuits were coming up on the calendar, they had produced a new aerodynamic package, which seemed to work incredibly well, both in qualifying and the race.

Sauber's result in the British Grand Prix was all the more remarkable, because only five cars retired from the race. Therefore, to finish at the front, you had to race at the front. *"I think I had a perfect race,"* reckoned fifth placed Kimi Raikkonen. *"I had to be patient behind Ralf Schumacher and then behind Jacques Villeneuve and, in the end, our strategy worked out just the way we had planned it."*

PRACTICE TIMES

No	Driver	Car/Engine/Chassis	Practice Friday	Pos.	Practice Saturday	Pos.	Qualifying	Pos.	Warm-up	Pos.
1.	Micahel Schumacher	Ferrari/F2001/210	1'23"619	4°	1'31"430	1°	1'20"447	1°	1'24"407	5°
2.	Rubens Barrichello	Ferrari/F2001/206	1'23"578	3°	1'32"128	5°	1'21"715	6°	1'24"657	9°
3.	Mika Häkkinen	McLaren/Mercedes/MP4/16/7	1'22"827	1°	1'31"849	3°	1'20"529	2°	1'23"416	3°
4.	David Coulthard	McLaren/Mercedes/MP4/16/6	1'22"894	2°	1'32"014	4°	1'20"927	3°	1'22"994	1°
5.	Ralf Schumacher	Williams/BMW/FW23/5	1'24"222	8°	1'34"248	10°	1'22"283	7°	1'24"631	8°
6.	Juan Pablo Montoya	Williams/BMW/FW23/6	1'25"267	17°	1'34"674	11°	1'22"219	8°	1'25"260	12°
7.	Giancarlo Fisichella	Benetton/Renault/B201/6	1'26"730	21°	1'35"624	15°	1'24"275	19°	1'27"198	18°
8.	Jenson Button	Benetton/Renault/B201/5	1'25"673	19°	1'35"974	17°	1'24"123	18°	1'27"987	19°
9.	Olivier Panis	BAR/Honda/003/6	1'24"562	12°	1'34"097	9°	1'22"316	11°	1'24"598	6°
10.	Jacques Villeneuve	BAR/Honda/003/7	1'24"436	11°	1'35"690	16°	1'22"916	12°	1'25"217	11°
11.	Heinz-Harald Frentzen	Jordan/Honda/EJ11/4	1'23"887	5°	1'31"580	2°	1'21"217	5°	1'24"052	4°
12.	Jarno Trulli	Jordan/Honda/EJ11/5	1'24"343	9°	1'33"879	7°	1'20"930	4°	1'23"182	2°
14.	Jos Verstappen	Arrows/Asiatech/A22/6	1'25"026	16°	1'35"173	13°	1'24"067	17°	1'25"581	13°
15.	Enrique Bernoldi	Arrows/Asiatech/A22/3	1'25"209	16°	1'35"402	14°	1'24"606	20°	1'25"658	14°
16.	Nick Heidfeld	Sauber/Petronas/C20/7	1'24"096	6°	1'33"837	6°	1'22"223	9°	1'25"734	15°
17.	Kimi Räikkönen	Sauber/Petronas/C20/6	1'24"387	10°	1'34"069	8°	1'22"023	10°	1'24"609	7°
18.	Eddie Irvine	Jaguar/R-2/4	1'24"733	13°	1'43"222	22°	1'23"439	15°	1'25"147	10°
19.	Pedro de la Rosa	Jaguar/R-2/6	1'24"116	7°	1'35"157	12°	1'23"273	13°	1'26"463	16°
20.	Tarso Marques	Minardi/European/PS01/4	1'27"203	22°	1'40"199	21°	1'26"506		-	
21.	Fernando Alonso	Minardi/European/PS01/3	1'26"695	20°	1'38"748	20°	1'24"792	21°	1'26"988	17°
22.	Jean Alesi	Prost/Acer/AP04/6	1'24"832	14°	1'36"193	18°	1'23"392	14°	1'28"060	20°
23.	Luciano Burti	Prost/Acer/AP04/5	1'25"448	18°	1'37"203	19°	1'23"735	16°	1'28"240	21°

MAXIMUM SPEEDS

No	Driver	P1 Qualifs	Pos	P1 Race	Pos	P2 Qualifs	Pos	P2 Race	Pos	Finish Qualifs	Pos	Finish Race	Pos	Trap Qualifs	Pos	Trap Race	Pos
1.	M. Schumacher	309,2	10°	306,0	16°	272,1	1°	252,9	6°	292,6	5°	291,4	10°	308,7	1°	299,6	7°
2.	R. Barrichello	310,8	6°	308,0	12°	262,9	9°	253,5	5°	292,7	4°	292,1	7°	305,6	4°	300,2	5°
3.	M. Häkkinen	309,8	8°	310,2	10°	269,1	3°	257,4	2°	293,5	3°	292,6	5°	305,6	5°	299,4	9°
4.	D. Coulthard	312,2	4°	305,0	17°	266,2	6°	245,9	15°	293,9	2°	287,1	18°	306,9	2°	293,2	18°
5.	R. Schumacher	314,0	2°	312,9	4°	252,8	18°	249,1	16°	296,3	1°	295,4	2°	306,4	3°	301,7	2°
6.	J. P. Montoya	313,8	3°	316,9	1°	257,7	14°	252,5	8°	-		297,0	1°	303,3	10°	305,0	1°
7.	G. Fisichella	308,2	12°	304,1	18°	255,3	16°	245,9	16°	288,5	16°	288,3	17°	298,0	18°	292,8	19°
8.	J. Button	309,2	9°	307,1	13°	252,9	17°	237,2	19°	288,9	15°	288,7	15°	300,3	15°	293,5	17°
9.	O. Panis	311,8	5°	-		261,9	10°	-		289,8	11°	-		303,9	8°	-	
10.	J. Villeneuve	308,9	11°	313,3	3°	256,4	15°	240,5	17°	289,6	12°	289,7	13°	304,3	6°	299,9	6°
11.	H.-H. Frentzen	307,1	16°	316,5	2°	260,1	12°	247,1	14°	290,4	8°	293,3	4°	301,2	14°	298,8	11°
12.	J. Trulli																
14.	J. Verstappen	303,4	19°	310,4	9°	260,5	11°	252,6	7°	287,4	17°	288,4	16°	297,3	19°	295,8	14°
15.	E. Bernoldi	307,5	15°	311,4	8°	263,4	8°	247,3	12°	285,3	19°	292,6	6°	298,2	17°	299,0	10°
16.	N. Heidfeld	307,8	13°	312,4	5°	268,1	4°	255,0	3°	290,4	9°	291,2	11°	304,3	7°	299,5	8°
17.	K. Räikkönen	306,8	17°	311,5	7°	269,3	2°	254,4	4°	288,9	14°	292,0	8°	301,5	12°	300,6	3°
18.	E. Irvine	306,1	18°	309,9	11°	264,6	7°	259,1	1°	290,2	10°	294,4	3°	300,2	16°	300,5	4°
19.	P. de la Rosa	307,6	14°	307,0	14°	265,9	6°	249,7	9°	289,6	13°	291,5	9°	301,3	13°	297,6	13°
20.	T. Marques	301,3	21°	-		241,1	20°	-		-		283,2	20°	-		292,3	21°
21.	F. Alonso	303,1	20°	306,2	19°	237,1	21°	247,2	13°	285,6	18°	286,6	19°	296,7	20°	295,0	16°
22.	J. Alesi	314,2	1°	306,4	15°	264,5	8°	247,7	11°	291,7	6°	289,6	14°	303,2	11°	298,0	12°
23.	L. Burti	309,9	7°	311,9	6°	247,0	19°	238,0	18°	290,8	7°	290,0	12°	303,9	9°	295,4	15°

PIT STOPS

	Driver	Time	Lap	Stop n°
1.	Räikkönen	34"160	20	1
2.	Häkkinen	31"259	21	1
3.	Heidfeld	32"603	21	1
4.	Verstappen	33"163	22	1
5.	Button	32"648	22	1
6.	Bernoldi	33"387	23	1
7.	Alonso	32"979	23	1
8.	Frentzen	34"009	24	1
9.	Fisichella	31"807	24	1
10.	Montoya	32"517	25	1
11.	Alesi	35"307	30	1
12.	Irvine	30"727	30	1
13.	Villeneuve	36"487	32	1
14.	de la Rosa	30"888	34	1
15.	R. Schum.	36"944	35	1
16.	de la Rosa	34"969	35	2
17.	Häkkinen	32"527	39	2
18.	M. Schum.	32"612	39	1
19.	Button	32"760	39	2
20.	Räikkönen	32"711	40	2
21.	Alonso	51"879	39	2
22.	Montoya	35"000	41	2
23.	Heidfeld	32"869	41	2
24.	Frentzen	32"477	41	2
25.	Verstappen	32"427	41	2
26.	Barrichello	33"040	42	1
27.	Bernoldi	32"347	42	2
28.	Fisichella	31"604	42	2
29.	Irvine	30"890	45	2

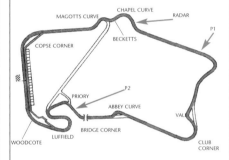

BRIDGESTONE

Best result for a driver running Bridgestone tyres :

M. Häkkinen, McLaren Mercedes, winner

CHAMPIONSHIP

(after eleven rounds)

Drivers :

1.	M. Schumacher	84
2.	D. Coulthard	47
3.	R. Barrichello	34
4.	R. Schumacher	31
5.	M. Häkkinen	19
6.	J. P. Montoya	15
7.	N. Heidfeld	10
8.	K. Räikkönen	9
	J. Trulli	9
10.	J. Villeneuve	7
11.	H.-H. Frentzen	6
12.	O. Panis	5
13.	E. Irvine	4
14.	J. Alesi	3
15.	J. Verstappen	1
	P. de la Rosa	1
	G. Fisichella	1

Constructors :

1.	Ferrari	118
2.	McLaren Mercedes	66
3.	Williams BMW	46
4.	Sauber Petronas	19
5.	Jordan Honda	15
6.	BAR Honda	12
7.	Jaguar Racing	5
8.	Prost Acer	3
9.	Arrows Asiatech	1
	Benetton Renault	1
11.	European Minardi	0

CLASSIFICATION & RETIREMENTS

Pos	Driver	Team	Time
1.	Häkkinen	McLaren Mercedes	1:25:33.770
2.	M. Schum.	Ferrari	+ 33.646
3.	Barrichello	Ferrari	+ 59.280
4.	Montoya	Williams BMW	+ 68.772
5.	Räikkönen	Sauber Petronas	+ 1 lap
6.	Heidfeld	Sauber Petronas	+ 1 lap
7.	Frentzen	Jordan Honda	+ 1 lap
8.	Villeneuve	BAR Honda	+ 1 lap
9.	Irvine	Jaguar Racing	+ 1 lap
10.	Verstappen	Arrows Asiatech	+ 2 laps
11.	Alesi	Prost Acer	+ 2 laps
12.	de la Rosa	Jaguar Racing	+ 2 laps
13.	Fisichella	Benetton Renault	+ 2 laps
14.	Bernoldi	Arrows Asiatech	+ 2 laps
15.	Button	Benetton Renault	+ 2 laps
16.	Alonso	European Minardi	+ 3 laps

Lap	Driver	Team	Reason
1	Panis	BAR Honda	accident
1	Trulli	Jordan Honda	accident
3	Coulthard	McLaren Mercedes	suspensions
7	Burti	Prost Acer	engine
37	R. Schum	Williams BMW	engine

FASTEST LAPS

	Driver	Time	Lap
1.	Häkkinen	1'23"405	34
2.	M. Schum.	1'23"928	42
3.	Montoya	1'24"437	23
4.	Barrichello	1'24"445	44
5.	Irvine	1'24"544	59
6.	Räikkönen	1'24"563	34
7.	Heidfeld	1'24"765	46
8.	Frentzen	1'25"029	23
9.	R. Schum.	1'25"188	33
10.	de la Rosa	1'25"739	33
11.	Villeneuve	1'25"809	27
12.	Verstappen	1'26"394	40
13.	Alesi	1'26"497	29
14.	Bernoldi	1'26"695	25
15.	Fisichella	1'26"778	41
16.	Button	1'26"963	24
17.	Alonso	1'27"091	30
18.	Coulthard	1'28"908	2
19.	Burti	1'29"252	4

THE CIRCUIT

ELEVENTH ROUND

THE 2001 FOSTER'S BRITISH GRAND PRIX, SILVERSTONE

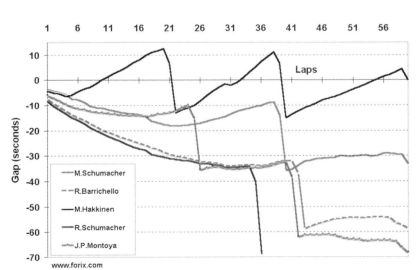

Date : July 15, 2001
Length : 5141 meters
Distance : 60 laps, 308.356 km
Waether : cloudy but dry, 19°

All results :
© 2001 Fédération Internationale de l'Automobile, 2, Ch. Blandonnet, 1215 Genève 15, Suisse

RACE SUMMARY

• When the red lights go out, Michael Schumacher takes the lead ahead of Häkkinen. Behind, it's carnage: Coulthard squeezes Trulli to the inside, the two men touch. Coulthard continues for three laps, but both men retire. Panis is pushed off by Villeneuve.

• Häkkinen pushes Michael Schumacher hard: on lap 3, as they cross the line, the gap is 0.1 seconds. On lap 4, it is 0.2 seconds.

• Lap 5 and Häkkinen gets past Michael Schumacher at Maggots.

LAP CHART

Pos.	Driver	2	10	20	30	40	50	60	
1	M. Schumacher								1
2	M. Häkkinen								2
3	D. Coulthard								3
4	J. Trulli								4
5	H.-H. Frentzen								5
6	R. Barichello								6
7	K. Räikknen								7
8	J. P. Montoya								8
9	N. Heidfeld								9
10	R. Schumacher								10
11	O. Panis								11
12	J. Villeneuve								12
13	P. de la Rosa								13
14	J. Alesi								14
15	E. Irvine								15
16	L. Burti								16
17	J. Verstappen								17
18	J. Button								18
19	G. Fisichella								19
20	E. Bernoldi								20
21	M. Alonso								21

GAPS ON THE LEADER BOARD

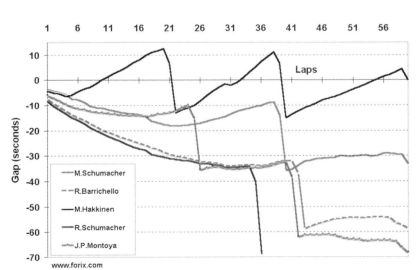

www.forix.com

Miracle at Hockenheim

A problem with Michael Schumacher's Ferrari. Luciano Burti unable to avoid the German's car and it's a recipe for disaster. It was one of those huge impacts that has everyone holding their breath.

In the 50s, 60s and 70s, tragedy was an everyday part of motor racing. Fatalities were common place, although always difficult to deal with. Even if Formula 1 was reckoned to be more fun in those far off times, those who lived through them retain an overall impression of sadness and hours spent waiting to hear the worst about good friends, in hospital corridors.

Today, Formula 1 is entertainment on a world stage and much safer. Luciano Burti's accident at Hockenheim left no one dead nor even injured.

However, there was a huge element of luck involved. In the modern era, carbon fibre, the survival cell and other advanced technologies have replaced luck and that is a more than fair swop for the "good times" of the past.

ROSSER MOBIL 1 PREIS VON DEUTSCHLAND HOCKENHEIM

It's One for Juan

Juan Pablo Montoya, despite his Latin origins, is not the sort to wear his heart on his sleeve. You won't see him embracing his mechanics or cuddling his engineers.

However, in Hockenheim, as he stepped out of the cockpit, the Colombian jumped for joy and showed a degree of exuberance we had never seen from him so far in his F1 career. And with good reason: using every inch of the Hockenheim track, making the most of the famous Motodrom section, the twisty part of the track, the Williams driver took his first F1 career pole position. It was a first, which would lead to more. *"I am really happy,"* he admitted. *"Everything went well and the car was fine. We worked hard and made a lot of changes to the set-up, which all went in the right direction and this is the result."*

Now, all the Colombian had to do was to convert pole into a suitable race result. *"The race should go well. We have had no problems this weekend and we should be competitive. I just hope the car will be reliable. We have had a few problems recently and I am worried it will be hot tomorrow."*

It was the third time this season that Ralf Schumacher had been out-paced by his team-mate. In Hockenheim, the gap was just 19 thousandths of a second, or the equivalent of 1.32 metres at the end of a 6.825 kilometre lap. *"It was very tough between me and Juan Pablo today,"* admitted Schumacher at the end of qualifying. *"I ran into traffic on my last two runs and that made the difference. The main thing is to be on the front row and I am. It will be a long race and a lot of things could happen."*

In Germany, the Williams were definitely way ahead of the rest, relegating Mika Hakkinen to third, almost seven tenths of a second behind. It was a major thrashing, inflicted mainly by the power of the BMW engine and the performance of the Michelin tyres. Because of this, Hakkinen was far from optimistic about the race. *"If these two guys can maintain this sort of pace in the race, we will have no chance,"* he complained. *"Let's hope they have some problems."*

For Ferrari, qualifying really had not gone at all to plan. Michael Schumacher was fourth and Rubens Barrichello could do no better than sixth. *"We knew it would be hard to get pole today, but we didn't expect to be that far off the pace,"* reckoned Jean Todt with a shrug of his shoulders.

> *"Don't worry darling, I won't be long." Juan Pablo Montoya kisses his fiancee before the start of qualifying. He should do more of that kissing that, as an hour later the Colombian took his first ever F1 pole position.*

> *Jos the Boss was still having trouble getting off the back end of the grid. In Germany, he had to settle for 19th place.*

> *In Hockenheim, despite his best wheel locking efforts, Jacques Villeneuve did not qualify any better than usual, making do with 12th on the grid. However, in the race, the Canadian would finish on the podium.*

STARTING GRID

J. P. MONTOYA 1'38"117	-1-	**R. SCHUMACHER** 1'38"136
Mika HÄKKINEN 1'38"811	-2-	**M. SCHUMACHER** 1'38"941
David COULTHARD 1'39"574	-3-	**R. BARRICHELLO** 1'39"682
Nick HEIDFELD 1'39"921	-4-	**Kimi RAIKKONEN** 1'40"072
Pedro De la Rosa 1'40"265	-5-	**Jarno TRULLI** 1'40"322
Eddie IRVINE 1'40"371	-6-	**Jacques VILLENEUVE** 1'40"437
Olivier PANIS 1'40"610	-7-	**Jean ALESI** 1'40"724
Ricardo ZONTA 1'41"174	-8-	**Luciano BURTI** 1'41"213
G. FISICHELLA 1'41"299	-9-	**Jenson BUTTON** 1'41"438
Enrique BERNOLDI 1'41"668	-10-	**Jos VERSTAPPEN** 1'41"870
Fernando ALONSO 1'41"913	-11-	**Tarso MARQUES** 1'42"716

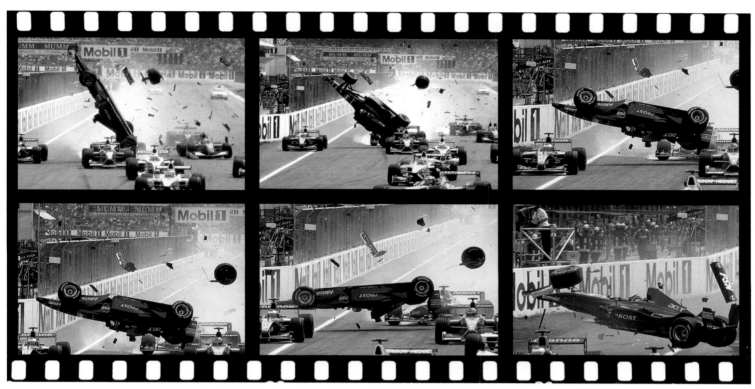

Luciano Burti had a very big scare, but so did Enrique Bernoldi. A wheel off the Prost crashed into the side pod of his Arrows. It was a close call.

Luciano Burti has a miracle escape and starts again!

Michael Schumacher had never won the German Grand Prix at the wheel of a Ferrari and, this year, he had every intention of putting right this omission on his record book. It wasn't to be, because this turned out to be rather a hectic afternoon for the local hero.

It all began at the beginning. Only fourth on the grid, the world champion got off the line, but was then struck with a gearbox problem, which stopped him changing up through the box. Flying up from the back of the grid, Luciano Burti's view was obscured by another car and rammed his Prost into the back of the stricken Ferrari. *"I saw him coming in my mirrors, but I couldn't move over to give him room,"* explained the Ferrari driver. *"It was a hell of a bang, but it could have been much worse."*

The Brazilian's Prost, rolled over the top of the other car and ended up in the tyre barrier at the first corner. The driver was unhurt. *"It all happened very quickly,"* said Burti later that day. *"The pack of cars in front meant I couldn't see Michael's car and when I did see it, it was too late. But actually, the accident looked much worse on television as, sitting in the cockpit, I didn't feel anything."*

At first the race was slowed by the arrival of the Safety Car. But then, the race officials realised there was too much debris on the track and the red flags were brought out. *"It had to be stopped,"* agreed Michelin's Pierre Dupasquier. *"There were fragments of carbon everywhere. They are very sharp and can get embedded in a tyre before causing a slow puncture."*

The track was thoroughly cleaned before a second start. Both Luciano Burti and Michael Schumacher sprinted back to the pits to take the re-start in their spare cars, but the German would eventually retire, a few hundred metres after his pit stop. *"I had a problem with lack of fuel pressure,"* he recounted calmly after the race, apparently unaffected by his accident. With

David Coulthard retiring, Schumacher's position in the championship classification looked even more secure. *"My lead over David is the same as before this weekend, but with one less race to go. And I am happy that Ralf has won here at our home event."*

For his part, Burti went off the track, halfway through the race. *"I took the spare, but I must have hurt myself in the accident, because my left arm started to hurt more and more. In the end, I could hardly hang onto the steering wheel and that's why I went off."* A day of miracles had come to an end for the Brazilian.

Williams win

A poll run by a German magazine, the month before the race, showed that Ralf Schumacher was regarded by his fellow countrymen as a more sympathetic character than his brother Michael.

The younger Schumi's win at Hockenheim would no doubt serve to increase this popularity. Certainly, the ovation he received as he appeared in the stadium section to complete his final lap, showed that the fans adored him. *"Winning here in Germany, in a German powered car and being German is really fantastic,"* exulted Ralf. *"This is the perfect scenario."*

It was a scenario that required the retirement of Juan Pablo Montoya to see it come to fruition. Having charged off into the lead, the Colombian was let down yet again by his equipment, having run into major problems during his pit stop. *"It's true that Juan was quicker than me today,"* conceded Ralf. *"I had brake problems and my first set of tyres wasn't fantastic. But when I saw Juan Pablo disappear into the lead, I told myself, "Ok you do what you like" and I slowed a bit to save the car. We knew this circuit would stretch our engine to the limit and I preferred to look after it. I did the right thing."*

Once in the lead, all the younger Schumacher had to do was keep an eye on the substantial lead he had over second placed Rubens Barrichello. *"I kept asking the team what lap times Rubens was doing. The more I slowed down, the more he did the same and the team kept telling me to back off. With a fifty second lead, that wasn't too difficult!"*

On Sunday night, in the Williams camp, it was laughing-Ralf and crying-Montoya. While one man celebrated victory, the other could only reflect on the constant mechanical problems which plagued him. Indeed, Juan Pablo Montoya

Ralf consoles the German fans

led the German Grand Prix for the first 22 laps. Then he came in for a pit stop and a recalcitrant fuel nozzle cost him around 20 seconds. Once under way, his car died on him two laps later. *"I am so disappointed, I can't find the words to express how I feel,"* he lamented after the race. *"Up until the pit stop, everything was going smoothly. Even with the problem in the pits, I could have finished second, if it hadn't been for the engine failing."*

◁◁
(above)
With all the debris on the track, the Safety Car was put into action.

(below)
The Ostkurve chicane was also the scene of collisions on the opening lap.

◁
Lap 25: Juan Pablo Montoya's fantastic charge comes to an end when his BMW V10 cries enough. His first win would have to wait.

△
"So, aren't I worth all the Montoyas in the world?" Ralf Schumacher took top honours in Hockenheim, but he lost out to the Colombian, who had qualified on pole.

"No, I still can't see anything coming." No matter how hard he looked into the distance, Giancarlo Fisichella could still not see any major signs of progress this season. Despite that, he came home an encouraging fourth in Hockenheim.
▷

"Eddie, let me remind you it's me who gives the orders." Niki Lauda gets forceful to make a point to his driver.
▽

Jean Alesi scores and leaves

"Alain, I've got you a point. It's my leaving present. Now, I'm off." The scene was one of calm, but it was obviously a serious discussion on Sunday afternoon, not long after the end of the German Grand Prix. Changed into civvies and with his briefcase in his hand, Jean Alesi told Alain Prost he was leaving the team - for good and without giving the slightest explanation to any of the journalists present.

Alain Prost also refused to be drawn on the matter, leaving the door open to all sorts of rumour and speculation. Because, if Jean Alesi would not be driving for Prost Grand Prix in the forthcoming Hungarian Grand Prix, what would he be doing? There were those in Hockenheim who reckoned Jordan was the most likely option.

Bridgestone continues

While everyone had been expecting a prolongation of the contract between Bridgestone and McLaren, it was Ferrari who announced in Germany that the two companies were extending their agreement to the end of the 2004 season.

Heinz-Harald Frentzen misses the party

A major drama was keeping the F1 gossips busy on the Wednesday. As the teams were quietly going about their business, setting everything up for the Hockenheim weekend, news arrived in the afternoon that Eddie Jordan had sacked his driver, Heinz-Harald Frentzen, "with immediate effect," terminating a contract which was not due to expire until the end of 2002.

According to a team member, who wished to remain anonymous, the Irishman and his driver had a huge row after the previous grand prix in England. Jordan justified his decision in an official statement, saying that the dismissal came as the result of an "exchange of views," between himself and his driver. Recently, the atmosphere had been tense between the two men, as the team had not exactly been getting great results. Currently eleventh in the classification, Heinz-Harald Frentzen had not finished in the points since the San Marino Grand Prix.

For his part, the German driver contested the reasons for his dismissal and was threatening to take his former employer to court. It was later learned that the amount he was after was a staggering nine million dollars!

Provisionally, Jordan had nominated their test driver, Ricardo Zonta, to stand in for Frentzen at the German Grand Prix. All options were still open for the remaining races however, especially that of employing Jean Alesi (see below.)

The exact reasons which led Eddie Jordan to take this action remained nebulous for the rest of the season.

Those close to the team reckoned Jordan wanted to take on the young Japanese driver, Takuma Sato for 2002 and so, he had to get rid of Heinz-Harald Frentzen, who was suddenly surplus to requirements. Jordan cited a non-competitive clause to get rid of the German and it was suggested that the team owner acted to sack him, in case his form picked up later in the year.

It was rumoured that "HH" might turn his attention to the States and the Indycar series, if he could not find another F1 berth. He had already looked at the American option back in 1998, when he had been "thanked" for his services by Frank Williams, before he was saved from that fate by none other than....Eddie Jordan!

Villeneuve confirmed....and on the podium!

The last few weeks had been pretty hectic for the BAR team. Jacques Villeneuve was regularly getting beaten by his team-mate and no longer seemed to have his heart in it or give it his all. *"Why should he? It would be a waste of his talent,"* said a sympathetic Jock Clear, his track engineer. The team's French driver had left the British Grand Prix in a black mood, having been knocked out of the race at the very first corner, by none other than his team-mate. Olivier Panis had reason to feel frustrated, given that Villeneuve was the protege of Craig Pollock, his team boss and former personal manager.

The 2001 car, the BAR03 was hardly a great success and had only been good enough to pick up the odd point here and there.

However, all this unrest did not seem to get in the way of progress in Germany. To start with, on Thursday in Hockenheim, the team confirmed that both its drivers were staying on until the end of 2002. This would represent Villeneuve's fourth season with the team. *"Since I have been here, I have noticed continuous progress being made,"* insisted the Canadian. *"I am sure that next year, we will be able to take a big step forward."*

Olivier Panis was all smiles when he arrived at the track on Thursday, along with his wife Anne. He was also clearly pleased to have renewed his deal. *"Things have not always gone the way we would have liked up until now, but I still have confidence in the team and they in me. In my opinion that is very important. I*
am also very happy that Jacques is staying too. We know one another better now and he is a great driver."

With the 2001 season already in its final third phase, the team was already working hard on the 2002 car. *"Now, we have to build a car capable of finishing in the top three on a regular basis,"* reckoned Craig Pollock. With Jacques Villeneuve and Olivier Panis the team could count on two super drivers. Now it just had to produce a super car. No easy task.

And a surprise third place

Jacques Villeneuve was definitely surprised to find himself in third place in Hockenheim and have something worth celebrating at last. All the more so, as he had started from a mediocre twelfth place on the grid. *"I knew we would need a bit of luck to finish in the points, but I never thought I could make it to the podium,"* he exclaimed. *"We were not at all competitive this weekend, except this morning in the warm-up. Then, the car was suddenly great on full tanks."*

Running relatively high downforce, the Canadian was not able to pass anyone. In fact, he even let team-mate Olivier Panis pass him. *"I knew Olivier was on a different strategy to me and that he would be stopping twice,"* continued the BAR driver. *"As I couldn't pass Trulli, I let Olivier by so that he could have some fun. Just as I had hoped, Jarno ended up going off! In fact, today, I was basically a privileged spectator, powerless to do anything."*

176

results

PRACTICE TIMES

No	Driver	Car/Engine/Chassis	Practice Friday	Pos.	Practice Saturday	Pos.	Qualifying	Pos.	Warm-up	Pos.
1.	Michael Schumacher	Ferrari/F2001/210	1'42"255	5°	1'39"937	3°	1'38"941	4°	1'42"747	4°
2.	Rubens Barrichello	Ferrari/F2001/206	1'41"953	4°	1'40"436	6°	1'39"682	6°	1'42"989	5°
3.	Mika Häkkinen	McLaren/Mercedes/MP4/16/7	1'41"949	3°	1'40"069	4°	1'38"811	3°	1'43"129	6°
4.	David Coulthard	McLaren/Mercedes/MP4/16/5	1'42"304	7°	1'40"697	9°	1'39"574	5°	1'42"743	3°
5.	Ralf Schumacher	Williams/BMW/FW23/5	1'42"987	10°	1'39"188	1°	1'38"136	2°	1'42"621	1°
6.	Juan Pablo Montoya	Williams/BMW/FW23/6	1'41"487	2°	1'39"469	2°	1'38"117	1°	1'42"651	2°
7.	Giancarlo Fisichella	Benetton/Renault/B201/6	1'43"014	11°	1'43"256	20°	1'41"299	17°	1'44"601	17°
8.	Jenson Button	Benetton/Renault/B201/5	1'43"496	15°	1'41"771	16°	1'41"438	18°	1'45"653	20°
9.	Olivier Panis	BAR/Honda/003/6	1'43"487	14°	1'40"575	8°	1'40"610	13°	1'43"615	10°
10.	Jacques Villeneuve	BAR/Honda/003/4	1'43"815	17°	1'41"683	15°	1'40"437	12°	1'43"570	9°
11.	Ricardo Zonta	Jordan/Honda/EJ11/4	1'43"461	13°	1'41"534	14°	1'41"174	15°	6'35"247	22°
12.	Jarno Trulli	Jordan/Honda/EJ11/6	1'42"941	9°	1'40"894	10°	1'40"322	10°	1'43"856	14°
14.	Jos Verstappen	Arrows/Asiatech/A22/6	1'44"143	18°	1'42"580	19°	1'41"870	20°	1'43"704	11°
15.	Enrique Bernoldi	Arrows/Asiatech/A22/3	1'44"549	20°	1'42"223	18°	1'41"668	19°	1'43"512	8°
16.	Nick Heidfeld	Sauber/Petronas/C20/7	1'43"211	12°	1'40"263	5°	1'39"921	7°	1'43"479	7°
17.	Kimi Räikkönen	Sauber/Petronas/C20/6	1'43"528	16°	1'41"153	12°	1'40"072	8°	1'43"986	15°
18.	Eddie Irvine	Jaguar/R-2/4	1'41"424	1°	1'40"443	7°	1'40"371	11°	1'43"851	13°
19.	Pedro de la Rosa	Jaguar/R-2/5	1'42"302	6°	1'40"905	11°	1'40"265	9°	1'43"706	12°
20.	Tarso Marques	Minardi/European/PS01/4	1'45"005	22°	1'43"909	22°	1'42"716	22°	1'45"981	21°
21.	Fernando Alonso	Minardi/European/PS01/3	1'44"730	21°	1'43"512	21°	1'41"913	21°	1'45"263	19°
22.	Jean Alesi	Prost/Acer/AP04/6	1'42"828	8°	1'41"428	13°	1'40"724	14°	1'44"300	16°
23.	Luciano Burti	Prost/Acer/AP04/5	1'44"162	19°	1'42"136	17°	1'41"213	16°	1'45"004	18°

MAXIMUM SPEEDS

No	Driver	P1 Qualifs	Pos	P1 Race	Pos	P2 Qualifs	Pos	P2 Race	Pos	Finish Qualifs	Pos	Finish Race	Pos	Trap Qualifs	Pos	Trap Race	Pos
1.	M. Schumacher	299,6	1°	274,8	11°	326,3	4°	323,4	13°	277,7	6°	267,8	13°	348,7	16°	350,9	13°
2.	R. Barrichello	280,5	7°	277,4	3°	324,8	7°	333,0	1°	276,9	8°	272,8	2°	346,3	19°	353,2	9°
3.	M. Häkkinen	281,3	4°	273,6	13°	325,9	5°	322,4	14°	277,9	5°	268,8	9°	359,2	1°	349,4	18°
4.	D. Coulthard	280,6	6°	277,9	2°	324,8	8°	326,3	5°	276,9	9°	270,5	5°	348,2	17°	350,4	14°
5.	R. Schumacher	284,3	3°	277,4	4°	327,3	2°	325,2	8°	281,7	2°	273,7	1°	350,7	6°	352,7	10°
6.	J. P. Montoya	285,3	2°	279,2	1°	327,6	1°	325,8	7°	282,3	1°	271,6	4°	350,8	5°	355,2	4°
7.	G. Fisichella	273,5	22°	273,0	15°	316,7	22°	320,9	18°	271,7	20°	268,7	10°	344,7	22°	354,3	7°
8.	J. Button	273,8	21°	270,8	20°	318,2	20°	320,0	19°	271,0	22°	266,6	17°	346,2	20°	350,1	15°
9.	O. Panis	278,2	15°	275,4	9°	323,5	10°	327,5	3°	277,0	7°	271,8	3°	348,7	14°	354,4	5°
10.	J. Villeneuve	276,7	18°	275,7	8°	323,2	13°	322,0	15°	276,5	10°	269,1	8°	348,8	13°	354,3	6°
11.	R. Zonta	280,4	8°	275,8	7°	325,9	6°	323,8	10°	276,2	12°	264,9	18°	349,8	10°	357,3	1°
12.	J. Trulli	280,2	9°	276,9	6°	326,5	3°	326,1	6°	279,9	3°	269,7	7°	352,0	2°	351,7	11°
14.	J. Verstappen	278,7	12°	275,2	10°	323,5	11°	324,2	9°	274,9	16°	270,5	6°	351,1	4°	354,2	8°
15.	E. Bernoldi	279,5	11°	277,3	5°	323,9	9°	328,3	2°	275,8	13°	268,5	11°	351,5	3°	355,4	3°
16.	N. Heidfeld	278,0	16°	-	-	321,6	17°	-	-	275,2	15°	-	-	349,2	11°	349,7	16°
17.	K. Räikkönen	278,4	13°	272,0	18°	322,7	15°	323,4	12°	274,6	17°	264,9	19°	349,1	12°	348,0	19°
18.	E. Irvine	279,8	10°	274,7	12°	323,3	12°	326,5	4°	276,4	11°	267,3	14°	347,9	18°	355,6	2°
19.	P. de la Rosa	281,1	5°			322,9	14°			278,5	4°			348,7	15°	347,2	21°
20.	T. Marques	275,2	20°	272,3	17°	317,2	21°	317,2	20°	271,1	21°	264,4	20°	345,4	21°	346,9	22°
21.	F. Alonso	276,0	19°	271,7	19°	319,5	19°	323,6	11°	273,4	19°	266,9	16°	350,4	7°	351,3	12°
22.	J. Alesi	276,9	17°	272,9	16°	322,4	16°	320,9	17°	274,6	18°	267,2	15°	349,9	8°	348,0	20°
23.	L. Burti	278,4	14°	273,2	14°	320,1	18°	321,5	16°	275,7	14°	268,4	12°	349,9	9°	349,5	17°

CLASSIFICATION & RETIREMENTS

Pos	Driver	Team	Time
1.	R. Schum.	Williams BMW	1:18:17.873
2.	Barrichello	Ferrari	+ 46.117
3.	Villeneuve	BAR Honda	+ 62.806
4.	Fisichella	Benetton Renault	+ 63.477
5.	Button	Benetton Renault	+ 65.454
6.	Alesi	Prost Acer	+ 65.950
7.	Panis	BAR Honda	+ 77.527
8.	Bernoldi	Arrows Asiatech	+ 1 lap
9.	Verstappen	Arrows Asiatech	+ 1 lap
10.	Alonso	European Minardi	+ 1 lap

Lap	Driver	Team	Reason
1	de la Rosa	Jaguar Racing	accident
1	Heidfeld	Sauber Petronas	accident
8	Zonta	Jordan Honda	accident
14	Häkkinen	McLaren Mercedes	engine
17	Irvine	Jaguar Racing	fuel pressure
17	Räikkönen	Sauber Petronas	transmission
24	Burti	Prost Acer	off
24	M. Schum.	Ferrari	fuel pressure
25	Montoya	Williams BMW	engine
27	Marques	European Minardi	gearbox
28	Coulthard	McLaren Mercedes	engine
35	Trulli	Jordan Honda	hydraulic pump

FASTEST LAPS

	Driver	Time	Lap
1.	Montoya	1'41"808 241,336 km/h	20
2.	R. Schum.	1'42"048	17
3.	Barrichello	1'42"638	10
4.	M. Schum.	1'42"853	21
5.	Panis	1'43"329	30
6.	Villeneuve	1'43"448	21
7.	Häkkinen	1'43"516	4
8.	Coulthard	1'43"571	26
9.	Trulli	1'43"740	33
10.	Fisichella	1'43"999	34
11.	Button	1'44"051	31
12.	Alesi	1'44"135	42
13.	Räikkönen	1'44"365	10
14.	Irvine	1'44"415	11
15.	Verstappen	1'44"681	35
16.	Burti	1'44"683	17
17.	Bernoldi	1'44"785	31
18.	Zonta	1'45"591	4
19.	Alonso	1'45"908	4
20.	Marques	1'46"013	12

All results : © 2001 Fédération Internationale de l'Automobile, 2, Ch. Blandonnet, 1215 Genève 15, Suisse

PIT STOPS

	Driver	Time	Lap	Stop n°
1.	Zonta	49"027	6	1
2.	Verstappen	31"177	7	1
3.	Irvine	29"653	12	1
4.	Bernoldi	33"380	12	1
5.	Alonso	31"064	13	1
6.	Barrichello	28"910	16	1
7.	Panis	31"247	16	1
8.	Marques	34"689	20	1
9.	Montoya	50"808	22	1
10.	M. Schum.	31"437	25	1
11.	R. Schum.	31"555	24	1
12.	Villeneuve	36"138	24	1
13.	Button	31"997	24	1
14.	Alesi	31"161	25	1
15.	Alonso	31"227	25	2
16.	Fisichella	29"541	26	1
17.	Coulthard	29"124	27	1
18.	Trulli	37"866	27	1
19.	Verstappen	29"437	27	2
20.	Bernoldi	30"057	28	2
21.	Panis	31"030	31	2
22.	Barrichello	39"835	32	2

BRIDGESTONE

Best result for a driver running Bridgestone tyres :

Ruben Barrichello, Ferrari, second

THE CIRCUIT

TWELFTH ROUND

GROSSER PREIS VON DEUTSCHLAND - HOCKENHEIM

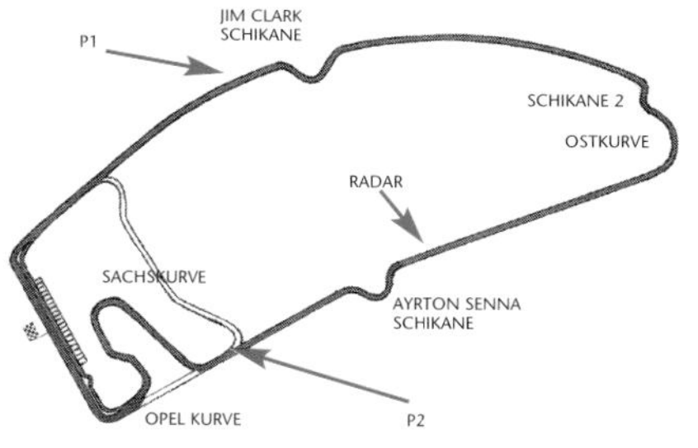

Date : July 30, 2001
Length : 6825 meters
Distance : 45 laps, 307.125 km
Weather : hot and sunny, 28°

CHAMPIONSHIP

(after twelve rounds)

Drivers :

1. M. Schumacher 78
2. D. Coulthard 47
3. R. Schumacher 41
4. R. Barrichello 40
5. M. Häkkinen 19
6. J. P. Montoya 15
7. J. Villeneuve 11
8. N. Heidfeld 10
9. K. Räikkönen 9
   J. Trulli 9
11. H.-H. Frentzen 6
12. O. Panis 5
13. E. Irvine 4
    G. Fisichella 4
    J. Alesi 4
16. J. Button 2
17. J.Verstappen 1
    P. de la Rosa 1

Constructors :

1. Ferrari 124
2. McLaren Mercedes 66
3. Williams BMW 56
4. Sauber Petronas 19
5. BAR Honda 16
6. Jordan Honda 15
7. Benetton Renault 6
8. Jaguar Racing 5
9. Prost Acer 4
10. Arrows Asiatech 1

RACE SUMMARY

- Both Minardis are in trouble at the start of the formation lap: one is on fire on the grid. Both take the start from the pit lane.
- After the start, Michael Schumacher's Ferrari has a problem and is almost motionless in the middle of the grid. Luciano Burti hits it from behind, flies over the car and lands back on the track. The race is interrupted so that the debris can be cleared away.
- At the second start, Montoya gets the better of Ralf Schumacher. Barrichello passes Hakkinen at the first chicane.
- Barrichello continues his charge, passing Michael Schumacher on lap 6, the German having taken the second start with the spare car.
- The order on lap 10: Montoya leads Ralf Schumacher by 6.1 seconds. 9.4 seconds back is Barrichello, 14.4 is Michael Schumacher and Hakkinen is 18.3 down, before retiring on lap 14.
- Montoya refuels at half-distance. A problem with the fuel line makes for a very long stop. He rejoins third, before retiring with a broken engine on lap 25. Michael Schumacher had pulled out a lap earlier, just after refuelling.
- Two laps later and Coulthard retires from third place.
- With 15 laps remaining, Ralf Schumacher leads Barrichello by 11.3 seconds. That says it all.

LAP CHART

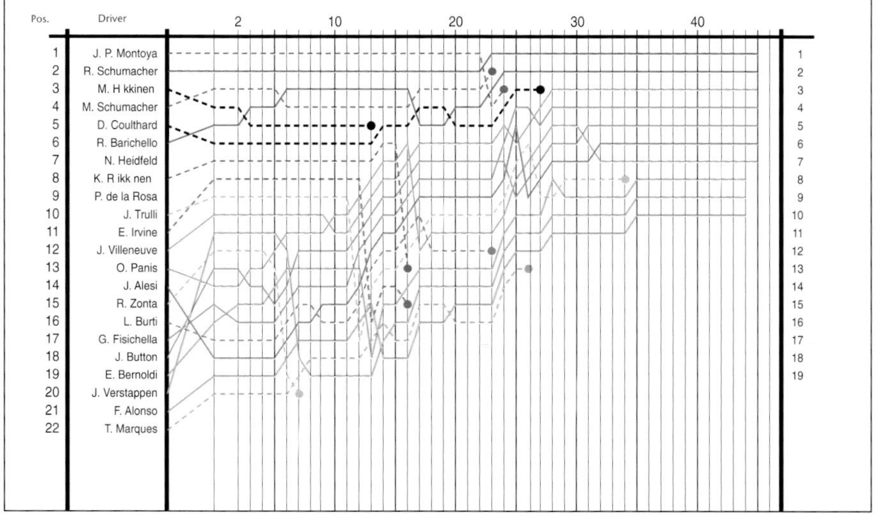

GAPS ON THE LEADER BOARD

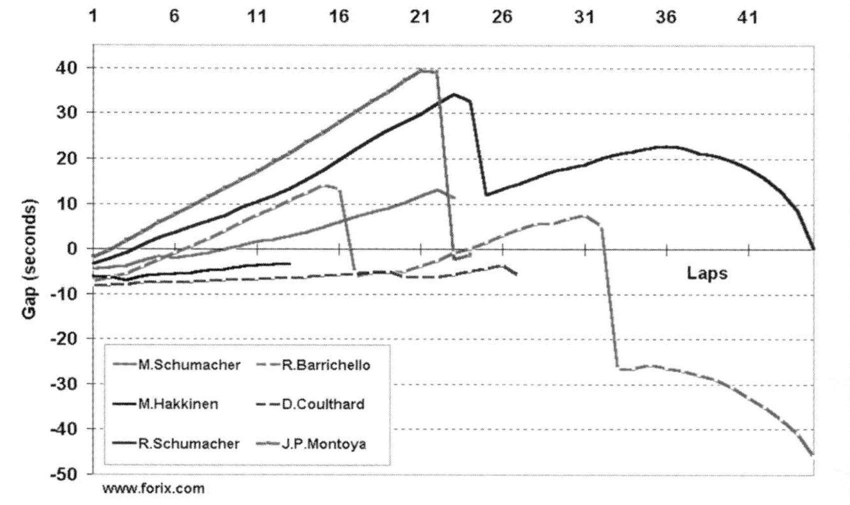

It's in the bag!

By winning the Hungarian Grand Prix, Michael Schumacher made sure of his fourth world title. True class. For Scuderia Ferrari it was a total triumph as, thanks to Rubens Barrichello's second place in Budapest, the Italian team lifted the Constructors' title, for the third year in succession. These achievements, coming so early in the season, were proof of the dominance exhibited by the red arrows in 2001.

MARLBORO MAGYAR NAGYDÍJ
BUDAPEST

practice

Heinz-Harald Frentzen in blue and Jean Alesi in yellow, alongside Jarno Trulli: this was the main novelty at the Hungarian Grand Prix after the summer three week break.

Debuts for Jean Alesi with Jordan and Heinz-Harald Frentzen with Prost.

Yellow suits him so well

In his new canary coloured race suit, Jean Alesi struts around with a giant grin on his face, signing every autograph asked of him. On this the first day of practice with his new team, the man from Avignon was the paddock's Mr. Congeniality personified. And setting the sixth fastest time on Friday was an added bonus.

Jean Alesi looked like making a successful transition to Jordan. Yet, some of his nearest and dearest were a bit worried on the eve of the grand prix weekend, given that he was getting in the car after the summer testing ban and had only completed a handful of laps in his new mount, prior to coming to Budapest. The EJ11 was fitted with two pedals, set up for left foot braking, while Alesi's driving style required three, as he brakes with the right foot. There was a risk the car could not be properly set up to suit the Frenchman, but the Jordan engineers managed it. *"As I brake and accelerate with the same foot, they had to rejig the pedal box,"* explained the

Michael Schumacher didn't need to hide away in the trees of the Budapest circuit, given he had just taken pole position; his ninth of the season.

driver. *"The problem is that there is very little room and there has to be enough between the pedals, so that I don't press both at once. The team has come up with a solution and everything is going very well."*

It was going even better, given that the Frenchman, who had everything to learn, had been a good half second quicker than team-mate Jarno Trulli. *"I was having to adapt to new tyres, a new engine, a new chassis and a new team. But it was fine. My biggest problem was that, at the end of a run, I tended to miss my pit, heading automatically for the last one and the*

mechanics had to come and drag me back!" He did the same thing in the race.

Saturday was not as good as the previous one for Alesi. He would start from 12th on the grid, pretty much where he was used to finding himself in the Prost. He was also a long way back from team-mate Trulli, who had qualified fifth.

The Frenchman fought hard all day to try and get his EJ11 balanced to his liking. *"We made some changes and the car isn't too bad. The only problem I have is adapting to the chassis."*

Yet another pole in passing

Michael Schumacher could become world champion this weekend, if he scored three little points more than David Coulthard.

However, doing it in style with a win would be the icing on the cake. On Saturday, Schumacher took out a serious option on that

eventuality, by setting pole position with a very impressive margin of over eight tenths of a second on David Coulthard. On top of that, he only took two runs to set the time. *"It wasn't really to spare the tyres, but mainly to save myself!"* he joked after the session.

STARTING GRID

M. SCHUMACHER 1'14"059	-1-	David COULTHARD 1'14"860	
R. BARRICHELLO 1'14"953	-2-	R. SCHUMACHER 1'15"095	
Jarno TRULLI 1'15"394	-3-	Mika HÄKKINEN 1'15"411	
Nick HEIDFELD 1'15"739	-4-	J. P. MONTOYA 1'15"881	
Kimi RAIKKONEN 1'15"906	-5-	Jacques VILLENEUVE 1'16"212	
Olivier PANIS 1'16"382	-6-	Jean ALESI 1'16"471	
Pedro De la Rosa 1'16"543	-7-	Eddie IRVINE 1'16"607	
G. FISICHELLA 1'16"632	-8-	H.-H. FRENTZEN 1'17"196	
Jenson BUTTON 1'17"535	-9-	Fernando ALONSO 1'17"624	
Luciano BURTI 1'18"238	-10-	Enrique BERNOLDI 1'18"258	
Jos VERSTAPPEN 1'18"389	-11-	Tarso MARQUES 1'19"139	

Schumi wins and gets it all!

Ferrari President Luca di Montezemolo, had demanded it the week before: he wanted the Scuderia to win the world championship this weekend in Budapest, so that the matter could be put to bed as soon as possible.

The team arrived in Budapest, with the cars set up specifically for the Hungarian circuit and everyone was in determined mood. A few minutes before the race, a mechanic explained that everyone was on edge within the Scuderia. The title was so close they could almost touch it. And that's exactly what Michael Schumacher did on the track on Sunday and seemingly without too much effort at that. Starting from pole, the German was never really troubled for the rest of the afternoon. *"I didn't feel I would do it this weekend,"* he admitted after stepping down from the podium. *"I had a bad feeling and it was only when there were three laps to go that I started to believe that it might be alright. That's when I got nervous."*

Once he had taken the chequered flag, the German felt emotions that he could not

describe, but they were strong enough to see him dissolve in tears during the post-race press conference. *"I'm not too bad when it comes to driving, but when it comes to describing my feelings, I'm rubbish,"* he admitted. *"It's just fantastic for me and for the team. They are all extraordinary people, so human and so hard working. This team is simply the best."*

Having picked up the 2001 title with four races in hand, it all looked rather "simple," compared with the down-to-the-wire tussles of previous years. Nevertheless, Schumacher did not feel it was any less satisfying. *"I don't feel less pride in this title than in the others,"* was his newly crowned analysis. *"If you look at the number of times our rivals failed to score, you can see that, when they were running, they were very competitive and we had to fight for it. Apart from in the first two grands prix maybe, they gave us a hard time."*

Even if the titles were wrapped up, there were still four grands prix remaining. Rubens Barrichello still had a chance of taking second spot in the Drivers' classification (he was currently five points behind David Coulthard.) Michael Schumacher maintained his motivation was still firing on all cylinders. *"I am here to win and I always want to win races,"* he concluded. *"If I get it wrong in Spa in a fortnight's time, no one will say to me, "you had a good race in Budapest" but they will criticise me in Spa. This constant pressure is*

what makes Formula 1 a bit special. On top of that, I still feel I have plenty of energy to carry on doing my maximum, even if the championship is over." He would prove two weeks later in Belgium and two months later in Japan, that the will to win still burned within him.

△

Jumping for joy in Budapest: Michael Schumacher on the podium with David Coulthard and Jean Todt. Below: the winner's trophy.

▽

Ferrari takes the Constructors' Championship

It really was Ferrari's day in Budapest. Apart from Michael Schumacher clinching the Drivers' title, Rubens Barrichello's second place also handed the Scuderia the 2001 Constructors' Championship for the third year in succession.

With 140 points to 72 for its closest rival, McLaren, the Scuderia was now home and dry. Luca di Montezemolo was not at the circuit in Budapest to see his team triumph. His absence was entirely down to superstition: in 1997, 1998 and 1999 he had turned up for the decisive race of the series, only for it to always end in defeat!

Once the title was in the bag, the Scuderia President immediately jumped on a plane to join in the Ferrari party at the swanky Kempinski Hotel in Budapest. The revels went on long into the night, with most of the team heading bleary eyed straight for the airport on Monday morning.

The Debutantes Ball

Michael Schumacher stormed away from pole, giving no one else a chance to lead into the first corner.

The singer Chris Rea has been a personal friend of Eddie Jordan's for many years and on the Monday before the Hungarian Grand Prix, he was at Silverstone circuit to watch Jean Alesi have his first ever run in the Jordan-Honda EJ11. *"It was a great day,"* recalled Alesi. Chris Rea had said to Eddie: *"I won't come back to see your car run at the track until you have employed Jean Alesi."* So on Monday, Eddie called him. *"You've been on my case for twelve years and now I've done it. Jean's in the car!"*

Jean Alesi arrived at the Hungaroring around three in the afternoon on Thursday, in civvies, but he was soon sporting his new yellow fire suit for the weigh in. He displayed all the enthusiasm of a kid with a new toy. *"I am extra-motivated,"* explained the Frenchman. *"I hardly did any running at Silverstone, but I get the impression the car is pretty good. The main thing is that the session allowed me to sort out a good driving position."*

Just like Heinz-Harald Frentzen, Alesi had only managed about fifty kilometres in his new mount. This year, the FIA had banned testing between the German and Hungarian Grands Prix, in order to give the teams a break. The 50 kilometres were allowed as a shake-down for the cars, but both Alesi and Frentzen made the most of it to get used to their new cars. *"I have to adapt to this new team as quickly as possible,"* explained the other new boy, Frentzen, all decked out in blue. *"I've got five races to get the job done and that's not a lot. For the moment, I have only been able to sort out the position of the steering wheel and the pedals. I'm starting from zero and we will have to see how I fit in with the team. I went to visit the factory before signing and everything seems very good. I think*

The splendour of Budapest at night

the team has a solid base with some very professional people working for Prost." For the German, this drive for the French team smacked of the Last Chance Saloon, as there was nothing else on the cards at the end of 2001.

In Budapest, the German refused to expand on the reasons for his sacking by Jordan. Some claimed it was because he wasn't physically fit enough, but this did not seem very plausible. *"I won't say anything about it,"* he insisted. *"I had a contract with Jordan, which I thought was valid and now the courts will decide who was right."* Even a judge would find in his favour, awarding him the

nine million dollars damages and interest he was demanding, Heinz-Harald Frentzen would never make up for the lost time.

The greatest?

Thanks to a fourth world title, Michael Schumacher was yet again kept busy rewriting his name in the motorsport book of legends. Naturally, people were beginning to ask themselves if he was perhaps the greatest driver of all time.

What is missing of course, is his duel with Ayrton Senna, which would have been fantastic. But we will never know, as fate robbed us of this thrilling possibility one black day in May 1994.

Since then, Michael Schumacher has been in a league of his own, without any real opposition worthy of the name. He would have to settle for setting his sights on Juan Manuel Fangio's record of five titles, set in 1957.

But, as the Ferrari driver himself explained in Budapest, it was impossible to draw any comparisons with the Argentinian. Fangio set his record in the days when much of the grid was made up of wealthy amateurs rather than professional drivers. The seasons consisted of just seven or eight races, as opposed to 17 in 2001 and the risks back then were much higher, not to say phenomenal.

However, even if Juan Manuel Fangio's record belongs to a different era, it was now the only record left for Michael Schumacher to aim for and from which to take some motivation.

Jean Alesi has just over-shot his pit when coming in to refuel. He has to be pulled back by his mechanics for them to work on the car.

Once again, the Saubers proved to be "the best of the rest" in Budapest. The two Ferraris, the two McLarens and Ralf Schumacher having all made it to the flag, the Swiss cars had to settle for feasting on the single point for sixth place. It went to Nick Heidfeld, with team-mate Kimi Raikkonen right behind in seventh.

PRACTICE TIMES

No	Driver	Car/Engine/Chassis	Practice Friday	Pos.	Practice Saturday	Pos.	Qualifying	Pos.	Warm-up	Pos.
1.	Michael Schumacher	Ferrari/F2001/211	1'16"651	1°	1'15"466	2°	1'14"059	1°	1'17"338	2°
2.	Rubens Barrichello	Ferrari/F2001/206	1'16"734	2°	1'15"650	3°	1'14"953	3°	1'17"360	3°
3.	Mika Häkkinen	McLaren/Mercedes/MP4/16/7	1'16"789	3°	1'15"839	5°	1'15"411	6°	1'17"704	5°
4.	David Coulthard	McLaren/Mercedes/MP4/16/6	1'18"182	10°	1'15"263	1°	1'14"860	2°	1'16"915	1°
5.	Ralf Schumacher	Williams/BMW/FW23/5	1'17"308	4°	1'16"033	7°	1'15"095	4°	1'17"608	4°
6.	Juan Pablo Montoya	Williams/BMW/FW23/6	1'18"524	13°	1'16"098	8°	1'15"881	8°	1'19"465	12°
7.	Giancarlo Fisichella	Benetton/Renault/B201/6	1'17"896	7°	1'16"513	10°	1'16"632	15°	1'19"704	15°
8.	Jenson Button	Benetton/Renault/B201/5	1'19"263	17°	1'16"619	13°	1'17"535	17°	1'21"397	22°
9.	Olivier Panis	BAR/Honda/003/6	1'17"970	9°	1'16"581	12°	1'16"382	11°	1'18"881	8°
10.	Jacques Villeneuve	BAR/Honda/003/7	1'19"238	16°	1'17"087	14°	1'16"212	10°	1'19"554	13°
11.	Jarno Trulli	Jordan/Honda/EJ11/7	1'18"277	12°	1'16"021	6°	1'15"394	5°	1'18"433	6°
12.	Jean Alesi	Jordan/Honda/EJ11/6	1'17"862	6°	1'17"334	16°	1'16"471	12°	1'19"581	14°
14.	Jos Verstappen	Arrows/Asiatech/A22/6	1'19"368	18°	1'18"954	21°	1'18"389	21°	1'19"887	16°
15.	Enrique Bernoldi	Arrows/Asiatech/A22/3	1'19"466	19°	1'18"533	20°	1'18"258	20°	1'20"500	17°
16.	Nick Heidfeld	Sauber/Petronas/C20/7	1'17"928	8°	1'15"821	4°	1'15"739	7°	1'18"851	7°
17.	Kimi Räikkönen	Sauber/Petronas/C20/6	1'18"834	15°	1'16"578	11°	1'15"906	9°	1'19"068	9°
18.	Eddie Irvine	Jaguar/R-2/4	1'17"409	5°	1'16"471	9°	1'16"607	14°	1'19"148	10°
19.	Pedro de la Rosa	Jaguar/R-2/7	1'18"195	11°	1'17"549	17°	1'16"543	13°	1'19"393	11°
20.	Tarso Marques	Minardi/European/PS01/4	1'20"981	22°	1'19"153	22°	1'17"981	22°	1'21"354	21°
21.	Fernando Alonso	Minardi/European/PS01/3	1'19"992	20°	1'18"234	19°	1'17"624	18°	1'20"965	20°
22.	Heinz-Harald Frentzen	Prost/Acer/AP04/6	1'18"724	14°	1'17"203	15°	1'17"196	16°	1'20"546	18°
23.	Luciano Burti	Prost/Acer/AP04/5	1'20"615	21°	1'17"992	18°	1'18"238	19°	1'20"652	19°

MAXIMUM SPEEDS

No	Driver	P1 Qualifs	Pos	P1 Race	Pos	P2 Qualifs	Pos	P2 Race	Pos	Finish Qualifs	Pos	Finish Race	Pos	Trap Qualifs	Pos	Trap Race	Pos
1.	M. Schumacher	286,9	4°	283,3	6°	244,7	6°	235,8	5°	251,9	5°	246,0	10°	295,8	3°	297,1	8°
2.	R. Barrichello	287,9	3°	284,2	5°	283,3	7°	237,8	2°	237,5	2°	253,1	3°	247,4	7°	295,1	14°
3.	M. Häkkinen	285,1	9°	283,3	7°	239,8	6°	237,3	3°	250,1	9°	249,9	4°	294,1	11°	297,8	4°
4.	D. Coulthard	286,0	6°	285,3	3°	238,3	11°	233,6	7°	252,4	4°	248,6	5°	294,8	9°	299,6	3°
5.	R. Schumacher	293,9	1°	286,9	2°	242,6	4°	235,9	4°	259,0	1°	253,8	1°	305,4	1°	303,2	2°
6.	J. P. Montoya	292,6	2°	289,0	1°	242,7	3°	238,2	1°	258,4	2°	252,8	2°	303,0	2°	304,7	1°
7.	G. Fisichella	284,5	10°	277,7	17°	235,6	15°	228,8	15°	249,3	12°	245,1	12°	295,2	17°	294,1	16°
8.	J. Button	283,3	13°	278,8	14°	235,6	16°	230,9	11°	248,6	15°	274,4	6°	295,0	8°	295,0	15°
9.	O. Panis	280,0	21°	280,4	11°	238,5	10°	228,9	14°	248,5	16°	244,6	16°	294,7	10°	296,6	9°
10.	J. Villeneuve	283,3	14°	279,5	12°	237,7	13°	232,7	9°	248,1	18°	243,6	18°	289,8	22°	294,0	17°
11.	J. Trulli	282,7	15°	277,9	15°	240,9	5°	229,2	13°	249,7	11°	244,9	15°	295,2	6°	296,2	10°
12.	J. Alesi	282,5	16°	-	-	238,8	9°	224,5	20°	248,7	14°	-	-	291,6	18°	-	
14.	J. Verstappen	281,0	19°	279,4	13°	234,9	19°	230,6	12°	246,5	21°	245,9	11°	293,2	14°	297,5	5°
15.	E. Bernoldi	281,4	18°	268,7	20°	235,4	18°	226,9	17°	247,7	19°	245,0	14°	291,1	20°	293,0	19°
16.	N. Heidfeld	286,1	5°	284,3	4°	239,0	7°	231,5	10°	250,9	6°	246,5	8°	293,9	12°	295,7	12°
17.	K. Räikkönen	285,4	7°	281,2	8°	238,7	9°	233,5	8°	250,6	7°	246,1	9°	295,7	4°	295,7	11°
18.	E. Irvine	283,8	11°	-	-	238,3	12°	-	-	250,4	8°	-	-	292,7	16°	254,5	21°
19.	P. de la Rosa	283,8	12°	280,9	9°	237,6	14°	234,6	6°	250,1	10°	250,5	3°	292,8	15°	297,5	6°
20.	T. Marques	278,7	22°	279,4	18°	231,6	22°	223,4	21°	244,5	22°	241,6	20°	291,4	19°	292,2	20°
21.	F. Alonso	280,9	20°	277,7	16°	233,4	21°	225,8	18°	247,3	20°	241,8	19°	290,3	21°	293,0	18°
22.	H.-H. Frentzen	285,3	8°	280,9	10°	235,5	17°	227,6	16°	248,2	17°	245,1	13°	295,4	5°	297,1	7°
23.	L. Burti	281,9	17°	272,0	19°	234,0	20°	224,6	19°	248,7	13°	244,5	17°	293,5	13°	295,4	13°

PIT STOPS

Driver	Time	Lap	Stop n°
1. Button	33"747	6	1
2. Frentzen	30"246	18	1
3. Alonso	32"297	20	1
4. Fisichella	28"102	21	1
5. Verstappen	31"743	24	1
6. Räikkönen	29"617	26	1
7. Heidfeld	29"522	27	1
8. Panis	30"052	27	1
9. M. Schum.	30"261	28	1
10. Marques	31"591	26	1
11. Button	29"851	27	2
12. Trulli	34"780	29	1
13. R. Schum.	31"270	30	1
14. Villeneuve	31"267	30	1
15. Barrichello	30"740	31	1
16. de la Rosa	32"546	30	1
17. Coulthard	29"548	32	1
18. Montoya	30"676	32	1
19. Häkkinen	28"630	38	1
20. Fisichella	33"640	45	2
21. Räikkönen	31"553	46	2
22. Trulli	32"377	48	2
23. Montoya	30"423	49	2
24. Villeneuve	30"994	49	2
25. Heidfeld	29"799	51	2
26. M. Schum.	30"755	52	2
27. R. Schum.	32"053	52	2
28. Barrichello	30"125	53	2
29. Coulthard	31"632	54	2
30. Frentzen	30"567	52	2
31. Panis	31"287	53	2
32. de la Rosa	30"989	53	2
33. Verstappen	30"480	53	2
34. Marques	31"750	52	2
35. Häkkinen	28"411	56	2
36. Panis	18'04"911	57	3
37. Häkkinen	26"245	71	3

BRIDGESTONE

Best result for a driver running Bridgestone tyres:

Michael Schumacher, Ferrari, winner

CHAMPIONSHIP

(after thirteen rounds)

Drivers:

1. M. Schumacher	94
2. D. Coulthard	51
3. R. Barrichello	46
4. R. Schumacher	44
5. M. Häkkinen	21
6. J. P. Montoya	15
7. J. Villeneuve	11
N. Heidfeld	11
9. K. Räikkönen	9
J. Trulli	9
11. H.-H. Frentzen	6
12. O. Panis	5
13. E. Irvine	4
G. Fisichella	4
J. Alesi	4
16. J. Button	2
17. J. Verstappen	1
P. de la Rosa	1

Constructors:

1. Ferrari	140
2. McLaren Mercedes	72
3. Williams BMW	59
4. Sauber Petronas	20
5. BARHonda	16
6. Jordan Honda	15
7. Benetton Renault	6
8. Jaguar Racing	5
9. Prost Acer	4
10 Arrows Asiatech	1

CLASSIFICATION & RETIREMENTS

Pos	Driver	Team	Time
1.	M. Schumacher	Ferrari	1:41:49.675
2.	Barrichello	Ferrari	+ 3.363
3.	Coulthard	McLaren Mercedes	+ 3.940
4.	R. Schumacher	Williams BMW	+ 49.687
5.	Häkkinen	McLaren Mercedes	+ 70.293
6.	Heidfeld	Sauber Petronas	+ 1 lap
7.	Räikkönen	Sauber Petronas	+ 1 lap
8.	Montoya	Williams BMW	+ 1 lap
9.	Villeneuve	BAR Honda	+ 2 laps
10.	Alesi	Jordan Honda	+ 2 laps
11.	de la Rosa	Jaguar Racing	+ 2 laps
12.	Verstappen	Arrows Asiatech	+ 3 laps

Lap	Driver	Team	Reason
0	Irvine	Jaguar Racing	spin
9	Burti	Prost Acer	spin
12	Bernoldi	Arrows Asiatech	spin
35	Button	Benetton Renault	spin
38	Alonso	European Minardi	spin
54	Trulli	Jordan Honda	hydraulic
59	Panis	BAR Honda	engine electrics
64	Marques	European Minardi	oil pressure
64	Frentzen	Prost Acer	spin
68	Fisichella	Benetton Renault	engine

All results :
© 2001 Fédération Internationale de l'Automobile, 2, Ch. Blandonnet, 1215 Genève 15, Suisse

FASTEST LAPS

	Driver	Time	Lap
1.	Häkkinen	1'16"723	51
		180,348 km/h	
2.	Coulthard	1'17"054	53
3.	R. Schum.	1'17"233	54
4.	Barrichello	1'17"274	51
5.	M. Schum.	1'17"436	23
6.	Montoya	1'18"030	34
7.	Heidfeld	1'18"165	50
8.	de la Rosa	1'18"186	51
9.	Räikkönen	1'18"216	28
10.	Trulli	1'18"536	50
11.	Alesi	1'19"134	32
12.	Panis	1'19"222	29
13.	Fisichella	1'19"471	24
14.	Button	1'19"475	29
15.	Villeneuve	1'19"494	75
16.	Frentzen	1'20"046	50
17.	Verstappen	1'20"401	51
18.	Marques	1'21"379	51
19.	Alonso	1'21"533	18
20.	Burti	1'21"912	8
21.	Bernoldi	1'22"045	7

THE CIRCUIT

THIRTEENTH ROUND

MALBORO MAGYAR NAGYDIJ, GRAND PRIX DE HONGRIE

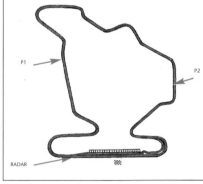

P1 P2 RADAR

Date :	August 19, 2001
Length :	3975 meters
Distance :	77 laps, 306.075 km
Weather :	hot and sunny, 31°

RACE SUMMARY

- Michael Schumacher has a trouble-free start, maintaining his pole position advantage into the first corner.
- The first corner in Budapest can be tricky, but everyone gets through, apart from Irvine who spins.
- Michael Schumacher cannot pull out a lead in the early stages. Barrichello and Coulthard are less than 3 seconds down. Ralf Schumacher is 8.3 seconds back.
- Michael Schumacher takes until lap 25 to shake off his team-mate. Behind, Trulli holds up Hakkinen, which allows Heidfeld, Montoya and Raikkonen to close up.
- After the first fuel stops, Michael Schumacher leads Coulthard by 11.6 seconds and Barrichello by 14.9.
- After the second stops, Michael Schumacher now leads the new Barrichello-Coulthard tandem by 6.9 seconds.
- Hakkinen is forced to make a third "splash 'n dash" stop.

LAP CHART

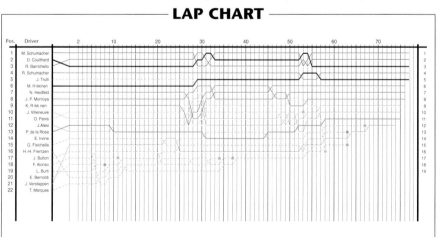

GAPS ON THE LEADER BOARD

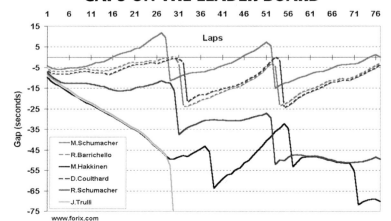

www.forix.com

One to forget

The Belgian Grand Prix turned out to be a strange event. The race was marred by a terrible accident, from which Luciano Burti was lucky to escape relatively unscathed. It was also a race in which the two front row starters dropped down the order even before the start.

Qualifying had set the tone, with the threat of disqualification hanging over no less than sixteen drivers!

The Sauber boys (photo) also had a weekend to forget. The two Swiss cars had qualified very badly and neither took the start, breaking down before the red lights went out.

**FOSTER'S BELGIAN GRAND PRIX
SPA-FRANCORCHAMPS**

A blue and white front row

Five weeks after taking pole position for the German Grand Prix, Juan Pablo Montoya did it again, setting the fastest lap in the qualifying session for the Belgian Grand Prix. It had rained heavily just a few minutes before the start of the session, after which, a watery sun gradually appeared. It was obvious therefore that all the quick times would come at the end of the hour. Juan Pablo Montoya timed his quickest lap to perfection, starting it just seconds before the chequered flag was waved to end the session. On an almost dry track on "dry" tyres, the Colombian set a time which gave an advantage over team-mate Ralf Schumacher of almost a second. *"It was very difficult today,"* reckoned the pole sitter after qualifying. *"I had chosen a basically dry set-up on the car. I did one run on the rain tyres, just to get a time in the bag and then I switched to the dry weather tyres. I did one cautious lap and then I told myself that it really was alright and I went for it. Actually, during my last lap, the track was dry apart from the chicane at Les Combes."*

Ralf Schumacher was second, to make it an all-Williams front row. *"I am not frustrated,"* he commented. *"The secret was to be on the track at the right time and I couldn't quite decide what to do. The Michelin intermediates are not great and we should have gone straight from rain tyres to slicks. But in the end, it all went better than expected."*

Sixteen drivers under threat!

Ron Dennis protests

After Nick Heidfeld went off at Stavelot, a few minutes before the end of the session, the yellow flags were hung out and waved to indicate that the Sauber was in trouble. In theory, the yellow flag means the drivers must show signs of taking precautions, although what they actually do is at their own discretion. One thing is clear however; one should not set one's best time when the yellow flags are out.

However, as the track was drying all the time, no less than 16 drivers improved their lap times in the final minutes of qualifying, just as these flags were being shown.

It was McLaren boss Ron Dennis who decided to protest all these drivers and, to cap it all, they included Mika Hakkinen as one of the 16 guilty men! *"I protested all those who had set quicker times, without considering whether this affected my drivers or not. It's a question of principle,"* he boomed.

A principle which would suit the Englishman as, if his protest had been upheld, all those at fault would have lost their times. That would have put Michael Schumacher on pole ahead of, well would you believe it, the two McLaren drivers, Mika Hakkinen and David Coulthard.

After over five hours of deliberation, the Stewards finally rejected Ron Dennis' protest. The classification was thus confirmed as was and sixteen drivers breathed a big sigh of relief. Phew!

STARTING GRID

-1-	Ralf SCHUMACHER	1'52"959		J. P. MONTOYA	1'52"072
-2-	Heinz-H. FRENTZEN	1'55"233		M. SCHUMACHER	1'54"685
-3-	Jacques VILLENEUVE	1'57"038		R. BARRICHELLO	1'56"116
-4-	Giancarlo FISICHELLA	1'57"668		Mika HAKKINEN	1'57"043
-5-	Pedro de la ROSA	1'58"519		David COULTHARD	1'58"008
-6-	Kimi RAIKKONEN	1'59"050		Olivier PANIS	1'58"838
-7-	Nick HEIDFELD	1'59"302		Jean ALESI	1'59"128
-8-	Jarno TRULLI	1'59"647		Jenson BUTTON	1'59"587
-9-	Luciano BURTI	1'59"900		Eddie IRVINE	1'59"689
-10-	Fernando ALONSO	2'02"594		Jos VERSTAPPEN	2'02"039
-11-	Tarso MARQUES	2'04"204		Enrique BERNOLDI	2'03"048

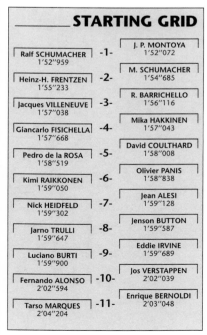

Number 52 for Michael Schumacher

With his main rivals, the two BMW-Williams, having eliminated themselves (see page 190,) Michael Schumacher had a relatively time of it in Spa. He led from the first lap, with second placed Giancarlo Fisichella holding up the McLarens, so that he only really had himself to contend with. That nearly cost him dear, as he briefly ran off the road on lap 17 when his concentration slipped. *"We have a lot of buttons on the steering wheel and I was playing with them when I ran a bit wide. I got a scare, but luckily I managed to control the car!"*

With win number 52, the German became the outright record holder for the most number of grand prix wins. *"Obviously, I didn't really have to fight today, apart from on the first lap with Ralf,"* he conceded. *"But it doesn't matter. It's nice to beat the previous record and on top of that, it's always a bit special winning on this track. This is where I made my debut. This is where I won my first grand prix in 1992 and it's not so far from my home."*

The Ferrari driver also felt this win would silence some of his critics. *"Some people thought we would not fight anymore, now that we have won the championship. Everyone can see that's not the case. My motivation is still intact. I race to enjoy myself and to win races. The records are fine, but they are not a goal on their own."*

Fisico on the podium

The big surprise on the podium in Spa came courtesy of Giancarlo Fisichella, who finished third. Up until this point, the Benetton-Renault season had been a catastrophe, with both its drivers skulking down the back of the pack far too often.

But this weekend in Belgium, the team fronted up with a new aerodynamic package which worked miracles. Giancarlo Fisichella qualified eighth and then made two lightning starts and was therefore second when the race finally got going for good.

He then fought off the attentions of David Coulthard, before giving best eight laps from the end. *"I was held up by Bernoldi when I came up to lap him and David made the most of it, to get past me on the next straight,"* explained "Fisico." *"But anyway, I'm very happy to be third. I could hear all the team cheering over the radio. The engineers kept telling me to push and not to let up."*

It was ironic that this return to form for the Benetton came just days after Eddie Jordan signed Giancarlo to drive for Jordan. *"Of course it won't be easy leaving a team I have worked with for the past four years. I am a bit sad to be going at the end of the year."*

Luciano Burti: a miracle escape on lap 5

Belgian Grand Prix, lap 5. Towards the back of the pack, at the exit to Stavelot corner, Luciano Burti mounts an optimistic attack on Eddie Irvine's Jaguar, in their battle for 16th place. The two cars were side by side, going into the double left hander at Blanchimont. Eddie Irvine cannot see the Brazilian's Prost and takes the corner, using the usual racing line. By this stage, Burti is already on the grass. He backs off, but it's too late and he hits the Jaguar and the front wing comes off. The Prost is therefore an out of control missile and it flies across the gravel trap, hitting the tyre barrier with such force, it bends the barrier behind the tyres. It is a huge impact, taken at 260 km/h. The Prost is buried under the tyres and a crane is required to free the driver.

The journalists watching on television in the media centre are stunned into silence. The Safety Car is called out, but the incident looks so serious that, a few minutes later, the race is stopped. At the scene of the accident, the marshals hold up sheets so the television cameras cannot show what is going on.

It is a normal procedure, but nevertheless, it sends shivers down the spine. Seen in slow motion, the crash has desperate similarities with Ayrton Senna's fatal accident seven years ago. The general consensus is that Luciano Burti will be lucky to get out of the situation alive.

And yet! In the hospital in Liege, a full examination a few hours after the incident, reveals that the Prost driver has not actually broken anything. He was just bruised. The impact had been so severe however, that the Brazilian would be out of action until the end of the season, suffering with severe headaches.

After the chequered flag, Eddie Irvine was called before the Stewards to explain his actions. They finally decided the Irishman was not to blame, declaring it was a straightforward racing incident and no action was taken against Irvine. *"I knew Luciano was there, but I would never have expected him to try and pass at that place,"* explained the Irishman. *"I took my usual line and I was hit from behind. From then on, I was just a passenger in my car."*

First on the scene of the accident, Irvine also added that the lateral head protection around the cockpit had done its job perfectly. *"Luciano's head was completely pushed over by the weight of the tyres,"* he continued. *"And it's clear that the neck protection absorbed the impact from the tyres."*

The race got underway again. With more than two laps, but less than 75% distance completed, it would be treated as a new race with only the second part counting. Eight laps were taken off the 44 laps originally scheduled: the four laps run before the crash, the two additional warm-up laps and the two laps run behind the Safety Car before the race was stopped.

Later in the evening, the first four laps were added to the classification. In order not to change the order, the time Michael Schumacher did, as leader of that "first leg" was simply added to everyone's time. Got that?

△
But what was Giancarlo Fisichella doing on the podium? It had to be a special occasion if the Italian got to swig the Champagne. In fact, it was the only time this year that he got to celebrate in front of the TV cameras.

No problems for Michael Schumacher, who basically cruised round for what amounted to a 43 lap victory parade.
◁

The wreck of Luciano Burti's Prost returns to the pits. The survival cell had done its job.
▽

 **FOSTER'S BELGIAN GRAND PRIX**

Nothing more spectacular than a blurred view of the Raidillon at Spa. Despite all the problems associated with Spa - terrible traffic jams, dreadful weather and slightly soggy chips - the Belgian circuit would deserve its place on the calendar for this corner alone.

FOSTER'S BELGIAN GRAND PRIX

The opening lap, at the braking point for Les Combes. Ralf Schumacher would lead for just a few more seconds and lights up his tyres.

Williams get it all wrong

What an afternoon! The Belgian Grand Prix was run in two legs, full of incident which made it the most action packed weekend of the year.

Having qualified on the front row, the BMW-Williams chances went out the window, even before the lights went out at the start of the race.

The facts: after a first warm-up lap, Heinz-Harald Frentzen stalls his Prost on the grid. As required by the rules, any driver stalling has to start from the back of the pack.

It was a terrible stroke of bad luck for the French team, as one of their cars had qualified on the second row of the grid, for the first time this season. During the qualifying session, Heinz-Harald Frentzen had made the most of a drying track, combined with his experience and that of Alain Prost. He was thus fourth on the grid.

At the start of the second warm-up lap, a similar fate befell Juan Pablo Montoya, who stalled and had to forsake pole position to move to the back of the class.

Once the race was finally underway, Ralf Schumacher took the lead, but was passed by Michael Schumacher two kilometres down the road. While the Ferrari pulled away, the Williams had to contend with the attentions of Rubens Barrichello. Then, Luciano Burti's accident forced the race to be

David Coulthard's car was not very clean at the end of the race. The Scotsman had spent a lot of time behind Giancarlo Fisichella's Benetton, before passing the Italian to finish second.

stopped, necessitating a new start.

This time, it was Ralf Schumacher who suffered: as the cars streamed off the grid to start the third formation lap, his FW20 was not ready. In fact it was still up on jacks! It seemed an incredible mistake by the Williams team and he too had to start the race from the back.

This final start saw Juan Pablo Montoya tangle with Pedro De La Rosa. *"I had made a super start, until Pedro ran into me,"* said the Colombian. *"After that, the car was pulling to the left and I was worried that part of the suspension might break. I backed off for a while, before pushing on again."*

It was a wasted effort, as a few laps later, Montoya had to retire with a blown engine. Ralf Schumacher was thus the only Williams driver to make it to the flag, in a modest seventh place. *"Nothing worked today,"* complained the world champion's little brother. *"I had understeer, then oversteer and we made a lot of mistakes. We have a lot to learn after today."*

Jean Alesi scored a point in Belgium, coming home sixth. He did better than his team-mate, Jarno Trulli, who had retired on lap 32.

Giancarlo Fisichella heading for third place. Just as his move to Jordan was confirmed, his Benetton had started to improve.

PRACTICE TIMES

No	Driver	Car/Engine/Chassis	Practice Friday	Pos.	Practice Saturday	Pos.	Qualifying	Pos.	Warm-up	Pos.
1.	Michael Schumacher	Ferrari/F2001/213	1'48"655	1°	1'57"257	19°	1'54"685	3°	1'49"495	1°
2.	Rubens Barrichello	Ferrari/F2001/26	1'49"456	3°	1'49"071	5°	1'56"116	5°	1'51"394	10°
3.	Mika Häkkinen	McLaren/Mercedes/MP4/16/7	1'50"239	5°	1'48"465	3°	1'57"043	7°	1'50"694	2°
4.	David Coulthard	McLaren/Mercedes/MP4/16/6	12'37"913	22°	1'48"698	4°	1'58"008	9°	1'51"750	12°
5.	Ralf Schumacher	Williams/BMW/FW23/7	1'50"801	7°	1'47"768	2°	1'52"072	1°	1'50"993	7°
6.	Juan Pablo Montoya	Williams/BMW/FW23/6	1'52"829	16°	1'47"494	1°	1'52"072	2°	1'50"993	7°
7.	Giancarlo Fisichella	Benetton/Renault/B201/6	1'50"192	4°	1'50"130	9°	1'52"436	14°	1'52"436	14°
8.	Jenson Button	Benetton/Renault/B201/5	1'51"673	10°	1'50"130	9°	1'59"587	15°	2'34"526	22°
9.	Olivier Panis	BAR/Honda/003/6	1'52"071	11°	1'50"501	12°	1'58"838	11°	1'52"519	16°
10.	Jacques Villeneuve	BAR/Honda/003/4	1'52"804	15°	1'49"953	8°	1'57"038	6°	1'25"903	17°
11.	Jarno Trulli	Jordan/Honda/EJ11/5	1'49"404	2°	1'50"494	11°	1'59"647	16°	1'51"062	8°
12.	Jean Alesi	Jordan/Honda/EJ11/4	1'51"631	9°	1'50"485	10°	1'59"128	13°	1'52"338	13°
14.	Jos Verstappen	Arrows/Asiatech/A22/6	1'52"955	19°	1'52"477	20°	2'02"039	19°	1'53"737	20°
15.	Enrique Bernoldi	Arrows/Asiatech/A22/3	1'55"491	20°	1'52"906	16°	2'03"048	21°	1'54"472	21°
16.	Nick Heidfeld	Sauber/Petronas/C20/7	1'52"436	14°	2'55"816	22°	1'59"302	14°	1'51"317	9°
17.	Kimi Räikkönen	Sauber/Petronas/C20/6	1'50"495	6°	1'58"547	21°	1'59"050	12°	1'50"738	3°
18.	Eddie Irvine	Jaguar/R-2/6	1'51"555	8°	1'49"857	7°	1'58"519	10°	1'50"818	5°
19.	Pedro de la Rosa	Jaguar/R-2/7	1'52"119	13°	1'52"267	14°	1'58"519	10°	1'51"418	11°
20.	Tarso Marques	Minardi/European/PS01/4	1'55"099	19°	1'53"861	18°	2'04"204	22°	1'52"908	18°
21.	Fernando Alonso	Minardi/European/PS01/2	1'55"021	18°	1'53"546	17°	2'02"594	20°	1'52"479	15°
22.	Heinz-Harald Frentzen	Prost/Acer/AP04/4	1'52"073	12°	1'50"765	13°	1'55"233	4°	1'50"908	6°
23.	Luciano Burti	Prost/Acer/AP04/4	2'11"037	21°	1'52"740	15°	1'59"900	18°	1'53"083	19°

MAXIMUM SPEEDS

No	Driver	P1 Qualifs	Pos	P1 Race	Pos	P2 Qualifs	Pos	P2 Race	Pos	Finish Qualifs	Pos	Finish Race	Pos	Trap Qualifs	Pos	Trap Race	Pos
1.	M. Schumacher	321,3	1°	323,4	12°	192,4	4°	188,9	3°	261,7	3°	270,6	5°	280,5	5°	304,6	2°
2.	R. Barrichello	315,0	5°	331,2	1°	183,2	11°	191,8	1°	258,8	7°	270,6	4°	277,1	8°	297,6	6°
3.	M. Häkkinen	312,2	9°	327,8	4°	183,4	10°	188,1	4°	258,4	8°	271,0	3°	282,4	3°	305,5	1°
4.	D. Coulthard	315,6	3°	329,3	2°	184,2	8°	189,9	2°	258,2	9°	270,0	6°	284,1	2°	302,3	3°
5.	R. Schumacher	314,8	6°	326,1	5°	194,8	2°	185,5	13°	268,5	2°	272,5	2°	281,0	4°	297,6	5°
6.	J. P. Montoya	315,6	4°	328,6	3°	199,8	1°	186,7	9°	269,8	1°	273,3	1°	297,1	1°	293,7	9°
7.	G. Fisichella	302,8	19°	320,6	17°	191,4	5°	187,1	6°	256,7	13°	263,8	17°	275,6	9°	295,4	7°
8.	J. Button	303,7	18°	321,5	15°	182,8	13°	186,7	8°	256,0	16°	264,7	16°	253,8	20°	291,9	11°
9.	O. Panis	307,7	15°	323,0	10°	182,9	12°	183,7	16°	254,1	20°	267,1	9°	256,9	19°	295,0	8°
10.	J. Villeneuve	311,4	11°	323,1	9°	193,2	3°	187,3	5°	261,4	4°	266,5	10°	260,8	17°	288,6	13°
11.	J. Trulli	310,4	14°	324,5	8°	174,2	22°	181,6	19°	258,0	10°	268,9	8°	270,0	10°	293,7	10°
12.	J. Alesi	314,4	7°	325,0	6°	174,5	21°	185,3	14°	260,5	5°	269,4	7°	277,9	7°	300,2	4°
14.	J. Verstappen	306,3	17°	318,8	18°	177,4	20°	186,1	10°	255,6	18°	265,2	14°	266,8	16°	286,5	14°
15.	E. Bernoldi	305,1	17°	314,0	20°	178,9	18°	186,0	12°	255,8	17°	263,6	19°	269,7	11°	281,8	17°
16.	N. Heidfeld	311,8	10°	323,5	11°	178,5	19°	178,9	22°	256,2	15°	266,2	11°	269,3	12°	279,2	19°
17.	K. Räikkönen	311,2	12°	324,7	7°	180,2	16°	184,8	15°	255,3	19°	265,8	12°	268,6	14°	285,7	15°
18.	E. Irvine	312,6	8°	323,1	14°	181,9	14°	180,4	21°	257,3	12°	261,3	21°	268,9	13°	280,0	18°
19.	P. de la Rosa	310,7	13°	321,4	16°	183,8	9°	182,0	18°	257,5	11°	263,6	18°	267,3	15°	282,3	16°
20.	T. Marques	299,1	21°	317,2	19°	180,4	15°	183,5	17°	247,8	22°	261,6	20°	244,4	22°	270,0	21°
21.	F. Alonso	300,6	20°	309,7	22°	178,9	17°	181,5	20°	250,4	21°	259,3	22°	259,9	18°	265,6	22°
22.	H.-H. Frentzen	320,2	2°	324,0	9°	189,9	6°	186,1	11°	259,7	6°	265,8	13°	280,1	6°	289,4	12°
23.	L. Burti	278,4	22°	313,4	21°	186,1	7°	186,8	7°	256,5	14°	265,0	15°	252,3	21°	278,4	20°

CLASSIFICATION & RETIREMENTS

Pos	Driver	Team	Time
1.	M. Schum.	Ferrari	1:08:05.022
2.	Coulthard	McLaren Mercedes	+ 10.098
3.	Fisichella	Benetton Renault	+ 27.742
4.	Häkkinen	McLaren Mercedes	+ 36.087
5.	Barrichello	Ferrari	+ 54.521
6.	Alesi	Jordan Honda	+ 59.684
7.	R. Schum.	Williams BMW	+ 59.986
8.	Villeneuve	BAR Honda	+ 64.970
9.	Frentzen	Prost Acer	+ 1 lap
10.	Verstappen	Arrows Asiatech	+ 1 lap
11.	Panis	BAR Honda	+ 1 lap
12.	Bernoldi	Arrows Asiatech	+ 1 lap
13.	Marques	European Minardi	+ 4 laps

Lap	Driver	Team	Reason
First start:			
3	Alonso	European Minardi	gearbox
4	Burti	Prost Acer	accident
4	Irvine	Jaguar Racing	accident
5	Räikkönen	Sauber Petronas	transmission
Second start:			
1	Heidfeld	Sauber Petronas	accident
1	de la Rosa	Jaguar Racing	accident
2	Montoya	Williams BMW	engine
18	Button	Benetton Renault	off
32	Trulli	Jordan Honda	accident

FASTEST LAPS

	Driver	Time	Lap
1.	M. Schum.	1'49"758 228,546 Km/h	7
2.	R. Schum.	1'51"058	25
3.	Coulthard	1'51"608	35
4.	Fisichella	1'51"725	14
5.	Häkkinen	1'51"741	13
6.	Barrichello	1'51"776	24
7.	Trulli	1'51"828	8
8.	Alesi	1'51"996	9
9.	Villeneuve	1'52"372	15
10.	Panis	1'52"533	28
11.	Button	1'53"409	21
12.	Räikkönen	1'53"595	2
13.	Frentzen	1'54"051	19
14.	Verstappen	1'54"095	8
15.	Bernoldi	1'55"196	8
16.	Heidfeld	1'55"805	4
17.	Montoya	1'55"832	4
18.	Burti	1'56"083	3
19.	de la Rosa	1'56"158	4
20.	Marques	1'56"484	12
21.	Irvine	1'56"746	2
22.	Alonso	1'59"814	2

PIT STOPS

	Driver	Time	Lap	Stop n°
1.	Trulli	30"386	6	1
2.	Häkkinen	29"850	7	1
3.	Alesi	31"149	7	1
4.	Panis	30"331	7	1
5.	Verstappen	30"840	8	1
6.	Barrichello	31"067	9	1
7.	Villeneuve	30"437	9	1
8.	R. Schum.	30"820	9	1
9.	Bernoldi	32"852	9	1
10.	Marques	31"732	9	1
11.	M. Schum.	31"443	10	1
12.	Coulthard	28"483	10	1
13.	Button	29"298	10	1
14.	Fisichella	28"708	11	1
15.	Panis	33"763	12	2
16.	Marques	30"786	15	2
17.	Frentzen	32"714	16	1
18.	Marques	46"104	16	3
19.	Barrichello	32"623	18	2
20.	Marques	4'23"021	17	4
21.	Trulli	32"910	19	2
22.	Alesi	31"401	20	2
23.	Villeneuve	30"146	21	2
24.	Panis	49"764	21	3
25.	Verstappen	30"636	22	2
26.	Fisichella	29"077	23	2
27.	Häkkinen	28"912	23	2
28.	Coulthard	28"569	24	2
29.	M. Schum.	29"779	25	2
30.	Bernoldi	34"320	24	2
31.	R. Schum.	31"092	25	2

BRIDGESTONE

Best result for a driver running Bridgestone tyres:

Michael Schumacher, Ferrari, winner

CHAMPIONSHIP

(after fourteen rounds)

Drivers :

1.	M. Schumacher	104
2.	D. Coulthard	57
3.	R. Barrichello	48
4.	R. Schumacher	44
5.	M. Häkkinen	24
6.	J. Montoya	15
7.	J. Villeneuve	11
	N. Heidfeld	11
9.	K. Räikkönen	9
	J. Trulli	9
11.	G. Fisichella	8
12.	H.-H. Frentzen	6
13.	O. Panis	5
	J. Alesi	5
15.	E. Irvine	4
16.	J. Button	2
17.	J. Verstappen	1
	P. de la Rosa	1

Constructors :

1.	Ferrari	152
2.	McLaren Mecedes	81
3.	BMW Williams	59
4.	Sauber Petronas	20
5.	BAR Honda	16
	Jordan Honda	16
7.	Benetton Renault	10
8.	Jaguar Racing	5
9.	Prost Acer	4
10.	Arrows Asiatech	1

THE CIRCUIT

— FOURTEENTH ROUND —

FOSTER'S BELGIAN GRAND PRIX, SPA-FRANCORCHAMPS

Date : September 2, 2001
Length : 6968 meters
Distance : 36 laps, 250.831 km
Weather : dry and cloudy, 17°

All results : © 2001 Fédération Internationale de l'Automobile, 2, Ch. Blandonnet, 1215 Genève 15, Suisse

RACE SUMMARY

- At the first start, Frentzen stalls on the grid and has to start from the back. As the second formation lap gets underway, it's Montoya who is left on the grid. The race has already lost a lot of its interest.

- As the field finally gets away, Ralf Schumacher gets the better of his brother, but the elder man gets by braking for Les Combes.

- On lap 5, Burti attacks Irvine at Blanchimont, an impossible move. The cars touch and fly into the tyre barrier. It's a big one, and the race is stopped.

- On the formation lap for the re-start, Ralf Schumacher's car is left up on jacks.

- Michael Schumacher leads from Fisichella. By lap 4, the German already has a 10 second lead over his pursuers, led by Fisichella. He wins from Coulthard, who passes Fisichella in the pit stops.

LAP CHART

GAPS ON THE LEADER BOARD

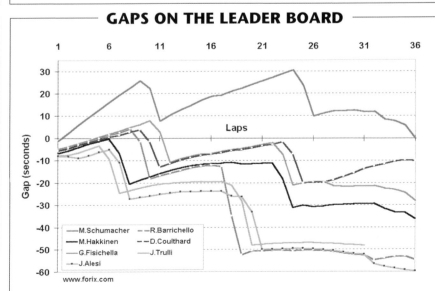

www.forix.com

Montoya at last!

At Monza, the Colombian finally threw off the jinx which had been following him since the start of the year to take his first ever Formula 1 win. No doubt it would not be his last. The Italian Grand Prix was run under a cloud, as it took place the weekend after the September 11th terrorist attacks in the United States. Not many were in the mood to go motor racing. All the parties planned for Monza, especially the Ferrari ones were all cancelled. For his part, Michael Schumacher really did not have his heart in it and finished an anonymous fourth, having failed to convince the other drivers not to race one another at the first two corners on the opening lap.

GRAN PREMIO CAMPARI D'ITALIA
MONZA

Monza feels the effects of the World Trade Center disaster

Sign of mourning: Scuderia Ferrari ran without any advertising on its cars in Monza.

The drama which had unfolded the previous Tuesday was the only talking point at this grand prix. On the Wednesday, the FIA announced that all three remaining grands prix would go ahead, but several other sporting events around the globe had been cancelled.

As a gesture of sympathy with the victims of the terrorist attacks, a minute's silence was observed at midday on the Friday, which meant practice was brought forward by ten minutes to accommodate it. Not a soul stirred in the pits nor in the grandstand during a very unusual silence for a race track.

Scuderia Ferrari cancelled its Saturday night gala dinner, which this year would have been used to celebrate their 2001 titles. For the entire weekend, its cars ran without any advertising decals and with a black nose section. *"With the full agreement*

of its sponsors and partners, Ferrari has decided to show its sympathy with the American people. For Ferrari, Sunday's race will be a purely sporting event, without any commercial implications and without any joy," explained a Ferrari release.

The Jaguar team, belonging to American car giant Ford had, for its part, hesitated before confirming

it would take part in the Italian Grand Prix. After a long meeting on the Thursday, the constructors involved in F1 all agreed to take part in the United States Grand Prix, two weeks later. FIA President Max Mosley, explained that there was no question of letting the terrorists win in this particular situation.

Juan Pablo quickest again

Two drivers made their debut this weekend: in the Prost camp, Tomas Enge was the first Czech to race in F1. He qualified 20th, while in the Minardi colours, Alex Yoong was last.

Once he stepped out of the cockpit, having put in his quick laps, Juan Pablo Montoya was calm personified. Everything had just been fine and dandy apparently. *"The car was really good this afternoon,"* he explained. *"We managed to improve it some more after the morning and I am very happy with it. I must say that beating the Ferraris on this track is something special. After yesterday's practice, I actually didn't think it would be possible."* The tifosi lining the track could not believe the Williams team could spoil their party either. Despite their best efforts to cheer him on, Michael Schumacher could "only" manage third place, behind his team-mate Rubens Barrichello. It said a lot about the German's motivation at Monza. He said he had been badly affected by events in the States.

It was therefore the first time this season that the Brazilian had out-qualified his team-mate. *"I am very happy,"* admitted "Rubinho." *The team helped me a lot in setting up the car since yesterday, including on the engine side. I knew qualifying would be very tight. I had to run on new tyres, because I flat spotted one of the set I had run in this morning. It was a risk, because the new tyres do not seem to work as well here, but it paid off in the end."*

Michael Schumacher claimed not to be too disappointed with third. *"I made several small mistakes on my best lap and this is the result. I pushed too hard and sometimes that means you go slower."*

Juan Pablo Montoya's Williams team-mate was fourth, never having found the right set up. He was ahead of Jarno Trulli who was an excellent fifth. While the Italian was jubilant in the Jordan camp, Jean Alesi was down in the dumps. Only 16th, the Frenchman was even beaten by Heinz-Harald Frentzen, in what used to be his Prost up to the German Grand Prix. *"It's much worse than I thought,"* moaned Jean. *"I could not find the right set-up, the balance of the car was wrong, I had problems braking and I ran into traffic on all my runs."* But apart from that, life was a bowl of cherries!

STARTING GRID

J. P. MONTOYA 1'22"216	-1-	R. BARRICHELLO 1'22"528
M. SCHUMACHER 1'22"624	-2-	R. SCHUMACHER 1'22"841
Jarno TRULLI 1'23"126	-3-	David COULTHARD 1'23"148
Mika HÄKKINEN 1'23"394	-4-	Nick HEIDFELD 1'23"417
Kimi RAIKKONEN 1'23"595	-5-	Pedro De la Rosa 1'23"693
Jenson BUTTON 1'23"892	-6-	H.-H. FRENTZEN 1'23"943
Eddie IRVINE 1'24"031	-7-	G. FISICHELLA 1'24"090
Jacques VILLENEUVE 1'24"164	-8-	Jean ALESI 1'24"198
Olivier PANIS 1'24"677	-9-	Enrique BERNOLDI 1'25"444
Jos VERSTAPPEN 1'25"511	-10-	Thomas ENGE 1'26"039
Fernando ALONSO 1'26"218	-11-	Alex YOONG 1'27"463

Juan Pablo says hello! With a third pole of the season, the Colombian was beginning to live up to his reputation. And all to the detriment of team-mate Ralf Schumacher.

Montoya's first first

For the first time in the history of Formula 1, the Colombian National Anthem rang out over a race track. It happened on the podium in Monza: a rousing tune which celebrated a superb victory for Juan Pablo Montoya, the first in his Formula 1 career. The Williams man definitely deserved it, having started from pole three times this season, especially given the bad luck he had experienced earlier in the year.

The Colombian was certainly ecstatic as he stepped out of the cockpit. *"I want to thank all my fans and the team, who gave me a fantastic car today,"* he said as he stepped off the podium.

He took the lead right from the start, before he had to give best to Rubens Barrichello. *"One of the rear tyres was blistered and the car started to slide under braking. I made a small mistake and Rubens made the most of it to get by,"* explained the Colombian. The Ferraris refuelled twice, while he and his Williams only needed refreshing once. Montoya moved back into the lead when the Brazilian came down pit lane for the second time and that was that.

With one win under his belt, the Colombian has no intention of leaving it at that. *"My run of bad luck is now behind me,"* he continued.

His team-mate Ralf Schumacher finished third. A good result in itself, but it was not enough to stop him looking particularly sulky after the race. In fact, Ralf did not come and congratulate Montoya when they drove into parc ferme and made a point of keeping himself to himself on the podium. He was now doubt figuring out how difficult life would be next year, alongside Montoya. In fact, a few weeks later, he suggested to Frank Williams, via the medium of the media, that he should impose team orders in 2002, *"otherwise we risk losing the title."* Given the current form of the Ferraris, that was a pretty big assumption in itself.

Michael Schumacher's words fall on deaf ears

His safety crusade failed. On Sunday morning, during the usual Drivers' Briefing. Michael Schumacher tried to get his 21 colleagues to sign a non-aggression pact. Its premise was that no one should try a passing move until after the first two corners on the opening lap, as these two chicanes were considered particularly dangerous. Indeed, the previous year, they had been the site of several collisions and a fire marshal had died as a result.

The drivers almost reached unanimity, with only Jacques Villeneuve opposed to the ideal. According to the Canadian, a driver is paid to race, not to take part in a fashion parade. Without unanimity, Michael Schumacher once again tried to canvas his fellow drivers during the lunch break. But several team bosses forbade their drivers to sign any such agreement. Amongst this group were Craig Pollock, Flavio Briatore, Tom Walkinshaw, Frank Williams and Paul Stoddart, the bosses of BAR, Benetton, Arrows, Williams and Minardi respectively.

Some, like Ron Dennis, said they would support their drivers, but regretted that the GPDA (Grand Prix Drivers Association) had waited until race morning to come up with the idea. Especially, as the first chicane which Schumacher was complaining about, had been modified since last year, and that its new design had been approved by the very same GPDA and Michael Schumacher himself, before any work was begun!

The world champion continued to argue his case on the starting grid and walked down it, talking to almost every driver to ask them not to attack in the first braking area. *"We all agreed to brake 200 metres before the first corner, rather than a hundred and I think everyone was happy to go along with that,"* explained Rubens Barrichello after the race. In the end, with or without an agreement, the start went well, with the exception of Jenson Button, who collided yet again with Jarno Trulli, thankfully without any serious consequences. The Englishman had indeed braked at the 200 metre mark, but he was on the dirty side of the track and it pitched him into sliding like a bar of soap. In the end, the first driver to cut the first chicane was none other than Michael Schumacher (photo above.) No man is a prophet in his own land.

△
That's done it: Michael Schumacher misses the chicane and will have to let Rubens Barrichello pass behind Juan Pablo Montoya.

◁
Race start: Montoya leads the two Ferraris. On lap 9, Rubens Barrichello finally gets past the Colombian, whose tyres are blistered. Much later, the Brazilian pulled off another very nice move to pass Ralf Schumacher, at the first chicane on lap 47. "Ralf was in trouble with his rear tyres and I made the most of it," explained "Rubinho," who went on to finish second.

◁
What a sulk! On the podium, Ralf Schumacher was not in the mood to celebrate with his team mate. Gerhard Berger had asked the team not to make too much of a fuss, given recent world events.

Alex Yoong did not have an easy F1 debut. He spun twice at the Lesmo corner, retiring after the second one.

Jarno Trulli had a troubled season, characterised by an awful run of bad luck, which continued at Monza. He had qualified a superb fifth, but was knocked out at the first corner when Jenson Button ran into him.

GRAN PREMIO CAMPARI D'ITALIA

Raikkonen moves to McLaren

Having ceaselessly repeated that his favourite little driver, Kimi Raikkonen, would be staying with him next season, Peter Sauber finally had to let him go to McLaren.

After a good month of negotiation, the Swiss boss and Jurgen Hubbert, the boss of DaimlerChrysler's "special vehicles" division, finally reached an agreement on how much the three pointed star company would pay the Swiss team to break the young prodigy's contract. There were rumours of it being as much as 18 million dollars!

So it was that on Saturday morning in Monza, at nine thirty, it was confirmed that Kimi Raikkonen would drive for McLaren next year.

For the young Finn, would turn 22 on 17th October, this transfer was an incredible opportunity. Recognised for his exceptional talent, he has often been compared with Michael Schumacher for his ability to learn quickly and his natural instinct. He had only taken part in 14 grands prix at this stage, but he had finished in the points on four occasions and was lying ninth in the 2001 world championship. Is a new star born? We would have to wait for next year to have an answer. One thing was certain, the atmosphere within the McLaren team would be tenser than in the familiar cocoon of the Sauber family.

Mika takes a "sabbatical"

Those who were close to Mika Hakkinen had felt since back in June, that he had changed. Never particularly outgoing, the Finn seemed even more introverted than usual. The rumours had thus started running around the paddock. Even David Coulthard admitted he did not know who would be his team-mate in 2002.

But while the man in question refused to be drawn on the subject, his manager Keke Rosberg, continued to deny the stories, stating his man would still be driving for McLaren next season. In fact, Mika Hakkinen had indeed signed a contract, tying him to the team for two more years.

For its part, McLaren kept delaying announcing its driver line-up for 2002, which only fuelled the rumours. In Monza, they were saying that Ron Dennis was determined to find a worthy replacement for Hakkinen, before letting the Finn escape from his contract. The Hakkinens were apparently keen to push the team into taking on Kimi Raikkonen.

At Spa, it was evident to what extent Hakkinen had had enough. Asked about the race, all he talked about was the risk, insufficient safety and badly sited guard rails. It seemed that his passion for racing had mutated into a malaise. Since his first child, Hugo, had come into the world at the end of last year, the Finn's sole objective seemed to be to live the quiet family life. After ten years in F1 and two world titles, what could be more natural? On Saturday, Mika Hakkinen insisted that he was not retiring, but only taking a year off.

The unlucky crown

Jarno Trulli was heading effortlessly for the title of *"unluckiest driver of the year."* In Monza, he was fifth on the grid, but he saw his efforts turn to nothing at the first corner, when Jenson Button rammed him with his Benetton. Button had only been tenth on the grid and evidently had ideas about winning the race at the first corner. *"I made a super start, but I was on the inside line, which no one uses and it was coated in oil,"* explained the Englishman. *"I braked at the same time as the others, but the car didn't stop and I ran into Trulli. I am very sorry for him."*

results

PRACTICE TIMES

No	Driver	Car/Engine/Chassis	Practice Friday	Pos.	Practice Saturday	Pos.	Qualifying	Pos.	Warm-up	Pos.
1.	Michael Schumacher	Ferrari/F2001/213	1'25"131	3°	1'23"178	1°	1'22"624	3°	1'26"029	1°
2.	Rubens Barrichello	Ferrari/F2001/206	1'25"311	5°	1'23"828	4°	1'22"528	2°	1'26"296	4°
3.	Mika Häkkinen	McLaren/Mercedes/MP4/16/4	1'25"343	6°	1'24"263	8°	1'23"394	7°	1'26"825	9°
4.	David Coulthard	McLaren/Mercedes/MP4/16/6	1'25"544	7°	1'23"873	5°	1'23"148	6°	1'26"086	2°
5.	Ralf Schumacher	Williams/BMW/FW23/7	1'24"667	1°	1'23"917	6°	1'22"841	4°	1'26"793	8°
6.	Juan Pablo Montoya	Williams/BMW/FW23/8	1'25"067	2°	1'23"477	2°	1'22"216	1°	1'26"247	3°
7.	Giancarlo Fisichella	Benetton/Renault/B201/6	1'25"911	11°	1'24"683	12°	1'24"090	14°	1'28"137	17°
8.	Jenson Button	Benetton/Renault/B201/5	1'26"197	13°	1'25"062	15°	1'23"892	11°	1'28"633	18°
9.	Olivier Panis	BAR/Honda/003/4	1'26"354	14°	1'24"990	14°	1'24"677	17°	1'27"708	15°
10.	Jacques Villeneuve	BAR/Honda/003/8	1'26"521	15°	1'25"258	16°	1'24"164	15°	1'27"161	10°
11.	Jarno Trulli	Jordan/Honda/EJ11/5	1'25"987	12°	1'23"762	3°	1'23"126	5°	1'26"446	6°
12.	Jean Alesi	Jordan/Honda/EJ11/4	1'25"849	9°	1'24"928	13°	1'24"198	16°	1'26"778	7°
14.	Jos Verstappen	Arrows/Asiatech/A22/6	1'27"900	21°	1'26"285	18°	1'25"511	19°	1'27"548	14°
15.	Enrique Bernoldi	Arrows/Asiatech/A22/3	1'27"217	18°	1'27"309	19°	1'25"444	18°	1'27"766	16°
16.	Nick Heidfeld	Sauber/Petronas/C20/5	1'25"740	8°	1'24"251	7°	1'23"417	8°	1'27"218	11°
17.	Kimi Räikkönen	Sauber/Petronas/C20/6	1'26"701	16°	1'24"586	10°	1'23"595	9°	1'26"389	5°
18.	Eddie Irvine	Jaguar/R-2/6	1'27"401	19°	1'24"642	11°	1'24"031	13°	1'27"458	13°
19.	Pedro de la Rosa	Jaguar/R-2/7	1'25"205	4°	1'24"575	9°	1'23"693	10°	1'27"351	12°
20.	Alex Yoong	Minardi/European/PS01/4	1'28"250	22°	36'03"692	21°	1'27"463	22°	1'29"826	21°
21.	Fernando Alonso	Minardi/European/PS01/2	1'26"972	17°	1'42"45"315	22°	1'26"218	21°	1'29"027	20°
22.	Heinz-Harald Frentzen	Prost/Acer/AP04/6	1'25"860	10°	1'25"600	17°	1'23"943	12°	1'28"752	19°
23.	Thomas Enge	Prost/Acer/AP04/2	1'27"662	20°	1'28"064	20°	1'26"039	20°	1'30"445	22°

MAXIMUM SPEEDS

No	Driver	P1 Qualifs	Pos	P1 Race	Pos	P2 Qualifs	Pos	P2 Race	Pos	Finish Qualifs	Pos	Finish Race	Pos	Trap Qualifs	Pos	Trap Race	Pos
1.	M. Schumacher	338,1	10°	344,1	5°	338,9	11°	340,2	8°	326,7	7°	324,3	5°	350,4	12°	356,0	7°
2.	R. Barrichello	339,4	6°	344,9	2°	341,3	3°	345,1	2°	326,8	4°	328,5	1°	352,1	7°	354,9	10°
3.	M. Häkkinen	338,0	12°	336,7	12°	337,7	14°	335,1	15°	324,4	11°	316,9	16°	349,4	17°	349,8	14°
4.	D.Coulthard	338,0	11°	332,0	18°	338,9	10°	331,4	18°	324,1	14°	315,5	18°	351,2	9°	346,9	18°
5.	R. Schumacher	339,4	5°	341,7	6°	338,5	13°	341,2	7°	326,8	6°	325,5	6°	350,0	15°	358,4	4°
6.	J. P. Montoya	338,6	3°	341,5	7°	339,0	8°	341,5	5°	324,7	3°	325,9	3°	351,1	10°	355,6	9°
7.	G. Fisichella	334,3	16°	337,9	9°	336,4	17°	341,3	6°	322,3	7°	323,4	7°	350,0	13°	356,7	5°
8.	J. Button	336,8	12°	346,4	21°	338,9	9°	327,4	21°	324,4	10°	314,0	19°	353,0	6°	344,4	20°
9.	O. Panis	333,9	17°	336,9	11°	337,3	15°	339,8	9°	323,4	16°	323,6	6°	350,0	14°	352,7	13°
10.	J. Villeneuve	334,4	15°	336,2	14°	337,1	16°	336,9	13°	324,0	15°	320,0	12°	346,4	18°	352,8	11°
11.	J. Trulli	342,7	1°	-	-	344,0	2°	-	-	327,9	2°	-	-	359,0	2°	259,5	22°
12.	J. Alesi	341,2	2°	346,4	14°	344,0	1°	344,7	3°	328,1	1°	327,8	2°	359,4	1°	363,2	1°
14.	J. Verstappen	336,3	13°	338,5	8°	340,5	6°	339,7	10°	324,1	12°	321,3	10°	350,5	11°	355,9	8°
15.	E. Bernoldi	333,7	18°	337,1	10°	338,8	12°	338,8	11°	322,3	18°	321,1	11°	349,6	16°	356,2	6°
16.	N. Heidfeld	341,1	3°	344,7	4°	341,2	4°	344,2	4°	326,5	8°	322,1	9°	356,5	3°	361,8	2°
17.	K. Räikkönen	338,5	8°	344,8	3°	340,9	5°	345,9	1°	324,7	9°	322,9	8°	355,9	4°	360,4	3°
18.	E. Irvine	333,0	19°	330,5	19°	334,6	19°	330,7	19°	319,5	20°	312,7	20°	344,6	21°	346,5	19°
19.	P. de la Rosa	332,8	20°	335,1	15°	333,8	20°	336,4	14°	321,6	19°	319,2	13°	345,6	19°	349,5	15°
20.	A. Yoong	325,7	22°	328,2	20°	327,3	22°	327,6	20°	313,4	22°	311,1	21°	341,2	22°	343,2	21°
21.	F. Alonso	329,3	21°	336,7	13°	329,8	21°	337,8	12°	315,2	21°	316,4	17°	344,7	20°	352,8	12°
22.	H.-H. Frentzen	339,5	4°	334,3	16°	340,0	7°	333,7	16°	326,8	5°	318,4	15°	353,6	5°	348,2	17°
23.	T. Enge	335,4	14°	333,6	17°	335,5	18°	332,6	17°	324,1	13°	318,5	14°	352,0	8°	348,3	16°

CLASSIFICATION & RETIREMENTS

Pos	Driver	Team	Time
1.	Montoya	Williams BMW	1:16:58.493
2.	Barrichello	Ferrari	+ 5.175
3.	R. Schum.	Williams BMW	+ 17.335
4.	M. Schum.	Ferrari	+ 24.991
5.	de la Rosa	Jaguar Racing	+ 74.984
6.	Villeneuve	BAR Honda	+ 82.469
7.	Räikkönen	Sauber Petronas	+ 83.107
8.	Alesi	Jordan Honda	+ 1 lap
9.	Panis	BAR Honda	+ 1 lap
10.	Fisichella	Benetton Renault	+ 1 lap
11.	Heidfeld	Sauber Petronas	+ 1 lap
12.	Enge	Prost Acer	+ 1 lap
13.	Alonso	European Minardi	+ 2 laps

Lap	Driver	Team	Reason
0	Trulli	Jordan Honda	spin
5	Button	Benetton Renault	engine
7	Coulthard	McLaren Mercedes	engine
15	Irvine	Jaguar Racing	engine
20	Häkkinen	McLaren Mercedes	transmission
26	Verstappen	Arrowa Asiatech	fuel pressure
29	Frentzen	Prost Acer	transmission
45	Yoong	European Minardi	spin
47	Bernoldi	Arrowa Asiatech	engine

FASTEST LAPS

	Driver	Time	Lap
1.	R. Schum.	1'25"073	39
		246,315 Km/h	
2.	Barrichello	1'25"221	39
3.	M. Schum.	1'25"525	52
4.	Montoya	1'25"657	52
5.	Alesi	1'26"365	28
6.	de la Rosa	1'26"381	34
7.	Panis	1'26"386	31
8.	Räikkönen	1'26"656	51
9.	Villeneuve	1'26"667	31
10.	Heidfeld	1'26"825	52
11.	Fisichella	1'27"283	29
12.	Coulthard	1'27"323	4
13.	Frentzen	1'27"394	28
14.	Häkkinen	1'27"627	15
15.	Enge	1'27"643	52
16.	Alonso	1'27"709	50
17.	Verstappen	1'27"945	22
18.	Button	1'28"268	4
19.	Bernoldi	1'28"578	24
20.	Irvine	1'29"262	2
21.	Yoong	1'30"605	21

PIT STOPS

	Driver	Time	Lap	Stop n°
1.	Button	25"200	1	1
2.	Alonso	24"267	17	1
3.	M. Schum.	24"881	18	1
4.	Verstappen	23"518	18	1
5.	Barrichello	30"765	19	1
6.	Alesi	22"885	22	1
7.	Räikkönen	27"724	22	1
8.	Bernoldi	26"349	27	1
9.	Montoya	26"581	28	1
10.	Heidfeld	23"546	28	1
11.	Yoong	26"975	27	1
12.	Fisichella	24"621	30	1
13.	Alesi	25"567	32	2
14.	Panis	24"463	32	1
15.	Enge	26"421	32	1
16.	Villeneuve	24"447	33	1
17.	Alonso	1'10"931	33	2
18.	R. Schum.	22"697	35	1
19.	de la Rosa	23"605	36	1
20.	M. Schum.	21"174	40	2
21.	Barrichello	20"754	41	2

THE CIRCUIT

FIFTEENTH ROUND

GRAN PREMIO CAMPARI D'ITALIA, MONZA

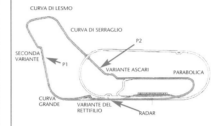

Date : September 16, 2001
Length : 5793 meters
Distance : 53 laps, 306.749 km
Weather : sunny and warm, 21°

All results :
© 2001 Fédération Internationale de l'Automobile, 2, Ch. Blandonnet, 1215 Genève 15, Suisse

BRIDGESTONE

Best result for a driver running Bridgestone tyres:

Ruben Barrichello, Ferrari, second

CHAMPIONSHIP

(after fifteen rounds)

Drivers :

1.	M. Schumacher	107
2.	D. Coulthard	57
3.	R. Barrichello	54
4.	R. Schumacher	48
5.	J. P. Montoya	25
6.	M. Häkkinen	24
7.	J. Villeneuve	12
8.	N. Heidfeld	11
9.	K. Räikkönen	9
	J. Trulli	9
11.	G. Fisichella	8
12.	H.-H. Frentzen	6
13.	O. Panis	5
	J. Alesi	5
15.	E. Irvine	4
16.	P. de la Rosa	3
17.	J. Button	2
18.	J. Verstappen	1

Constructors :

1.	Ferrari	161
2.	McLaren Mercedes	81
3.	Williams BMW	73
4.	Sauber Petronas	20
5.	BAR Honda	17
6.	Jordan Honda	16
7.	Benetton Renault	10
8.	Jaguar Racing	7
9.	Prost Acer	4
10	Arrows Asiatech	1

RACE SUMMARY

- Montoya maintains his pole advantage and swerves ahead of Barrichello and Michael Schumacher. Button loses control and knocks Trulli out of the race.

- Barrichello hangs onto Montoya, who leads him by 1 second on lap 5. Michael Schumacher is 2.3 down, Ralf Schumacher is at 5.9 and Coulthard is at 10.6.

- Lap 9 and Barrichello passes Montoya.

- On lap 15, Barrichello has a 7.4 second advantage over Montoya, 7.8 over Michael Schumacher and 20.0 on Ralf Schumacher.

- Lap 19, Barrichello refuels and loses a lot of time.

- On lap 27, Montoya who has yet to pit, is in the lead, 22.6 seconds ahead of Ralf Schumacher, 25.8 up on Barrichello and 31.1 on Michael Schumacher.

- Montoya refuels one lap later and rejoins third. Ralf Schumacher leads up to his pit stop, a late one on lap 35.

- Laps 40 and 41 see Michael Schumacher and Barrichello refuel and rejoin behind the two Williams.

- Lap 46 and Barrichello manages to pass Ralf Schumacher and closes on Montoya, but does not pass. First F1 career win for the Colombian.

LAP CHART

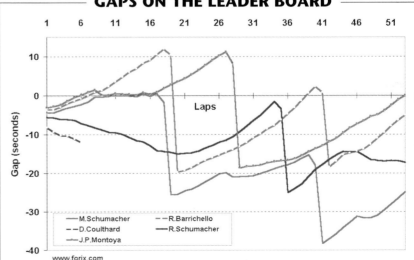

GAPS ON THE LEADER BOARD

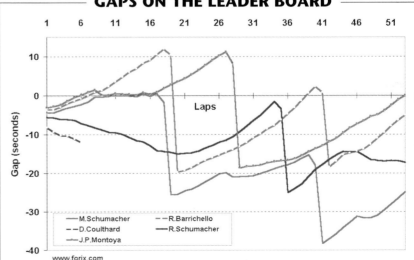

www.forix.com

Retirement suits you

Mika Hakkinen was planning to retire in a fortnight's time, but not just yet! In Indianapolis, thanks to a well thought out strategy, he took his second grand prix win of the season. Michael Schumacher and David Coulthard joined him on the podium, after bad luck and a faulty engine robbed Rubens Barrichello of second place. In the pack, confusion reigned, as Jarno Trulli was disqualified from fourth place. The Jordan team appealed against the decision and the FIA tribunal finally reinstated the Italian, but not until one month later.

**THE SAP UNITED STATES GRAND PRIX
INDIANAPOLIS**

That makes 10! Michael Schumacher destroyed the opposition with a lap which even he described as "perfect."

Indianapolis and its "Circle Centre," its restaurants and shopping malls. It is a lively place at night, unlike many sleepy American cities.

Another pole position for the German

Schumacher makes it look easy

Relaxed and sitting on a packing case at the back of the garage, Michael Schumacher watched the end of qualifying on a television. While his rivals were still giving it their all, right up to the bitter end of the session, he did not even bother to use all the twelve laps available to him. *"It's not that I was particularly confident at that point,"* he explained later. *"What I was certain of though, was that I couldn't improve my time. I had got the maximum out of the car, so there was no point in trying to do better."*

The German went to the trop of the time sheet on his third run. Until then, Mika Hakkinen, who was on top form on the American track - he had been fastest on the Friday - was quickest. The Finn was

working with a new race engineer this weekend and it seemed he had found that missing something that signalled a return to the Hakkinen of old. *"Of course, every engineer has a different way of working, but I am not sure if that is the reason for my being back on form,"* remarked Mika on Saturday afternoon.

Michael Schumacher was hoping to repeat his performance in the race. *"The car has definitely been getting better over the weekend and things look like going well,"* he maintained. *"We have a lot of supporters at this track. After every-*

thing that has happened recently, I would like to give them something to smile about. Everyone at Ferrari wants to do that and win the race."

David Coulthard in silhouette. The man who hoped to be world champion one day, could only manage 7th place in qualifying on the Indy track, a long way behind his pole sitting team-mate Mika Hakkinen.

STARTING GRID

M. SCHUMACHER 1'11"708	-1-	R. SCHUMACHER 1'12"986
J. P. MONTOYA 1'12"252	-2-	Mika HÄKKINEN 1'12"309
R. BARRICHELLO 1'12"327	-3-	Nick HEIDFELD 1'12"434
David COULTHARD 1'12"500	-4-	Jarno TRULLI 1'12"605
Jean ALESI 1'12"607	-5-	Jenson BUTTON 1'12"805
Kimi RAIKKONEN 1'12"881	-6-	G. FISICHELLA 1'12"942
Olivier PANIS 1'13"122	-7-	Eddie IRVINE 1'13"189
H.-H. FRENTZEN 1'13"281	-8-	Pedro De la Rosa 1'13"679
Fernando ALONSO 1'13"991	-9-	Jacques VILLENEUVE 1'14"012
Enrique BERNOLDI 1'14"129	-10-	Jos VERSTAPPEN 1'14"135
Thomas ENGE 1'14"185	-11-	Alex YOONG 1'15"247

Mika has lost none of his bite

The United States Grand Prix was not shaping up well for Mika Hakkinen. Having qualified a brilliant second on Saturday, he saw his fastest lap from that session disallowed, after he left the pit lane during the Sunday morning warm-up, while the lights were still red.

That meant he would start from fourth on the grid, instead of being on the front row! To make matters worse, he crashed during the warm-up, seriously damaging his car. *"What with the accident and going back on the grid, I was really angry and very frustrated,"* explained Hakkinen after the race. *"Naturally, that frustration made me drive in a rage for the whole race. And this is the result!"*

The result was a brilliant victory, taken fair and square, beating Michael Schumacher and David Coulthard in the other McLaren. The Finn took the lead thanks to a very late pit stop. Delaying his one and only refuelling until lap 46, he was able to run for longer on light tanks than the Ferraris.

As he came out of the pit lane, he found himself in the lead and there he stayed to the chequered flag. *"There were two races I really wanted to win this season: the British Grand Prix and the one in the United States,"* he continued. *"And now I've managed to win both of them."*

Despite this success, nothing would make the Finn change his mind about next season. *"Obviously, I've had a difficult 2001 season and that's part of the reason why I have decided to stop. But even if I go on to win in Suzuka, I will not go back on my decision. I will not be in Formula 1 next season."*

△ It's Tony George himself, the owner of the Indianapolis circuit, who waved the flag as Mika Hakkinen won the United States Grand Prix.

The Italian lost his fourth place for the sake of half a millimetre.

Peter Sauber was unusually excited a few hours after the end of the United States Grand Prix. The Swiss team boss had until 17h15 local time to protest Jarno Trulli's Jordan as the post-race scrutineering had revealed that the plank under the car had worn more than the legal limit of 9 millimetres (or 10 millimetres, plus or minus 1 millimetre.) Apparently, it was out by half a millimetre!

The problem was, that in order to make the protest, he had to put down $2500 in cash. The team had not actually got the money. Therefore, Peter Sauber had to borrow the money, from mechanics and even from journalists who had passed by the garage. In the end, he just got the cash together in time and was able to lodge the protest.

In the end he need not have bothered: Jarno Trulli's Jordan did not comply with the rules and the Stewards at Indianapolis would disqualify the Ita-

Trulli disqualified then reinstated

lian anyway.

At least, that was the situation on the evening of the grand prix. Because the Jordan team appealed against the decision of the Stewards and their case was finally heard on 26th October, a month after the race. Against all odds, the FIA Appeal Tribunal found in favour of Jordan, on the grounds that the original decision was rendered null and void by the fact one of the stewards had not been present when Jordan was called up after the race.

This came as a great relief to Jarno Trulli, who had not enjoyed much success in 2001. This decision also meant that Jordan got back its two points, which put it ahead of BAR in the 2001 Constructors' classification.

Bad luck for Barrichello

In the Ferrari camp, it was Barrichello who was once again the victim of bad luck. He had to retire on the penultimate lap, while lying second and about to challenge David Coulthard for second place in the world championship.

"It's our first engine failure of the season, so on its own, it's not that serious," commented Michael Schumacher. *"But, of course it would have been* better if it had happened to me rather than Rubens!" Third in Indianapolis, David Coulthard now had a seven point lead over Barrichello in the race for the 2001 runner-up spot. *"Of course, I profited from the bad luck of the others,"* admitted the Scotsman. *"But I think I've had enough bad luck in my career for things to go the other way for a change."*

◁ It was the final grand prix in a long career for Jo Ramirez, the McLaren team coordinator. What better way to end it than with a win for one of his drivers.

◁◁ The Finn was particularly pleased to win this event, possibly the last of his career. But he was not spared the full podium treatment.

 **THE SAP UNITED STATES GRAND PRIX**

Mika Hakkinen in full flight in the United States Grand Prix. Playing a tactical game, the Finn and the McLaren team managed to do better than Ferrari, which was no mean feat.

paddock

On the start grid, an enormous American flag was unfurled. Patti LaBelle sang "God Bless America," after the national Anthem, "The Star Spangled Banner" had been performed by a children's choir. It was a very emotional moment, with plenty of tears in the grandstands.

After making a great start, Eddie Irvine finished fifth, allowing Jaguar to catch up with Benetton in the Constructors' classification.

It was a tough day for many of the teams and especially for Williams. Juan Pablo Montoya had gone for a one stop strategy, which should have seen him win the race. He pulled a great move to get past Michael Schumacher on lap 34, before retiring with engine failure. Ralf Schumacher made a driving error and went off the track. In the Jordan camp, Jean Alesi was taking part in his 200th grand prix and the team had decorated the side-pods with a huge "200." He finished seventh, just out of the points.

A lot of support

In Indianapolis, there were several initiatives planned to help the victims of the 11th September attacks. The race organisers arranged a collection for the Red Cross. At 37 points around the circuit, the spectators were encouraged to donate. The race title sponsor, SAP, announced it was donating three million dollars to the victims. Then, on Sunday, SAP and Bridgestone handed out a hundred thousand stars and stripes flags to the spectators. For his part, Jarno Trulli had a new helmet design, featuring the American flag, as indeed did some of the other drivers.

Rubinho had not wanted to come

Rubens Barrichello would have far rather stayed at home in Brazil than come to the States. He had only been a father for a few days and, very much the family man, the Brazilian had been upset at leaving his new son for the austere surroundings of the American paddock.

He had been very nervous about making the trip, when the time came to get on a plane. "I wanted to check out the security precautions," he admitted in all innocence. "When I got to Customs and passport control, the officer checking my papers was very kind and reassuring. In the hotel, or when I was walking around the city, everyone seemed very calm and everything seemed alright. There are American flags everywhere and everyone is thinking about what happened on 11th September, but life goes on."

200,000 people for a big party

For several days after the Italian Grand Prix, the United States Grand Prix looked as though it might not go ahead. Five teams, including Jaguar and Ferrari, were putting pressure on for it to be cancelled. However, Bernie Ecclestone was adamant; "We have a contract with Indianapolis and the teams have a contract with us," he announced. "I see no reason why these contracts should not be respected. We will not give in to terrorism." He was right. On Sunday night, race over, the event had been a total success. Large numbers of spectators had turned up at the last minute, without knowing anything about F1, just to thank the European circus for having had the courage to cross the Atlantic. The weekend became a party and everyone was very happy to have been part of it.

Despite the threat of germ warfare which hung over the circuit, almost 200,000 spectators massed around the famous Speedway. 200,000 people who, more than anything, wanted to attend a motor race and underline the fact they were proud to be American and would not give in to terrorism. Of course, the terrible events of 11th September had not been forgotten. The skies were empty. Very often, a grand prix is the setting for an air dis-play and all races feature constant helicopter traffic. But on the Sunday, all air traffic had been banned in the vicinity of the Speedway, in case of a terrorist attack. The army was even authorised to shoot down any planes which headed over the track.

On the grid, the singing of the famous "Star Spangled Banner" by a choir of children had an immediate effect. There was total silence from the grandstands, until it was over, at which point, thousands of Stars and Stripes flags were unfurled. America wanted to live again, but it would not forget.

Michael Schumacher did not look happy when he showed up in the Indianapolis paddock. The German had not wanted to make the journey to the USA, but Bernie Ecclestone made sure he did. The F1 boss had threatened to dock him some of his points if he did not show up in Indy. Obviously lacking motivation in Monza, the German seemed to find it hard to deal with events of 11th September. He went on to explain that his children had given him the strength to get over it. "The kids didn't realise what had happened. They are too young. They just want to get on with their lives, to play and have fun. It's thank to them that I got back to normal."

results

PRACTICE TIMES

No	Driver	Car/Engine/Chassis	Practice Friday	Pos.	Practice Saturday	Pos.	Qualifying	Pos.	Warm-up	Pos.
1.	Michael Schumacher	Ferrari/F2001/213	1'13"552	2°	1'12"078	1°	1'11"708	1°	1'14"029	4°
2.	Rubens Barrichello	Ferrari/F2001/206	1'13"584	3°	1'12"463	5°	1'12"327	5°	1'14"220	9°
3.	Mika Häkkinen	McLaren/Mercedes/MP4/16/4	1'13"387	1°	1'12"330	2°	1'11"945	2°	1'14"025	3°
4.	David Coulthard	McLaren/Mercedes/MP4/16/6	1'13"656	4°	1'12"724	8°	1'12"500	7°	1'13"982	2°
5.	Ralf Schumacher	Williams/BMW/FW23/7	1'13"919	9°	1'12"454	4°	1'11"986	3°	1'13"912	1°
6.	Juan Pablo Montoya	Williams/BMW/FW23/8	1'13"983	10°	1'12"668	6°	1'12"252	4°	1'14"063	6°
7.	Giancarlo Fisichella	Benetton/Renault/B201/6	1'14"911	17°	1'12"672	7°	1'12"942	12°	1'14"979	13°
8.	Jenson Button	Benetton/Renault/B201/5	1'14"186	13°	1'12"955	9°	1'12"805	10°	1'15"122	14°
9.	Olivier Panis	BAR/Honda/003/8	1'14"368	15°	1'13"521	12°	1'13"122	13°	1'15"201	15°
10.	Jacques Villeneuve	BAR/Honda/003/4	1'14"999	18°	1'14"346	19°	1'14"012	18°	1'15"958	19°
11.	Jarno Trulli	Jordan/Honda/EJ11/4	1'14"215	14°	1'13"205	11°	1'12"605	8°	1'14"778	12°
12.	Jean Alesi	Jordan/Honda/EJ11/5	1'14"057	12°	1'13"675	13°	1'12"607	9°	1'15"344	16°
14.	Jos Verstappen	Arrows/Asiatech/A22/4	1'15"547	21°	1'14"902	21°	1'14"138	20°	1'14"036	5°
15.	Enrique Bernoldi	Arrows/Asiatech/A22/6	1'15"449	20°	1'13"978	16°	1'14"129	19°	1'15"649	18°
16.	Nick Heidfeld	Sauber/Petronas/C20/7	1'13"827	6°	1'12"407	3°	1'12"434	6°	1'14"528	10°
17.	Kimi Räikkönen	Sauber/Petronas/C20/5	1'14"027	11°	1'13"186	10°	1'12"881	11°	1'14"145	8°
18.	Eddie Irvine	Jaguar/R-2/4	1'13"806	5°	1'14"052	17°	1'13"189	14°	1'14"597	11°
19.	Pedro de la Rosa	Jaguar/R-2/7	1'13"917	8°	1'13"753	14°	1'13"679	16°	1'14"083	7°
20.	Alex Yoong	Minardi/European/PS01/4	1'16"318	22°	1'15"604	22°	1'15"247	22°	1'16"646	22°
21.	Fernando Alonso	Minardi/European/PS01/3	1'15"131	19°	1'14"867	20°	1'13"991	17°	1'16"332	21°
22.	Heinz-Harald Frentzen	Prost/Acer/AP04/6	1'13"858	7°	1'13"870	15°	1'13"281	15°	1'16"037	20°
23.	Thomas Enge	Prost/Acer/AP04/5	1'14"767	16°	1'14"205	18°	1'14"185	21°	1'15"437	17°

MAXIMUM SPEEDS

No	Driver	P1 Qualifs	Pos	P1 Race	Pos	P2 Qualifs	Pos	P2 Race	Pos	Finish Qualifs	Pos	Finish Race	Pos	Trap Qualifs	Pos	Trap Race	Pos
1.	M. Schumacher	266,5	4°	257,4	2°	170,3	16°	162,5	19°	331,2	1°	331,3	9°	332,8	4°	336,9	9°
2.	R. Barrichello	266,7	3°	253,6	3°	173,3	10°	170,1	2°	329,7	2°	333,5	6°	335,7	1°	339,6	4°
3.	M. Häkkinen	264,7	6°	251,2	6°	177,9	1°	169,5	3°	324,1	11°	337,3	2°	328,2	10°	337,9	6°
4.	D. Coulthard	263,8	8°	251,2	7°	177,6	2°	168,7	5°	324,9	9°	329,1	14°	329,9	6°	337,1	8°
5.	R. Schumacher	266,7	2°	252,1	4°	174,0	8°	163,0	16°	327,3	5°	333,6	5°	331,1	5°	340,5	3°
6.	J. P. Montoya	268,5	1°	257,4	1°	173,2	11°	161,5	20°	329,5	3°	338,6	1°	333,3	2°	348,1	1°
7.	G. Fisichella	264,2	7°	250,4	9°	175,2	3°	167,9	8°	326,8	6°	329,1	13°	328,9	7°	337,5	7°
8.	J. Button	260,8	10°	250,0	11°	174,7	5°	163,0	17°	329,0	4°	335,7	3°	332,9	3°	338,6	5°
9.	O. Panis	257,9	19°	250,0	12°	171,1	14°	167,2	10°	320,6	18°	328,9	15°	326,0	14°	335,5	12°
10.	J. Villeneuve	256,4	22°	241,1	21°	167,4	20°	165,4	14°	316,3	22°	330,0	10°	320,6	22°	333,5	13°
11.	J. Trulli	261,5	9°	244,1	20°	171,0	15°	165,8	13°	318,9	20°	332,4	8°	325,7	16°	336,0	11°
12.	J. Alesi	265,4	5°	250,1	10°	172,2	13°	166,4	12°	323,0	14°	334,0	4°	325,5	17°	342,0	2°
14.	J. Verstappen	260,3	14°	247,4	15°	172,3	12°	169,0	4°	321,1	17°	323,6	21°	325,3	18°	330,2	19°
15.	E. Bernoldi	259,0	18°	249,0	13°	169,1	18°	166,6	11°	318,3	21°	329,8	12°	322,6	21°	330,7	18°
16.	N. Heidfeld	259,6	17°	244,8	18°	169,2	17°	168,6	6°	324,5	10°	332,7	7°	326,1	13°	336,6	10°
17.	K. Räikkönen	260,0	15°	223,9	22°	166,7	22°	162,5	18°	321,4	16°	327,3	16°	326,0	15°	326,4	22°
18.	E. Irvine	260,0	16°	247,8	14°	174,0	7°	171,7	1°	323,4	13°	323,4	22°	327,3	12°	328,8	21°
19.	P. de la Rosa	260,5	12°	251,8	5°	173,6	9°	167,6	9°	324,0	12°	329,9	11°	324,6	20°	331,7	17°
20.	A. Yoong	256,6	21°	245,9	17°	167,3	21°	164,9	15°	325,3	8°	327,1	17°	328,0	11°	332,5	15°
21.	F. Alonso	260,6	11°	244,5	19°	168,3	19°	159,2	21°	325,5	7°	326,3	18°	328,9	8°	333,2	14°
22.	H.-H. Frentzen	260,4	13°	247,3	16°	174,9	4°	168,0	7°	322,4	15°	325,3	19°	328,5	9°	332,0	16°
23.	T. Enge	256,8	20°	250,9	8°	174,3	6°	158,8	22°	320,3	19°	323,7	20°	324,8	19°	329,1	20°

CLASSIFICATION & RETIREMENTS

Pos	Driver	Team	Time
1.	Häkkinen	McLaren Mercedes	1:32:42.840
2.	M. Schum.	Ferrari	+ 11.046
3.	Coulthard	McLaren Mercedes	+ 12.043
4.	Irvine	Jaguar Racing	+ 72.434
5.	Heidfeld	Sauber Petronas	+ 72.996
6.	Alesi	Jordan Honda	+ 1 lap
7.	Fisichella	Benetton Renault	+ 1 lap
8.	Button	Benetton Renault	+ 1 lap
9.	Frentzen	Prost Acer	+ 1 lap
10.	Panis	BAR Honda	+ 1 lap
11.	de la Rosa	Jaguar Racing	+ 1 lap
12.	Bernoldi	Arrows Asiatech	+ 1 lap
13.	Enge	Prost Acer	+ 1 lap
14.	Barrichello	Ferrari	engine

Lap	Driver	Team	Reason
3	Räikkönen	Sauber Petronas	transmission
37	Alonso	Minardi European	transmission
37	R. Schum.	Williams BMW	spin
39	Yoong	Minardi European	gearbox
39	Montoya	Williams BMW	hydraulic
45	Verstappen	Arrows Asiatech	engine
46	Villeneuve	BAR Honda	accident
73	Trulli	Jordan Honda	disqualified

FASTEST LAPS

	Driver	Time	Lap
1.	Montoya	1'14"448 202,707 km/h	35
2.	Häkkinen	1'14"481	45
3.	Barrichello	1'14"629	47
4.	Coulthard	1'14"641	39
5.	R. Schum.	1'14"706	22
6.	M. Schum.	1'14"841	32
7.	Irvine	1'15"139	58
8.	Heidfeld	1'15"169	29
9.	Trulli	1'15"199	63
10.	Button	1'15"252	71
11.	Frentzen	1'15"296	38
12.	Fisichella	1'15"457	40
13.	Alesi	1'15"659	67
14.	de la Rosa	1'15"758	68
15.	Panis	1'15"919	67
16.	Bernoldi	1'16"068	68
17.	Enge	1'16"155	71
18.	Verstappen	1'16"342	35
19.	Villeneuve	1'16"680	40
20.	Alonso	1'16"694	30
21.	Yoong	1'17"079	25
22.	Räikkönen	1'51"518	2

PIT STOPS

	Driver	Time	Lap	Stop n°
1.	Räikkönen	30"837	2	1
2.	R. Schum.	26"975	24	1
3.	Barrichello	22"874	27	1
4.	Yoong	25"011	26	1
5.	Heidfeld	22"423	27	1
6.	Button	26"662	35	1
7.	Montoya	27"484	36	1
8.	Verstappen	25"916	36	1
9.	Alesi	26"611	37	1
10.	Bernoldi	27"648	37	1
11.	Enge	27"132	37	1
12.	M. Schum.	25"569	39	1
13.	Trulli	25"918	39	1
14.	Yoong	58"200	39	2
15.	Fisichella	24"460	41	1
16.	Frentzen	25"112	42	1
17.	Coulthard	23"067	43	1
18.	Villeneuve	13"083	43	1
19.	Panis	26"324	44	1
20.	Villeneuve	24"738	44	2
21.	Häkkinen	23"350	46	1
22.	Heidfeld	22"457	48	2
23.	Barrichello	22"214	50	2
23.	de la Rosa	28"429	50	1
24.	Irvine	22"560	52	1

BRIDGESTONE

Best result for a driver running Bridgestone tyres:

M. Häkkinen, McLaren Mercedes, winner

CHAMPIONSHIP

(after sixteen rounds)

Drivers :

1. M. Schumacher 113
2. D. Coulthard 61
3. R. Barrichello 54
4. R. Schumacher 48
5. M. Häkkinen 34
6. J. P. Montoya 25
7. J. Villeneuve 12
   N. Heidfeld 12
   J. Trulli 12
10. K. Räikkönen 9
11. G. Fisichella 8
12. E. Irvine 6
    H.-H. Frentzen 6
14. O. Panis 5
    J. Alesi 5
16. P. de la Rosa....................................3
17. J. Button 2
18. J. Verstappen 1

Constructors :

1. Ferrari...167
2. McLaren Mercedes 95
3. Williams BMW 73
4. Sauber Petronas...........................21
5. Jordan Honda 19
6. BAR Honda 17
7. Benetton Renault..........................10
8. Jaguar Racing 9
9. Prost Acer 4
10. Arrows Asiatech 1

THE CIRCUIT

SIXTEENTH ROUND

2001 SAP UNITED STATES GRAND PRIX

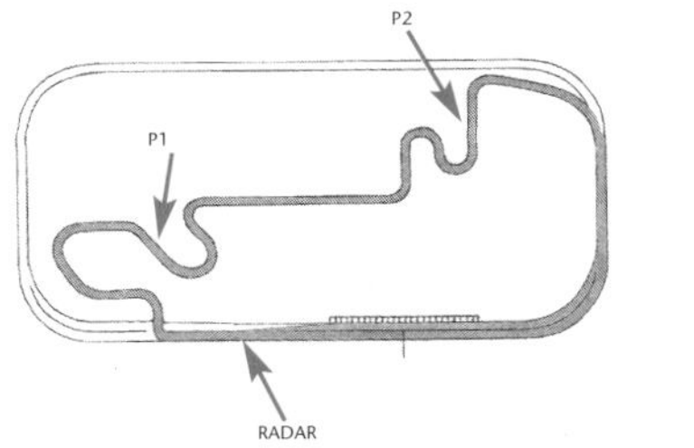

Date :	September 30, 2001
Length :	4192 meters
Distance :	73 laps, 306.016 km
Weather :	dry and sunny, 20°

RACE SUMMARY

- Michael Schumacher leads from pole, ahead of Montoya.
- At the end of the opening lap, Raikkonen tries to pass Heidfeld and Trulli. He hits the Jordan and retires.
- At the front, Barrichello makes short work of passing Montoya and Michael Schumacher. He is on a two stop strategy as opposed to one for his rivals.
- By lap 10, Barrichello leads Michael Schumacher by 5.2 seconds and Montoya by 8.5.
- Montoya closes on Michael Schumacher. When Barrichello makes his first pit stop on lap 27, the gap from Michael Schumacher to the Colombian is less than a second.
- On lap 34, Montoya goes round the outside of the German at the first corner. Two laps later, the Colombian pits and one lap after that he retires.
- On lap 39, Michael Schumacher refuels and Hakkinen finds himself in the lead. When the Finn pits, Barrichello is briefly in the lead, before making his second stop.
- Mika Hakkinen is thus back in the lead and takes his second win of the season.

LAP CHART

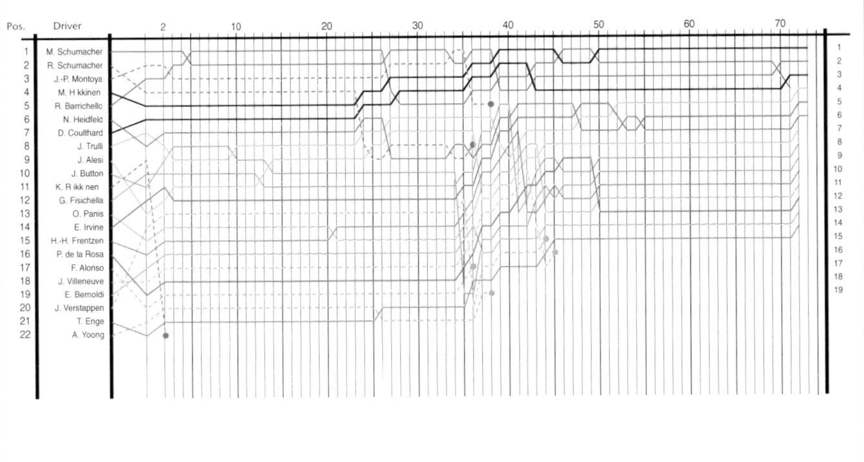

GAPS ON THE LEADER BOARD

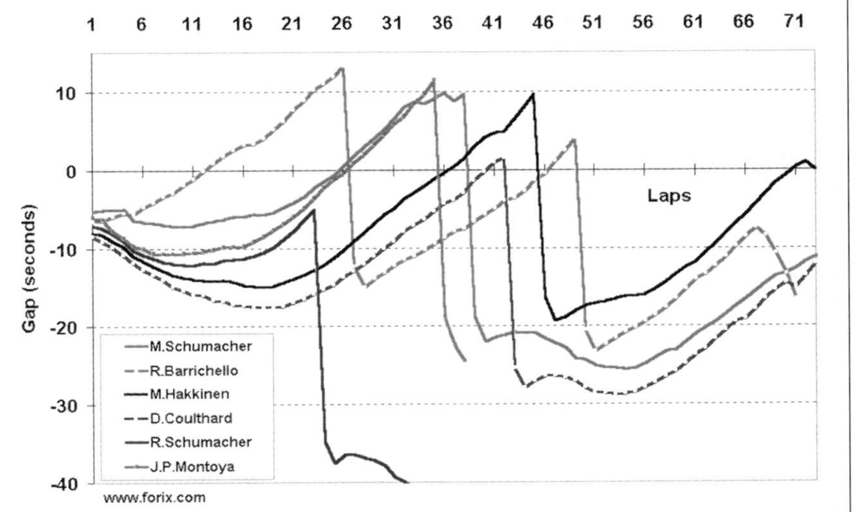

All results : © 2001 Fédération Internationale de l'Automobile, 2, Ch. Blandonnet, 1215 Genève 15, Suisse

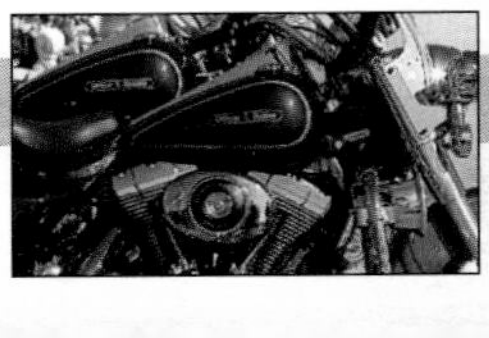

A last one for the road

For Scuderia Ferrari, the Japanese Grand Prix was very much the icing on the cake, a supreme coronation and a final slap in the face for the opposition.

Michael Schumacher was more than unbeatable on the Suzuka circuit, sticking over a second on his pursuers in the first sector of the track alone. How? It seemed to be down to a brand new chassis, which might well turn out to be the 2002 version. If it does, then the rest might as well pack up now.

FUJI TELEVISION JAPANESE GRAND PRIX
SUZUKA

Japan makes a comeback

In 2001, the Japanese Grand Prix was not what it used to be a decade earlier. There was no longer any need for a lottery to decide who would be lucky enough to get tickets. No longer did the fans sleep on the pavement outside the gates to be sure of getting the best viewing point. But it now seemed that the downturn had reached its limit. With Takuma Sato signed up to Jordan and Toyota entering the sport, the Nippon spectators would no doubt get fired up about F1 once again. In Suzuka, Honda was of course racing at home, which was a good reason to bring out a new engine. *"It is not a small step forward, it's a significant advance,"* insisted Kazutoshi Nishizawa, the man in charge of the Honda project.

Despite giving it his all and locking his wheels, Juan Pablo Montoya was powerless against the Schumacher-Ferrari-Bridgestone trio in Suzuka.

Some fans will go to any lengths to resemble their idol. Except that Michael Schumacher does not wear spectacles!

Tomas Enge did a good job in his last grand prix. In Suzuka, rumours were flying that this was also the Prost team's last race, or at least in its present form.

Michael Schumacher in a league of his own

Michael Schumacher was easily quickest in qualifying for the Japanese Grand Prix. With the 2001 title safely in his pocket, the German might have tackled this final round with a light heart and equally light pressure on the throttle. But in Suzuka, he proved he doesn't do things by half.

Improving every time he left the pits, he ended the day on a 1.34.484 which left the others struggling in his wake. Shortly after the session, he said he was prepared to let Rubens Barrichello pass him, if it would help the Brazilian to second place in the championship. It was not the usual sort of behaviour from the German, but it showed how united Scuderia Ferrari had been in 2001.

It fell to the two BMW-Williams to offer the strongest resistance. Juan Pablo Montoya qualified on the front row, but 7 tenths down on Schumacher's Ferrari. It was a major pasting! *"I am not too unhappy,"* commented the Colombian after qualifying. *"I am particularly surprised to see the Ferrari's times in the first sector, but I think that Suzuka is primarily down to experience. As it's the first time I'm driving here, I can be satisfied with second place."* It was yet another dig at Ralf Schumacher, who knew the track really well, having encountered it a few times in F1 as well as competing in a the Japanese F3000 series.

Sauber signs Massa

In Italy, they already called him "the new Senna." While that might be premature, it had to be said that 20 year old Felipe Massa already had a impressive cv. After eight years in karting, the Brazilian had meticulously picked off the titles in the last three series he had contested, ending with the European F3000 series.

Massa did two tests at the wheel of a Sauber C20. Those two outings were enough to convince Peter Sauber to take him on for 2002, replacing Kimi Raikkonen and the news was confirmed in Suzuka on the Friday.

STARTING GRID

M. SCHUMACHER 1'32"484	-1-	J. P. MONTOYA 1'33"184
R. SCHUMACHER 1'33"297	-2-	R. BARRICHELLO 1'33"323
Mika HÄKKINEN 1'33"662	-3-	G. FISICHELLA 1'33"830
David COULTHARD 1'33"916	-4-	Jarno TRULLI 1'34"002
Jenson BUTTON 1'34"375	-5-	Nick HEIDFELD 1'34"386
Jean ALESI 1'34"420	-6-	Kimi RAIKKONEN 1'34"581
Eddie IRVINE 1'34"851	-7-	Jacques VILLENEUVE 1'35"109
H.-H. FRENTZEN 1'35"132	-8-	Pedro De la Rosa 1'35"639
Olivier PANIS 1'35"766	-9-	Fernando ALONSO 1'36"410
Thomas ENGE 1'36"446	-10-	Enrique BERNOLDI 1'36"885
Jos VERSTAPPEN 1'36"973	-11-	Alex YOONG 1'38"246

And two more records for Schumacher, yes two!

Right from the start of the Japanese Grand Prix, Michael Schumacher was keen to make his opponents realise that he had every intention of winning the final race of the season. As soon as the grand prix was underway, he pulled out a 3.6 second advantage by the end of the opening lap, which increased to 6 seconds after two laps! *"Our Bridgestone tyres gave us a clear advantage when they were new, but it would not last and we knew that,"* explained Schumacher after the race. *"I tried to make the most of it, as we weren't sure if the Williams were on a one or a two stop strategy."*

Behind him, Juan Pablo Montoya was having a hard time fighting off the attentions of Rubens

Barrichello, who was planning to refuel three times; an aggressive strategy decided on by Jean Todt, with the aim of getting the Brazilian into the lead. If he had managed it, Michael Schumacher would have slowed the rest of the pack, to allow his colleague to finish second in the world championship.

Unfortunately, stuck behind Montoya, Barrichello never managed to get into the lead and ended up a long way back in fifth place.

By winning this grand prix, Michael Schumacher equalled Nigel Mansell's 1992 record of nine wins in a season. But more than that, the German also broke the record for the greatest number of points scored in a career. He now had 801, against the

798.5 scored by Alain Prost. Finally, he also established a new record for the most number of points scored in a season with 123. In short, it was a total success. *"I would say it has been a perfect season in all senses,"* admitted Schumacher. *"Finishing the season with a win is really nice. We went through two rather difficult races in Monza and Indianapolis. But here, we are back to normal. It's great and it's a super way to end the season, for the whole team."*

△ *And they're off for the final time this season. It was a perfect start for Michael Schumacher, who managed to keep Juan Pablo Montoya behind him.*

◁ *David Coulthard's latest girlfriend, Simone, was on hand to support him in his fight for second place in the world championship.*

By finishing second, David Coulthard claimed the runner-up spot in the championship. Rubens Barrichello missed out. It was the only blemish on Ferrari's season.

▽

No fanfare

With none of the three teams in contention for fourth place in the series scoring any points at Suzuka, Sauber hung onto this position, at the end of a tight fight with Jordan and BAR.

However, come Sunday night and there was little sign of celebration in the Sauber garage. The team did gather for a little end of term photo, but that was about it and there was no champagne to be

had. With night falling quickly in Suzuka, the mechanics worked flat out to pack up all the team equipment. They just wanted to leave the track as quickly as possible.

It has to be said that the race was not exactly a success for the Swiss lads. Kimi Raikkonen had been knocked out in a spectacular crash and Nick Heidfeld finished ninth.

For the Benetton team, the Japanese Grand Prix meant just one thing: putting an end to a disastrous 2001 season. It had been a year spent perfecting a revolutionary engine, which was expected to produce miracles in 2002.
In the meantime, the 2001 show was over and it was time to pack everything away in the containers.

FUJI TELEVISION JAPANESE GRAND PRIX

The remains of Jean Alesi's and Kimi Raikkonen's cars show what a big impact they had survived. The young Finn crashed heavily into the barrier after his rear suspension collapsed.

Mika Hakkinen was given several kiddy's toys by his mechanics, to help him fill the role of father. (on right:) the final goodbye for two legends of today's F1 era.

Lap six: a brutal way for Jean Alesi to say farewell to F1

201 grands prix were reason enough to head for retirement. In the history of Formula 1, only Ricardo Patrese, Gerhard Berger, Andrea de Cesaris and Nelson Piquet had sat on the grid more often. Alain Prost had stopped at 199 grands prix. In Suzuka, Jean Alesi brought his racing career to an end, despite the fact that, two weeks earlier at the United States Grand Prix, the Frenchman said he had not idea of throwing in the towel. *"I will only retire when I no longer feel capable of driving at the top level. That's a long way off,"* he had declared. Nevertheless, he knew his fate was in Eddie Jordan's hands, depending on whether or not he was kept on for 2002. On the Sunday prior to Japan, the Irishman had told him he had decided to sign the young and very promising Takuma Sato. So Jean Alesi had no real option but to retire. *"I'll finish this grand prix, then I'll do*

something else,"* he admitted in Suzuka. *"For the moment, I'm not sure exactly what. I am having serious talks with Eddie Jordan. Maybe we will work on a project together as we have a few ideas."*
Alesi seemed keen to persuade himself that it was all for the best. *"It's time to stop, even if racing is what I love best. After 200 grands prix, it's time to make way for younger drivers. When you like something, you never think about stopping, but all the same you have to be realistic. I enjoyed everything I have done and I have liked everyone I have worked with, through the good and the bad times. But everything has a beginning and an end."*
The Frenchman might have an opportunity to head off for the American Indycar series, like Nigel Mansell did in 1993. *"One thing is certain. I will not stay quietly at home, even if I love Kumiko and the children,"* he added. *"I have to decide on something. I am not ruling anything out and I am*

just waiting to see what offers come my way. As long as it involves four wheels and a steering wheel, I will be happy. But I don't want to say any more at the moment, because it's bound to be wrong."*
After a fine showing on Friday, Alesi was only eleventh on the grid. In the race, he was knocked out on lap 6, after colliding with Kimi Raikkonen's spinning Sauber, which he was unable to avoid.
It was the first time this season that Alesi had not been classified as a finisher! *"It's a shame to end like this, but we were not quick enough today,"* he concluded. After the race, Michael Schumacher paid tribute to his friend, the Frenchman being one of the German's few close friends in the paddock. *"I am very sad to see him go. He is still very quick and a close look shows that there are many other drivers who should retire before he does!"*

The end of a demon partnership

The Suzuka race also marked the end of a long partnership; that between Mika Hakkinen and David Coulthard. With the Finn taking a sabbatical year, it was unlikely they would be seen in the same team kit again. With McLaren they had competed alongside one another in 99 grands prix; the longest partnership in the history of F1. They racked up 85 podium finishes, had 13 one-two finishes to their name

and monopolised the front row of the grid 18 times. All weekend in Suzuka, the Finn had endlessly repeated he was not retiring, but only taking a year's break.
However, after the race, he admitted this might have been his last grand prix. *"It's my last grand prix for some time and maybe even for forever,"* he declared. *"Even I don't know what my future will be."*

PRACTICE TIMES

No	Driver	Car/Engine/Chassis	Practice Friday	Pos.	Practice Saturday	Pos.	Qualifying	Pos.	Warm-up	Pos.
1.	Michael Schumacher	Ferrari/F2001/214	1'36"727	8°	1'34"711	4°	1'32"484	1°	1'36"231	1°
2.	Rubens Barrichello	Ferrari/F2001/206	1'36"994	10°	1'35"222	9°	1'33"323	4°	1'37"813	7°
3.	Mika Häkkinen	McLaren/Mercedes/MP4/16/4	1'36"430	4°	1'35"043	8°	1'33"662	5°	1'37"584	6°
4.	David Coulthard	McLaren/Mercedes/MP4/16/6	1'36"638	7°	1'34"562	3°	1'33"916	7°	1'36"685	2°
5.	Ralf Schumacher	Williams/BMW/FW23/7	1'36"874	9°	1'33"969	1°	1'33"297	3°	1'38"183	11°
6.	Juan Pablo Montoya	Williams/BMW/FW23/8	1'35"977	2°	1'34"301	2°	1'33"184	2°	1'39"182	17°
7.	Giancarlo Fisichella	Benetton/Renault/B201/6	1'38"398	16°	1'36"114	16°	1'33"830	6°	1'38"641	14°
8.	Jenson Button	Benetton/Renault/B201/5	1'37"645	12°	1'34"735	5°	1'34"375	9°	1'38"740	15°
9.	Olivier Panis	BAR/Honda/003/8	1'39"108	18°	1'36"051	14°	1'35"766	17°	1'39"091	16°
10.	Jacques Villeneuve	BAR/Honda/003/4	1'38"312	14°	1'35"457	10°	1'35"109	14°	1'38"604	13°
11.	Jarno Trulli	Jordan/Honda/EJ11/4	1'37"564	11°	1'34"909	6°	1'34"002	8°	1'37"140	4°
12.	Jean Alesi	Jordan/Honda/EJ11/5	1'35"454	1°	1'35"719	13°	1'34"420	11°	1'37"361	5°
14.	Jos Verstappen	Arrows/Asiatech/A22/4	1'39"511	19°	1'37"805	21°	1'36"973	21°	1'40"482	20°
15.	Enrique Bernoldi	Arrows/Asiatech/A22/6	1'39"744	20°	1'37"514	20°	1'36"885	20°	1'39"295	18°
16.	Nick Heidfeld	Sauber/Petronas/C20/7	1'37"665	13°	1'35"037	7°	1'34"386	10°	1'36"966	3°
17.	Kimi Räikkönen	Sauber/Petronas/C20/5	1'38"315	15°	1'35"672	12°	1'34"581	12°	1'37"942	9°
18.	Eddie Irvine	Jaguar/R-2/4	1'36"589	6°	1'36"060	16°	1'34"851	13°	1'38"263	12°
19.	Pedro de la Rosa	Jaguar/R-2/7	1'36"225	3°	1'36"144	17°	1'35"639	16°	1'37"970	10°
20.	Alex Yoong	Minardi/European/PS01/4	1'39"952	21°	1'38"839	22°	1'38"246	22°	1'41"104	21°
21.	Fernando Alonso	Minardi/European/PS01/3	1'38"961	17°	1'37"429	19°	1'36"410	18°	1'42"142	22°
22.	Heinz-Harald Frentzen	Prost/Acer/AP04/4	1'36"439	5°	1'35"483	11°	1'35"132	15°	1'37"891	8°
23.	Thomas Enge	Prost/Acer/AP04/5	1'41"216	22°	1'37"246	18°	1'36"446	19°	1'40"324	19°

MAXIMUM SPEEDS

No	Driver	P1 Qualifs	Pos	P1 Race	Pos	P2 Qualifs	Pos	P2 Race	Pos	Finish Qualifs	Pos	Finish Race	Pos	Trap Qualifs	Pos	Trap Race	Pos
1.	M. Schumacher	287,8	4°	282,5	6°	312,8	4°	312,5	6°	288,0	4°	285,6	4°	304,1	4°	293,1	2°
2.	R. Barrichello	288,9	3°	283,9	3°	314,3	3°	321,7	1°	289,1	3°	285,4	5°	299,8	4°	283,1	7°
3.	M. Häkkinen	286,6	5°	283,6	4°	311,3	10°	314,5	3°	285,9	10°	282,0	12°	301,6	2°	293,9	1°
4.	D. Coulthard	284,2	12°	283,3	5°	311,8	8°	312,0	7°	285,8	11°	283,9	6°	301,0	3°	287,4	3°
5.	R. Schumacher	290,4	2°	286,0	2°	314,5	2°	315,0	2°	289,2	2°	288,2	1°	291,3	10°	284,0	5°
6.	J. P. Montoya	290,4	1°	286,4	1°	315,9	1°	313,5	4°	290,1	1°	287,3	2°	297,1	5°	286,4	4°
7.	G. Fisichella	284,4	9°	282,0	7°	312,5	5°	311,9	8°	287,6	5°	283,6	7°	292,4	9°	274,1	14°
8.	J. Button	284,6	8°	280,3	11°	312,4	6°	308,0	20°	286,5	6°	282,2	11°	285,1	15°	275,2	11°
9.	O. Panis	282,2	17°	277,4	16°	309,6	15°	311,2	9°	282,5	17°	280,4	18°	287,3	14°	274,5	13°
10.	J. Villeneuve	281,5	19°	278,4	12°	310,5	12°	309,7	15°	282,6	16°	281,1	17°	297,1	6°	283,2	6°
11.	J. Trulli	282,8	15°	278,1	13°	309,8	14°	308,3	19°	286,3	7°	281,8	14°	297,0	7°	275,2	12°
12.	J. Alesi	284,7	7°	275,5	20°	310,4	13°	308,3	18°	286,1	9°	281,4	15°	293,1	8°	276,2	10°
14.	J. Verstappen	280,4	20°	276,9	18°	307,7	17°	311,0	11°	281,6	20°	280,0	19°	280,1	18°	271,0	17°
15.	E. Bernoldi	281,6	18°	277,4	17°	307,2	18°	309,2	17°	281,8	19°	279,5	20°	280,0	19°	267,7	20°
16.	N. Heidfeld	284,3	10°	277,4	15°	309,2	16°	311,2	10°	283,0	15°	283,0	9°	290,0	11°	272,4	16°
17.	K. Räikkönen	282,3	16°	274,3	21°	306,7	19°	309,3	16°	282,0	18°	277,5	21°	282,6	13°	270,6	18°
18.	E. Irvine	283,3	14°	280,8	8°	305,9	20°	310,4	13°	284,1	14°	281,8	13°	281,1	16°	273,6	15°
19.	P. de la Rosa	285,9	6°	280,4	10°	311,8	7°	309,8	14°	286,1	8°	283,0	8°	280,8	17°	265,1	21°
20.	A. Yoong	276,9	22°	269,5	22°	303,2	21°	304,1	22°	279,8	21°	277,1	22°	264,1	22°	253,2	22°
21.	F. Alonso	277,3	21°	276,8	19°	303,0	22°	306,2	21°	279,6	22°	281,4	16°	279,4	20°	278,4	9°
22.	H.-H. Frentzen	284,2	11°	280,8	9°	310,4	13°	313,3	5°	285,1	12°	286,8	3°	289,7	12°	281,6	8°
23.	T. Enge	284,1	13°	277,5	14°	311,7	9°	310,7	12°	284,5	13°	282,2	10°	277,4	21°	269,7	19°

CLASSIFICATION & RETIREMENTS

Pos	Driver	Team	Time
1.	M. Schum.	Ferrari	1:27:33.298
2.	Montoya	BMW Williams	+ 3.154
3.	Coulthard	McLaren Mercedes	+ 23.262
4.	Häkkinen	McLaren Mercedes	+ 35.539
5.	Barrichello	Ferrari	+ 36.544
6.	R. Schum.	BMW Williams	+ 37.122
7.	Button	Benetton Renault	+ 97.102
8.	Trulli	Jordan Honda	+ 1 lap
9.	Heidfeld	Sauber Petronas	+ 1 lap
10.	Villeneuve	BAR Honda	+ 1 lap
11.	Alonso	European Minardi	+ 1 lap
12.	Frentzen	Prost Acer	+ 1 lap
13.	Panis	BAR Honda	+ 2 laps
14.	Bernoldi	Arrows Asiatech	+ 2 laps
15.	Verstappen	Arrows Asiatech	+ 2 laps
16.	Yoong	European Minardi	+ 3 laps
17.	Fisichella	Benetton Renault	gearbox

Lap	Driver	Team	Reason
6	Alesi	Jordan Honda	accident
6	Räikkönen	Sauber Petronas	accident
25	Irvine	Jaguar Racing	refuelling problem
43	Enge	Prost Acer	brakes
46	de la Rosa	Jaguar Racing	oil leak

FASTEST LAPS

	Driver	Time	Lap
1.	R. Schum.	1'36"944	46
		217,573 km/h	
2.	Barrichello	1'36"970	17
3.	Montoya	1'37"017	20
4.	M. Schum.	1'37"133	29
5.	Häkkinen	1'37"298	40
6.	Coulthard	1'37"313	51
7.	Frentzen	1'38"240	48
8.	Fisichella	1'38"361	13
9.	Button	1'38"526	36
10.	Irvine	1'38"620	22
11.	Heidfeld	1'38"647	21
12.	Trulli	1'38"857	28
13.	Villeneuve	1'38"887	22
14.	Alonso	1'39"153	36
15.	de la Rosa	1'39"182	40
16.	Panis	1'39"299	44
17.	Enge	1'39"827	27
18.	Räikkönen	1'39"991	4
19.	Alesi	1'40"225	4
20.	Bernoldi	1'40"940	46
21.	Verstappen	1'41"383	16
22.	Yoong	1'42"915	42

PIT STOPS

	Driver	Time	Lap	Stop n°
1.	Frentzen	35"314	3	1
2.	Barrichello	28"936	15	1
3.	Trulli	29"898	16	1
4.	Fisichella	29"771	16	1
5.	Panis	41"709	16	1
6.	Verstappen	30"053	17	1
7.	M. Schum.	30"512	18	1
8.	Yoong	32"183	18	1
9.	Villeneuve	29"437	19	1
10.	Heidfeld	29"333	19	1
11.	Bernoldi	31"590	19	1
12.	Button	32"568	20	1
13.	Montoya	30"030	21	1
14.	Alonso	31"228	21	1
15.	Enge	31"712	21	1
16.	Bernoldi	33"542	21	2
17.	R. Schum.	30"467	23	1
18.	Frentzen	30"105	22	2
19.	Coulthard	28"174	23	2
20.	Irvine	28"285	23	2
21.	Häkkinen	28"918	24	1
22.	de la Rosa	33"548	26	1
23.	Barrichello	34"586	29	2
23.	R. Schum.	32"021	29	2
24.	Panis	31"260	32	2
25.	Trulli	32"093	33	2
26.	Heidfeld	30"071	33	2
27.	Verstappen	31"065	33	2
28.	Montoya	30"562	34	2
29.	Fisichella	30"040	35	2
30.	M. Schum.	30"039	36	2
31.	Enge	25"302	35	2
32.	Yoong	31"806	34	2
33.	Verstappen	31"666	35	3
34.	Enge	39"235	36	3
35.	Montoya	29"195	38	2
36.	Alonso	30"653	37	2
37.	Häkkinen	28"774	38	2
38.	Button	29"450	38	2
39.	Bernoldi	30"606	37	3
40.	Coulthard	27"890	39	2
41.	R. Schum.	30"682	39	3
42.	Frentzen	28"720	38	3
43.	Barrichello	28"534	41	3
44.	de la Rosa	29"570	41	2
45.	Enge	1'09"393	41	4

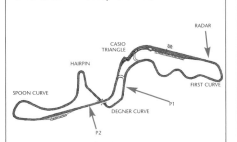

BRIDGESTONE

Best result for a driver running Bridgestone tyres:

Michael Schumacher, Ferrari, winner

CHAMPIONSHIP

(after seventeen rounds)

Drivers :

1.	M. Schumacher	123
2.	D. Coulthard	65
3.	R. Barrichello	56
4.	R. Schumacher	49
5.	M. Häkkinen	37
6.	J. P. Montoya	31
7.	J. Villeneuve	12
	N. Heidfeld	12
	J. Trulli	12
10.	K. Räikkönen	9
11.	G. Fisichella	8
12.	E. Irvine	6
	H.-H. Frentzen	6
14.	O. Panis	5
	J. Alesi	5
16.	P. de la Rosa	3
17.	J. Button	2
18.	J. Verstappen	1

Constructors :

1.	Ferrari	179
2.	McLaren Mercedes	102
3.	Williams BMW	80
4.	Sauber Petronas	21
5.	Jordan Honda	19
6.	BAR Honda	17
7.	Benetton Renault	10
8.	Jaguar Racing	9
9.	Prost Acer	4
10.	Arrows Asiatech	1

THE CIRCUIT

SEVENTEENTH ROUND

FUJI TELEVISION JAPANESE GRAND PRIX, SUZUKA

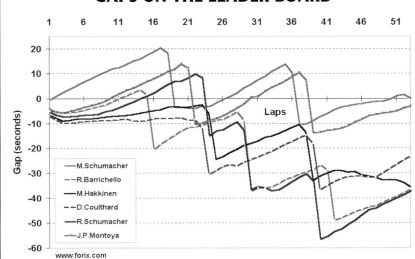

Date : October 14, 2001
Length : 5859 meters
Distance : 53 laps, 310.331 km
Weather : sunny, 23°

RACE SUMMARY

- At the start, Michael Schumacher swerves over to the right to block Montoya who made a great start.
- Barrichello passes Ralf Schumacher and then Montoya in the two opening laps, but Montoya fights back again at the chicane.
- Lap 9 and Raikkonen's suspension collapses and he goes into a slide. Alesi cannot avoid ramming the Sauber and both men are out.
- After 10 laps, Michael Schumacher has destroyed the opposition. He leads Montoya and Barrichello by 11.2 seconds.
- Michael Schumacher refuels on lap 18, handing the lead to Montoya. He stops on lap 21, so that Ralf Schumacher now leads for two laps before his pit stop.
- Lap 29 Ralf Schumacher is given a 10 second penalty for having gained advantage from cutting the chicane.

LAP CHART

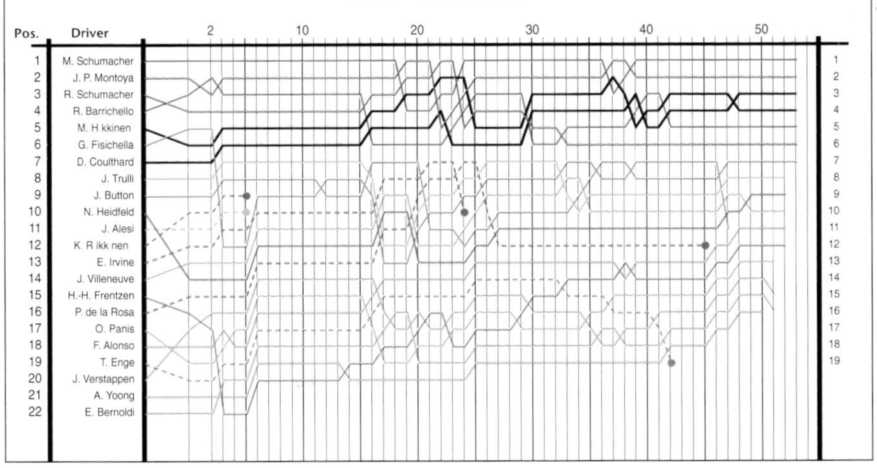

Pos.	Driver
1	M. Schumacher
2	J. P. Montoya
3	R. Schumacher
4	R. Barrichello
5	M. Häkkinen
6	G. Fisichella
7	D. Coulthard
8	J. Trulli
9	J. Button
10	N. Heidfeld
11	J. Alesi
12	K. Räikkönen
13	E. Irvine
14	J. Villeneuve
15	H.-H. Frentzen
16	P. de la Rosa
17	O. Panis
18	F. Alonso
19	T. Enge
20	J. Verstappen
21	A. Yoong
22	E. Bernoldi

GAPS ON THE LEADER BOARD

- M.Schumacher
- R.Barrichello
- M.Hakkinen
- D.Coulthard
- R.Schumacher
- J.P.Montoya

www.forix.com

All results :
© 2001 Fédération Internationale de l'Automobile, 2, Ch. Blandonnet, 1215 Genève 15, Suisse

Raikkonen, the McLaren baby

Sauber started trying out Kimi Raikkonen back in the autumn of 2000, before signing him up for this season. Of all the drivers of the modern era, the Finn is the one who has made the biggest jump. Before he began his F1 career, he had only competed in 23 Formula Renault races, where he had five times less power under his right foot than the eight hundred at his disposal this season. Of course, he started in karts. So remarkable was this rapid ascent, that FIA only granted him his superlicense on a provisional probationary period of four races. Having completed 3,500 kilometres in winter testing, the young lad showed right from the first race in Melbourne, that he already had the hang of it. Classified sixth, he became the fiftieth driver, since 1950, to score points at his first attempt. Further results with Sauber confirmed his talent and the top teams began to circle like sharks. In September in Monza, it was announced that he would replace fellow countryman Mika Hakkinen at McLaren in 2002.

Not only that, but Ron Dennis, well known for never taking risks with inexperienced drivers, had to pay a large amount to buy him out of a long-term Sauber contract. The fact he now becomes the new McLaren baby, certainly did not impress his current team-mate Nick Heidfeld. The young German has contractual links to Mercedes and actually out-qualified the Finn ten times out of seventeen, but he was left on the side lines. Next year, Heidfeld will have to contend with another young charger. Peter Sauber tested the young Brazilian Felipe Massa, just as he did with Kimi and the 20 year old European F3000 champion will step up to F1 next year.

Toyota: the shadow of a giant

F1 can accommodate 12 teams maximum. Those are the rules, so if a major car company wants in, it has to buy out one of the existing teams. And just as FIA had always hoped, this naturally increases the value of the teams already in the game. This twelfth place has been booked since 1999, when Toyota put its name down. So, next March, the Japanese company which has done everything else in motorsport, from the world rally championship to the 24 Hours of Le Mans, will finally step up to the plate in the world's most prestigious series. It is based in Cologne and at the Paul-Ricard circuit.

Under the direction of Ove Andersson, Toyota has decided to do things big. It has a big factory and a big number of employees and just like Ferrari, it is building the entire car from chassis to engine. This year, their first car has tested relentlessly from March to November on a variety of circuits. Behind the wheel were Mika Salo, with 99 grand prix to his credit and Alan McNish, who starts from zero. Toyota has now confirmed this will be their driver line-up in 2002. Not very impressive. But before they can attract a superstar driver, they will need to prove they are up to the task. On the technical side, this has already necessitated a palace coup.

Andre Cortanze was not considered hard headed enough to be technical director and he was replaced by Gustav Brunner, poached from Minardi.

The decision certainly proved Toyota had learned how to move at the right pace for F1. But now we must wait and see if their car can do the same.

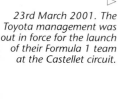

Hand signals
Ron Dennis in animated conversation with his technical director, Adrian Newey. The body language speaks volumes about a 2001 season full of worries for the McLaren team and its boss: from technical problems in all areas - failures, launch control computer glitches etc. to internal strife. Previously, a tightly knit squad, McLaren almost lost a big part of its technical team to Jaguar. As if that wasn't enough, Ron Dennis had to deal with the fact Mika Hakkinen wanted to take a year off in 2002, even if he had already signed a contract.
In 2002, the silver arrows team will face a number of challenges, including switching to Michelin tyres, integrating the still inexperienced Kimi Raikkonen into a top team and getting back on track to success. Ron Dennis is unlikely to have an easier time next year.

Renault: the big comeback

Renault quit F1 at the end of 1997, having won everything they could as an engine supplier to Williams and Benetton.

However, the effect of picking up five Drivers' titles and six Constructors' was almost becoming negative, in that Renault was so successful that only its failures made the headlines. After nine years, the time had come to call it a day. But under the guise of Mecachrome and then Supertec, Renault maintained its presence in the sport up to the end of 1999.

This strategy allowed it to keep its engineering brains busy, while training new ones. And then, almost out of the blue, Renault bought Benetton in 1999. The Anglo-Italian squad had been in the sport since 1985, under the Toleman banner.

This was its final year in the sport. It ran a very experimental and top secret engine, reputed to have a 111 degree V angle and designed by Jean-Jacques His, the team's charismatic leader.

Renault would thus race under its own name in 2002, with the clear aim of picking up more titles, but this time, as its own team. It marks a return to the period from 1977 to 1985 and the turbo era. In 1983, the Renault team just missed out on taking the title.

Up against the top teams and with Toyota joining the fray, it is a risky challenge. But Renault reckons it has the edge over the Japanese and maybe over all the others too, if the opposition is forced to copy the new generation of engines. In Viry-Chatillon, they reckon to push it right to the limit.

◁
Flavio Briatore had run the Benetton-Renault team in its glory days and he was brought back to run it by Renault, after they bought the team. This time they aim to win the championship with their own car, chassis and engine both bearing their name. It will not be an easy task.

Recap of the 2001 season

Position in Championship	Driver	Team	Australian Grand Prix	Malaysian Grand Prix	Brazilian Grand Prix	San Marino Grand Prix	Spanish Grand Prix	Austrian Grand Prix	Monaco Grand Prix	Canadian Grand Prix	European Grand Prix	French Grand Prix	British Grand Prix	German Grand Prix	Hungarian Grand Prix	Belgium Grand Prix	Italian Grand Prix	United States Grand Prix	Japanese Grand Prix	Number of poles	Number of victories	Number of fastest laps	Number of laps in the lead	Number of km in the lead	Nber of points
1	Michael SCHUMACHER	Ferrari	**1**	**1**	2	A	**1**	2	**1**	2	**1**	**1**	2	A	**1**	**1**	4	2	**1**	11	9	3	533	2513,662	123
2	David COULTHARD	McLaren Mercedes	2	3	**1**	2	5	**1**	5	A	3	4	A	A	3	2	A	3	3	2	2	3	77	349,608	65
3	Rubens BARRICHELLO	Ferrari	3	2	A	3	A	3	2	A	5	3	3	2	2	5	2	(15)	5	-	-	-	64	267,898	56
4	Ralf SCHUMACHER	Williams BMW	A	5	A	**1**	A	A	A	**1**	4	2	A	**1**	4	7	3	A	6	1	3	5	141	718,544	49
5	Mika HÄKKINEN	McLaren Mercedes	A	6	A	4	(9)	A	A	3	6	A	**1**	A	5	4	A	**1**	4	-	2	3	110	525,405	37
6	Juan Pablo MONTOYA	Williams BMW	A	A	A	A	2	A	A	A	2	A	4	A	8	A	**1**	A	2	3	1	3	122	633,798	31
7	Jacques VILLENEUVE	BAR Honda	A	A	7	A	3	8	4	A	9	A	8	3	9	8	6	A	10	-	-	-	-	-	12
	Nick HEIDFELD	Sauber Petronas	4	A	3	7	6	9	A	A	A	6	6	A	6	A	11	6	9	-	-	-	-	-	12
	Jarno TRULLI	Jordan Honda	A	8	5	5	4	A	A	(11)	A	5	A	A	A	A	A	4	8	-	-	-	1	5,543	12
10	Kimi RÄIKKÖNEN	Sauber Petronas	6	A	A	A	8	4	10	4	10	7	5	A	7	A	7	A	A	-	-	-	-	-	9
11	Giancarlo FISICHELLA	Benetton Renault	13	A	6	A	14	A	A	A	11	11	13	4	A	3	10	8	(17)	-	-	-	-	-	8
12	Eddie IRVINE	Jaguar	11	A	A	A	A	7	3	A	7	A	9	A	A	A	A	5	A	-	-	-	-	-	6
	Heinz-Harald FRENTZEN	Jordan Honda / Prost Acer	5	4	(11)	6	A	A	A		A	8	7		A	9	A	10	12	-	-	-	-	-	6
14	Olivier PANIS	BAR Honda	7	A	4	8	7	5	A	A	A	9	A	7	A	11	9	11	13	-	-	-	-	-	5
	Jean ALESI	Prost Acer / Jordan Honda	10	9	8	9	10	10	6	5	(15)	12	11	6	10	6	8	7	A	-	-	-	-	-	5
16	Pedro de la ROSA	Jaguar					A	A	A	6	8	14	12	A	11	A	5	12	A	-	-	-	-	-	3
17	Jenson BUTTON	Benetton Renault	(14)	11	10	12	15	A	7	A	13	(16)	15	5	A	A	A	9	7	-	-	-	-	-	2
18	Jos VERSTAPPEN	Arrows Asiatech	9	7	A	A	12	6	8	(10)	A	13	10	9	12	10	A	A	15	-	-	-	-	-	1
	Then:																								
	Ricardo ZONTA	Jordan Honda								7				A						-	-	-	-	-	-
	Luciano BURTI	Jaguar / Prost Acer	8	10	A	11	11	11	A	8	12	10	A	A	A	A				-	-	-	-	-	-
	Enrique BERNOLDI	Arrows Asiatech	A	A	A	10	A	A	9	A	A	A	14	8	A	12	A	13	14	-	-	-	-	-	-
	Tarso MARQUES	Minardi European	A	14	9	A	16	A	A	9	A	15	NQ	A	A	13				-	-	-	-	-	-
	Fernando ALONSO	Minardi European	12	13	A	A	13	A	A	A	14	(17)	16	10	A	A	13	A	11	-	-	-	-	-	-
	Tomas ENGE	Prost Acer															12	14	A	-	-	-	-	-	-
	Gaston MAZZACANE	Prost Acer	A	12	A	A														-	-	-	-	-	-
	Alex YOONG	Minardi European															A	A	16	-	-	-	-	-	-

Overall grid of the season 2001

1. **M. SCHUMACHER** 23'23.568 (216,720 Km/h)
2. **R. SCHUMACHER** 23'29.600
3. **MONTOYA** 23'33.538
4. **BARRICHELLO** 23'33.768
5. **HÄKKINEN** 23'34"464
6. **COULTHARD** 23'36.314
7. **TRULLI** 23'42"994
8. **HEIDFELD** 23'50"169
9. **VILLENEUVE** 23'51"507
10. **RÄIKKÖNEN** 23'51"943
11. **PANIS** 23'53"201
12. **IRVINE** 23'58"301
13. **ALESI** 24'03"046
14. **FISICHELLA** 24'06"257
15. **BUTTON** 24'14"831
16. **VERSTAPPEN** 24'18"812
17. **ALONSO** 24'26"075

Did not enter all qualifying sessions:

18. **DE LA ROSA** 18'15"396 (211,672 Km/h)
19. **FRENTZEN** 20'48"887 (211,145 Km/h)
20. **BURTI** 19'59"542 (206,031 Km/h)
21. **MARQUES** 20'24"759 (201,789 Km/h)
22. **BERNOLDI** 23'42"496 (199,808 Km/h)
23. **ZONTA** 2'58"502 (226,807 Km/h)
24. **ENGE** 4'16"670 (222,224 Km/h)
25. **YOONG** 4'20"956 (218,574 Km/h)
26. **MAZZACANE** 5'54"074 (204,242 Km/h)

Number of poles

Senna	65	Fittipaldi	6
M. Schumacher	43	P. Hill	6
Prost	33	Jabouille	6
Clark	33	Jones	6
Mansell	32	Reutemann	6
Fangio	28	Amon	5
Häkkinen	26	Farina	5
Lauda	24	Regazzoni	5
Piquet	24	Rosberg	5
D. Hill	20	Tambay	5
Andretti	18	Hawthorn	4
Arnoux	18	Pironi	4
Stewart	17	De Angelis	3
Moss	16	Brooks	3
Ascari	14	T. Fabi	3
Hunt	14	Gonzales	3
Peterson	14	Gurney	3
Brabham	13	Jarier	3
G. Hill	13	Scheckter	3
Ickx	13	Barrichello	3
J. Villeneuve	13	Montoya	3
Coulthard	12		
Berger	12	Then :	
Rindt	10	Alesi	2
Surtees	8	Frentzen	2
Patrese	8	Fisichella	1
Laffite	7	R. Schumacher	1

Number of fastest laps

M. Schumacher	44	Hunt	8
Prost	41	Laffite	7
Mansell	30	G. Villeneuve	7
Clark	28	Farina	6
Lauda	25	Fittipaldi	6
Häkkinen	24	Gonzalez	6
Fangio	23	Gurney	6
Piquet	23	Hawthorn	6
Berger	21	P. Hill	6
Moss	20	Pironi	6
Senna	19	Scheckter	6
D. Hill	19	Frentzen	6
Coulthard	17	R. Schumacher	6
Regazzoni	15	Pace	5
Stewart	15	Watson	5
Ickx	14	Alesi	4
Jones	13	Alboreto	4
Patrese	13	Beltoise	4
Arnoux	12	Depailler	4
Ascari	11	Reutemann	4
Surtees	11	Siffert	4
Andretti	10	Barrichello	3
Brabham	10	Montoya	3
G. Hill	10		
Hulme	9		
Peterson	9	Then :	
J. Villeneuve	9	Irvine	1

Number of GP contested

Patrese	256	Frentzen	129	Capelli	94
Berger	210	Ma. Andretti	128	Salo	93
DeCesaris	208	Brabham	126	Hunt	92
Piquet	204	Coulthard	124	Fisichella	91
Alesi	201	Peterson	123	Verstappen	91
Prost	199	Martini	119	Beltoise	86
Alboreto	194	Ickx	116	Gurney	86
Mansell	187	Jones	116	Palmer	84
G. Hill	176	D. Hill	116	R. Schumacher	83
Laffite	176	Rosberg	114	Surer	82
Lauda	171	Tambay	114	Trintignant	82
Boutsen	163	Hulme	112	Trulli	80
M. Schumacher	162	Scheckter	112		
Häkkinen	162	Surtees	111	Then :	
Herbert	162	De Angelis	108	de la Rosa	46
Senna	161	Panis	108	Button	34
Brundle	158	Alliot	107	Heidfeld	33
Watson	152	Mass	105	Zonta	31
Arnoux	149	Bonnier	102	Marques	26
Barrichello	147	McLaren	101	Mazzacane	21
Warwick	147	J. Villeneuve	99	Alonso	17
Reutemann	146	Stewart	99	Bernoldi	17
E. Fittipaldi	144	Diniz	98	Montoya	17
Jarier	135	Siffert	97	Räikkönen	17
Cheever	132	Amon	96	Burti	15
Regazzoni	132	Depailler	95	Enge	3
Irvine	130	Katayama	95	Yoong	3

Nber of laps and Km completed into 2001

Maximum	1069	5140,794
M. Schumacher	1009	4803,190
Alesi	1002	4772,335
Barrichello	932	4538,359
Coulthard	930	4377,810
Verstappen	893	4296,901
Button	865	4135,059
Fisichella	814	4004,016
R. Schumacher	810	3955,185
Panis	788	3858,862
Villeneuve	794	3819,271
Trulli	759	3658,947
Heidfeld	768	3628,973
Frentzen	723	3487,089
Räikkönen	760	3482,607
Alonso	709	3469,531
Häkkinen	693	3418,778
Montoya	684	3315,975
Irvine	661	3042,064
Burti	602	2847,063
Bernoldi	572	2845,702
Marques	582	2723,483
de la Rosa	583	2693,559
Enge	166	848,662
Yoong	132	706,662
Mazzacane	135	664,322
Zonta	75	348,403

Number of victories

M. Schumacher	53	Arnoux	7
Prost	51	Brooks	6
Senna	41	Laffite	6
Mansell	31	Rindt	6
Stewart	27	Surtees	6
Clark	25	G. Villeneuve	6
Lauda	25	Patrese	6
Fangio	24	Alboreto	5
Piquet	23	Farina	5
D. Hill	22	Regazzoni	5
Häkkinen	20	Rosberg	5
Moss	16	Watson	5
Brabham	14	Gurney	4
Fittipaldi	14	McLaren	4
G. Hill	14	Boutsen	3
Ascari	13	P. Hill	3
Andretti	12	Hawthorn	3
Jones	12	Pironi	3
Reutemann	12	R. Schumacher	3
Coulthard	11	Irvine	3
J. Villeneuve	11	Frentzen	3
Hunt	10	Herbert	3
Peterson	10	Then :	
Scheckter	10	Montoya	1
Berger	10	Panis	1
Hulme	8	Alesi	1
Ickx	8	Barrichello	1

Total number of points scored

M. Schumacher	801	Alboreto	186.5
Prost	798.5	Moss	186.5
Senna	614	Irvine	183
Piquet	485.5	Arnoux	181
Mansell	482	Ickx	181
Lauda	420.5	Ma. Andretti	180
Häkkinen	420	Surtees	180
Berger	386	Hunt	179
Stewart	360	Watson	169
D. Hill	360	Frentzen	159
Coulthard	359	R. Schumacher	135
Reutemann	310		
G. Hill	289	Then :	
E. Fittipaldi	281	Herbert	98
Patrese	281	Fisichella	75
Fangio	277.5	Panis	61
Clark	274	Montoya	31
Brabham	261	Trulli	29
Scheckter	259	Wurz	26
Alesi	241	Verstappen	17
Laffite	228	Button	14
Regazzoni	212	Heidfeld	12
J. Villeneuve	209	Diniz	10
Jones	206	Räikkönen	9
Peterson	206	de la Rosa	6
McLaren	196.5	Zonta	3
Barrichello	195	Gené	1

Number of laps in the lead

M. Schumacher	3'097	Hulme	436
Senna	2'982	Rindt	387
Prost	2'712	Regazzoni	361
Mansell	2'099	Surtees	310
Clark	2'039	Pironi	295
Stewart	1'893	Watson	287
Lauda	1'620	Laffite	279
Piquet	1'572	Alesi	265
Häkkinen	1'490	Alboreto	218
D. Hill	1'352	Barrichello	210
G. Hill	1'073	Tambay	197
Brabham	827	Gurney	191
Andretti	799	P. Hill	189
Coulthard	760	Jabouille	184
Peterson	706	Amon	183
Berger	695	Brooks	173
Scheckter	671	Depailler	165
Reutemann	648	Irvine	156
Hunt	634	Frentzen	149
J. Villeneuve	634	R. Schumacher	148
Jones	594	Montoya	122
Patrese	568		
G. Villeneuve	533	Then :	
Ickx	529	Herbert	44
Arnoux	506	Trulli	38
Rosberg	506	Fisichella	35
Fittipaldi	459	Panis	16

Number of km in the lead

M. Schumacher	14'318	Fittipaldi	2'122
Senna	13'613	Rindt	1'905
Prost	12'575	Hulme	1'900
Clark	10'189	Regazzoni	1'855
Mansell	9'642	P. Hill	1'715
Stewart	9'077	Brooks	1'525
Piquet	7'465	Gurney	1'518
Häkkinen	7'201	Laffite	1'476
Lauda	7'188	Alesi	1'285
D. Hill	6'248	Watson	1'245
G. Hill	4'618	Pironi	1'238
Brabham	4'541	Barrichello	979
Coulthard	3'669	Jabouille	978
Andretti	3'577	Tambay	975
Berger	3'456	Alboreto	927
Reutemann	3'309	Irvine	838
Peterson	3'304	Von Trips	787
Hunt	3'229	Amon	784
Ickx	3'067	R. Schumacher	751
J. Villeneuve	2'970	Frentzen	746
Jones	2'877	Montoya	634
Scheckter	2'837		
Patrese	2'571	Then :	
Arnoux	2'561	Herbert	226
G. Villeneuve	2'244	Fisichella	172
Rosberg	2'137	Trulli	165
Surtees	2'131	Panis	53

Abbreviations : A = retired; NQ = not qualified; DNF = did not finished; F = withdrawal; D = disqualified; NC = finished, but not classified (insufficient distance covered); ARG = Argentina; AUS = Australia; AUT = Austria; BEL = Belgium; BRE = Brazil; CAN = Canada; DAL = Dallas; ESP = Spain; EUR = Europe; FIN = Finland; FRA = France; GB = Great Britain; GER = Germany; HOL = Holland; ITA = Italy; JAP = Japan; MEX = Mexico; MON = Monaco; NZ = New Zealand; PAC = Pacific; POR = Portugal; RSM = San Marino; SA = South Africa; SUE = Sweden; SUI = Switzerland; USA = United States; USAE = United States (East); USAW = United States (West); VEG = Las Vegas; NB = Laps in the lead only since 1957.

The 52 World Champions

Year	Driver	Nationality	Make	Nber of races	Nber of poles	Nber of victories	Nber of fastest laps
1950	Giuseppe Farina	ITA	Alfa Roméo	7	2	3	3
1951	Juan Manuel Fangio	ARG	Alfa Roméo	8	4	3	5
1952	Alberto Ascari	ITA	Ferrari	8	5	6	5
1953	Alberto Ascari	ITA	Ferrari	9	6	5	4
1954	Juan Manuel Fangio	ARG	Mercedes/Maserati	9	5	6	3
1955	Juan Manuel Fangio	ARG	Mercedes	7	3	4	3
1956	Juan Manuel Fangio	ARG	Lancia/Ferrari	8	5	3	3
1957	Juan Manuel Fangio	ARG	Maserati	8	4	4	2
1958	Mike Hawthorn	GB	Ferrari	11	4	1	5
1959	Jack Brabham	AUS	Cooper Climax	9	1	2	1
1960	Jack Brabham	AUS	Cooper Climax	10	3	5	3
1961	Phil Hill	USA	Ferrari	8	5	2	3
1962	Graham Hill	GB	BRM	9	1	4	3
1963	Jim Clark	GB	Lotus Climax	10	7	7	6
1964	John Surtees	GB	Ferrari	10	2	2	2
1965	Jim Clark	GB	Lotus Climax	10	6	6	6
1966	Jack Brabham	AUS	Brabham Repco	9	3	4	1
1967	Dennis Hulme	NZ	Brabham Repco	11	0	2	2
1968	Graham Hill	GB	Lotus Ford	12	2	3	0
1969	Jackie Stewart	GB	Matra Ford	11	2	6	5
1970	Jochen Rindt	AUT	Lotus Ford	13	3	5	3
1971	Jackie Stewart	GB	Matra Ford	11	6	6	3
1972	Emerson Fittipaldi	BRE	Lotus Ford	12	3	5	0
1973	Jackie Stewart	GB	Tyrrell Ford	15	3	5	1
1974	Emerson Fittipaldi	BRE	McLaren Ford	15	2	3	0
1975	Niki Lauda	AUT	Ferrari	14	9	5	2
1976	James Hunt	GB	McLaren Ford	16	8	6	2
1977	Niki Lauda	AUT	Ferrari	17	2	3	3
1978	Mario Andretti	USA	Lotus Ford	16	8	6	3
1979	Jody Scheckter	SA	Ferrari	15	1	3	1
1980	Alan Jones	AUS	Williams Ford	14	3	5	5
1981	Nelson Piquet	BRE	Brabham Ford	15	4	3	1
1982	Keke Rosberg	FIN	Williams Ford	16	1	1	0
1983	Nelson Piquet	BRE	Brabham BMW Turbo	15	1	3	4
1984	Niki Lauda	AUT	McLaren TAG Porsche Turbo	16	0	5	5
1985	Alain Prost	FRA	McLaren TAG Porsche Turbo	16	2	5	5
1986	Alain Prost	FRA	McLaren TAG Porsche Turbo	16	1	4	2
1987	Nelson Piquet	BRE	Williams Honda Turbo	16	4	3	4
1988	Ayrton Senna	BRE	McLaren Honda Turbo	16	13	8	3
1989	Alain Prost	FRA	McLaren Honda	16	2	4	5
1990	Ayrton Senna	BRE	McLaren Honda	16	10	6	2
1991	Ayrton Senna	BRE	McLaren Honda	16	8	7	2
1992	Nigel Mansell	GB	Williams Renault	16	14	9	8
1993	Alain Prost	FRA	Williams Renault	16	13	7	6
1994	Michael Schumacher	GER	Benetton Ford	14	6	8	9
1995	Michael Schumacher	GER	Benetton Renault	17	4	9	7
1996	Damon Hill	GB	Williams Renault	16	9	8	5
1997	Jacques Villeneuve	CAN	Williams Renault	17	10	7	3
1998	Mika Häkkinen	FIN	McLaren Mercedes	16	9	8	6
1999	Mika Häkkinen	FIN	McLaren Mercedes	16	11	5	6
2000	Michael Schumacher	GER	Ferrari	17	9	9	2
2001	Michael Schumacher	GER	Ferrari	17	11	9	3

Constructor's championship 2001

Position	Team	Nber of points	Nber of poles	Nber of victories	Nber of fastest laps	Nber of laps in the lead	Nber of km in the lead
1.	Ferrari	179	11	9	3	597	2,781,560
2.	McLaren-Mercedes	102	2	4	6	187	875,013
3.	Williams-BMW	80	4	4	8	263	1,352,342
4.	Sauber-Petronas	21	-	-	-	-	-
5.	Jordan-Honda	19	-	-	-	1	5,543
6.	BAR-Honda	17	-	-	-	-	-
7.	Benetton-Renault	10	-	-	-	-	-
8.	Jaguar	9	-	-	-	-	-
9.	Prost-Acer	4	-	-	-	-	-
10.	Arrows-Asiatech	1	-	-	-	-	-
-.	Minardi-European	0	-	-	-	-	-

Nber of constructor's championship
(exist since 1958)

11 : Ferrari
  1961 - 64 - 75 - 76 - 77 - 79 - 82 - 83 - 99 - 2000 - 2001
9 : Williams
  1980 - 81 - 86 - 87 -92 - 93 - 94 - 96 - 97
8 : McLaren
  1974 - 84 - 85 - 88 - 89 - 90 - 91 - 98
7 : Lotus
  1963 - 65 - 68 - 70 -72 - 73 - 78
2 : Cooper   1959 - 60
    Brabham 1966 - 67·
1 : Vanwall   1958
    BRM   1962
    Matra   1969
    Tyrrell   1971
    Benetton 1995

Number of poles per make

Ferrari	148
Williams	112
McLaren	112
Lotus	107
Brabham	39
Renault	31
Benetton	16
Tyrrell	14
Alfa Roméo	12
BRM	11
Cooper	11
Maserati	10
Ligier	9
Mercedes	8
Vanwall	7
March	5
Matra	4
Shadow	3
Lancia	2
Jordan	2
Arrows	1
Honda	1
Lola	1
Porsche	1
Wolf	1
Stewart	1

Number of victories per make

Make	
Ferrari	144
McLaren	134
Williams	107
Lotus	79
Brabham	35
Benetton	26
Tyrrell	23
BRM	17
Cooper	16
Renault	1
Alfa Roméo	10
Maserati	9
Matra	9
Mercedes	9
Vanwall	9
Ligier	9
March	3
Wolf	3
Jordan	3
Honda	2
Hesketh	1
Penske	1
Porsche	1
Shadow	1
Stewart	1

Number of fastest laps per make

Ferrari	147
Williams	118
McLaren	107
Lotus	70
Brabham	41
Benetton	37
Tyrrell	20
Renault	18
BRM	15
Maserati	15
Alfa Roméo	14
Cooper	13
Matra	12
Ligier	11
Mercedes	9
March	7
Vanwall	6
Surtees	4
Eagle	2
Honda	2
Shadow	2
Wolf	2
Ensign	1
Gordini	1
Hesketh	1
Lancia	1
Parnelli	1
Jordan	1

Family picture of the 2001 Championship. From left to right and from top to bottom: Jos Verstappen, Enrique Bernoldi, Heinz-Harald Frentzen, Tomas Enge, Giancarlo Fisichella, Jenson Button, Alex Yoong, Fernando Alonso, Juan Pablo Montoya, Ralf Schumacher, Michael Schumacher, Rubens Barrichello, David Coulthard, Mika Häkkinen, Olivier Panis, Jacques Villeneuve, Nick Heidfeld, Kimi Räikkönen, Jarno Trulli, Jean Alesi, Eddie Irvine and Pedro de la Rosa.

Sporting regulations

The FIA will organise the FIA Formula One World Championship (the Championship) which is the property of the FIA and comprises two titles of World Champion, one for drivers and one for constructors. It consists of the Formula One Grand Prix races which are included in the Formula One calendar and in respect of which the ASNs and organisers have signed the organisation agreement provided for in the 1998 Concorde Agreement (...)

LICENCES

10. All drivers, competitors and officials participating in the Championship must hold a FIA Super Licence. Applications for Super Licences must be made to the FIA through the applicant's ASN.

CHAMPIONSHIP EVENTS

11. Events are reserved for Formula One cars as defined in the Technical Regulations.

12. Each Event will have the status of an international restricted competition.

13. The distance of all races, from the start signal referred to in Article 141 to the chequered flag, shall be equal to the least number of complete laps which exceed a distance of 305 km. However, should two hours elapse before the scheduled race distance is completed, the leader will be shown the chequered flag when he crosses the control line (the Line) at the end of the lap during which the two hour period ended. The Line is a single line which crosses both the track and the pit lane.

14. The maximum number of Events in the Championship is 17, the minimum is 8.

16. An Event which is cancelled with less than three months written notice to the FIA will not be considered for inclusion in the following year's Championship unless the FIA judges the cancellation to have been due to force majeure.

17. An Event may be cancelled if fewer than 12 cars are available for it.

WORLD CHAMPIONSHIP

18) The Formula One World Championship driver's title will be awarded to the driver who has scored the highest number of points, taking into

consideration all the results obtained during the Events which have actually taken place.

19. Points will not be awarded for the Championship unless the driver has driven the same car throughout the race in the Event in question.

20. The title of Formula One World Champion for Constructors will be awarded to the make which has scored the highest number of points, taking into account all the results obtained by a maximum of 2 cars per make.

21. The constructor of an engine or rolling chassis is the person (including any corporate or unincorporated body) which owns the intellectual property rights to such engine or chassis. The make of an engine or chassis is the name attributed to it by its constructor. If the make of the chassis is not the same as that of the engine, the title will be awarded to the former which shall always precede the latter in the name of the car.

22. Points for both titles will be awarded at each Event according to the following scale :

1st : 10 points; 2nd : 6 points; 3rd : 4 points; 4th : 3 points; 5th : 2 points; 6th : 1 point.

23. If a race is stopped under Articles 155 and 156, and cannot be restarted, no points will be awarded in case A, half points will be awarded in case B and full points will be awarded in case C.

24. Drivers finishing first, second and third in the Championship must be present at the annual FIA Prize Giving ceremony. Any such driver who is absent will be liable to a maximum fine of US $ 50,000.00. All competitors shall use their best endeavours to ensure that their drivers attend as aforesaid.

DEAD HEAT

25. Prizes and points awarded for all the positions of competitors who tie, will be added together and shared equally.

26. If two or more constructors or drivers finish the season with the same number of points, the higher place in the Championship (in either case) shall be awarded to :

a) the holder of the greatest number of first places,

b) if the number of first places is the same, the holder of the greatest number of second places,

c) if the number of second places is the same, the holder of the greatest number of third places and so on until a winner emerges.

d) if this procedure fails to produce a result, the FIA will nominate the winner according to such criteria as it thinks fit.

COMPETITORS APPLICATIONS

42. Applications to compete in the Championship may be submitted to the FIA at any time between 1 November and 15 November each year, on an entry form as set out in Appendix 2 hereto accompanied by the entry fee provided for in the Agreement. Entry forms will be made available by FIA who will notify the applicant of the result of the application no later than 1 December. Successful applicants are automatically entered in all Events of the Championship and will be the only competitors at Events.

44. A competitor may change the make and/or type of engine at any time during the Championship. All points scored with an engine of different make to that which was first entered in the Championship will count (and will be aggregated) for the assessment of Benefits and for determining team positions for pre-qualifying purposes, however such points will not count towards (nor be aggregated for) the FIA Formula One Constructors Championship.

45. With the exception of those whose cars have scored points in the Championship of the previous year, applicants must supply information about the size of their company, their financial position and their ability to meet their prescribed obligations. All applicants who did not take part in the entire Championship for the previous year must also deposit US$500,000.00 with the FIA when submitting their application. This sum will be returned to them forthwith if their application is refused or at the end of their first Championship season provided they have met all the requirements of the Agreement and its schedules.

46. All applications will be studied by the FIA which will publish the list of cars and drivers accepted together with their race numbers on 1 December (or the following Monday if 1 December falls on a week-end), having first notified unsuccessful applicants as set out in article 42.

47. No more than 24 will be accepted from any one competitor.

INCIDENTS

53. Incident means any occurrence or series of occurrences involving one or more drivers, or any action by any driver, which is reported to the stewards by the race director (or noted by the stewards and referred to the race director for investigation) which :

- necessitated the stopping of a race under Article 155;
- constituted a breach of these Sporting Regulations or the Code;
- caused a false start by one or more cars;
- caused an avoidable collision;
- forced a driver off the track;
- illegitimately prevented a legitimate overtaking manoeuvre by a driver;
- illegitimately impeded another driver during overtaking.

54. a) It shall be at the discretion of the stewards to decide, upon a report or a request by the race director, if a driver or drivers involved in an incident shall be penalised.

b) If an incident is under investigation by the stewards, a message informing all Teams of this will be displayed on the timing monitors.

c) If a driver is involved in a collision or Incident (see Article 53), he must not leave the circuit without the consent of the stewards.

55. The stewards may impose a 10 second time penalty on any driver involved in an Incident. However, should such penalty be imposed during the last five laps, or after the end of a race, Artice 56b) below will not apply and 25 seconds will be added to the elapsed race time of the driver concerned.

56. Should the stewards decide to impose a time penalty, the following procedure will be followed :

a) The stewards will give written notification of the time penalty which has been imposed to an official of the team concerned and will ensure that this information is also displayed on the timing monitors.

b) From the time the steward's decision is notified on the timing monitors the relevant driver may cover no more than three complete laps before entering the pits and proceeding to his pit where he shall remain for the period of the time penalty. During the time the car is stationary for the time penalty it may not be worked on. However, if the engine stops, it may be started after the time penalty period has elapsed.

c) When the time penalty period has elapsed the driver may rejoin the race.

d) Any breach or failure to comply with Articles 56 b) or 56 c) may result in the car being excluded.

57. Any determination made or any penalty imposed pursuant to Article 55 shall be without prejudice to the operation of Articles 160 or 161 of the Code.

PROTESTS

58. Protests shall be made in accordance with the Code and accompanied by a fee of 2500.00 Swiss Francs or its equivalent in US Dollars or local currency.

SANCTIONS

59. The stewards may inflict the penalties specifically set out in these Sporting Regulations in addition to or instead of any other penalties available to them under the Code.

CHANGES OF DRIVER

60. During a season, each team will be permitted one driver change for their first car and will be permitted to have three drivers for their second car who may be changed at any time provided that any driver change is made in accordance with the Code and before the start of qualifying practice. After 18.00 on the day of scrutineering, a driver change may only take place with the consent of the stewards. In all other circumstances, competitors will be obliged to use the drivers they nominated at the time of entering the Championship except in cases of force majeure which will be considered separately. Any new driver may score points in the Championship.

PIT LANE

66. a) For the avoidance of doubt and for description purposes, the pit lane shall be divided into two lanes. The lane closest to the pit wall is designated the "fast lane", and the lane closest to the garages is designated the "inner lane", and is the only area where any work can be carried out on a car.

b) Competitors must not paint lines on any part of the pit lane.

c) No equipment may be left in the fast lane. A car may enter or remain in the fast lane only with the driver sitting in the car behind the steering wheel in his normal position, even when the car is being pushed.

d) Team personnel are only allowed in the pit lane immediately before they are required to work on a car and must withdraw as soon as the work is complete.

e) It is the responsibility of the Competitor to release his car after a pit stop only when it is safe to do so.

SPORTING CHECKS

67. Each competitor must have all relevant Super Licences available for inspection at any time during the Event.

SCRUTINEERING

70. Initial scrutineering of the car will take place three days (Monaco : four days) before the race between 10.00 and 16.00 in the garage assigned to each team.

71. Unless a waiver is granted by the stewards, competitors who do not keep to these time limits will not be allowed to take part in the Event.

72. No car may take part in the Event until it has been passed by the scrutineers.

73. The scrutineers may :

a) check the eligibility of a car or of a competitor at any time during an Event,

b) require a car to be dismantled by the competitor to make sure that the conditions of eligibility or conformity are fully satisfied,

c) require a competitor to pay the reasonable expenses which exercise of the powers mentioned in this Article may entail,

d) require a competitor to supply them with such parts or samples as they may deem necessary.

74. Any car which, after being passed by the scrutineers, is dismantled or modified in a way which might affect its safety or call into question its eligibility, or which is involved in an accident with similar consequences, must be re-presented for scrutineering approval.

75. The race director or the clerk of the course may require that any car involved in an accident be stopped and checked.

77. The stewards will publish the findings of the scrutineers each time cars are checked during the Event. These results will not include any specific figure except when a car is found to be in breach of the Technical Regulations.

SUPPLY OF TYRES IN THE CHAMPIONSHIP AND TYRE LIMITATION DURING THE EVENT

78. Supply of tyres : No tyre may be used in the Championship unless the company supplying such tyre accepts and adheres to the following conditions :

- one tyre supplier present in the Championship: this company must equip 100% of the entered teams on ordinary commercial terms.

- two tyre suppliers present : each of them must, if called upon to do so, be prepared to equip up to 60% of the entered teams on ordinary commercial terms.

- three or more tyre suppliers present : each of them must, if called upon to do so, be prepared to equip up to 40% of the entered teams on ordinary commercial terms.

- each tyre supplier must undertake to provide only two specifications of dry-weather tyre and three specifications of wet-weather tyre at each Event, each of which must be of one homogenous compound only;(...)

79. Quantity and type of tyres :

a) The same driver may not use more than a total of thirty two dry-weather tyres and twenty eight wet-weather tyres throughout the entire duration of the Event. Prior to the qualifying practice each driver may use two specifications of dry-weather tyres but must, before qualifying practice begins, nominate which specification of tyre he will use for the remainder of the Event. For qualifying practice, warm up and the race each driver may use no more than twenty eight tyres (fourteen front and fourteen rear).

b) All dry-weather tyres must incorporate circumferential grooves square to the wheel axis and around the entire circumference of the contact surface of each tyre.

c) Each front dry-weather tyre, when new, must incorporate 4 grooves which are :

- arranged symmetrically about the centre of the tyre tread ;

- at least 14 mm wide at the contact surface and which taper uniformly to a minimum of 10 mm at the lower surface ;

- at least 2.5 mm deep across the whole lower surface ;

- 50 mm (+/- 1.0 mm) between centres.

Furthermore, the tread width of the front tyres must not exceed 270 mm.

d) Each rear dry-weather tyre, when new, must incorporate 4 grooves which are:

- arranged symmetrically about the centre of the tyre tread ;

- at least 14 mm wide at the contact surface and which taper uniformly to a minimum of 10 mm at the lower surface ;

- at least 2.5 mm deep across the whole lower surface ; - 50 mm (+/- 1.0 mm) between centres.

The measurements referred to in c) and d) above will be taken when the tyre is fitted to a wheel and inflated to 20 psi.

e) A wet-weather tyre is one which has been designed for use on a wet or damp track.

All wet-weather tyres must, when new, have a contact area which does not exceed 300 cm? when fitted to the front of the car and 475 cm? when fitted to the rear. Contact areas will be measured over any square section of the tyre which is normal to and symmetrical about the tyre centre line and which measures 200 mm x 200 mm when fitted to the front of the car and 250 mm x 250 mm when fitted to the rear. For the purposes of establishing conformity, only void areas which are greater than 2.5 mm in depth will be considered.

Prior to use at an Event, each tyre manufacturer must provide the technical delegate with a full scale drawing of each type of wet-weather tyre intended for use. With the exception of race day, wet-weather tyres may only be used after the track has been declared wet by the race director and, during the remainder of the relevant session, the choice of tyres is free.

80. Control of tyres :

a) All tyres which are to be used at an Event will be marked with a unique identification.

b) At any time during an Event, and at his absolute discretion, the FIA technical delegate may select the dry-weather tyres to be used by any Team from among the total stock of tyres which such Team's designated supplier has present at the Event.

c) During initial scrutineering, each competitor may have up to forty four dry-weather tyres and thirty six wet-weather tyres for each of his drivers ready for marking in his garage. Tyres not marked during initial scrutineering can be marked at other times by arrangement with the FIA technical delegate.

d) From among the twenty-eight dry-weather tyres chosen for each car for qualifying practice, warm up and the race, the FIA technical delegate will choose at random sixteen tyres (eight front and eight rear) which are the only dry-weather tyres which such car may use in qualifying practice.

e) A competitor wishing to replace an already marked unused tyre by another unused one must present both tyres to the FIA technical delegate.

f) The use of tyres without appropriate identification is strictly forbidden.

81. Wear of tyres :

The Championship will be contested on grooved tyres. The FIA reserve the right to introduce at any time a method of measuring remaining groove depth if performance appears to be enhanced by high wear or by the use of tyres which are worn so that the grooves are no longer visible.

WEIGHING

82. The weight of any car may be checked during the Event as follows :

a) all drivers entered in the Championship will be weighed, wearing their complete racing apparel, at the first Event of the season. If a driver is entered later in the season he will be weighed at his first Event.

b) During qualifying practice :

1) the FIA will install weighing equipment in an area as close to the first pit as possible, this area will be used for the weighing procedure ;

2) cars will be selected at random to undergo the weighing procedure. The FIA technical delegate will inform the driver by means of a red light at the pit entrance that his car has been selected for weighing

3) having been signalled (by means of a red light), that his car has been selected for weighing, the driver will proceed directly to the weighing area and stop his engine ;

4) the car will then be weighed and the result given to the driver in writing ;

5) if the car is unable to reach the weighing area under its own power it will be placed under the exclusive control of the marshals who will take the car to be weighed ;

6) a car or driver may not leave the weighing area without the consent of the FIA technical delegate.

c) After the race :

Each car crossing the Line will be weighed. If a car is weighed without the driver, the weight determined under a) above will be added to give the total weight required under Article 4.1 of the Technical Regulations.

d) Should the weight of the car be less than that specified in Article 4.1 of the Technical Regulations when weighed under b) or c) above, the car and the driver will be excluded from the Event save where the deficiency in weight results from the accidental loss of a component of the car due to force majeure.

e) No solid, liquid, gas or other substance or matter of whatsoever nature may be added to, placed on, or removed from a car after it has been selected for weighing or has finished the race or during the weighing procedure. (...)

f) Only scrutineers and officials may enter the weighing area. No intervention of any kind is allowed there unless authorised by such officials.

83. Any breach of these provisions for the weighing of cars may result in the exclusion of the relevant car.

SPARE CAR

86. A competitor may use several cars for practice and the race provided that :

a) he uses no more than two cars (one car for a one car Team) for free practice sessions on each of the two practice days held under Article 115 a) and b) ;

b) he uses no more than three cars (two cars for a one car Team) during qualifying practice;

c) they are all of the same make and were entered in the Championship by the same competitor,

d) they have been scrutineered in accordance with these Sporting Regulations,

e) each car carries its driver's race number.

87. Changes of car may only take place in the pits under supervision of the marshals.

88. No change of car will be allowed after the green light (see Article 139) provided always that if a race has to be restarted under Article 157 Case A, the moment after which no car change will be allowed shall be when the green light for the subsequent start is shown.

GENERAL SAFETY

90. Drivers are strictly forbidden to drive their car in the opposite direction to the race unless this is absolutely necessary in order to move the car from a dangerous position. A car may only be pushed to remove it from a dangerous position as directed by the marshals.

91. Any driver intending to leave the track or to go to his pit or the paddock area must signal his intention to do so in good time making sure that he can do this without danger.

93. A driver who abandons a car must leave it in neutral or with the clutch disengaged and with the steering wheel in place.

94. Repairs to a car may be carried out only in the paddock, pits and on the grid.

96. Save as provided in Article 138, refuelling is allowed only in the pits.

99. Save as specifically authorised by the Code or these Sporting Regulations, no one except the driver may touch a stopped car unless it is in the pits or on the starting grid.

101. During the periods commencing 15 minutes prior to and ending 5 minutes after every practice session and the period between the green lights being illuminated (Article 139) and the time when the last car enters the parc fermé, no one is allowed on the track with the exception of :

a) marshals or other authorised personnel in the execution of their duty ;

b) drivers when driving or under the direction of the marshals ;

c) mechanics under Article 140 only.

102. During a race, the engine may only be started with the starter except in the pit lane where the use of an external starting device is allowed (...)

104. A speed limit of 80 km/h in practice and 120 km/h during the warm up and the race, or such other speed limits as the Permanent Bureau of the Formula One Commission may decide, will be enforced in the pit lane. Except in the race, any driver who exceeds the limit will be fined US$250 for each km/h above the limit (this may be increased in the case of a second offence in the same Championship season). During the race, the stewards may impose a time penalty on any driver who exceeds the limit.

105. If a driver has serious mechanical difficulties during practice or the race he must leave the track as soon as it is safe to do so.

106. The car's rear light must be illuminated at all times when it is running on wet-weather tyres.

107. Only six team members per participating car (all of whom shall have been issued with and wearing special identification) are allowed in the signalling area during practice and the race.

109. The race director, the clerk of the course or the FIA medical delegate can require a driver to have a medical examination at any time during an Event.

110. Failure to comply with the general safety requirements of the Code or these Sporting Regulations may result in the exclusion of the car and driver concerned from the Event.

FREE PRACTICE, QUALIFYING PRACTICE AND WARM UP

112. No driver may start in the race without taking part in qualifying practice.

113. During all practices there will be a green and a red light at the pit exit. Cars may only leave the pit lane when the green light is on (...)

115. Free practice sessions will take place :

a) Two days (Monaco : three days) before the race from 11.00 to 12.00 and from 13.00 to 14.00.

b) The day before the race from 09.00 to 09.45 and from 10.15 to 11.00.

116. Qualifying practice will take place :

a) The day before the race from 13.00 to 14.00.

b) Each driver is allowed a maximum of 12 laps qualifying practice. Should a driver complete more than 12 laps all times recorded by the driver will be cancelled.

117. Warm up : a free practice session will take place on race day; it will last 30 minutes and start 4 hours and 30 minutes before the starting time of the race.

118. The interval between the free and qualifying practice session may never be less than 1 hour and 30 minutes. Only in the most exceptional circumstances can a delay in free practice or other difficulty on race morning result in a change to the starting time of the race.

119. If a car stops during practice it must be removed from the track as quickly as possible so that its presence does not constitute a danger or hinder other competitors. If the driver is unable to drive the car from a dangerous position, it shall be the duty of the marshals to assist him. If any such assistance results in the car being driven or pushed back to the

pits, the car may not be used again in that session. Additionally, if the assistance is given during a pre-qualifying or qualifying practice session, the driver's fastest lap time from the relevant session will be deleted. In the event of a driving infringement during practice, the stewards may delete any number of qualifying times from the driver concerned. In this case, a Team will not be able to appeal against the steward's decision.

120. The clerk of the course may interrupt practice as often and for as long as he thinks necessary to clear the track or to allow the recovery of a car. In the case of free practice only, the clerk of the course with the agreement of the stewards may decline to prolong the practice period after an interruption of thiskind.Furthermore, if in the opinion of the stewards, a stoppage is caused deliberately, the driver concerned may have his times from that session cancelled and may not be permitted to take part in any other practice session that day.

122. Should one or more sessions be thus interrupted, no protest can be accepted as to the possible effects of the interruption on the qualification of drivers admitted to start.

123. All laps covered during qualifying practice will be timed to determine the driver's position at the start in accordance with the prescriptions of Article 129. With the exception of a lap on which a red flag is shown (see Article 155), each time a car crosses the Line it will be deemed to have completed one lap.

STOPPING THE PRACTICE

124. Should it become necessary to stop the practice because the circuit is blocked by an accident or because weather or other conditions make it dangerous to continue, the clerk of the course shall order a red flag and the abort lights to be shown at the Line. Simultaneously, red flags will be shown at all marshal posts. When the signal is given to stop, all cars shall immediately reduce speed and proceed slowly back to their respective pits, and all cars abandoned on the track will be removed to a safe place. Any lap during which the red flag is shown will not be counted towards a car's total lap allocation for that session. At the end of each practice session all drivers may cross the Line only once.

PRESS CONFERENCES AND DRIVERS PARADE

125. The FIA press delegate will choose a maximum of five drivers who must attend a press conference in the media centre for a period of one hour at 15.00 on the day before first practice. These driver's Teams will be notified no less than 48 hours before the conference. In addition, a maximum of two team personalities may be chosen by the FIA press delegate to attend this press conference. On the first day of practice, a minimum of three and a maximum of six drivers and/or team personalities, (other than those who attended the press conference on the previous day and subject to the consent of the team principal) will be chosen by ballot or rota by the FIA press delegate during the Event and must make themselves available to the media for a press conference in the media centre for a period of one hour at 15.30.

126. Immediately after qualifying practice the first three drivers in qualifying will be required to make themselves available for television interviews in the unilateral room and then attend a press conference in the media centre for a maximum period of 30 minutes.

THE GRID

128. At the end of qualifying practice, the fastest time achieved by each driver will be officially published (see Article 51).

129. The grid will be drawn up in the order of the fastest time achieved by each driver. Should two or more drivers have set identical times, priority will be given to the one who set it first.

130. The fastest driver will start the race from the position on the grid which was the pole position in the previous year or, on a new circuit, has been designated as such by the FIA safety delegate.

131. Any driver whose best qualifying lap exceeds 107% of the pole position time will not be allowed to take part in the warm up or race. Under exceptional circumstances however, which may include setting a suitable lap time in a previous free practice session, the stewards may permit the car to start the race. Should there be more than one driver accepted in this manner, their order will be determined by the stewards. In either case, a Team will not be able to appeal against the stewards' decision.

132. The starting grid will be published after the warm up on race day. Any competitor whose car(s) is (are) unable to start for any reason whatsoever (or who has good reason to believe that their car(s) will not be ready to start) must inform the clerk of the course accordingly at the earliest opportunity and, in any event, no later than 45 minutes before the start of the race. If one or more cars are withdrawn, the grid will be closed up accordingly. The final starting grid will be published 45 minutes before the start of the race.

134. Any car which has not taken up its position on the grid by the time the ten minute signal is shown, will not be permitted to do so and must start from the pits in accordance with Article 137.

BRIEFING

135. A briefing by the race director will take place at 10.00 on the first day of practice. All drivers entered for the Event and their Team Managers must be present . Should the race director consider another briefing is necessary, it will take place one hour after the end of warm up. Competitors will be informed no later than three hours after the end of qualifying practice if this is deemed necessary.

STARTING PROCEDURE

136) 30 minutes before the time for the start of the race, the cars will leave the pits to cover a reconnaissance lap. At the end of this lap they will stop on the grid in starting order with their engines stopped.

Should they wish to cover more than one reconnaissance lap, this must be done by driving down the pit lane at greatly reduced speed between each of the laps.

137) 17 minutes before the starting time, a warning signal announcing the closing of the pit exit in 2 minutes will be given. 15 minutes before the starting time, the pit exit will be closed and a second warning signal will be given. Any car which is still in the pits can start from the pits provided it reached the pit exit under its own power. If more than one car is affected they must line up in the order in which they reached the pit exit.

Where the pit exit is immediately after the Line, cars will join the race when the whole field has passed the pit exit on its first racing lap. Where the pit exit is immediately before the Line, cars will join the race as soon as the whole field has crossed the Line after the start.

138) Refuelling on the starting grid may only be carried out prior to the 5 minute signal and by using one unpressurised container with a maximum capacity of 12 litres. Any such container may not be refilled during the starting procedure and must be fitted with one or more dry break couplings connecting it to the car.

139) The approach of the start will be announced by signals shown ten minutes, five minutes, three minutes, one minute and fifteen seconds before the start of the formation lap, each of which will be accompanied by an audible warning.

When the ten minute signal is shown, everybody except drivers, officials and team technical staff must leave the grid. When the five minute signal is shown all cars must have their wheels fitted. After this signal wheels may only be removed in the pits. Any car which does not have all its wheels fitted at the five minute signal must start the race from the back of the grid or the pit lane.

When the one minute signal is shown, engines should be started and all team personnel must leave the grid by the time the 15 second signal is given. If any driver needs assistance after the 15 second signal he must raise his arm and, when the remainder of the cars able to do so have left the grid, his team may attempt to rectify the problem. In this case, marshals with yellow flags will stand beside any car (or cars) concerned to warn drivers behind.

When the green lights are illuminated, the cars will begin the formation lap with the pole position driver leading. When leaving the grid, all drivers must proceed at a greatly reduced speed until clear of any Team personnel standing beside the track.

During the formation lap practice starts are forbidden and the formation must be kept as tight as possible. Overtaking during the formation lap is only permitted if a car is delayed when leaving its grid position and cars behind cannot avoid passing it without unduly delaying the remainder of the field. In this case, drivers may only overtake to re-establish the original starting order.

Any driver who is delayed leaving the grid may not overtake another moving car if he was stationary after the remainder of the cars had crossed the Line, and must start the race from the back of the grid. If more than one driver is affected, they must form up at the back of the grid in the order they left to complete the formation lap. If the Line is not situated in front of pole position, for the purposes of this Article only, it will be deemed to be a white line one metre in front of pole position.

A time penalty will be imposed on any driver who, in the opinion of the Stewards, unnecessarily overtook another car during the formation lap.

140) Any driver who is unable to start the formation lap must raise his arm and, after the remainder of the cars have crossed the Line, his mechanics may attempt to rectify the problem under the supervision of the marshals. If the car is still unable to start the formation lap it will be pushed into the pit lane by the shortest route and the mechanics may work on the car again.

141) When the cars come back to the grid at the end of the formation lap, they will stop on their respective grid positions, keeping their engines running. Once all the cars have come 2001 F1 Sporting Regulations 15 to a halt the five second signal will appear followed by the four, three, two and one second signals. At any time after the one second signal appears, the race will be started by extinguishing all red lights.

142) There will be a standing start. The starting signal will be given by means of starting lights activated by the permanent starter. During the start of a race, the pit wall must be kept free of all persons with the exception of properly authorised officials and fire marshals all of whom shall have been issued with and shall be wearing the appropriate pass.

143) Any car which is unable to maintain starting order during the entire formation lap or is moving when the one second light comes on must enter the pit lane and start from the pits as specified in Article 137.

This will not apply to any car which is temporarily delayed during the lap and which is able to regain its position, without endangering itself or any other car, before the leading car has taken up its position on the grid.

144) If, after returning to the starting grid at the end of the formation lap, a car develops a problem that could endanger the start, the driver must immediately raise his hands above his head and the marshal responsible for that row must immediately wave a yellow flag.

If the start is delayed as a result, a marshal with a yellow flag will stand in front of the car concerned to prevent it from moving until the whole field has left the grid on the new formation lap. The driver concerned may then start the race from the back of the grid and any vacant positions will not be filled. Should there be more than one car involved, their new positions at the back of the grid will be determined in accordance with their respective final grid positions.

If a problem cannot be rectified before the commencement of the new formation lap the car must be pushed into the pit lane by the shortest route. The Team may then attempt to rectify the problem and, if successful, the car may then start from the pit lane. Should there be more than one car involved their starting order from the pit lane will be determined by the order in which they reached the pit exit under their own power.

145) If a problem arises when the cars reach the starting grid at the end of the formation lap the following procedure shall apply :

a) If the race has not been started, the abort lights will be switched on, all engines will be stopped and the new formation lap will start 5 minutes later with the race distance reduced by one lap. The next signal will be the three minute signal.

b) If the race has been started the marshals alongside the grid will wave their yellow flags to inform the drivers that a car is stationary on the grid.

c) If, after the start, a car is immobilised on the starting grid, it shall be the duty of the marshals to push it into the pit lane by the fastest route. If the driver is able to re-start the car whilst it is being pushed he may rejoin the race.

d) If the driver is unable to start the car whilst it is being pushed his mechanics may attempt to start it in the pit lane. If the car then starts it may rejoin the race. The driver and mechanics must follow the instructions of the track marshals at all times during such a procedure.

146) Should Article 145 apply, the race will nevertheless count for the Championship no matter how often the procedure is repeated, or how much the race is shortened as a result.

147) No refuelling will be allowed on the grid if more than one start procedure proves necessary under Article 145.

148) A time penalty will be imposed for a false start judged using an FIA supplied transponder which must be fitted to the car as specified.

149) Only in the following cases will any variation in the start procedure be allowed :

a) If it starts to rain after the five minute signal but before the race is started and, in the opinion of the race director Teams should be given the opportunity to change tyres, the abort lights will be shown on the Line and the starting procedure will begin again at the 15 minute point. If necessary the procedure set out in Article 145 will be followed.

b) If the start of the race is imminent and, in the opinion of the race director, the volume of water on the track is such that it cannot be negotiated safely even on wet-weather tyres, the abort lights will be shown on the Line simultaneously with a "10" board with a red background.

This "10" board with a red background will mean that there is to be a delay of ten minutes before the starting procedure can be resumed. If weather conditions have improved at the end of that ten minute period, a "10" board with a 2001 F1 Sporting Regulations 16 green background will be shown. The "10" board with a green background will mean that the green light will be shown in ten minutes. Five minutes after the "10" board with the green background is shown, the starting procedure will begin and the normal starting procedure signals (i.e. 5, 3, 1 min., 15 second) will be shown.

If however, the weather conditions have not improved within ten minutes after the "10" board with the red background was shown, the abort lights will be shown on the Line and the "10" board with the red background will be shown again which will mean a further delay of ten minutes before the starting procedure can be resumed.

This procedure may be repeated several times. At any time when a "10" board (with either a red or green background) is shown, it will be accompanied by an audible warning.

c) If the race is started behind the safety car, Article 154n) will apply.

150) The stewards may use any video or electronic means to assist them in reaching a decision. The stewards may overrule judges of fact. A breach of the provisions of the Code or these Sporting Regulations relating to starting procedure, may result in the exclusion of the car and driver concerned from the Event.

THE RACE

151. A race will not be stopped in the event of rain unless the circuit is blocked or it is dangerous to continue (see Article 155).

152. If a car stops during the race (except under Article 145c and d), it must be removed from the track as quickly as possible so that its presence does not constitute a danger or hinder other competitors. If the driver is unable to drive the car from a dangerous position, it shall be the duty of the marshals to assist him. If any such assistance results in the engine starting and the driver rejoining the race, the car will be excluded from the results of the race.

153. During the race, drivers leaving the pit lane may only do so when the pit exit light is green and on their own responsibility. A marshal with a blue flag, or a flashing blue light, will also warn the driver if cars are approaching on the track.

SAFETY CAR

154 (...)b) 30 minutes before the race start time the safety car will take up position at the front of the grid and remain there until the five minute signal is given. At this point (except under n) below) it will cover a whole lap of the circuit and enter the pit lane. If Article 149a) applies, the safety car will take up its position at the front of the grid as soon as the 15 minute practice session has finished.

c) The safety car may be brought into operation to neutralise a race upon the decision of the clerk of the course. It will be used only if competitors or officials are in immediate physical danger but the circumstances are not such as to necessitate stopping the race.

d) When the order is given to deploy the safety car, all observer's posts will display immobile yellow flags and a board "SC" which shall be maintained until the intervention is over.

e) During the race, the safety car with its revolving lights on, will start from the pit lane and will join the track regardless of where the race leader is.

f) All the competing cars will form up in line behind the safety car no more than 5 car lengths apart. All overtaking is forbidden (except under n) below), unless a car is signalled to do so from the safety car.

g) When ordered to do so by the clerk of the course the observer in the car will use a green light to signal to any cars between it and the race leader that they should pass. These cars will continue at reduced speed and without overtaking until they reach the line of cars behind the safety car.

h) The safety car shall be used at least until the leader is behind it and all remaining cars are lined up behind him.(...)

i) While the safety car is in operation, competing cars may stop at their pit, but may only rejoin the track when the green light at the pit exit is on. It will be on at all times except when the safety car and the line of cars following it are about to pass or are passing the pit exit. A car rejoining the track must proceed at reduced speed until it reaches the end of the line of cars behind the safety car.

j) When the clerk of the course calls in the safety car, it must extinguish all the revolving lights, this will be the signal to the drivers that it will be entering the pit lane at the end of that lap. At this point the first car in line behind the safety car may dictate the pace and, if necessary, fall more than five car lengths behind it. As the safety car is approaching the pit entrance the yellow flags and SC boards at the observer's posts will be withdrawn and green flags will be displayed for one lap.

k) When the safety car has pulled off the circuit and the cars are approaching the Line, green lights will be shown. Overtaking remains strictly forbidden until the cars pass the green light at the Line.

l) Each lap completed while the safety car is deployed will be counted as a race lap.

m) If the race is stopped under Article 156 Case C, the safety car will take the chequered flag and all cars able to do so must follow it into the pit lane and into the parc fermé.

n) In exceptional circumstances the race may be started behind the safety car. In this case, at any time before the one minute signal, its revolving yellow lights will be turned on. This is the signal to the drivers that the race will be started behind the safety car. When the green lights are illuminated the safety car will leave the grid with all cars following in grid order no more than 5 car lengths apart. There will be no formation lap and race will start when the leading car crosses the line for the first time. Overtaking, during the first lap only, is permitted if a car is delayed when leaving its grid position and cars behind cannot avoid passing it without unduly delaying the remainder of the field. In this case, drivers may only overtake to re-establish the original starting order. Any driver who is delayed leaving the grid may not overtake another moving car if he was stationary after the remainder of the cars had crossed the Line, and must form up at the back of the line of cars behind the safety car. If more than one driver is affected, they must form up at the back of the field in the order they left the grid. A time penalty will be imposed on any driver who, in the opinion of the Stewards, unnecessarily overtook another car during the first lap.

STOPPING A RACE

155) Should it become necessary to stop the race because the circuit is blocked by an accident or because weather or other conditions make it dangerous to continue, the clerk of the course shall order a red flag and the abort lights to be shown at the Line. Simultaneously, red flags will be shown at all marshal posts.

When the signal is given to stop all cars shall immediately reduce speed in the knowledge that :

- the race classification will be that at the end of the lap two laps prior to that during which the signal to stop the race was given,
- race and service vehicles may be on the track,
- the circuit may be totally blocked because of an accident,
- weather conditions may have made the circuit undriveable at racing speed, - the pit lane will be open.

156) The procedure to be followed varies according to the number of laps completed by the race leader before the signal to stop the race was given :

Case A. Less than two full laps. If the race can be restarted, Article 157 will apply. Case B. Two or more full laps but less than 75% of the race distance (rounded up to the nearest whole number of laps). If the race can be restarted, Article 158 will apply.

Case C. 75% or more of the race distance (rounded up to the nearest whole number of laps). The cars will be sent directly to the parc fermé and the race will be deemed to have finished when the leading car crossed the Line at the end of the lap two laps prior to that during which the signal to stop was given.

RESTARTING A RACE

157) Case A.

a) The original start shall be deemed null and void.

b) The length of the restarted race will be the full original race distance.

c) The drivers who are eligible to take part in the race shall be eligible for the restart either in their original car or in a spare car.

d) Any driver who was forced to start from the back of the grid or the pit lane during the original start may start from his original grid position ;

e) After the signal to stop the race has been given, all cars able to do so will proceed directly but slowly to either :

- the pit lane or ;
- if the grid is clear, to their original grid position or ;
- if the grid is not clear, to a position behind the last grid position as directed by the marshals. 2001 F1 Sporting Regulations 18

f) Cars may be worked on in the pits or on the grid. If work is carried out on the grid, this must be done in the car's correct grid position and must in no way impede the re-start. g) Refuelling will be allowed until the five minute signal is shown.

158) Case B.

a) Other than the race order at the end of the lap two laps prior to that during which the signal to stop was given and the number of laps covered by each driver, the original race will be deemed null and void.

b) The length of the re-started race will be three laps less than the original race distance less the number of classified laps completed by the leader before the signal to stop was given.

c) The grid for the re-started race will be arranged in the race order at the end of the lap two laps prior to that during which the signal to stop was given.

d) Only cars which took part in the original start will be eligible for the re-start and then only if they returned under their own power by an authorised route to either :

- the pit lane or ;
- to a position behind the last grid position as directed by the marshals.

e) No spare car will be eligible.

f) Cars may be worked on in the pits or on the grid. If work is carried out on the grid, this must be done in the car's correct grid position and must in no way impede the re-start.

g) Refuelling is only permitted in the pits. If a car is refuelled it must take the re-start from the back of the grid and, if more than one car is involved, their positions will be determined by their race order at the end of the lap two laps prior to that during which the signal to stop was given. In this case their original grid positions will be left vacant.

159) In both Case A and Case B :

a) 10 minutes after the stop signal, the pit exit will close.

b) 15 minutes after the stop signal, the five minute signal will be shown, the grid will close and the normal start procedure will recommence.

c) Any car which is unable to take up its position on the grid before the five minute signal will be directed to the pits. It may then start from the pits as specified in Article 137. The Organiser must have sufficient personnel and equipment available to enable the foregoing timetable to be adhered to even in the most difficult circumstances.

FINISH

160. The end-of-race signal will be given at the Line as soon as the leading car has covered the full race distance in accordance with Article 13. Should two hours elapse before the full distance has been covered, the end-of-race signal will be given to the leading car the first time it crosses the Line after such time has elapsed.

161. Should for any reason (other than under Article 155) the end-of-race signal be given before the leading car completes the scheduled number of laps, or the prescribed time has been completed, the race will be deemed to have finished when the leading car last crossed the Line before the signal was given. Should the end-of-race signal be delayed for any reason, the race will be deemed to have finished when it should have finished.

162. After receiving the end-of-race signal all cars must proceed on the circuit directly to the parc fermé without stopping, without receiving any object whatsoever and without any assistance (except that of the marshals if necessary). Any classified car which cannot reach the parc fermé under its own power will be placed under the exclusive control of the marshals who will take the car to the parc fermé.

PARC FERME

163. Only those officials charged with supervision may enter the parc fermé. No intervention of any kind is allowed there unless authorised by such officials.

164. When the parc fermé is in use, parc fermé regulations will apply in the area between the Line and the parc fermé entrance.

165. The parc fermé shall be sufficiently large and secure that no unauthorised persons can gain access to it.

CLASSIFICATION

166. The car placed first will be the one having covered the scheduled distance in the shortest time, or, where appropriate, passed the Line in the lead at the end of two hours. All cars will be classified taking into account the number of complete laps they have covered, and for those which have completed the same number of laps, the order in which they crossed the Line.

167. If a car takes more than twice the time of the winner's fastest lap to cover its last lap this last lap will not be taken into account when calculating the total distance covered by such car.

168. Cars having covered less than 90% of the number of laps covered by the winner (rounded down to the nearest whole number of laps), will not be classified.

169. The official classification will be published after the race. It will be the only valid result subject to any amendments which may be made under the Code and these Sporting Regulations.

PODIUM CEREMONY

170. The drivers finishing the race in 1st, 2nd and 3rd positions and a representative of the winning constructor must attend the prize-giving ceremony on the podium and abide by the podium procedure set out in Appendix 3 (except Monaco); and immediately thereafter make themselves available for a period of 90 minutes for the purpose of television unilateral interviews and the press conference in the media centre.

Meaning of the flags

White flag : service vehicle on track

Blue flag : (immobile) : a car is close behind you
(waving) : a car is about to overtake you

Yellow flag : (immobile) : overtaking is prohibited, danger
(waving) immediate danger, slow down

Red flag : (by marshals and the Clerk of the race) : stopping of the race on the Line

Green flag : end of danger, free track

Yellow with red stripes flag : danger, slippery surface

Black flag : (with car number) : stop on the next lap

Black with yellow circle flag : your car is in danger

Black and white flag : non-sporting behaviour, warning

Chequered flag : end of the race or of the practice

BRIDGESTONE
A GRIP ON THE FUTURE
ONE MAN
ONE CAR
ONE TYRE
Pictures from 2001 FIA Formula One Championship